MURDER U.S.A.

MURDER U.S.A.

The Ways We Kill Each Other

———————

John Godwin

BALLANTINE BOOKS · NEW YORK

For Don Congdon,
who made this book possible

Manufactured in the United States of America

First Edition: October 1978

Library of Congress Cataloging in Publication Data
Godwin, John
  Murder U. S. A.
  Bibliography: p. 375
  Includes index.
  1. Murder—United States. 2. Crime-prevention—
United States. I. Title.
HV6529.G6 1978   364.1'523'0973   78-4662
ISBN 0-345-27721-X

Acknowledgments

I wish to thank, first and foremost, my two invaluable and indefatigable researchers, Genevieve Strobel and Catherine Blake Jenkins, without whose assistance this book would have taken several years longer to produce.

A great many other collaborators are identified within the text. It would be redundant to name them here, but I want to express my gratitude to them collectively as well as my appreciation for the patience and occasional forbearance they displayed during lengthy interviews.

My special thanks go to the following persons, whose contributions were specific and in some cases vital: attorneys Vincent Bugliosi, Robert M. Moll, and Jack Burnam; Special Agent Andrew McKean of the Federal Bureau of Investigation; Patrick V. Murphy and Thomas V. Brady, respectively President and Director of Communications of the Police Foundation; Detective Sergeant Gerald T. McQueen of the Manhattan Homicide Task Force Command; Police Lieutenant Harold Kneeland and Sergeants Leo Vinelli and Stanley P. Howe; District Attorney Joseph Freitas; Assistant District Attorney Paul Flaxman; James O. Golden and John Lucy of the Law Enforcement Assistance Administration; Janet Mole, Lois Morris, Marilyn Wood, Caren B. Rubio, Connie Turner, Relly Weiner, Dr. Albert Sterner, and the Reverend Charles W. Breel.

Finally, I must thank those members of the Prisoners' Union, the Department of Corrections, the Legal Aid Society, the New York Dragons, and various law-enforcement bodies throughout the nation who supplied me with valuable information but who must, for pertinent reasons, remain anonymous.

Contents

Prologue on a Crisis

If we wanted to typify contemporary American homicide, we could find all the ingredients of our current murder epidemic in a double slaying that occurred in a scabby high-rise slum on Delaware Avenue, Washington, D.C., during 1975.

On October 22 four men visited the apartment belonging to one Curtis Arrington. Ranging in age from eighteen to twenty-eight, the four were drug addicts and functional illiterates whose reading skills were barely above third-grade level. They had actually come to kill Arrington's friend Slim in the aftermath to an earlier neighborhood fight. When Arrington insisted that he didn't know Slim's whereabouts, they decided to kill him instead. The youngest of them later testified:

> I got a butcher knife out of the kitchen. We tied him up and led him to the bathroom. And we all stabbed him good. Then, when we started to leave, I heard somebody at the door. Lois [Lois Ann Davis, Arrington's sixteen-year-old girl friend] came in. She asked for Curtis. So we took her back to the bathroom and showed her his body. She started begging, "Please don't kill me. I ain't gonna tell nobody. Just don't kill me, please." She said we all could have sex with her if we wouldn't kill her.
>
> After we finished with her, Jack Bumps told her, "Bitch, I ain't takin' no chances. I'm gonna kill you anyway." We put a pillow over her head, and we stabbed her till she stopped wiggling. Then we set fire to the sheets in the bedroom and went out to buy us some liquor.

Minutes later flames were leaping from the windows, and fire trucks roared up with screeching sirens. The four men mingled with the excited crowd below, nudging one another and asking loudly, "Hey, what's going on here, man?" When firemen broke into the apartment they found two bound and scorched bodies. Arrington had been stabbed sixty-one times, Lois forty-three times.

The killers were tracked down fast enough, but the process of trying them turned out to be vastly more complicated. They had piled up crime records that at times appeared to swamp the capacity of the D.C. court system. Two of the group, Eddie Wilson and Warren Peters, pleaded guilty to 103 charges apiece—including kidnapping, rape, armed robbery, burglary, and auto theft—*apart* from the double homicide counts. The four had perfected a style of approaching motorists at gunpoint, forcing the drivers to take them to their homes, raping any young women present, plundering the premises, and escaping in their victims' automobiles. Whatever loot they collected went to buy narcotics.

That they were well known to the police didn't curtail their activities in the slightest. The oldest—Larry Hallman, nicknamed Jack Bumps—boasted three assault and robbery convictions and was living in a halfway house, supposedly under official supervision. The supervision was such that it hampered neither his dope shooting, nor his holdups, nor the final killings.

Superior Court Judge Nicholas Nunzio found his hands tied by a rash promise when it came to passing sentences. At the time that Wilson and Peters made their wholesale guilty pleas he was—unaccountably—ignorant of their roles in the murders. The judge had therefore agreed to limit the lower range of the penalty to twenty-eight years—an important consideration, because the minimum must be served before prisoners become eligible for parole. "That," commented Nunzio, "was the biggest mistake I ever made. I didn't know then what I know now. . . . You stabbed those two people just for the hell of it."

Jack Bumps Hallman had to be tried twice. The first round was declared a mistrial because of legal technicalities. He drew two consecutive twenty-years-to-life sentences, plus an extra nine years for arson. In practice, this meant that he wouldn't become eligible for parole for forty-three years.

Almost every detail of this episode was symptomatic of the malaise that has turned Americans into a people obsessed by fear of violence. The murders themselves were remarkable only for their idiotic pointlessness and sheer brutality. They were committed on a whim, the impromptu escapade of unthinking and drug-stunted primitives who had embarked on a series of depredations that—sooner or later—had to produce homicide. The fact that the victims happened to be their acquaintances was merely coincidental. It could have been anyone.

The entire career of these men exemplifies the bankruptcy of U.S. law enforcement. Spawned by a social system that dehumanized them, they collided with a legal system that was patently unable to cope with them until they had destroyed two lives. Even at their trials, they were confronted by a judge who had been kept partly unaware of their actions through the deficiencies of the court machine over which he presided. Their victims represented two out of 20,510 people who died that year in America as a result of criminal violence. That casualty list amounted to well over ten times the total of U.S. combat dead for the last three years of the Vietnam war. It meant that every twenty-six minutes a man, woman, or child was slaughtered in one fashion or another in this country.

There are at least two ways in which one might depict this crisis situation. One would be to point out that our national murder rate more than doubled in one decade and that certain cities experienced five- or six-fold increases in their homicide rates while their populations actually declined. Another would be to describe the impact of this crisis on our daily lives—an impact that everybody feels in his or her bones. It manifests itself in what might be called the Urban American After-Dark Look: a panicky glance over the shoulder the moment footsteps sound down a lonely street. It condemns older people to a unique kind of permanent house arrest—to "golden years" spent in barred and barricaded apartment cells, interrupted by scuttling forays into the outside world to buy the groceries necessary to prolong the prison term.

In a 1976 CBS television special on New York's stricken South Bronx, police official Tony Bouza addressed viewers: "America, take a look around," he said. "Look what you're doing in your ghettos. You're creating a permanent underclass of the disaffected and poor, drugged on alcohol, on welfare, living in bombed-out situations, with an educational system that doesn't educate, police that don't police. . . . We're all failing, and we're just a holding operation."

The failure of our response to the scourge of homicide is only indirectly connected with the existence of ghettos. It has the same basis as the helplessness of medieval Europeans against bubonic plague: ignorance of the causes. As Franklin E. Zimring, a University of Chicago law professor, summarized the situation: "Considering how much money is spent, the really shocking thing is how little we know about murder in this country. The number of important things we don't know amount to a national scandal."

Instead of knowledge we have myths, some of them accepted as gospel by people who should know better—police officers among them. Liberals, conservatives, and radicals all cherish their respective pet fables, which usually contain just enough truth to make them dangerously misleading.

The most widespread of these myths holds that the entire world is passing through an era of violence and that America, by and large, is no worse afflicted than others. Now there has indeed been some increase in global mayhem. And some countries do show a proportionally higher violence score than the United States. But all those countries—Thailand, Burma, Mexico, Colombia, Nicaragua, et al.—fall within the "underdeveloped" class of nations. Among its industrialized peers, America stands in grim solitude.

Canada's proportional homicide rate is less than one fifth of ours, despite a similar pioneer and melting-pot background. The whole of Great Britain (population 54 million) has fewer annual killings than Manhattan (population 1.7 million). Philadelphia, with 2 million people, had 430 murders in 1973; Toronto, Canada, with the same population, had 45. Greater London, containing about 8 million people, has half the yearly homicides of Atlanta, Georgia, with just half a million. From 1972 to 1974 a total of 372 law-enforcement officers were slain in the United States. Over the same period Japan had 13 police killings; Great Britain had 3.

A second myth, promulgated by the political left, is embodied in the slogan "Poverty breeds murder"—the implication being that if you alleviate poverty you automatically diminish homicide. Unfortunately, this has never been true, in this country or anywhere else.

The poorest patch in the Western Hemisphere is Haiti, where the per capita income hovers around $130 a year and poverty, in the phrase of one writer, "is something to which you aspire." Yet Haiti is one of the safest places on earth. You can wander around the pestilential slums of Port-au-Prince at any hour without risking more than heat rash. Three of the poorest nations in Europe—Spain, Portugal and Ireland—also share the lowest murder rates. Both France and West Germany suffered fewer murders during the starvation years after World War II than during the booming 1950s. And in America the current surge in the homicide rate began in the peak prosperity period of the 1960s.

It isn't poverty as such that generates murder but the special ingredients we infuse into the condition. The nature of these ingredients forms a clue as to the *why* of our violence chart.

A third myth, espoused mainly by conservatives, puts the blame on the loosening of family ties and waning church influence. The facts tell a different story. The nations that surpass America's murder statistics all boast extremely strong family bonds and even stronger religious attachments. And in the U.S. it is the South—the region with the least-eroded home and church structure—that heads the homicide list. Thirteen out of every 100,000 persons are murdered in the South in an average year, compared with 4 out of 100,000 in

New England. With only 31 percent of the country's population, the Southern states account for 43 percent of the killings.

Contrary to the conservative tenet, strong family ties and regular church attendance can coexist with a sky-high murder rate when a tradition of violence exists, as it does in the South. Almost a matter of regional pride, this tradition cuts right across racial lines. Southerners show the nation's highest homicide figures for whites and blacks alike.

Several other myths will be dealt with in the relevant chapters; right now we are concerned with sketching the overall picture of a crisis situation. Here, however, we run into the worst obstacle in the way of outlining a pattern of American crime: the lack of reliable figures. In a country positively inundated with statistics, there is no such thing as a dependable nationwide crime index. Umpteen governmental and private organizations spew out reams of documentation on the subject, but since they apply different yardsticks and use different sources, they seldom arrive at the same totals.

Even the FBI's *Uniform Crime Report*, quoted reverently by every newspaper, offers no more than approximations. These annual reports are based on figures supplied by local police chiefs, most of whom are deeply concerned with not rocking political boats. They therefore tend to understate crime in their territories by anything up to 100 percent. As one Detroit patrolman told me casually, "I'd be surprised if the public ever learned about even a quarter of the rapes that happen in this town." *

Homicide figures are the most trustworthy of the lot: Since for each slaying there is usually a corpse, the authorities can arrive at a fairly accurate tally by counting the bodies. Here the problem lies in obtaining any kind of historical perspective. The FBI didn't begin compiling its reports until 1933. Before that national crime statistics were gathered haphazardly,

---

* One example of the extent of these discrepancies will suffice. The FBI's report for 1976 showed 11.3 million "victimizations" by rape, robbery, assault, burglary and larceny. The Census Bureau's projections for the same year gave 41.1 million such crimes.

and not at all before 1900. Prior to the turn of the century national figures were largely surmises backed by guesswork.

So far as a historical pattern can be discerned, America's murder rate climbed and fell, peaked and flattened like a stock-market graph, but without apparent connection to the country's prosperity cycles. There seem to have been four major upsurges of homicide over the past century. The first occurred in the wake of the Civil War. The second lasted from about 1900 to 1910. The third began in the boom period of the late 1920s, reached its pinnacle in Depression-wracked 1933, then ebbed gradually. There was no real increase in the homicide rate from the 1940s through the early 1960s, despite a rapid rise in population. Then, in 1965, the figures started to climb again. The upward trend has continued ever since, an occasional minor drop notwithstanding.

Some optimistic sociologists, maintaining that the rate is bound to fall to "acceptable" levels by the same mysterious process that operated in the past, draw comfort from the previous ups and downs of our murder chart. But several features of the current wave give it an ominously different character. The differences lie in the *types* of slayings that are becoming more and more prevalent—differences that don't register on graphs.

One of them is the terrifying increase of stranger-to-stranger killings, the form of violence that arouses more general fear than any other. Whereas the overall homicide rate doubled over the last decade, stranger-to-stranger slayings have more than quadrupled. Most of these are felony murders, meaning that they occur in the course of another crime, such as a mugging, rape, robbery, or burglary. Herein lies the sinister difference between our current wave and the earlier versions. In the past bandits killed almost invariably because they met resistance or while fighting the law. Today's specimens slaughter batches of people for the sole purpose of eliminating witnesses.

John Dillinger once remarked about Bonnie and Clyde: "Folks like them give bank-robbing a bad name." His quip was prompted by the pair's habit of leaving a corpse or two at the scene of every one of their peddling heists. It would have been interesting to hear the great John D.'s comments on the Washington, D.C., holdup man who blew out the brains of four unresisting men and women in a grocery store for a take of $117; about the two bandits who struck a hi-fi shop in Ogden, Utah, tied up four employees, and tortured them to death by making them swallow drain cleaner, which burned holes in their stomachs; or about the Kansas teenager who shot three men simply in order to steal their cars.

In each of these cases compliance with the demands of the criminals meant death. Multiply them by several thousand and you will get an idea of the new breed of outlaw in our midst: a species of moral cretin either incapable of weighing the enormity of their actions against their gains or so disoriented by drugs as to preclude any weighing process. They make the Pretty Boy Floyds, the Machine Gun Kellys, the Underhills, Nashes, and Baileys of the 1930s appear oddly innocuous. Their methods are mostly clumsy, their criminal skills mediocre, their planning often asinine, but by sheer weight of numbers they can stymie a flaccid, badly coordinated, sorely perplexed, and frequently demoralized law apparatus.

Ellsworth Smith, for example, was no slick underworld operator. His career as a holdup man, bank robber, mugger, and murderer revealed far more brutality than brains. He got caught thirty-two times in fourteen years. Yet he spent less than five years in jail, although he cold bloodedly shot a liquor-store clerk in the stomach and a mugging victim in the head. Between 1971 and 1975 he was wanted in New Jersey, New York, Washington, D.C., Georgia, and California, but nobody seemed capable of holding him for any length of time. Despite the fact that his fingerprints were on file with the FBI, Smith again and again threw the law-enforcement system into disarray by simply changing aliases. He got off on parole, on probation, on suspended sentence, by jumping bail, and once by escaping from prison. Several judges showed him leniency amounting to culpable negligence. Far more often the courts were in ignorance about his past because of overloaded schedules, mislaid records, clerical errors, and the confusion arising from incompetence. Smith kept right on robbing and shooting people, kept getting arrested, and kept getting free. His third victim died after Smith smashed his skull with a bullet. Even then his conviction came about by pure coincidence. Using yet another alias, he had nonchalantly gone to the Washington D.C. Superior Court to bail out his girl friend on a shoplifting charge. A detective recognized him in the corridor and snapped handcuffs on him. Smith is now serving a life sentence for first-degree murder in the Atlanta federal penitentiary. What is significant is that in no other civilized country could he have been at liberty to commit his ultimate deed after so many dress rehearsals.

Little research has gone into fathoming the grimmest manifestation of our violence epidemic—the growth of the multiple-murder syndrome. The second half of the twentieth century could be called America's Age of Mass Murder. Triple and quadruple slayings are so commonplace that unless they involve celebrities they hardly make the news outside of the states in which they are committed. The mass murderer was a rarity in every previous crime wave; today he has almost become its symbol. The baffling part of this phenomenon is that it has no visible connection with social or racial conflicts, with poverty, illiteracy, alienation, or any of the other causes usually mentioned as a factor in our crisis. A large proportion of the killers are, of course, insane, at least in the colloquial sense. The question is: Are there proportionately more of them today or do they have greater opportunities for killing?

English criminologist Grierson Dickson coined the word "multicide" to designate the type of series murderer who has put his imprint on our era. In order to compile a chronological table of multicides in this century we have to whittle down the list to the top scorers—those who claimed seven or more victims. We have to ignore the professional triggermen of the underworld, since they usually work in squads. The same applies to group killers, such as the Manson "family," whose concerted action makes it impossible to pinpoint individual guilt. Finally, we must eliminate those who wiped out large numbers while actually aiming at only one victim. This would rule out killers like Jack Graham, who planted a bomb in an airplane and blew up forty-four passengers for the purpose of destroying just one, his mother.

The survey below, therefore, includes only those multicides who murdered each of their victims individually, deliberately, and single-handed.

	Numbers of Victims	Apprehended
Belle Gunness	14–17	Vanished 1908
Earle Nelson	18–26	1927
Carl Panzram	21?	1928
Albert Fish	8–15	1934
Jarvis Catoe	7	1941
Howard Unruh	13	1949
Ernest Ingenito	7	1950
Charles Starkweather	11	1958
Melvin Rees	9	1960
Albert DeSalvo	13	1964
Richard Speck	8	1966
Charles Whitman	16	Killed 1966
John Freeman	7	1971
Dean Corll	27–?	Killed 1973
Edmund Kemper	10	1973
Herbert Mullin	13	1973
Paul Knowles	18–?	Killed 1974
Calvin Jackson	9	1974
James Ruppert	11	1975
Vaughn Greenwood	9–11	1975
Edward Allaway	7	1976

The first thing that should be noted about this roll is that it contains only one woman (Belle Gunness) and only three blacks (Catoe, Jackson, and Greenwood). The second is the relative absence of the profit motive. Only Mrs. Gunness and Paul Knowles killed for loot. Seven of the slayers acted on sudden berserk impulses that in several cases seemed to have no motivation at all. Another, Herbert Mullin, was a textbook example of paranoid schizophrenia: He obeyed "divine" voices that ordered him to go forth and kill. Twelve—more than half of the entire roster—followed manic sexual urges.

Three of those were homosexuals, one of whom, the Texan Dean Corll, may have achieved America's all-time homicide record before an associate finished him off. The heterosexuals had widely differing *modi operandi:* from Earle Nelson, who raped and murdered elderly landladies, to Albert Fish, who killed—and often ate—children. The alcoholic pill popper Speck stabbed and throttled eight student nurses in a single night. Albert DeSalvo, the Boston Strangler, never touched drugs or liquor, and terrorized an entire city during two years of leisurely slaughter. The trim, handsome jazz musician Rees slowly tortured his prey to death. The bloated giant Kemper killed quickly, then did unspeakable things to the corpses.

The most telling feature of this survey, however, is not method but sequence. During the first fifty years of this century we had only seven major multicides. Then, over the past twenty-six years, the number shot up to sixteen—ten of them in the 1970s, which aren't over yet. You don't have to be a statistician to observe that an acceleration process is taking place and that it is gathering momentum. As a Los Angeles homicide detective commented, "Maybe it's something in the air. They all seem to be crawling out of the woodwork."

"Something in the air" is a ubiquitous sense of menace currently felt by Americans, to which millions react with a troubled rage that becomes self-destructive for want of tangible targets. It camouflages itself in a blend of callousness and cowardice and emerges as the kind of crowd behavior that shocked New York in September 1976.

Calvin Springs, a Queens diamond cutter, was sitting in

a parked car with his three young children a few blocks from his home when a shooting match erupted in a barbecue restaurant across the street. A stray bullet struck the back of his head. He slumped over the wheel, pumping blood, while the screaming children desperately tried to "wake up Daddy." A large crowd gathered, watching with great interest and not stirring a finger. A nurse pushed her way through, looked at the head wound, and decided that Springs needed an ambulance—fast. She asked the bystanders to call one. Nobody moved. She then tried to call herself, but none of the shopkeepers or residents would allow her to use their telephone.

"I tried and tried, one place after another, but no one wanted to get involved," she related. "I told them it was an emergency—I begged them—I said please help, please help, a man's life was in danger. None of them helped. Not a single one."

Finally the nurse got into Spring's car and drove to Jamaica Hospital, where he died nine hours later.

This is the callousness; the rage lies only one layer deeper. It surfaces in response to a new entertainment genre created expressly for this mood: the revenge movie. It comes as grade-B schlock or Academy Award contender, but its theme is always the same: Some decent citizen, tormented beyond endurance, takes vengeance into his own hands and goes after "them" with blazing guns. It doesn't much matter whether "they" are muggers, pimps, pushers, or gangsters. What counts is the orgiastic joy of seeing them riddled, watching them spurt realistic blood while the hero, in a cold fury of sadistic justice, reloads his weapon for the next round. All these films emphasize the powerlessness or corruption of official law enforcement and demonstrate that direct counter-violence is the only policy that works. They strike ominously responsive chords in the audience; sometimes the squeals of "Go get 'em!" drown out the gunfire and groans on the screen.

Those are the voices of a multitude who feel abandoned by their traditional protective forces, the police and the courts, and to whom the spectacle of bloody retribution comes as an almost physical relief. Sociologist Edward McNaren zeroed in on the basis of that emotion when he wrote: "People sense that the margin of safety in their lives is daily being eroded, and that the authorities are quite unresponsive to their fears. A new term, 'victimology,' has been coined, which subtly shifts the onus of guilt from the attackers to the victims. It assumes that victims of assaults are somehow guilty by having exposed themselves to attack in the first place."

Erosion of our safety margins—always slender enough— leads to an erosion in the quality of our lives. Sitting behind bars, chains, and triple locks, guarded by TV monitors and watchdogs, prevented from taking a stroll through the park in the evening or buying a newspaper at night, hurrying furtively past dark alleys, battling clammy terror on entering deserted parking lots, climbing stairs rather than taking elevators—these are some of the symptoms of this erosion. We are just beginning to take them for granted as part of urban existence, the price of daily survival. What is worse is that our children may accept them as normal.

Metropolitan areas are now mushrooming with so-called fortress apartments, buildings made practically inaccessible by high walls, steel grills, electronic monitors, and armed guards, where visitors and delivery boys need signed passes to enter. The security systems of these blocks usurp as much as 20 percent of the construction costs, and the expense is added to the rents. Thus, a huge burden is piled on the inflation-wracked housing market solely for the privilege of dwelling in a cross between an army base and a penitentiary.

As a cheaper alternative architect Oscar Newman has projected a form of urban housing utilizing the concept of "defensible space." His units are strategically positioned in blocked cul-de-sacs, with all stairways, corridors, and recreation areas easily viewable from each apartment. Residents would act as their own housing police, instantly spotting strangers who entered, watching their movements, and noting their destination and times of arrival and departure. This might indeed render the occupants somewhat safer, but would give them all the privacy of a goldfish bowl.

Both alternatives shift the task of vigilance to the private sector. This is another giant step backward, a regression into medieval conditions, with armed retainers or householders mounting guard over their fortress homes. And it is quite in keeping with a general acceptance of mayhem as a fact of city life, about which the police can do little—certainly less than a well-trained Doberman pinscher.

This nadir of public confidence has been fostered by the lame response of governments at every level to the rising tide of violence. It reached a point of near resignation after the departure of Agnew, Mitchell, Kleindienst, & Co., who had entered bellowing law-'n'-order incantations and turned them into obscene jokes by their own contempt for the law.

A side effect of this mood has been a curious downgrading of the seriousness of criminal acts. Rapes, muggings, and assaults have been changed into something like misdemeanors; in the case of juveniles, to pranks. One scribe of the underground press even referred to the Manson clan as "just doing their own thing," perhaps the greatest banality ever bestowed on mass murder. But it offers a whiff of the almost nonchalant attitude toward homicide that permeates the country, extending from courts of law to neighborhood police stations.

This attitude, which conservatives so often mistake for permissiveness, actually expresses nothing beyond a very low regard for human lives. It reflects a scale of values that places numerous things well above the prevention of killings: convenience, profit, entertainment, political expediency, macho complexes, regional traditions, ethnic sensitivities, and psychiatric experimentation. The courts adhere to this lopsided value ladder by handing down wrist slaps to drunk or doped motorists who massacre entire families (often their own). Most of them receive fines or suspended sentences. In Scandinavia, Holland, and Switzerland—countries noted for their otherwise lenient penal codes—such offenders collect prison terms of up to ten years. Our practice probably has no *direct* bearing on the homicide rate, but it gives powerful psychological reinforcement to potential murderers. It demonstrates to all and sundry the esteem in which judges hold human safety.

Some law-enforcement bodies tend to view this mood as a form of heavenly visitation akin to drought and volcanic eruption—an evil that descends and will presumably pass in its own good time. All this attitude achieves is to further aggravate the malaise. For the condition is the manifest result of interlocking causes and it can be alleviated, providing the will to do so exists; but it can also deteriorate beyond repair if left untreated.

The *will* is the paramount factor. As we spotlight the problems in the course of this book it will become apparent that none of them requires a change in human nature. They may require certain constitutional amendments, the trimming of huge amounts of deadwood, and the liquidation of several sacred cows. Above all, they require the investment of labor, determination, ingenuity, and funds hitherto reserved for military enterprises. These problems simply cannot be solved with the resources we have so far been ready to make available.

Fortunately, the decision is still in our hands. As the late Walt Kelly expressed it by way of the immortal Pogo: "We have met the enemy, and he is us."

1

Murder as a Family Affair

If you are afraid of being murdered, there is more safety in deserting your family and having no friends than in additional police, who rarely have the opportunity to prevent friends and relatives from murdering each other.
—Former U.S. Attorney General Ramsey Clark

When sticky darkness sinks over the metropolis and the air enfolds you like a warm dishrag soaked in urine, the murder rate rises hand in hand with the humidity count. At such times, hundreds of thousands of cramped apartments become pressure cookers in which sweat, anger, frustration, and jealousy combine to form a highly volatile stew. Suddenly come the breathless screams, the glass-splintering crashes, and the thuds of crumpling bodies.

I once asked a veteran New York City patrolman what he considered to be the potentially most dangerous situation confronting a cop. Without hesitating, he answered: "Trying to stop a family brawl on a hot night." Later I checked his reply against the records and found that statistics confirmed his personal impression. Approximately one of every five policemen killed on duty dies while intervening in a domestic dispute. More cops are injured in this fashion than in any other type of violent encounter.

"I'd rather arrest an armed criminal in the street any time," my patrolman said. "The trouble with these damned family fights is you're never quite prepared for what can happen. One moment they're still yelling at each other, then . . . wham! There's a kitchen knife between your ribs or a bullet in your

17

guts. And it's liable to come from anybody—husband, wife, a kid, grandpa—just anybody."

In large cities patrolmen may have to spend up to 40 percent of their duty time trying to settle family brawls. Accordingly, a fair amount of their training is devoted to "domestic intervention." Yet much of this has no practical value, for unless a cop has learned the language and social patterns of ethnic minorities (or belongs to one himself), he still won't be able to read danger signals until it is too late.

Domestic murders play a curious role in our homicide statistics. For one thing, they are the only category of homicide in which the sex balance of the killers is nearly equal—clear evidence that in America almost as many women as men kill their mates, their children, or sundry relatives.

The second oddity is the fact that criminologists prefer that the proportion of intrafamily slayings remain high. They become alarmed when the percentage goes *down*, and for good reason: A declining ratio of domestic homicides usually indicates an equivalent increase of stranger-to-stranger murders, which not only inspire more public fear but are also vastly more difficult to solve. Domestic murders are mostly unpremeditated. The killers rarely flee; even if they do, their arrest is usually just a routine matter. In stranger murders, on the other hand, investigators often face a blank wall. Thus, New York City owes its deplorable "clearance" record (only 64.5 percent of homicide cases solved in 1975, compared with San Diego's 93 percent and London's 97.5 percent) not to police incompetence but to that city's exceptionally high rate of stranger-to-stranger slayings.

Nationwide our ratio of domestic homicides has been declining for years. However, they still form the second biggest category on the chart, following felony murders. Of the 20,600 murders listed in the FBI's *Uniform Crime Report* for 1974, approximately one fourth were family affairs. Of these, slightly over one half involved spouse killing spouse. The remainder were parents killing their children or vice versa, plus every possible permutation of relatives doing away with each other.

Most of these 5,200 family murders occurred where the majority of all our killings take place—in the urban poverty regions housing some 40 million Americans. Nevertheless, an astonishing number were committed in middle-class and upper-income circles. The circumstances of all these murders are strangely similar, like mass-produced movie scripts, regardless of whether the background happens to be a blighted tenement or a suburban luxury residence.

The case of Bernard Castro, Jr., for instance, could serve as a textbook example. The twenty-six-year-old heir to the Castro Convertible fortune had married a slender blonde with whom he had little in common. The dark, chunky Bernard was a loner with an abrasive temper, a sporadic drinking problem, and an obsession with body building and firearms. Julie Ann's tastes and manners were conventional; she was far more concerned about social niceties than her husband. The couple had two children and three homes—one of them a beach house in the exclusive Coral Ridge section of Fort Lauderdale, Florida.

Bernard's penchant for armaments revealed itself in "his and hers" automatics, plus another pistol and a mounted shotgun for his car—all perfectly legal in Florida. A few times, while "likkered up," he waved his weapons at people with whom he was arguing—actions which were not so legal but resulted in nothing worse than a fine.

During six years of marriage the millionaire's son's behavior grew steadily more erratic, his periodic drinking bouts more truculent. Julie Ann remained sweetly genteel in public, but became gradually tougher and more strident in private, offering Bernard stronger resistance than he was used to encountering. With so many guns around the house, they eventually took to pointing them at each other in moments of fury.

At this point, as Julie Ann explained later, she became frightened of her husband and afraid for herself and her children. Around midnight on October 29, 1974, Bernard arrived at the beach house after hitting several bars. The couple promptly continued an argument that had raged throughout dinner. In the early-morning hours it apparently got out of control. When Bernard whipped out the automatic that he kept under the guest-room mattress and threatened to shoot his wife, she fled to her own room and came back with her Colt Junior. According to her version, she then fired five shots at her husband, killing him. Accepting her account unanimously, the Broward County Grand Jury refused to indict Mrs. Castro on any grounds.

The validity of their verdict doesn't concern us here. The really interesting aspect of the case is that it represents what might be called the "standard American spouse murder." There was the fatal availability of weapons and the effect of liquor in dissolving inhibitions. There was a history of mounting friction and, before the final explosion, several small warning combustions, laughed off by acquaintances and half ignored by the law. The Castros happened to be rich and socially prominent, but the ingredients of their tragedy were the same as those in thousands of slum killings.

Beneath these surface manifestations we find most of the motivations sparking marital homicide throughout our social structure. They closely matched the results of a study conducted by psychotherapist Dr. George Bach, who interviewed seventy-four spouse-slayers in connection with his work on violence prevention.

Dr. Bach's subjects were thirty-eight men and thirty-six women from white, black, Polynesian, and West Indian backgrounds, their ages ranging from twenty-two to sixty-two. The most striking parallel in their marriages was a sharp disparity of power. One partner was the aggressive ruler, the other the passive, often tyrannized, subject—yet there were more killers among the passive group than among the tyrants. Similarly their marriages showed an extreme imbalance in the daily giving and taking: One mate was required to give and give incessantly, while the other demonstrated utter insatiability in taking. Frequently the giver felt drained, exhausted, and used up, but was nevertheless expected to continue the one-sided relationship. Matching this were drastic differences in social contacts: One partner was far more socially oriented than the other, with the withdrawn one coming to feel increasingly insecure and threatened.

All of Dr. Bach's killers tended to have rigid ideas on how marriage partners should behave. They entered wedlock with a fixed set of expectations for which they demanded fulfillment. When this was not provided, they refused to modify their expectations. Instead, they attempted in one way or another to manipulate their mates into living up to them.

All these contrasts combined in pushing the couple toward a crisis point. The explosion occurred either immediately or shortly after when one partner announced a decision to leave the other. The mate responded with an attempt at blocking—an attempt that often turned out to be fatal for one of them. In the Castro case, Julie Ann had mentioned divorce during their ultimate quarrel. This apparently provoked her husband into brandishing a gun—a threat that culminated in his own death. Most often it is the mate attempting the blocking who ends up as the victim.

Sociologists, psychologists, and criminologists seem to agree on one point: Most marital murders are preceded by distinct warning signs, which often can be read quite plainly even by untrained observers. The trouble lies with our inability to act upon such perceptions, since our laws provide marriage partners with only the barest minimum of protection from each other.

The most ubiquitous of these signals is wife-beating, which also ranks as the most consistently ignored. There is an ineradicable myth—part of a legendary working-class tradition —that maltreated wives are a blue-collar phenomenon, whereas they can actually be found in all social strata, to the very top.

America is no worse afflicted than other nations in this respect but is doing less about it. England has fifty shelters in which wives can find refuge from physical assault; West Germany has thirteen; America has three. Yet these shelters are often the only preventive means available for marital situations quite obviously drifting toward homicide. Large numbers of battered wives, especially those with young children and no money of their own, have absolutely no place to escape to. Retreat is blocked, leaving them no alternatives but to continue being beaten or striking back with a weapon.

Marta Segovia Ashley, who heads a refuge organization in San Francisco, has a very personal stake in the venture: Her mother was a victim of just the kind of trap she is trying to save others from. "The first time my stepfather hit my mother she forgave him," she told an interviewer. "The second time he did it, he broke her jaw. But nobody in the family said it was wrong because in a Latino community it is the woman who keeps the harmony in the house. You can't even say, 'Listen, my husband is beating me,' for they say it's your fault. The third time he attacked her, he killed her."

Ms. Ashley's organization is unfortunately called *La Casa de Las Madres*—unfortunately because such a title conveys the impression that only Hispanic mothers stand in need of it. Actually, the Latino community's proportion of wife assaults is about "normal" by contemporary standards. According to FBI figures, wife-beating is the most common form of violence committed against women nationwide, outnumbering rape, the next most prevalent, by about three to one. In 1975 New York State, for example, had 14,000 reported (and, therefore, at least ten times that many unreported) cases of wife-beating.

It is difficult to describe the helplessness of some of the victims in our supposedly "liberated" age. Their impotence may be psychological as much as physical, but it is nevertheless as real as the pain of a psychosomatic illness. Here, as a sample, is the account given to me by a Chicago housewife in her thirties, whose husband is a sales executive with a large engineering firm. They are white, Catholic, have three children, and own a comfortable home in suburban Highland Park:

> I was married at twenty-three, and my husband has been beating, kicking, and manhandling me periodically ever since. Mostly he beat me with his fists, but on several occasions he

used a long metal ruler. He has thrown hot soup in my face, pushed my head into a basin of hot water, broken one of my fingers, blackened both my eyes, and knocked out a front tooth. He kicked me in the stomach when I was pregnant. As a result my youngest daughter was born with a deformed leg. Once he threw a hammer at me, hitting my left ear. I haven't been hearing well on that ear since then.

I've called the police twice, but they never came. I think it was because I was kind of incoherent each time. I've talked to our priest, and he told me that I should forgive him for the sake of our children. I also told our family doctor. He prescribed tranquilizers for me and said we should go to a family-guidance clinic. My husband won't hear of it. I would like to leave him, but I've never held a job. I have no skills and no money and no living relatives who could support me. I **don't** want to leave the children with my husband.

Most of the victims seeking outside help will turn to the clergy or the police—two equally unhappy choices. Clergymen, by and large, must rank among the least effective marriage counselors in the business. The majority imagine that their duty lies in holding a marriage together and suppose that even wedded martyrdom is preferable to separation. They will usually trot out some platitude about broken homes being bad for children—as if battered mothers weren't infinitely worse. Most of the clergy instinctively favor the status quo, even at the expense of a spouse's physical safety. Some will go to fantastic lengths to block out the wife's suffering if the husband is a regular church or synagogue attendant. I was able to tally nineteen marital-murder cases in which the killing occurred after some gentleman of the cloth had advised a desperate woman to "show forbearance" for the sake of her offspring. Those who commented on the slayings at all invariably voiced "unbelieving shock" at the bloody denouement—for which they were at least partly responsible.

The police are of little help because wife-beating falls into a category they fear like the plague: the shadowy borderline between criminal and civil offenses. My Chicago informant was probably wrong when she blamed her incoherence for the cops' failure to respond to her calls. Family disputes get the lowest priority on police networks. In some cities the squad cars will follow them up only if the complaint comes from a neighbor, not from the actual parties involved. The fault there lies not so much with the cops as with our legislators, who have done their damnedest to conceal marital violence behind a thicket of legalistic paradoxes.

The police can lock up a husband only if his wife files an assault charge against him. Many women won't do this or—if they do—promptly withdraw the charge the next day. Some act like this from fear, others in the vapid hope that "he'll be different from now on." The fear motivation, however, is only too realistic. For when a woman's husband gets free and continues to threaten her, all she can do is obtain a restraining order to keep him away from the house.

Such a restraining order is an extremely dubious document; one feminist lawyer characterizes it as "useful only for toilet purposes." It can be interpreted as a civil matter, in which case it is out of police jurisdiction. Most cops prefer that interpretation, seeing it as a valid excuse for their reluctance to make arrests for violations. One reason for this reluctance is that such orders are rarely recorded in headquarters files, and checking them out represents a hellishly time-consuming task.

My New York patrolman mentioned another reason for their reluctance to intervene: "Very often when you try to arrest a husband you get attacked by his old lady—the same dame he's just been beating the crap out of. I don't know why they do it; maybe they think he'll be nicer to them for wading in—I dunno. But I can tell you, it's not funny. Not when you're in the middle, getting it from both sides. I've been hit with a meat cleaver by a woman I tried to rescue from being throttled by her guy. And a buddy of mine had half his skull blown off by a gun he'd wrestled away from a husband. The gun dropped on the floor and the wife grabbed it. Only she didn't turn on the guy who'd been aiming it at her. She shot the cop instead."

The utterly harebrained behavior of some maltreated women undoubtedly contributes to the tardiness of the police. So does the macho notion, rampant among cops, that a male has some kind of divine dispensation to slap his woman around occasionally (". . . way deep down she probably enjoys it"). The fact that this exercise frequently precedes murder doesn't seem to have fully sunk in yet.*

The few attempts made to provide alternatives to an appeal to the police have proved more or less abject failures. One of them, the Citizens' Complaint Center, opened in Washington, D.C., in 1970. Intended as a criminal-justice agency, the Center quickly became a bureaucratic futility slot remarkable even by capital standards. When I visited the place, six years after its inauguration, I saw why. The entire full-time staff consisted of one receptionist and one paralegal employee. Between them, they were supposed to evaluate and process a daily average of seventy complaints, many from women in fear of their lives—this in a city literally awash with legal practitioners of every stripe.

A report issued in 1976 by the American Law Institute conveys an idea of the Center's protective worth. The report quoted two former assistant U.S. attorneys who handled the cases of eleven women who had been unable to convince Center staffers that they were in imminent physical danger. All of them were killed after lawyers connected with the center refused to apply for arrest warrants for their mates.

Diane Hallman, who worked in a Superior Court office, applied for a Civil Protection Order barring her husband from coming near her. Two days before the CPO hearing was scheduled, the husband walked into her office and shot her dead.

Alicha Warren came to the Center in November 1975, requesting a CPO against her husband. Four days later, while her request was still being considered, her husband shot her fatally.

In October 1975 the Center wrote a letter to the common-law spouse of Geraldine Bessie Williams, warning him to stay away from her. He killed her the same day.

---

* A study conducted in Kansas City revealed that in 85 percent of family homicides the police had been called one to five times before each murder occurred.

One woman (unnamed in the report) called at the Center twice in two months to complain about her husband's assaults. The first time she waited several hours without being able to speak to anyone. The second time her complaint was ignored. She didn't appear a third time, because her husband murdered her a month later.

In these and the seven other cases cited, the subsequent legal procedure was simplicity itself. All the slayers either pleaded or were found guilty and went to prison. Which must have been a great comfort to the eleven dead women who had approached the Center in the hope of help. "In almost every case," the report said ponderously, "the initial expectation of help is destroyed and most complainants leave the facility with the view that the center has done nothing to ameliorate their difficulties."

Except, possibly, to hasten their deaths.

While wife-beating is the most common signal predicting worse violence to come, it is not the only one. The others, however, are more difficult to spot. They may seem obvious to those enjoying the omniscience of hindsight, but the people involved at the time have no such vantage point. They may be quite unable to see that a person with a naturally combustive temperament is being pushed over the edge. This happened in America's bloodiest marital drama, the Ingenito case.

Ernest Ingenito was a tall, handsome muscle boy of twenty-three when he married Theresa Mazzoli in 1947. He had a bad track record that included a youthful burglary conviction, a disastrous teenage marriage, and a dishonorable discharge from the Army (for assaulting three superior officers simultaneously). Ernie had the kind of coiled-spring intensity that attracts women but requires delicate handling. Delicacy was not, however, a Mazzoli characteristic. Fiercely proud, hard-working, hardheaded, and clannish, they were prosperous Italian truck farmers in Gloucester County, New Jersey. Theresa, the dark family beauty, was the apple of their eye.

The young couple made a tragic mistake by moving into

the Mazzoli home, for, against Theresa's parents and uncles
and aunts, Ernie had to back down—a response to which
he was not accustomed. After the birth of their two sons,
the situation grew worse: Theresa became more headstrong;
Ernie more resentful; the air more sulfurous. Old Mike
Mazzoli had quietly decided that his son-in-law was a brain-
less bum, and Pearl, Ernie's mother-in-law, told him so daily
in very loud tones, often in front of the children. Ernie took
his bruised ego to the neighborhood bars. He drank and
picked fights, wading into one opponent after another with
a joyous ferocity that stopped only just short of murder. As
an added ego boost he had extracurricular affairs. This finished him so far as the Mazzolis were concerned. Mike threw
his son-in-law out of the house. Theresa refused to meet him
or let him near his sons. Almost crying with anger and frustration, Ernie contacted a lawyer and demanded his right as
a father to see his children. The attorney informed him that
this would require a court order and court orders took time.
Weeks . . . months . . . no telling how long.

At that point something happened to Ernie that had happened before in the Army. Only now it came on him a
hundred times stronger. A berserk bubble of rage burst inside his head, blowing away every thought except fury. None
of this showed on his face. Throughout everything that followed he maintained a curiously detached half-smile, like
someone perpetrating a practical joke.

On the evening of November 17, 1950, Ingenito dragged
out his weapons: two Luger pistols, a .32-caliber carbine, and
a paratrooper's knife. He emptied his pockets and filled them
with ammunition until they bulged grotesquely. Then he
marched over to the Mazzoli home. Theresa opened the door
but backed away when she saw the pistol in his hand. "I
want to see my kids," Ernie said quietly and shot her twice.
Mike Mazzoli rushed to the aid of his daughter, the evening
paper still under his arm. Again Ernie shot twice, and watched
the old man crumple. He stepped over his body and went
in search of his hated mother-in-law. Pearl heard him coming
and ran out the back door while he searched the house for

her. Meanwhile, Theresa, trailing blood over the carpet, crawled to the telephone. "For God's sake, get Ernie," she gasped to the police. "He's killing everybody—everybody." But Ernie had only just begun.

He guessed where Pearl had fled—to the home of her parents, the Pioppis, just down the block. Shouldering his carbine, infantry-style, he bounded after her. This time he didn't knock, but hurled himself bodily through the screen door, carbine blazing. The first bullets riddled Mrs. Pioppi. The next burst caught Marion Pioppi, Pearl's sister-in-law. Ernie tore open the kitchen door and came upon Pearl's two brothers, trying to shield their young children with their bodies. The maniac first emptied the carbine into them, then the clip of a Luger.

Leaving the bodies on the kitchen floor, Ernie panted up the stairs to the bedroom. First he looked under the beds; then he wrenched open the closet. There, frantically trying to hide between the clothes, was Pearl. Ernie shot her nine times.

He wasn't through yet; there were still Mazzolis left alive. Reloading his arsenal, Ernie climbed into his car and drove to Minotola, N.J., where Frank and Hilda Mazzoli lived. He caught the entire family at home. Screaming, "I'm getting even . . . all of you . . ." he pushed aside ten-year-old Barbara and opened fire on her parents. The house lay silent when Ernie staggered outside and into his car again.

For some reason he drove back to Mike Mazzoli's home. A squad car intercepted him two blocks from the massacre scene. The cops grabbed Ernie, still wearing his absent-minded grin, as he was trying to open his wrists with a rusty tin can. It was midnight. The entire rampage had taken three hours. Seven Mazzolis lay dead, but Theresa survived, badly wounded. She no longer had a family. Doctors declared Ernie insane, and he was sent to the New Jersey State Hospital in Trenton.*

---

* The same institution already housed another veteran, Howard Unruh, who just fourteen months earlier had gone on an even grimmer rampage. Also wielding two Lugers, Unruh killed thirteen neighbors and strangers

There are significant differences between spouse-slayings and the next-largest category of domestic murders: infanticide. Parents killing their children account for 600 to 700 cases a year, or over 3 percent of our total homicide score. But here the killers are overwhelmingly female, particularly when the victims are babies. (This does not indicate that fathers are more tolerant toward infants, merely that they have less contact with them.) Women who kill their children usually suffer from severe emotional disturbances and seldom commit the deed spontaneously. Often they go through long preliminary traumas, abusing and maltreating the child as they build up to the final step.

Children, however, are considerably better protected against ill-treatment than their mothers. Although child abuse is at least as widespread as wife-beating, every American city boasts half a dozen or more organizations to deal with it. These bodies can intervene on their own volition and do so forcefully and frequently. It is this intervention that quite probably prevents infanticide from becoming anywhere near as numerous as spouse murder.

When fathers turn killers they are most likely to murder their teenage sons, seldom daughters or babies. The reasons are nearly always emotional: clashes of temperament, drunken rages, struggles for household supremacy. The profit motive rarely enters these situations. But occasionally it does, and one of those instances gave a Texas town the worst bout of communal jitters in memory.

Pasadena, near Galveston Bay, is a drably streamlined blue-collar center, redolent with petrochemical fumes and proud of having one of the lowest crime rates in the nation. But in the days following Halloween of 1974, its citizens became panicky with the knowledge that somewhere among them dwelled a fiend who fed poisoned candy to trick-or-

---

within ten minutes in the streets of Camden, New Jersey. Unlike Ingenito, he had an excellent service record and was neither married nor reacting against any discernible social pressures. Contacted by the Camden *Courier Post*, Unruh amiably told the editor on the telephone: "Nope, nobody's done anything to me yet, but I'm doing plenty to them."

treating children. How many kids had taken his treats and were destined to die, no one could say.

The one known victim was eight-year-old Tim O'Bryan. His father and a friend had taken him, his sister, and two other children on a Halloween goodies hunt. Someone gave the youngsters five large tubes of a sweet called "Giant Pixy Stix." Tim was the only one who ate some, shortly after getting home. Minutes later he fell into convulsions, then lapsed into a coma. His father called an ambulance. Despite emergency treatment, the boy died that night, while the father paced the hospital waiting room beating his fists against the walls, crying, "Dear God, save my son . . ."

The first act of the police was to collect all the Giant Pixy Stix the children had carried home. They found that the top of each tube had been sliced open and resealed after the candies were mixed with enough potassium cyanide to kill a dozen adults. If, by sheer luck, the other children hadn't decided to postpone their candy feast, there would have been four small corpses instead of one.

The O'Bryans were what used to be termed "pillars of the community." Tim's father, Ronald, worked as an optometrist and sang solo tenor in his church choir. A large florid man, with a high forehead that made him appear rather more intelligent than he was, he laced his conversation with appeals to God and assured everyone that little Tim was "happy in heaven now."

But the more Homicide Captain R. E. Rhodes delved into O'Bryan's circumstances, the more suspicious he became. He discovered that the church tenor was also a known incompetent who had lost twenty-one jobs in ten years, had habitually lived beyond his means, and had piled up so many debts that a credit union was pressing for payment of his last car installment. Rhodes further discovered that, without having informed his wife, O'Bryan carried the rather extraordinary amount of $65,000 in life insurance on his two young children. Indeed, according to an insurance agent, one month before Tim's death O'Bryan had even begun procedures to collect immediately following the boy's demise. Rhodes also learned that O'Bryan had made several inquiries regarding the names of stores selling cyanide.

The captain's most startling discovery was that it was O'Bryan himself who had actually given the fatal candy to the kids. The children remembered knocking at a door on Donarail Street where no one had answered. They went away, but O'Bryan remained behind for a few moments. When he caught up with them he explained that someone had opened the door after all and had given him the first tubes of Pixy Stix, which he then distributed among the group.

Although Captain Rhodes's evidence was admittedly circumstantial, some circumstantial evidence, such as, in Thoreau's words, "finding a trout in your milk," can be powerful. The day after O'Bryan sang the evening solo service for Tim (he chose "Blessed Assurance"), the police arrested him on the charge of murdering his son and on three counts of attempted murder. Now that the child-poisoner was no longer anonymous, the people of Pasadena breathed easier. But everyone who knew the O'Bryans shared a sense of disturbed bewilderment: "Ron, of all people! What got into him?"

The subsequent trial didn't shed much light on that question. The prosecution presented a painstakingly assembled pattern of evidence indicating that the accused intended to murder both his children for the sake of the insurance money, as well as another two, possibly three, in order to divert suspicion. The scheme combined so much detailed cunning with so much slipshod stupidity that it was hard to decide whether to think of O'Bryan as a diabolical conniver or a prize idiot. He had, for example, actually asked a fellow member of his church how much cyanide it took to kill a human being. The jury seems to have arrived at the former conclusion in finding O'Bryan guilty and fixing his punishment at death. But hardly anything emerged about the mental processes that might have induced a zealous religionist to become a potential mass murderer of children. There are, after all, easier ways of making money illicitly.

If the O'Bryan case stands as a freakish phenomenon, the tragedy of the Diener family reads like a larger-than-life scenario of the generation gap. Instinctively a million fathers must have identified with George Edward Diener, the all-American dad who slew his heir.

The Dieners had a small house in East Meadow, Long Island, which, when they moved in, epitomized America's proliferating dormitory suburbs as well as political Archie Bunkerism. A food-company salesman with the Stars and Stripes tattooed on one arm, George Diener loved outdoor sports with a passion matched only by his devotion to his son, Richie. Indeed, so devoted was Diener to his son that he never showed his disappointment at the boy's total lack of interest in football and baseball.

Nor was this his only disappointment. Having reached his mid-teens in the early 1970s, Richie was even more caught up in the dangerous fads of the period than were most of his peers. He smoked grass and hashish, blasted the house with acid rock, grew a beard, let his red hair grow into a jungle mop, and turned his den into a black-lit shrine of the counterculture. For the solidly bourgeois suburbanites they were, the Dieners displayed remarkable tolerance toward their son, if little understanding. Nevertheless, they did throw out his marijuana stashes whenever they came across them, and George periodically tried to impose some semblance of order on his boy's lifestyle. Ultimately, however, even his attempt to initiate the traditional "man-to-man" talks had to be abandoned when he found absolutely no common ground between them.

On the one hand, George Diener was a man who believed in eternal verities: He knew who he was, where he stood, and what he wanted. On the other hand, his son knew nothing of the kind and seemed to have no ideas beyond doing "what the other kids do." In George's eyes this amounted to avoiding all work, lying in bed listening to ear-shattering torrents of noise, and getting high.

Matters were to deteriorate still further when, following his seventeenth birthday, Richie stopped getting high and took to getting low instead. He became a heavy user of Seconal, "goofers" or "reds" in pill poppers' parlance. A powerful barbiturate used as a sleeping pill, Seconal is a depressant that disturbs transmissions from the central nervous system and can lead to behavioral changes—though no more so than massive doses of alcohol. Now the alienation between father and son flared into hostility. There were tremendous rows—George bellowing, Richie yelling obscenities or wailing, "You don't love me! You never wanted me!"—both hurling all the clichés of father-son confrontations.

These flashes were followed by long periods of stalemate, each withdrawing further from the other, each nursing his own bitterness. Then, on February 27, 1972, Richie wrecked his mother's car. That Sunday morning he had swallowed some Seconals and knocked down a fence at sixty miles per hour. George Diener went to the scene, sent his unhurt son home, and talked to the police. That evening they had their final clash.

Richie swallowed four more pills and announced that he was going out. His mother barred the way, insisting that he was in no condition to go anywhere. When George appeared, his son went into a paroxysm of fury. "You told the cops that I was on dope when I had that accident," he screamed. "Did you? Answer me! I want an answer!" His face twitched uncontrollably; his whole body shook with rage. Diener felt that he and his wife were in danger at that moment. He went to his room and took out his automatic pistol. Then the couple went down into the basement, George with the gun tucked into his belt.

Richie came down the stairs twice, the first time with an ice pick, which he dropped when George cocked his pistol. The second time he descended clutching a steak knife. Holding it in his raised fist, the boy advanced on his parents. "Go on," he spat. "Shoot. Use your fucking gun."

George pushed his wife behind him and took aim at the shambling creature coming toward them. He fired once, killing him instantly. Then he called the police.

The Nassau County Grand Jury found that Diener had acted in self-defense and refused to indict him. The verdict met with almost unanimous approval in East Meadow. Only a few people were disturbed by the fact that George was an excellent marksman who might have aimed for his son's legs instead of his heart.

While we have fairly accurate figures on the prevalence of spouse murder and infanticide, the remaining varieties of intrafamilial homicide are shrouded in statistical darkness. According to the FBI, this is because their computer does not break down the rest categorically but lumps them together as "Other Family Killings." Therefore we have no way of knowing either how many patricides, matricides, fratricides, and sororicides occur in the United States, or even whether their numbers are rising or declining. We can surmise that they happen frequently, however, simply by looking at the newspapers.

All civilized societies, and most primitive ones,* stand in atavistic horror of parricide: killing one's parents. Yet for poets and dramatists it has always held a peculiar macabre fascination as the ultimate and simultaneously most immediate gesture of rebellion. Freud theorized that this is one crime all humans fantasize about although very few reach the point of acting it out. Who are these few? Frequently they are sons protecting mothers against assaults by their fathers. Whether these sons are motivated purely by protective instincts, are acting out the ancient Oedipus syndrome, or are combining both motives is a conundrum for psychiatrists to solve. Undoubtedly, though, the killing of a father often symbolizes a blow against *all* established authority; conversely, an attack on the state may be a proxy for the suppressed desire to kill a father.

The parallel crime, matricide, can usually be interpreted as a cutting of the umbilical cord—a violent assertion of the killer's personal independence. This may be the case even if the murder involves an ostensible profit motive. Although Jack Gilbert Graham, the pampered misfit whose bomb killed

---

* Among certain African and New Guinea tribes it is the duty of sons to club their parents to death, to spare them the miseries of old age.

not only his mother but also the forty-three other passengers on the airplane in which she was riding, did it in order to collect his inheritance, along with the insurance money, he told interrogators before he died in the Colorado gas chamber in 1957: "She [his mother] held something over me that I couldn't get out from under. When the plane left the ground a load came off my shoulders. I watched her go off for the last time, and I felt freer than I ever felt before in my life."

One of the most grotesquely hideous matricides on record, the murder of Mrs. Marilyn Gerson in New Jersey, was also rooted in overdependence. Robert Gerson loathed his mother because she continually had to rescue him from the troubles created by his own stupidity. Things came to a head on Christmas Eve, 1974, when, in order to give him Christmas dinner at home, she bailed him out of the jail cell in which he resided because of a botched restaurant robbery, during which a Chinese waiter felled him with a karate chop. While basting the turkey, Mrs. Gerson asked Robert to turn down the television. Instead he screamed, "You're always ordering me around!" and leaped on her with a child's jump rope. Proving as inept at strangling as at everything else, he needed help from his sweetheart, Lorraine. While Robert held the half-choked woman, Lorraine plunged a kitchen knife into her a dozen times.

Although the goateed, twenty-three-year-old Robert had written a lengthy death-list of "useless people" he intended to liquidate subsequently, rather than following through with further murders, the couple just ran and spent Mrs. Gerson's money until they were caught. Robert drew a fifteen-year stretch. Lorraine, although equally guilty, plea-bargained herself a much shorter sentence by testifying against him.

Delving further into "Other Family Killings," we come to the ultimate perpetrators: those who wipe out their entire family. Although this group accounts for some of the most spectacular mass slaughters in recent history, the murderers themselves are anything but spectacular. If they share a common characteristic, it is their colorlessness, their *lack* of vivid overtones. None was a domestic bully. Nearly all led

unusually passive lives right to the moment of their outbursts. The shock effect of their deeds lay mainly in their
total unexpectedness—as if white-bellied newts had suddenly
grown teeth and gobbled up all the fish in the aquarium.
Even if all of them could be called mentally unbalanced,
rarely could they be classified as legally insane. The tempests
and furies of their makeup churned only inside their heads.

The classic example of this type was Lowell Lee Andrews,
the elephantine Kansas honor student whom his home-town
newspaper dubbed "The Nicest Boy in Wolcott." At eighteen, Andrews weighed three hundred pounds, wore horn-
rimmed glasses, regularly attended church, never touched
liquor, and never took out a girl. His only visible passions
were for food and his studies. But Andrews had a secret
dream: to run away to Chicago and become a "hired gun."
In order to accomplish this he needed money, and he decided that to get the necessary funds he would kill off his
prosperous farming family and sell their property.

On the evening of November 28, 1958, having armed
himself with an automatic rifle and a revolver, Andrews
waited until his parents and older sister had gathered before
the television set. He then marched into the parlor, switched
on the light, and shot his sister between the eyes. He shot
his mother three times, and his father twice. Both parents
were still alive, so the son reloaded and shot them until both
weapons were empty. Andrews had concocted an alibi of
sorts, claiming that he found the riddled corpses when he
returned from a trip to town. But a few days later, as if
bored with the comedy, he confessed the triple killing to his
late family's pastor. The only explanation he offered was
"Well, the time had come, and I did what I had to do."

Although the psychiatric team of the famous Menninger
Clinic that examined Andrews subsequently diagnosed him
as schizophrenic, they did not in his case equate this condition with the presence of delusions or hallucinations. According to Dr. Joseph Satten, his schizophrenia was of the
type in which thinking is separated from feeling. While perfectly aware of the criminal nature of his acts, Andrews ex-

perienced no emotion whatsoever about them. The doctors considered him a perfect example of diminished responsibility, but the Kansas courts thought otherwise. The judges applied the old English M'Naghten Rule, which recognizes as insanity only the culprit's explicit inability to distinguish between right and wrong. Andrews was sentenced to death and duly hanged in Leavenworth Prison. He ate two whole fried chickens with double helpings of potatoes and ice cream before they led him out to the leaky shed that housed the gallows.

James Ruppert was fortunate to have extirpated his family sixteen years later, when the death penalty was in abeyance. Although his crime ranks among the worst multicides in American annals, he escaped with his life, if the remainder of his existence can be called that. On the morning of Easter Sunday, 1975, police in Hamilton, Ohio, found that a two-story frame house in the Lindenwald section had been turned into a morgue. There were eleven bodies inside, all of them shot: widowed Mrs. Charity Ruppert, her son Leonard, his wife, Alma, and their eight children, aged four to seventeen. The sprawling heaps of corpses lying amid spent cartridges combined with the pervasive smell of cordite to give the place the character of an indoor battlefield when the police responded to a call from the sole survivor: Mrs. Ruppert's second son, James—a small, dough-faced bachelor of forty-one, wearing thick glasses and a startlingly flamboyant necktie that was strangely at odds with the rest of his appearance. He was charged with eleven counts of aggravated (second degree) murder the following day.

James Ruppert was a withdrawn, faintly effeminate person, highly intelligent but without a spark of temperament. He seemed unable to assert himself at any time, and the only topics that kindled some form of enthusiasm in him were firearms and the stock market. He was a crack shot and possessed three revolvers and a rifle. According to police evidence, he had used three handguns to shoot down eleven people in the house before they could run or hide. Having felled all of them, he leisurely dispatched those still showing signs of life, firing a total of thirty-five shots without missing once. He accomplished the largest indoor massacre in criminal history.

More elusive than the killer's identity was the question of why he had done this. Here, as usual, the psychiatric teams hired by the defense and prosecution contradicted each other flatly. Defense mentalists maintained that Ruppert was a paranoid psychotic, obsessed with the delusion that his family conspired with the FBI and CIA "to make him look small" and convinced that his mother was trying to turn him into a homosexual by combing his hair and talking baby talk to him. To the prosecution a less exotic motive for his crime presented itself: Ruppert had obliterated his family in order to leave himself the nearest and only heir to three hundred thousand dollars. He had also "planned, calculated and designed to be apprehended as part of his master plan." Ruppert did this, the prosecutor contended, in order to lay the basis for an anticipated verdict of not guilty by reason of insanity, to be followed by a brief stay in an institution "until such time as the psychiatrists determine he has been restored to reason, when he would walk out a free man with $300,000 in his pocket." Given the present state of our mental-health facilities, this wasn't nearly as phantasmagoric as it sounded (as we shall see in later chapters, asylum panels have pulled more preposterous boners than that), but the three trial judges found Ruppert sane and guilty. They sentenced him to eleven consecutive life terms in prison—a sentence that, while not assuring him even one lifetime behind bars, at least made certain that he wouldn't be out on parole in under twenty years.

Fratricides and sororicides have never been as prevalent in America as they used to be among the ruling nobility of Europe and the Orient. We have no equivalent for the wholesale elimination of brothers and sisters that frequently cleared the road to a throne or a fiefdom. Nevertheless, the murder of one sibling by another is far more common in this country than people assume.

In his study *Children Who Kill,* psychologist Douglas Sargent suggested that many such murders may be prompted by a parent. A mother or father can goad a child into the act, sometimes subconsciously, by fostering sibling rivalry, and thereby obtain the benefits of the deed without the responsibility.

The police tend to blame incest for most such killings, since it often involves a combination of guilt feelings and sexual jealousy—a lethal mixture at any age. Since incest is still under a powerful media taboo, such sibling slayings tend to receive much less publicity than their frequency might suggest. By the time news editors can assure themselves that the dreaded deviation is not involved, the case is usually old news.

An exception to this rule was to be found on front pages in February 1975, perhaps because the participants were the children of one of America's greatest publicists. Advertising wizard Howard Gossage (who created, among other things, paper-airplane contests and the Beethoven sweat shirt), died of leukemia in 1969. His divorced wife succumbed to acute alcoholism five years later. Their marriage had been a major social event in the West, and while it lasted the Gossages ranked among the cultural and creative elite of San Francisco. The couple left a boy and a girl about whom the best that can be said is that they were beautiful people. Eben Gossage, at twenty, resembled a permanently sulking version of Mick Jagger. His nineteen-year-old sister, Amy, had the kind of frail, blond, child-woman loveliness that affects older men like catnip. The two came into a dangerous heritage. With no usable skills, little education, and fifty thousand dollars apiece, they had just enough to afford them a whiff of *la dolce vita.*

Eben went through his share in five months flat. While his mother was still alive he first begged, then began stealing money from her. Forging checks to the tune of ten thousand dollars in her and his grandmother's names, he finally left Mrs. Gossage no means of stopping him, short of prosecution. After spending nine months in the Marin County jail, he emerged frayed but no wiser in November 1974.

Amy Gossage was more fortunate in that her tastes ran to bohemianism and did not entail a flashy lifestyle. A college dropout like her brother, she made at least a pretense of doing something. She enrolled in the San Francisco Art Institute and, although she attended few classes, carried a sketchbook and called herself an artist. She accordingly blended well with the North Beach area, which had once spawned Jack Kerouac and the poets of the Beat Generation but has since withered into a melancholy fata morgana. Part strippers' showcase, part panhandlers' row, and wholly unproductive, it still retained a certain blowzy charm. Its characteristic mingling of the aroma of roasting espresso, fresh sourdough bread, and stale reefers provided the closest facsimile of a Montparnasse scene that this country offers.

Amy used some cocaine and drank a little. Most of her time was spent in the coffeehouses along Upper Grant Avenue, sitting, sketching, and talking—always talking. "She had no talent," one of her fellow habitués at the Café Trieste told me. "That's no handicap around here. And she sure turned on the guys. Old guys, young guys—all of them. They thought she was a goddess in jeans." Sex was either Amy's main weakness or her chief strength, and her fancies were catholic to a fault. She went for loaded socialities and struggling musicians, young rock stars and aging alcoholics, streetwise locals and grass-green tourists. The one attribute all her partners had to share was the willingness to listen and nod with profound understanding while Amy expounded on her dreams, her ambitions, and her fantasies, including one in which she would play the title role in a movie on Joan of Arc. She took money from some; she gave it to others; frequently it just vanished. The final balance was a decided debit.

When Eben came out of jail, he turned to Amy for money. With his heroin suppliers getting tough about the sums he owed them, and the craving eating him up, he had no one else. He appeared regularly at her ill-furnished apartment on

Telegraph Hill, his hand outstretched, his whining voice tinged with desperation, until his sister had no more money to give him. According to rumors she too owed dealers who were growing impatient with her. Amy did expect to get $5,500, the last part of her inheritance. Eben told several people that the two of them intended to use the sum to go to Spain. (Why they should want to go to Spain was unclear. Eben usually talked in such nebulous spirals that nobody, perhaps not even himself, could distinguish his projects from his pipe dreams.) When Amy apparently proved reluctant to part with the money, their quarrels swelled into a blazing series of rows. On Wednesday, February 12, Amy telephoned two friends, saying that for the first time she was frightened of her brother. "What should I do?" she asked.

"Get out fast," one of them told her. "Like, today."

Amy didn't, and the following morning she woke up to the last day of her life.

Shortly after 11:00 A.M., Eben called at the building manager's office and asked him to open his sister's apartment. "It's so quiet in there . . . and strange," he mumbled. "I got a bad feeling."

When the manager unlocked the door, the entire bed-sitting room was spattered with blood, flecking the walls and the crucifix hanging above the bed. Amy lay on a drenched sheet beside the bed, clad in a T-shirt and panties. Blood was still trickling from where her head had been smashed in by some heavy instrument and from jagged stab wounds about her neck and breasts. Dozens of her sketches littered the floor. Her two small dogs crouched whimpering under the bed.

Eben gave a sobbing scream and rushed over to his sister. Cradling her in his arms, he pressed his mouth to hers in a clumsy attempt at artificial respiration. When he rose again his face was smeared, his hands dripping, with her blood. Weakly shouting for help, he tottered outside.

After the manager called the police and Homicide Inspector Ken Manley took Eben into custody, a search of his apartment, two blocks away, uncovered not only a blood-

stained claw hammer and pair of scissors, but also a bloody
shirt and trousers belonging to Eben. An hour later he was
charged with the murder of his sister.

Facing a throng of reporters and cameramen outside his
cell the next morning, Eben talked in a slow, bemused
voice with a slight stutter, his sentences trailing into space,
his full drooping lips fluttering with half-hysterical smiles.
"I d-don't know why they're k-keeping me here. But I want
you to promise me you'll put in your story that I'm not
g-getting p-proper medical treatment at all. I need sedatives.
I need h-hot chocolate or warm milk so I don't wake up
screaming. I woke up three times during the night, screaming."

Eben stuck to his innocent plea until the actual start of
his trial, two months later. Only after listening to the county
coroner testify that Amy had died from seventeen blows with
a hammer before being stabbed forty-five times with a pair
of scissors did the tall, stooping young man finally admit the
murder. It was self-defense, he told the jury.

They had argued about the trip to Spain, and "she started
bad-mouthing me," he said. "She yelled that I'd always
caused the family so much trouble and did I think I'd become a b-brand-new person by moving to Spain? I snapped
back at her about how she used cocaine and was screwing
around all the time, living like a tramp."

At this point, Eben stated, the fight began. Amy grabbed
a hammer with one hand, the scissors with the other. Then
they were grappling on the bed. "I tried to get off," he said,
his voice almost inaudible, "but she stayed on top of me,
and every time I pushed her off, she scooted back on top.
I ended up begging her to stop. She said she was going to
stab my eyes out. She was yelling, she was screaming: 'I'll
stab your eyes out!' All of a sudden I felt overpowered. I was
exhausted. I had a cramp across my back. I was scared. I
d-didn't have much strength left. I was scared b-bad."

He got hold of the hammer and swung it against her skull,
eight or ten times. She slid on the floor and lay limp, and
he knew then that he had killed her. "Then," he whispered,

"I got angry with her. I blamed her for what had happened. I started stabbing her with the scissors, cursing her. I don't know how many times I stabbed her. I was crying. I only stopped when I got exhausted."

Looking at the jury, he added: "I d-didn't do it on purpose. There's a great deal of difference between what I did and murder." The jury agreed. They found Eben guilty of voluntary manslaughter.

Before he was taken out on his way to state prison, Eben faced the reporters again. He stared at the ground, his mouth trembling. "Now I've lost everything," he said. "Everyone. My father, my mother, my sister. There's nobody left. I'm the last one . . . the last one." *

* Eben Gossage was paroled in 1978, after serving two years and 359 days in prison.

2

The Bloody Background

If once a man indulges himself in murder, very soon
he comes to think little of robbing: and from robbing
he comes next to drinking and Sabbath-breaking—
and from that to incivility and procrastination.
—Thomas De Quincey

On the afternoon of October 27, 1881, nine armed men
confronted each other across a fenced enclosure off Fremont
Street in Tombstone, Arizona. The "Gunfight at the O. K.
Corral," the most illustrious in the history of the Old West,
was about to commence. In precisely three minutes it was
all over. Three men lay dead, four retired wounded, and
Tombstone sheriff Behan hastily swore out murder warrants
for the two victors still on their feet.

In several ways the Tombstone encounter epitomized how
law enforcement was practiced in vast portions of the United
States during that period. The fact that three of the participants, Wyatt, Morgan, and Virgil Earp, wore official badges
was almost beside the point. The locals regarded it as strictly
a family feud, with the Earp brothers and Doc Holliday on
one side against the Clantons and McLowerys on the other,
and divided their sympathies about evenly between them.

Almost as evenly divided was the aura of criminality that
adhered to the fighters. Although the Earps were deputy
marshals, they did not hesitate to accept illicit employment
as bouncers and bodyguards from the Oriental Saloon, a
wide-open gambling den. Their civilian ally, the half-de-
mented Doc Holliday, was a consumptive dentist who
cheated at cards and reputedly shotgunned more than a
dozen men before expiring at the age of thirty-five. The opposing Clantons were widely known to be part-time thieves,
whose quarrel with the Earps erupted only when the two
groups accused each other of having robbed a Wells Fargo

stage and murdered the driver. And a fair section of Tombstone's citizens believed that the Earps possibly, and Doc Holliday probably, had something to do with the holdup.

The same ambiguity of character surrounded most of the other famous "lawmen" of the West. Some of them changed roles with downright dazzling alacrity, riding with their posses one month and on the "hoot-owl trail" of banditry the next. Others found it both more expedient and more profitable to live with one boot planted on each side of the law simultaneously. Typical of their kind was the celebrated James Butler Hickok—better known as Wild Bill. Hickok sported a town marshal's star throughout most of his career, during which he blew away an estimated sixty-three assorted cutthroats, cattle rustlers, and fighting-drunk cowhands. Yet, while safeguarding the muddy streets of Abilene, Kansas, he spent much of his time sampling the whores of the red-light district called Devil's Half Acre, running his own poker game, and selling protection to the crooked gamblers and brothel madams of the neighborhood, until he was shot down from behind at the poker table.

Alongside the well-earned notoriety of the law enforcers was the less-deserved tendency to whitewash the reputations of their opponents. Of the tens of thousands of horse thieves, holdup men, cardsharps, pimps, and thugs-for-hire infesting the West, few found themselves branded with their true irons. The majority enjoyed the much milder sobriquet "outlaw," evoking romantic overtones of Robin Hood and his Merry Men, to whom they bore little resemblance.

There were several reasons for this trend. One was the enduring bitterness of the defeated South. Since a large proportion of the outlaws happened to be former Confederate soldiers, their sympathizers chose to regard them more or less as guerrillas carrying on the old struggle by somewhat unorthodox means. This sentiment culminated in the near-hysterical glorification of the James and Younger brothers. Even today many Southerners view them as gallant and chivalrous crusaders rather than murderous bandits whose rampant racism was in keeping with their Southern orientation. Doc Holliday once remarked that he "never bothered to keep score of the niggers I plug." And John Wesley Hardin, perhaps the deadliest of the Texas gunfighters, first became a fugitive after shooting down a Negro armed, according to his own description, "with a big stick."

In addition to the animosities inherited from the Civil War, the West was also seething with resentments of more indigenous origin: Small ranchers hated and feared the large cattle companies, farmers dreaded the banks that held mortgages on their crops, homesteaders and pastoralists detested the railroads that crisscrossed the open plains with endless iron tracks. All these separate resentments converged to generate lasting sympathy for virtually anyone who struck a blow against the symbols of an impersonal, inexorably encroaching money power. So enduring was the imagery of the outlaw as heroic rebel that when the Great Depression half a century later again spawned bands of freelancing desperados, they were the beneficiaries of the same widespread public support their predecessors had enjoyed.

Such a lasting glamorization of Western gunmen would never have been possible without the efforts of a horde of Eastern hacks who had rarely ventured farther west than Illinois and frequently were unable to tell the difference between a Derringer and a single-action Colt. Embroidering a paragraph or two clipped from the newspapers of the time with hundreds of pages of invented heroics, they produced a steady flow of immensely popular pulp novels celebrating the mainly mythical exploits of manufactured heroes. They made a killing with Buffalo Bill Cody, who inspired entire dime libraries and ended up believing a goodly portion of the hokum they piled around his name. They made a gallant martyr of the alcoholic terrorist Clay Allison; they turned the female fence and lifelong prostitute Myra Belle Shirley into "Belle Starr, the six-gun Amazon," a creature of saintly virtue and steadfast loyalty; and they transformed Martha Jane Canary, a common harlot and camp follower who probably never fired a gun or mounted an express pony, into "Calamity Jane, intrepid Army Scout and deadshot Pony Express Rider." The ultimate feat of the dime-novel bards was the metamorphosis of William H. Bonney into Billy the Kid. Born in a New York slum tenement, Billy was taken to Kansas and later New Mexico, where he became an unwashed, reeking, fabulously foul-mouthed juvenile delinquent who knifed his first man (in the back) at the age of fourteen and went on to kill fifteen to twenty more (including three unarmed Indians), mostly from ambush. About the only detail the pulp writers got right was his youth: Sheriff Pat Garrett shot him dead shortly before his twenty-second birthday.

The pulps were largely to blame for the impossibility of even roughly assessing the killings notched by these pistoleers. The process used by the authors resembled the body counts of the Vietnam war, which totaled several times the actual strength of the Viet Cong. If only a fraction of the numbers claimed were true, they must have decimated whole townships.

Hollywood took over where the pulps left off. Aside from inventing the six-shooter that never needed reloading, Hollywood also produced the clean-cut collegiate gunslinger, although most of them wore drooping mustaches and shoulder-length hair. It churned out twenty movies on Billy the Kid, a dozen each on Wild Bill Hickok and Wyatt Earp, seven on Jesse and Frank James, plus hundreds more featuring the Youngers, the Daltons, the Renos, Bat Masterson, John Ringgold (Johnny Ringo), Butch Cassidy, Ben Thompson, etc. By the time television arrived the Western scene had acquired a kind of mystical hue, firmly imprinted in the minds of two generations of Americans.

The era of horseback desperadoes ended in Coffeyville, Kansas, in October 1892, when the Dalton gang perished amidst a hail of vigilante bullets. But the heritage they left still hangs like an albatross around America's neck: a heritage of gleeful mayhem, of counting corpses as so many notches on a revolver butt, of semi-crooked lawmen and half-straight outlaws, of romantic auras wreathing multiple murderers. Whereas other nations managed to outgrow equally gory frontier backgrounds, in America the entertainment industry carefully perpetuated the very worst aspects of frontier mentality: the toleration of violence, disregard for human lives, and a sly nudging admiration for the lawbreaker who could shoot his way out of trouble. We are paying a terrible price for this social infantilism glorified in millions of feet of film strip.

No such phony glamor surrounded the urban thugs, who in some respects were even more destructive. The rural Western gangs rode into immortality on Hollywood's back, but who today has heard of the Plug Uglies, the Blood Tubs, the Dead Rabbits, Bowery Boys, Roach Guards, Five Pointers, Whyos, Gophers, Sydney Ducks, Potato Peelers, or Chichesters? Of the hundreds of city gangs, only the Sicilian Black Hand and the Chinese tongs still strike some vague response. One cause for their oblivion may have been their lack of camera appeal. They were guttersnipes and, with few exceptions, looked it. Although a handful carried pistols, the fact that the majority used knives, blackjacks, nailed clubs, or paving stones turned their killings into un-aesthetic butcheries compared to the neat holes drilled by Western weaponry. They were also overwhelmingly of foreign origin, drawn from whichever immigrant group ran in the rear of the gravy train in their particular locale.

In New York this meant mainly the Irish, packed tightly into the stinking malarial rat-swarming boglands of the Fourth Ward, which occupied long stretches of the East River water-front, and the Sixth Ward, also known as Five Points, which was bounded by the present Canal Street, Broadway, Bowery, and Park Row. It remained the ghastliest slum in America until surpassed by the Chicago stockyards. Together these two areas spawned an immense proliferation of criminal gangs and subgangs that fought, merged, splintered, allied, disbanded, and reunited like a whirling kaleidoscope smudged with blood. During the 1850s the New York police estimated that around thirty thousand men and women owed allegiance to one or another of the city gangs.

Most of these mobs were brawlers first and only secondarily criminals, whose activities, in any case, rarely rose beyond mugging and thievery. Their killings, though numerous, were quite haphazard, more often resulting from the weakness of a victim's skull than from homicidal intent. But at least one of them moved in a more sinister direction. In 1874 a new outfit, calling themselves the Whyos, established head-quarters in a Bowery saloon. Quickly attracting the most lethal thugs in the city because they offered considerably higher earnings than other mobs, the Whyos were primitive forerunners of Murder, Inc., performing "jobs" for whoever met their fixed prices, ranging from two dollars for a punch in the nose to one hundred dollars for murder. Though they were never more than locally based, they were the most effec-tive terrorist organization in the city, exacting tribute from every other gang that roamed the Five Points, until their eventual demise around 1895.

This demise was in part a product of the Whyos' crude operating methods, which constantly involved them in fighting other gangs instead of dividing territory with them. It was also a consequence of their attempting to get by without political influence at a time when political pull had become the paramount factor in the survival of a New York mob. As the center from which all pull radiated, Tammany Hall, the Democratic political machine that ran the city, found the mobs useful on election days to herd people to the polling stations, strong-arm opposition herders, stuff the ballot boxes or, if necessary, toss them into the river. The degree of pull they enjoyed was measured precisely by the number of votes they mustered. Tammany repaid them by providing lenient judges, myopic cops, and, to a certain de-gree, freedom from prosecution. There were definite limits to this magnanimity: The gangs had to confine themselves to their territories; they couldn't openly carry arms; they had to contribute regularly to the Tammany war chest; and they couldn't tangle with the heavyweights in the New York arena.

Thus, Tammany Hall laid the groundwork for conditional collaboration between the underworld and elected authority, out of which, though along infinitely more sophisticated lines, evolved today's syndicated crime. First, however, the mobs had to learn the hard way that it doesn't pay to step out of your class. Just after the turn of the century, the Gophers mob had grown so large that they felt strong enough to challenge a corporate giant like the New York Central Railroad, whose freight cars and warehouses they systematically plundered. They enjoyed a relative tolerance on the part of the public authorities, but they did not anticipate the railroad's ability to mobilize a virtual army of detectives and private cops against them. As a result, the Gophers were crushed, their morale, unity, and prestige shattered.

Their demise marked the fading of New York's all-Irish rowdy gangs. It ushered in the era of specialized and purely criminal outfits that wasted no energy on unprofitable street brawls. The Mafia in particular was to grow rich by preying upon Italian immigrant communities and extorting protection money through anonymous notes that threatened the victim with death and usually ended with a courtly "Believe us to be your true friends . . ."

The Mafia operated with the tremendous advantage of being virtually unknown outside Italian circles. Although it dated back to thirteenth-century Sicily and came over with the first shiploads of immigrants, American authorities remained unaware of its existence or knew of it only by one of its numerous euphemisms such as "The Honored Society." Yet among Italians the Society inspired an almost psychotic fear, based only partly on its murderous reputation. More dreaded than death were the Mafia torture methods, derived from ancient Arabic knowledge of which nerve centers of the human anatomy would produce the most unbearable pain when pricked with a knife. Prosecution witnesses in court could be reduced to quivering silence by a spectator's waving a red handkerchief—the Mafia signal for "Your blood will flow."

Unlike its Irish predecessors, moreover, the Mafia learned from early mistakes just what it could and could not get away with. Such mistakes, while costly at the time, were invaluable lessons in the longer run. For example, New

Orleans Police Chief David Peter Hennessey accidentally stumbled across Mafia operations while investigating the murder of a Sicilian whose head had been cut off and stuffed in a fireplace. An enormously popular official despite—or because of—his blatant xenophobia, Hennessey was able to identify and indict two brothers who captained the local Mafia faction. Before the case could be tried in October 1890, however, Hennessey, who had planned to take the witness stand himself, was cut down on his doorstep by shotgun blasts.

An ill-conceived, badly planned, and poorly executed killing, it betrayed the organization's inexperience. The nine alleged assassins who were indicted for the slaying were shortly after to be acquitted for lack of evidence. But before they could be released from custody a furious crowd proceeded to storm the jail. Howling "We want the Dagos!" and swarming through the prison corridors, the lynchers proceeded to shoot, stab, or hang the nine suspects, as well as two other Sicilians who hadn't been indicted. It was the worst and—inasmuch as the mob included a number of Negroes—most unusual mass lynching in American history.

Although newspaper headlines at the time announced "The Mafia Exterminated," the Honored Society had hardly been dented. It was only a brief interruption in the rise to heights of wealth and power that would have been unimaginable to its humble forebears, but the bloody lesson of New Orleans was not forgotten by the Mafia. Despite the many occasions on which it must have been tempted to do so, never again did the Society harm a top-echelon public official. It was a policy of restraint that paid off handsomely in the long run.

In contrast to the shadowy stealth of the Mafia, the tongs, as the Chinese underworld bodies were called, were neither ancient nor camouflaged nor of Old World origin. Dating back only as far as the California gold fields of the 1860s, they were originally organized by Chinese prospectors and work gangs as protection against the white hoodlums who adored beating up pigtailed coolies.

"The complete history of these extraordinary associations probably never will be written," Herbert Asbury stated in his definitive volume, *The Barbary Coast*. "It is extremely doubtful if any white man has ever thoroughly understood the innumerable ramifications of tong influence or been privy to the intricacies of their organization and methods, despite the fact that they are as American as chop suey. Like that celebrated dish, they are unknown in China."

We do know that within a remarkably short time the tongs changed from protective to criminal bodies, from defenders of the community to its exploiters. (This is by no means a peculiarly Oriental development. Exactly the same process can be seen in the history of the successive San Francisco vigilante committees. Each of them, losing sight of their original function and becoming increasingly corrupt, gave rise to a new crop of vigilantes who eventually turned to gangsterism themselves.) Twenty years after their formation, the tongs virtually ruled San Francisco's Chinatown. They extorted protection money from the till of every respectable merchant, they monopolized the lucrative opium trade, ran the busy gambling establishments, and controlled the importation of child slaves, whom they bought from their starving parents in China, imprisoned in shacks called crib houses, and either killed or kicked out to die when they had wasted to disease-riddled old prostitutes of twenty-five.

In order to secure and maintain this pervasive control, the tongs employed professional killers. Initially these were known as "highbinders," but their preferred weapons—razor-sharp hatchets worn under their cloaks led journalists to christen them "hatchet men"—a term that subsequently was to take on much wider connotations. Drawing regular salaries, plus sick pay and danger bonuses, the original hatchet men were full-time soldiers of the tongs, whom the ordinary Chinese citizens were far too terrified to resist. Generally, the only alternative to total submission was to return to China—for, unlike the Mafia, the tongs had no network in their homeland.

In the absence of any civilian resistance, most casualties among the soldiery were the results of internecine battles, which occurred frequently and could be horrifying slaughters. Usually they were announced by one tong's soldiery posting blood-red challenge-to-mortal-combat notices in Chinese at a prominent intersection. The police rarely attempted to prevent them, generally arriving belatedly as the victorious warriors faded like shadows into the yards and alleys of Chinatown, leaving behind five or six hideously chopped and mangled bodies.

Thriving under the benign sufferance, and often active connivance, of the white city authorities, the tongs' decline was not the work of their human foes but the immediate consequence of an act of God: the San Francisco earthquake of 1906. Chinatown and the Barbary Coast were reduced to ashes, and although the city was quickly rebuilt, most of the vice had been seared from its bones. Gone were the cribs, the opium cellars and gambling holes, and with them the chief sources of tong revenue. Some of the organizations lingered on, but they never again played a prominent role in the community.

They could not, in any case, have survived the great metamorphosis of American gangsterism that occurred fourteen years later. With the coming of Prohibition—the "Noble Experiment of a Christian Society"—all bets were off, and an entirely new ball game commenced. It commenced quietly enough, for the consequences of the Noble Experiment astonished the mobsters no less than the authorities. The difference was that the hoodlums recovered faster.

For generations Prohibition had been the fond dream of the Anti-Saloon League and an assortment of reformers ranging from the clownish Yahoo evangelist Billy Sunday to the crusader of puritanical socialism, Upton Sinclair. Few of them imagined they would live to see their dream come true. In due course most of them wished they hadn't.

Propelled by the odd patriotic belief that teetotaling soldiers fought better, the Eighteenth Amendment to the Constitution went through Congress shortly after America had entered World War I, but did not become law until the

Armistice was fourteen months old. If the nation's Spartan spirit had correspondingly waned, nevertheless, in Frederick Lewis Allen's words, the country accepted dryness "not only willingly, but almost absent-mindedly."

The same blithe optimism went into the arrangements for enforcing the law. The government mandated the raising of a force of 1,520 special Prohibition Agents and allocated five million dollars for their annual upkeep. Not surprisingly, given the vast extent of our coastland and border stretches and the huge number of potential lawbreakers to be policed, before the debacle was over the force had grown to 2,836 men, and the government footed a bill exactly *one hundred times* larger than the original estimate.

The nation's big thirst broke out the moment liquor was officially declared taboo. American men had always been fairly heavy imbibers, but now, for the first time, women joined the drinking class in enormous numbers. During one average Prohibition year the country consumed an estimated 684 million gallons of beer, 200 million gallons of spirits, and 118 million gallons of wine. And every drop of this tidal wave had to be purchased from criminal sources.

Not only for America's underworld, but also for hundreds of thousands of folks who up to then had been more or less law-abiding, opportunity didn't so much knock as thunder. The organized gangs dropped virtually every other activity in favor of bootlegging. Only a small section of them became rumrunners engaged in smuggling liquor from abroad; the great majority engaged in illegal distilling, or "alky cooking." Within a few years bootlegging had expanded into the country's single largest industry, employing eight hundred thousand people all told and hauling in an annual revenue of around four billion dollars.

Even more profound than the figures were the social and psychological changes wrought in that period. To begin with, since bootlegging, much like any other industrial enterprise, became more profitable the bigger the scale of the operation, Prohibition encouraged the agglomeration of gangs into larger and larger bodies. As small outfits were swallowed up or wiped out, the new giants leaped at one another's throats, each striving for a monopoly of the hooch market.

Since the sums at stake in this struggle equaled the budget of a middling European country, it not surprisingly came about that the armament used took on distinctly military overtones. The gangs went to war equipped with armored cars, "pineapple" hand grenades, sniper rifles, and occasionally aircraft and army tanks. The most characteristic gangster weapon was one the U.S. Army had refused to buy in any quantity because it was too expensive.

Invented by John T. Thompson, formerly an Army ordnance officer, and put into production by Colt in 1921, the "tommy gun," as it came to be called, was one of the first and perhaps the finest submachine gun ever marketed. Weighing only nine pounds and firing standard .45 caliber bullets from a circular magazine, the Thompson had an effective range of 600 yards and could pump out lead at a rate of 1,500 rounds a minute. Those early models sold for a modest $175 each, but their prodigious rate of fire kept the Army from purchasing large quantities; the gun used too much ammunition. But if it was too expensive for the Army, the warring bootleggers found it ideal. Here was a weapon that could turn an automobile into a sieve in thirty seconds, leaving not a living soul inside. Moreover, unlike weapons which required a degree of skill not possessed by the average mobster, all you had to do was squeeze the trigger and hang on. This weapon, first used in Chicago in 1925, was so successful that within six months "choppers" were barking from coast to coast. The peculiar shrill chattering of these guns became the signature tune of the Great Experiment. The fact that they were extremely noisy didn't worry the gunners. By then they fought more or less openly and as often as not, without interference by the law.

Even as the bombs roared, the guns rattled, and the death toll mounted, an astonishing mutation was altering America's social character: Gangsters, who had in earlier times been confined to pariah status, were becoming respectable. As almost overnight they gained not only acceptance but desirability, and knowing them became chic, the presence of at least one was *de rigueur* at smart parties. They hobnobbed with Congressmen, mayors, business tycoons, movie stars, and the better-heeled literati. They conferred with newspaper editors and police chiefs. They endowed hospitals and orphanages (after helping to fill them), opened sports events, posed for newsreel cameras, and were quoted profusely in the gossip columns.

Underlying this change was more than the fact that hoodlums were becoming fabulously wealthy. Prohibition had the quite unforeseen effect of rubbing out the traditional borderline between honest citizens and crooks. If honest citizens wanted a drink, not only did they have to purchase it from and through a crook, but the act of drinking turned *them* into outlaws, too. Thus, the respectable majority became a de facto criminal element by raising a glass. And raise it they did, for Prohibition proved the greatest boost alcohol had ever received in this country. Whereas New York, for instance, managed on fifteen thousand saloons in pre-Volstead days, it boasted thirty-two thousand speakeasies a decade after going dry.

Historian Edward Waldis described the process as "spreading a coat of criminality over the entire populace. The neighborhood bootlegger became an indispensable social aide, helping Mom and Dad entertain visitors and frequently turning up at the party in person. After all, as anyone could see, there wasn't very much difference between the man who furnished the liquor and those who consumed it."

Helping the process along was the public's relative immunity to the mass mayhem of the bootleg wars. Although the casualties of the "beer battles" have never been assessed with any degree of accuracy, the Justice Department claimed that in twelve years of Prohibition 1,056 bootleggers were shot and killed by agents, who in turn suffered 494 fatalities in the course of duty. Meanwhile, the intergang struggles resulted in 500 murders officially classified as "unsolved." Altogether around 4,000 men fell in the bootleg combat— about as many as died of all causes in the Spanish-American

War. Most of these casualties were confined to professional participants; the average citizen's life had actually become safer because the hoodlums had turned to booze for their main source of income. By and large the battling gangsters took care not to harm the general public—their customers. The public in turn didn't blame the bootleggers for the multitudes who died or went blind or mad from drinking some of the poisonous concoctions sold as bona fide liquor. They blamed Prohibition instead.

Some of the gang lords achieved levels of genuine popularity that aroused the envy of politicians. Foremost among them was Mr. Alphonse Capone, whom Chicagoans called "our Al," an abbreviation which, incidentally, he strongly resented. Capone, who was New York–born and of Neapolitan—*not* Sicilian—parentage, worked as a strong-arm pimp in Brooklyn before being summoned to Chicago at the age of nineteen by Johnny Torrio, whom Capone affectionately named "Johnny Papa." Torrio himself had gone to Chicago to work for the city's bordello czar, Big Jim Colosimo. When Big Jim's refusal to allow Torrio to branch into bootlegging led to a bitter falling out between the two, Capone settled the dispute by shooting Colosimo at his nightclub. Having made it possible for Torrio to inherit the vice empire, Capone inherited it from him, quite amiably, when Johnny Papa retired to Italy five years later.

Capone's career resembled nothing so much as one of the stage caricatures of American capitalism etched by Bertolt Brecht. Personally killing or ordering the death of over five hundred people in Chicago, Capone was never indicted for murder. Although he earned roughly five million dollars a year and accrued a fortune computed at fifty million, he paid no income tax for ten years. He controlled most of the liquor, prostitution, and gambling in Illinois, yet talked as if he were engaged in missionary work. When London *Times* reporter Claud Cockburn interviewed him at the Lexington Hotel, Capone dabbed his fat fingers in a bowl of rose water and fulminated against "foreign radicals and Anarchist bums invading this country. All my rackets," he shouted, waving his dripping hands, "are clean American rackets, run on strictly American lines and they're gonna stay that way. I don't hold with none of that socialist bunk. This American system of ours which is our heritage, call it Americanism, call it Capitalism, call it what you like, gives to each and every one of us a great opportunity if we only seize it with both hands and make the most of it." Americans saw nothing even faintly ironic in this diatribe. It sounded comfortably akin to what statesmen, preachers, and editorials were telling them. Capone was roundly cheered when he attended baseball games. People waved when his specially built armor-plated McFarland limousine roared past.

Meanwhile, if the extent of the damage he and his ilk were inflicting on the national fiber was not immediately apparent, it was lasting. It lay in civic corruption on a scale unknown since the days of Byzantium. With the stupendous sums now at their disposal, the crime bosses no longer bribed police officers but bought them outright. They no longer influenced judges and administrators but elected their own. They no longer had to intimidate witnesses but could get almost any case simply thrown out of court. The only level of government still beyond their reach was federal. They could not command Washington. Not quite. Not yet.

As a whole, America's urbanites were inured to palm-greased cops and venal mayors. But to realize that such men were actually on the payrolls of the underworld was an entirely different matter. The spectacle of gang lords holding court like royalty, attended by aldermen, district attorneys, and police commissioners, did something to the public psyche that was beyond repair. Citizens watched state governors issue pardons at the behest of characters straight out of Hell's Kitchen. They watched grinning professional killers stroll free after mowing down people in broad daylight on crowded streets. They saw armed thugs in control of the ballot boxes at local elections. And they became permeated with a feeling entirely new to the country's character: a mixture of self-doubt, helplessness, and pervasive cynicism.

This was expressed by the public's ambivalence toward

Prohibition itself. Although everybody could see that the Noble Experiment lay in bloody shambles, nevertheless it was allowed to drag on year after year, upheld by a weird conglomeration of forces that ranged from blinkered fundamentalists to the beer barons who had grown rich from it. In 1931 the New York *World* pinpointed the situation with a scathing little jingle:

> Prohibition is an awful flop.
> We like it.
> It can't stop what it's meant to stop.
> We like it.
> It's left a trail of graft and slime,
> It's filled our land with vice and crime,
> It don't prohibit worth a dime,
> Nevertheless we're for it.

It took the Great Depression and the advent of Roosevelt to bring down the curtain on the sorry farce that had run for thirteen years. By cutting off the flow of easy millions to the underworld, repeal heralded the demise of those of its elements that could not adapt to new circumstances. Most of the old ethnic-neighborhood combines, rooted in local Irish, Italian, and Jewish communities, faded out with the Roaring Twenties. A new trend emerged toward the nationwide syndication of crime—a trend that led to the formation of gigantic cartels combining criminal, business, and labor-union activities and employing armies that dwarfed even Capone's one thousand professional gunsels. But before this national conglomeration was completed, there occurred a brief period of regression to still-earlier types of criminality.

Suddenly there reappeared small, mobile packs of freelance bandits that closely resembled the Western badmen of the past. Although they rode cars instead of horses and used submachine guns rather than six-shooters, they remained anachronisms, whose brief resurrection from 1930 to 1937 was possible only in the conditions characterizing the Depression years. Nevertheless, John Dillinger, Ma Barker, Bonnie and Clyde, Pretty Boy Floyd, Baby Face Nelson, Creepy Karpis, and Machine Gun Kelly left behind a crop of legendary names that have become as integral a part of the imagery of the Hungry Thirties as Bonus Marchers, apple sellers, soup kitchens, and migrating Okies.

Whereas the Prohibition hoods sprang from cosmopolitan cities and evoke a skyscraper background, the Depression desperadoes were not only social but demographic throwbacks to an earlier era, conjuring up dusty Main Streets, sagging storefronts, and little red-brick banks. Hailing more often than not from the rural Midwest and Southeast, they shared the rustic values, fierce clan loyalty, fundamentalist narrow-mindedness, and unemotional hardihood characteristic of that milieu.

They also shared a peculiar bitter pride in their atavistic brand of banditry that makes little sense to outsiders. Alvin Karpis, our last "Public Enemy No. 1," always resented being termed a gangster. "I was no gangster; I was a thief," he corrected an interviewer after emerging from thirty years spent in federal penitentiaries. "Gangsters are scum. They get paid for bumping guys off—guys they've never seen before even. A thief is someone who works for a living. Like robbing banks, or breaking into places stealing stuff, or kidnaping somebody. Putting effort into it. I had the opportunity to become a gangster. Handling a machine gun for the Chicago Syndicate. I turned it down cold. Maybe you don't understand—but I was a thief, you see."

Despite similar backgrounds and *modus operandi*, their personalities were highly individualized. The shrewd, autocratic Donnie Clark, better known as Ma Barker, was a product of the Missouri Ozarks. A fat, frumpish shrew with the brain of a business executive, she led three near-moronic sons, plus Alvin Karpis, on a robbery-and-kidnapping campaign that cost ten lives before, her favorite boy dead beside her, she died shooting it out with the law, a machine gun in her fist.

Charles Arthur "Pretty Boy" Floyd, whom neighbors called Chock, came out of Oklahoma's Cookson Hills and took it on the lam back there whenever the heat was on. Nobody turned him in regardless of rewards. He could roll into Salli-

saw cradling a tommy gun and have straw-chewing locals
wave at him. "Howdy, Chock—come to rob the bank? Give
'em hell." Floyd killed six men, but always firing back at
someone shooting at him . . . or so the folks insisted, though
the newspapers said otherwise.

People didn't hail Lester Gillis, alias Baby Face Nelson, a
homicidal pipsqueak weighing 120 pounds, possessed with the
hysterical blood lust of a piranha. Or the celebrated duo of
Bonnie Parker and Clyde Barrow, perhaps the most detested
outlaws of the thirties. The paper-thin, urchin-faced Bonnie
was unique in that she abandoned waitressing and took up
robbing from sheer ennui. Finding herself "bored crapless"
when she met the ex-convict Clyde in Dallas, Bonnie
promptly turned the former burglar into an enthusiastic man-
killer—though Bonnie herself was probably responsible for
most of their thirteen victims. A nymphomaniac and a homosexual, whose only shared passion was for firearms, they were
bungling amateurs at everything except shooting and driving.
Living in their cars and sleeping with their guns, they confined their amateurish heists mainly to gas stations and lunch
counters, running up a reputation for brutality and murder
so vicious that even the underworld breathed sighs of relief
when a posse shot them to ribbons near Gibland, Louisiana.

If the Barrow gang was the most hated, then John Dillinger was unquestionably the most admired of the Public
Enemies. The mythology surrounding him went so far as to
assert that he had an eight-inch penis and that it is preserved
in some government vault. Although apocryphal, the legend
is illustrative of the larger-than-life image Dillinger projected
throughout his career. Specializing in robbing banks, he did
so with an artistry only partly suggested by his reputation
as "the fastest mind and slowest gun in the business." He
was certainly a dangerous man, but what set him apart was
his continual attempt to substitute skill, speed, planning, and
diplomacy for gunplay. Despite his indirect involvement in a
series of killings by his associates, it is quite possible that he
never killed anybody. Possessed of a solid portion of humanity and a sardonic sense of humor that made even his

victims grin, he severed his brief association with Baby Face Nelson because "That little squirt is too quick on the fireworks." On occasion he allowed elderly bank customers to lower their hands and sit down during holdups. He treated the staff so courteously that a female clerk described him as "the politest fella I've ever seen behind a tommy gun." Once he waved away fifty dollars a farmer had been depositing when the raiders entered: "Aw, let him keep it. We want the bank's dough, not his."

But, as the banks toppled, Dillinger became an obsession with law-enforcement officials. Hunted as no American criminal has been hunted since, he was trapped time and again, only to shoot or drive his way out. Dillinger was in the end the victim of a woman's betrayal. Anna Sage, an illegal alien threatened with deportation, offered to finger Dillinger in return for the reward and a residence permit. On a broiling night in July 1934, the Feds shot him dead as he emerged from a Chicago theater. A hundred thousand Chicagoans filed past his body as it lay on display at the morgue. Anna Sage collected only five thousand dollars; then they deported her just the same.

Ultimately, none of the Depression bandits got away. A few went to prison; the majority were, like Dillinger, gunned down by lawmen. Although their depredations were minor and the number of their victims minuscule compared with the liquor barons, ironically they fostered the growth of a hitherto quite obscure branch of the Justice Department. The Federal Bureau of Investigation, almost unheard of before the Depression, became an American household term. This was largely due to its young, bulldog-jawed director, J. Edgar Hoover, and his immediate superior, Attorney General Homer Cummings.

The two men were painfully aware that the public imagination needed a legal counterweight to the gritty toughguy glamor surrounding the outlaws. They determined to supply Hollywood, in particular, with a cop hero to supplant the endless succession of bandit heroes dominating the screen. (Humphrey Bogart rose to fame mainly because of his resemblance to John Dillinger, whom he played over and over.) The FBI stepped in to fill that role.

The full glare of media publicity was turned on the Bureau's operation, often to the exclusion of everybody else involved. The Feds—the G-men*—Hoover's Boys—roared across the nation in planes and high-powered cars, killing or capturing the infamous outlaws in a blaze of gunfire, heroics, and newspaper headlines. Hoover had a wonderful knack for giving the press exactly what it needed. He invented the term "Public Enemy," and assigned the "No. 1" tag to a fresh candidate the moment his predecessor had fallen. When Alvin Karpis announced that he was planning to "get" Hoover, the FBI chief made a point of arresting him personally. If six Feds and sixty local cops participated in a gun battle, the locals were lucky if they received a mention. Within a year Hoover had his FBI heroes on the screen and kids playing G-men in the streets.

The heroics were by no means mock. FBI agents died in droves during those years; Baby Face Nelson alone killed three. Similarly real was the fear they inspired. Bandits dreaded their firepower, the cool ferocity of their attacks, the relentlessness of their pursuit. Not only were the Feds far better equipped, cleverer, and infinitely better trained than local minions, but they were above all distinguished by the single-mindedness of purpose that gave hunted criminals the feeling of having them constantly breathing down their necks. "Federal heat," to the underworld, denoted the very worst heat extant.

It has recently become fashionable to denigrate the FBI as so many "programmed rednecks in business suits" and to dismiss the Bureau's fame as a Madison Avenue ploy. This is partly a reaction to the nauseating personality cult built around the late Mr. Hoover. Despite that man's unfortunate character flaws, however, this sort of reaction is at least as errant in one direction as the deification that preceded it was

---

* The title *G-Man* was supposedly bestowed by George "Machine Gun" Kelly during his capture in 1933. Caught without his weapon, Kelly was said to have screamed, "It's the Government men—don't shoot, G-men, don't shoot!"

in another. What such critics have forgotten—or never knew —is the deplorable state which characterized local law enforcement in the early 1930s. Prohibition had left a legacy of demoralization, corruption, and plain inefficiency so pervasive as to turn some police departments into collections of Keystone Cops. Police-training academies hardly existed. Radio communications, if used at all, were primitive. Identification systems were chaotic. Above all, the locals were handicapped by continual petty antagonisms among city, county, and state authorities, and by conflicting jurisdictions that could be used as shields against prosecution by criminals. Some city officials even worked hand in glove with the gangs for appropriate fees. St. Paul and Kansas City, for instance, were known as "cooling resorts": places where cops tipped off wanted criminals. Given the nature of these conditions, the tendency for the Feds to ignore or circumvent local lawmen cannot be characterized solely as a form of elite-force arrogance. Much of it stemmed from security needs. There were just too many mysterious leaks when the local boys participated in the planning.

The fateful error Hoover made lay elsewhere. By deliberately magnifying a bunch of armed heisters into supervillains, he distracted attention from the incomparably greater menace of syndicated crime. The Dillinger gang stole perhaps $270,000 in its entire career—less than a day's take in any of a dozen syndicate rackets. If the Barrow-Parker outfit, bloodiest of the Depression robbers, killed thirteen people over twenty-six months, a single mob war claimed that many victims in a fortnight. While Floyd, Dillinger, Nelson, and Karpis all, in turn, became Public Enemy No. 1, not one of the real enemies of the public who ran the great cartels was ever branded with that label. And, during the whole time that the bandits were going down in the searchlight glare of publicity, the syndicate executives were quietly gnawing their way like termites into the timbers of our national economy. They're still there, still gnawing, to the point where by now the FBI may not be able to dig them out for fear of bringing the whole structure crashing over our heads.

3

Crimes Passionnels

I killed Amos because I loved him . . . I didn't
mean to hurt him . . . I wouldn't have hurt him for
anything in the world.
                    —Convicted murderess Ann Tracy

You can get a good indication of America's emotional state
at any given period from the amount of news coverage devoted to so-called crimes of passion. In times of tranquility
this coverage is extensive, occasionally stupendous.* But the
moment the nation's blood pressure soars for some reason,
passion killings—no matter how juicy—fade out of the media.

It is no coincidence that within such halcyon years of
prosperity and relatively little social unrest can be found all
our great romantic *cause célèbres:* the shooting of Stanford
White by Harry Thaw in 1906 for the sake of "the Girl in
the Red Velvet Swing"; the mysterious murders of the
Reverend Edward Hall and Mrs. Eleanor Mills in a New
Jersey lovers' lane in 1920; the alleged bludgeoning of his
pregnant wife by Dr. Sam Shepherd of Cleveland in 1954.
These and half a dozen other courtroom spectacles generated
a level of journalistic ballyhoo appropriate to the launching
of a middle-size war. Today it is doubtful whether any of
them would capture a single morning-edition headline.

The current minimization of *crimes passionnels* does not

---

* During the opening days of the Hall-Mills trial of the 1920s, reporters
used five million words to describe the event—more than were written about
the first moon landing. Yet the case was devoid of any significance, except,
perhaps, that of clergymen dating married choir singers.

mean that they have become any scarcer but only that their titillation quotient has decreased sharply. Twenty years ago an event like the Hollister case would have been milked to the last lachrymose driblet and splashed from coast to coast for the benefit of fifty million viewers, readers, and listeners. If once it would have been the sort of stuff circulation managers dreamed about, by the time it occurred, in 1974, it attracted little notice outside New York State.

Burr C. Hollister was the scion of a wealthy Boston family, a graduate of both Yale and Harvard, a Fulbright fellowship teacher, and one of the most brilliant young attorneys in New York. Although his swashbuckling red beard and mustache matched his courtroom manner, Hollister had a deeply concerned social conscience and devoted part of his driving energy to giving free legal service to poor and disadvantaged minorities. He worked as law secretary to a State Supreme Court Justice, a highly paid position, but he was better known as Long Island's foremost poverty lawyer.

His private life raised a lot of eyebrows among his colleagues—not so much because he lived with an attractive black woman (a dead ringer for Eartha Kitt) but because she was a former client of his. In 1969, Hollister had obtained a divorce for Mrs. JoAnne Brown. Shortly after the decree became final, JoAnne and her two children moved into Hollister's charming little Cape Cod house in Uniondale—an arrangement considered severely *de trop* in the legal profession. The stormy romance that followed more than once saw the pair split up, only to return to each other a few weeks later, unable to live together and equally unable to bear separation. Their turbulent relationship contained all the fundamental ingredients for a tragedy.

When, early on the morning of September 30, 1974, an attendant found Hollister dead on the carpet of the judge's chambers in the State Supreme Court, he had a small hole from a .22-caliber bullet in his head, while his flaming beard was streaked with darker bloodstains. Unable to find a gun in the room, investigators immediately ruled out suicide. Instead they tended initially to speculate that some irate plaintiff might have killed the lawyer—hardly a difficult task given the fact that during the previous night, a Sunday, the entire Nassau County court complex had been left without a security guard.

Hollister's wake drew an impressively mixed throng of mourners. Ivy League types and Long Island's social elite mingled with welfare families paying their last respects to the man who had been their friend and champion. All were deeply moved by JoAnne's farewell gesture. Kneeling beside the open casket, she laid her cheek against the dead man's face, placed her hands on his shoulders, gazed at his closed eyes, and whispered to him, in a voice so faint that not even those standing closest could hear her words.

Under the circumstances, who could have anticipated that only three weeks later JoAnne Brown would voluntarily surrender at the Nassau County police headquarters and confess to shooting her lover? The couple, it seemed, had been on the brink of another of their periodic breakups. Hollister had threatened to leave her, this time for good. JoAnne had not been able to take the idea of another separation and ended the affair with a gun.

Then followed one of those half-sad, half-ludicrous divergences that can happen only in contemporary American jurisprudence. Informing the press that his client was insane, Mrs. Brown's attorney remarked, "I can't be responsible for what she says. I believe she is sick." JoAnne, however, insisted that she was perfectly rational. When the lawyer demanded a mental examination for her, she opposed him. As she was being led from the courthouse to undergo tests at the county hospital, she turned tearfully to the waiting reporters. "I'm being framed for this," she shouted. "I killed Burr. I'm ready to talk about it, to tell everything. And they're trying to make me think I'm sick!"

What did she mean by "being framed"? Nobody knew. For her attorney this inconsistency constituted simply another proof of mental derangement—a compulsion to confess, which in JoAnne's case he believed was rooted in her delusory, unfounded conviction that the police and neighbors were harassing her children. From the legal point of view, regardless of the woman's feelings, the lawyer had struck exactly the right chord. At her trial Mrs. Brown was found "innocent of murder by reason of mental disease or defect." The judge ordered her confined to an institution. Whether JoAnne was in fact any more unbalanced than the thousands of other people who kill "for love" must remain moot, despite the official verdict of the court.

Although the phrase "crime of passion" automatically conjures up an image of emotional fever heat, of a deed perpetrated while at least temporarily non compos mentis, the term actually embraces a much wider spectrum, including some coldly calculated and meticulously planned slayings. If the basic motivation is usually sexual, this still offers a pretty vast scope. Within this broad category can be placed murder for revenge, from jealousy, from the desire to eliminate an obstacle to romance, or in order to determine that no one else should possess a certain lover.

During 1974, 6 percent of all our homicides were the direct result of romantic triangles or lovers' quarrels. If you add to this those passion killings that occurred among married couples, the total comes to about one in every seven murders committed in this country. This proportion is remarkably low by some international standards. In Italy, Spain, Portugal, and several Latin American countries, crimes passionnels account for more than half of the annual murder rate. This is only partly due to the famous erotic hair-trigger of the Latins. Much more decisive is the fact that the unavailability of legal divorce frequently makes homicide the only method available for getting rid of an unwanted spouse. In Italy, prior to the recent social reforms, the practice had become something of a bitter national joke, as anyone who has seen the movie Divorce Italian Style can attest.

The law's attitude toward murder from passion varies according to local temperament. The last woman hanged in England, for instance, was nightclub hostess Ruth Ellis, who riddled her philandering lover outside a London pub in 1955 and paid the supreme penalty the same year. In France the same deed would have earned her no more than two years' imprisonment. Most Latin juries will acquit the slayer of a spouse found *in flagrante delicto* with somebody else. This also used to be the rule in the Southern and Western United States, though jury sentiments there have changed over the past decade.

Nevertheless, Southern justice still tends to deal leniently with husbands who suffered what lawyers call "extreme humiliation" before resorting to drastic measures. This was demonstrated during the 1976 trial of Joseph Lippart, a truck driver, in Gaithersburg, Maryland. Lippart, his twenty-nine-year-old wife, Betty, and their four children lived next door to the Childress family. Kenneth Childress, a strapping, bearded lad of seventeen, caught Betty's eye at a neighborhood swimming party. The mother of four and the boy next door had a torrid affair that lasted until Joe Lippart discovered a rather compromising letter in his wife's handwriting.

"Dear Kenny," it ran, "I miss you so much. . . . I love you. Nobody has ever made me feel the way you do when you kiss and make love to me, not even Sonny. . . . I wish we could be together all the time. I feel I belong more to you than to Sonny."

Joe—the "Sonny" of the letter—delivered a stormy ultimatum to Kenny's mother, threatening to kill the boy. The Childress parents did their best to ground junior by taking away his car and restricting his outings. By skipping school, however, Kenneth managed to circumvent the restrictions and continue the affair. Now seriously worried, the parents called on the State Attorney's Office for disciplinary help. The state authorities worked out a formal agreement, stipulating that Kenny and Mrs. Lippart would henceforth stop seeing each other. But in the following months, Joe related, "Betty got mean as hell. All she cared about was saying mean things. She'd cuss me out before I went to work and when I got to work I couldn't work. I was sick on my stomach. My nerves got to me, she'd been so mean and nasty. She'd say 'Love it or leave it.'"

Things came to a head one hot June morning when Joe awoke with stomach pains and asked his wife to take him to a doctor. "I begged and begged and begged and she wouldn't do it." Instead, he related, "she said she was going next door. When it hit me, I couldn't take it no more." He took his double-barreled shotgun from beneath the bed and fired both barrels into Betty's chest. Then he telephoned the police. "I'll be sitting in front of my house and I'll surrender peacefully," he told the dispatcher.

At his trial at the Montgomery County Circuit Court, Lippart was found guilty of second-degree murder: killing with malice but without premeditation. Judge John Mitchell handed him one of those sentences that resemble movie punches—a tremendous swing but hardly any impact. He gave Lippart twenty years in prison but, by suspending all but eighteen months, made the wronged husband eligible for parole after only four and a half months behind bars.

Even in the days when death penalties were handed out wholesale in the U.S., American courts treated murders motivated by jealousy far more leniently than their British equivalents. While Caryl Chessman, who had murdered no one, went to the San Quentin gas chamber in 1960, in the same year and state confessed murderess Ann Tracy got away with a life sentence. In Britain the respective allocation of punishment would have been reversed. Despite her claim that her boy friend "taunted" her with his other conquests, Tracy would have gone to the gallows while Chessman would have escaped the death penalty.

One of the experts studying the Tracy case, crime psychiatrist Richard Auber, pointed to her tragedy as typical of the entire genre. "If you looked at the two protagonists," he told me, "you'd almost believe that they were specially designed to kill each other.

"She was a pretty cocktail waitress in Laguna Beach. Terribly insecure, highly romantic, with a strong taste for histrionics. Amos Stricker was twenty years older, a successful businessman who fancied himself a Casanova. He had to boast about his sexual prowess in order to enjoy it. She had to cling to him to live up to her self-image as a poor lost waif. So they both play their respective roles: He is constantly flaunting other women at her, she is constantly 'forgiving' him for it. He asks her melodramatic questions like 'Why do you waste your love on me?' And she answers, 'Because all the love I have is yours!' Both behaving like actors in a corny play . . . and enjoying it.

"But then," Dr. Auber added, "comes a point where the play takes over. In their case, when Amos told her to get out of his apartment because he was expecting another lady for the weekend. That, according to their script, calls for some grand dramatic gesture on her part. She takes his gun out of the drawer and shoots him. Only grazing him, mind you. But then he goes for her—all ready to strangle her in true Othello style. And now she *has* to shoot in earnest to save her neck. So she does. Five times. Until he's really dead. And the lady exits into prison—her life in shambles but her pose intact. Curtain."

Such murders undoubtedly do exhibit a pervasive theatrical element since the majority of them occur during escalating verbal confrontations. Both slayer and victim tend to work up to a climactic situation, sometimes over a period of years. Each seems to have a neurotic need that the other satisfies within the escalating drama. It doesn't much matter whether the passion between them is love or hatred, just so long as it can be made to appear larger than life and to convey a feeling of extraordinary intensity. Having drawn such a couple together in the first place, it is probably this penchant for melodrama that later prevents them from separating in anything like a normal fashion. That, together with a certain essential humorlessness, enables them to transform their every word and gesture into cataclysmic events that darken the horizon. For a sense of humor is basically a sense of proportion. If they had it, they would see their clash in something like its true perspective and possibly become bored rather than lethal. As it is, they constantly help each other magnify their emotions until they reach a stage where anything short of violence seems unbearably anticlimactic.

How else can one explain why two people, whose sole investment in a situation is emotional, should turn to murder instead of simply walking out? Too ego-involved to withdraw without leaving part of themselves behind, it almost seems that the two are bound by an unwritten contract that contains no viable escape clause. It should be noted that in most cases this contract expresses a *mutual* agreement—a compact establishing the rules of the game as both want to play it. But the scenario becomes a nightmare when only one of the partners pays in dead earnest. In such cases, the other may not feel committed to the unwritten rules—may, in fact, not even be aware of them until it is too late to back off. As a result of either inexperience or an irremediable ignorance of human psychology, such unfortunates seem to be unable to read any of the signs that would spell danger to a more knowledgeable partner. It is rather like embarking on a romance with one of the Borgias in the belief that if you don't like it, you can always call it quits.

Shelley Sperling and Louis Acevedo, for example, were high-school sweethearts for years, without Shelley's learning anything essential about her friend's emotional traits. What for her was a teenage exploration was for him a blood bond. When Shelley enrolled as a freshman at Marist College in Poughkeepsie, New York, it meant a new lifestyle to her— but not to Louis. First gently, then with an increasing sense of panic, she tried to sever their relationship. Louis would not be cast aside. The fact that the girl no longer wanted him was immaterial from his point of view. With the egotism of the unrequited lover, he felt himself committed; therefore, she had to be.

As the eighteen-year-old honor student's days at college turned into an unending cycle of terror, Shelley learned just how unprotected our society leaves those who can't protect themselves. In September 1974, she agreed to meet Louis near the waterworks adjacent to the college campus apparently for what she hoped would be a "final talk." It very nearly was for her. She was attacked with a brick, which fractured her skull and smashed the hand with which she tried to shield herself. Louis was charged with felony assault and released on bail of ten thousand dollars. Although a grand jury later indicted him for attempted murder, he nevertheless remained free on the same bail. Then his case was adjourned, still leaving him at liberty.

Although all of the girl's friends as well as the police, the college authorities, and the courts knew she was terrified of Louis, nobody stirred in her defense. Although Louis was then working as a part-time therapy aide at an institution for the mentally retarded, it apparently occurred to no one—least of all the court system that had blithely tuned him loose—to offer him psychiatric help. And despite the fact that his acquaintances were aware that Louis kept a gun in his locker, this went unreported—apparently an irrelevant detail about a man under indictment for attempted homicide. To be sure, the director of student life at Marist recalled that the security guards had been alerted to watch out for Louis (heaven help you if your safety depends on the alertness of underpaid private watchmen), and Shelley was told to "phone for help" if he ever confronted her on campus. But Louis had no difficulty entering the college grounds on the evening of February 18, 1975. He was waiting for Shelley outside the cafeteria when she spotted him. She raced back to the nearest telephone, past hundreds of milling students, and was actually calling for help—as she had been told—when she was shot dead.

There is a bewildering, infuriating note of avoidability about this death—a feature we will encounter over and over with sickening frequency as we go on. The life of a promising young woman was perhaps snuffed out because those mighty forces on which her safety depended prove blind, dumb, and paralyzed when it comes to taking even the simplest preventive measures. They were not dealing with an anonymous menace striking unexpectedly out of the dark. Nor is Poughkeepsie a ghetto jungle where surveillance might have proved difficult. The suspect had been photographed, fingerprinted, and indexed. His avowed intentions were known to a grand jury, his residence and employment recorded by the police.

In June 1976, for the second time, Acevedo was pronounced incompetent and unable to stand trial. Judge Raymond Aldrich, of Dutchess County Court, ordered that he be recommitted to the custody of the State Department of Mental Hygiene.

So far we have dealt with passion killings that actually occurred in the heat of passion and between directly involved partners. Although statistics suggest that these constitute the majority, this preponderance may be illusory, because other variations of *crime passionnel* can be disguised as accidents or suicides and may never enter our crime charts at all. The most pernicious type—the one to which we are most vulnerable—is the murder for elimination. Traditionally, this entails the classic romantic triangle, with two people conspiring to eliminate a third, usually a spouse, who blocks their relationship. The husband or wife in question may refuse a divorce or set too high a price on it. This was demonstrated during the celebrated trials of Dr. Bernard Finch and his pretty receptionist, Carole Tregoff, in 1961. The two were convicted of plotting the murder of Mrs. Finch because, as the doctor explained to his paramour, a divorce settlement would have cost him too much cash and property.*

The special peril of this situation lies in the potential victims' not realizing that they are standing in anyone's way. Not noticing anything amiss in their marriage until the actual moment of murder, and sometimes not even then, their blindness makes them uniquely helpless targets. The other members of the triangle may not strike themselves but engage another person to do it for them. Alternatively, either of them may act on his or her own volition without informing their partner. Most of our "contract murders" are the results of triangle affairs, with women doing the larger share of the hiring. As a rule they will try to enlist the services of a com-

---

* Finch and Tregoff both drew life sentences for the murder, which amounted to, respectively, ten and eight years in prison for them before they got out on parole. According to unconfirmed reports, Carole went to live with another woman under an assumed name and will have nothing further to do with men.

plete outsider—either someone with a reputation for violence or, if they can afford it, an underworld "hit man." But there have been some startling exceptions, such as the Midwestern kidnap-slaying that brought a mother and son, simultaneously, into death row for the first time in U.S. history.

Around eight o'clock on a chilly December morning in 1974, two men abducted a middle-aged woman from a parking lot in downtown Columbus, Ohio. Battering her with pistol butts and forcing her into a car, they drove to a lonely country road facing an old abandoned village schoolhouse. Half dragging, half carrying their captive into the crumbling building, one of the men then held her up while the other pumped two bullets through her skull.

The killers drove off, but a housewife on an adjacent farm had watched part of the action from her window. She called the police, and a squad car sped to the scene within minutes. The officers found the dead woman face down on the rotting floorboards of the school, surrounded by blood, rusty beer cans, and yellowing scraps of newspaper. Homicide detectives later identified her as Mrs. Hermalee Ross, a cashier in a Columbus department store. They also got a good description of her abductors: One was a light-skinned black man, the other white, young, and exceptionally handsome, with long dark hair falling to his shoulders.

Since the woman's purse was gone, the Columbus police first assumed that they were dealing with a robbery. But they changed their minds when, four days later, they arrested the black man, James Weind, and identified his companion as twenty-year-old Carl Osborne. Osborne's name rang bells with the investigators, since they had meanwhile discovered that the murdered woman's husband had been carrying on a long-standing affair with a Mrs. Alberta Osborne—Carl's divorced mother. They also found out that Mr. Ross had decided to terminate his extramarital fling, move to Kentucky with his wife, and "get a fresh start."

Alberta Osborne, it turned out, was something of a Corn Belt *femme fatale*. In her fifties, thin-lipped, bespectacled, and distinctly uncharming, she nevertheless boasted at least three other lovers aside from Mr. Ross. Two of her beaux were also her former employers in the tavern business. She had worked for Ross as a barmaid before entangling him in a torrid relationship lasting six years, despite the fact that she was much plainer than his legal wife.

Alberta was one of those women who make up in dynamic energy, sexual prowess, and sheer panache what they lack in physical allure. History is full of that breed—on the positive as much as the negative side of the ledger. In the higher social circles they often become masterful political organizers or financial manipulators. Lower down the social scale, they frequently turn to crime. They make valuable allies for their friends but can be extremely dangerous when thwarted or humiliated. The same pile-driving willpower that goes into their amours is then turned to destructive ends.

When Ross informed Alberta that he intended to take his wife to Kentucky, she took the news quietly at first; then, he remembered, "she got madder than hell and yelled she'd never let me go. Never." Six weeks later Mrs. Ross lay dead in the abandoned schoolhouse, murdered by two men, one of whom was Alberta's son.

Police suspicion centered on her when detectives recovered the murder weapon from a creek. A .25-caliber automatic, it had been presented to Mrs. Osborne by another of her bosses-turned-lovers while she still worked for him and had to guard the till. Eleven days after the killing, she was arrested on a charge of aggravated murder. Young Carl's arrest followed shortly.

The chief witness against the murder trio turned out to be Alberta's eighteen-year-old daughter. The girl obviously hated the entire Osborne household. In particular, she told the court how her mother and brother had introduced her to the drug scene, with Alberta helping her cultivate a marijuana crop in the back yard and Carl supplying her with "every kind of stuff except heroin." James Weind's role in the arrangement remained obscure. Apparently he was an outsider enlisted for the purpose of killing Mrs. Ross. Referring to her mother, the girl testified: "She told me that she paid

Jimmy $125 and Carl $200 to kill Mrs. Ross. Jimmy was supposed to do the actual shooting, but his gun broke while he was hitting her on the head when they jumped her in that parking lot. . . . Since Jimmy's gun was broke, Carl shot her in the back of the head."

Divided between two men, the grand total of $325 must have constituted one of the lowest murder fees on record. It bore out Carl's plea that he did what he did because he was completely under his mother's dominance: "She was always stronger mentally than I was; I could never break away from her." Nobody in the court doubted the good-looking youngster's mental inferiority. They had heard two separate witnesses declare that Carl, for no other reason than to demonstrate what a tough guy he was, had boasted of the slaying in their presence. He didn't mention the ludicrous fee involved. All three trials ended in guilty verdicts for the trio. All three were sentenced to die in the electric chair.

Why the possible departure of *one* of her lovers should have aroused such deadly fury in Mrs. Osborne is a secret she will probably take to her grave. One thing is certain: At no time did Hermalee Ross feel an inkling of the danger she was in. Even during those dreadful final moments of her life, she probably didn't connect her abductors with a woman rival. She died without knowing who was really killing her, or why.

It is useless to search for logic behind most crimes of passion. This is chiefly because passion per se is not a very logical emotion, but also because within the scenarios of murders sparked by love or hatred, there is often an extra element of irrationality—of motivation so oblique and convoluted that it becomes difficult to decide where passion ends and latent insanity begins. In many triangle murders the physical liquidation of the third party is totally unnecessary. Given our current matrimonial laws, the other two could just as easily depart together without risking a homicide investigation. To be sure, additional factors, such as money, property rights, or the custody of children, may intrude. Yet an astonishing number of killings occur where no such considerations exist, when the victim could have been simply left deserted, but alive. Such murders, although carried out ostensibly for the purpose of elimination, are more apt to be acts of revenge—a sort of retribution often for nothing more specific than unhappiness suffered in the past.

They can also stem from the romantic notion that in order to make a genuinely fresh start with a new partner you must wipe the slate clean (eradicate the old one). This form of romanticism, which is actually a lopsided brand of morality, causes much more bloodshed than rational criminologists tend to believe. As a concept it seems quaintly archaic, yet it frequently offers the only explanation of why certain marriages are terminated by violence.

Clover Edwards, for one, would certainly still be alive if her husband and his girl friend hadn't been such romantics. A couple in their twenties, the Edwardses were childless and without property that might otherwise have had to be divided. They managed a modern apartment complex in Stone Mountain, Georgia's most popular vacation resort. Paul Edwards, himself trim and wiry, had a penchant for Junoesque females: His wife, Clover, was a blonde Amazon; his girl friend, Jill Shaw, was a tall, broad-shouldered brunette with the proportions of a Russian discus thrower. Jill met Paul while she was a lodger in the Edwards home and had to leave hurriedly when Clover caught on to their relationship.

Her departure did not end that relationship, though it rendered their meetings rather less comfortable. There was nothing to prevent Paul from walking out on his wife, not even affection. At that stage their marriage had soured to the point where tenants complained about the screaming rows going on daily in the manager's apartment. Such an obvious solution apparently never occurred to the pair. Instead they concocted an elaborately foolish plot to eliminate Clover—a scheme that combined maximum risks with minimum gains.

On the evening of January 30, 1975, Paul gave Jill his revolver—an act of singular stupidity, since the weapon was registered in his name. Early the next morning, he went to make a deposit at the bank, chatting at length with the teller in order to establish an alibi. Meanwhile having asked Clover if she might be allowed to visit her "to talk things over," Jill drove up in an ostentatious scarlet Vega, which guaranteed that her arrival would be noticed by the tenants. In the course of their talk Jill drew the revolver and fired three shots, one hitting the wall and the other two Clover's face. Then she roared off in her beaconlike automobile.

Returning home to find his wife dead, Paul, as per arrangement, called an ambulance, but somehow forgot to call the police. This was the worst mistake he could have made for when the cops did arrive, in response to a neighbor's call, the distraught husband told them that Clover *must* have been murdered by robbers. Thus, he raised the question of why, if he was so sure of this, he hadn't brought in the law. In any case, investigators abandoned the robbery theory as soon as they searched Clover's purse and found fifty dollars left inside. If this were not enough, Jill was not only waiting for Paul in the lounge of the nearby Atlanta airport but had even left a message for him with an airport security guard, explaining that it was for a friend whose wife had been *shot in the face*—a detail she could not have known at the time if she hadn't done the shooting herself.

The two committed such a string of blunders in such a short period that we might well surmise that they acted from some unconscious desire for punishment—the old Freudian trap that has betrayed so many killers. Both received life imprisonment. As if to offer final proof of their romanticism, they petitioned the court for permission to marry—a purely symbolic gesture in view of the fact that Georgia's penal system does not allow conjugal visits between convicts.

In order to understand the romantic-idealistic trait in homicide, we must view the notion of *crime passionnel* in a context broader than the customary interpersonal framework. Crimes of passion can also be inspired by abstract *ideas*. Author Colin Wilson, for instance, noted the link between the prose of H. P. Lovecraft and the deeds of Charles Manson. Lovecraft, who wrote macabre fantasy tales and died in 1937, has today become the center of a youthful literary cult.

His paperback spine-chillers crowd drugstore shelves; their covers—in poster form—sell in head shops. There is even a rock group named after him. Wilson, in his *Order of Assassins*, points out: "It is the underlying spirit of Lovecraft, the revolt against civilization, the feeling that the material success by which the modern world justifies itself is the shallowest of all standards, that has made him a cult. Lovecraft was not a democrat; like Nietzsche, he felt that democracy is the rise of botchers and bunglers and mediocrities against the superior type of man."

Manson gave physical form to Lovecraft's nightmare imageries. He transmuted the author's cerebral horror visions into warm, twitching bodies and metamorphosed Lovecraft's dream monstrosities into the reality of California police files. Both men felt themselves outcasts from a materialistically structured society; both sought refuge in grotesque worlds of their own making. Basically romantics gone sour and twisted, both expressed their private rage against society in their own fashion: one by words, the other through murder.

They were true disciples of that archetypal romantic philosopher, Jean-Jacques Rousseau, though Manson had probably never heard of him. Two centuries ago Rousseau laid the foundations of a back-to-nature creed that has flourished off and on whenever the pressures of industrialization become too strong for sufficient numbers of people. He asserted that mankind can find happiness only in small, rustic communities, away from the soul-destroying din of large cities. Our civilization, he taught, has taken a false path by nurturing artificiality which alienates man from his basic virtues of kindness, generosity, and honesty. Instead society puts a premium on pride, ruthlessness, egoism and avarice and by constantly rewarding those destructive values moves further and further away from the pastoral tranquility that *could* be our lot. Our main enemy, therefore, is social convention as practiced by those who have achieved power through it.

Rousseau died, embittered to the point of paranoia, in 1778. But ours is by no means the first era in which his gently pacific creed has been revamped into a sword blade.

The most violently radical champions of the French Revolution were, in historian Stanley Loomis's phrase, "drunk on
Rousseau." Figures like Robespierre, St. Just, and Hébert
elevated his philosophy to a religion and—as so often happens—achieved the diametrical opposite of his ideals. They
reasoned that man's "natural virtues" are stymied by the
very existence of the "unvirtuous," and that only their ex-
termination would enable him to return to his primeval
benevolence. Thus the guillotine creaked and crashed to hack
a path for Rousseau's dream of selfless brotherhood, de-
capitating thousands accused of lacking in that terrible catch-
word, vertu. Among them, incidentally, were nearly all the
people who had made the Revolution in the first place, including the great Danton.*

Instead of free village communes dwelling in bucolic bliss,
the Terror spawned a centrally ruled nation-state, a rigid
bureaucracy, and Europe's biggest army, recruited by levée
en masse. Not to speak of a hidebound censorship that suppressed every book, play, and picture considered "lascivious"
by the petit-bourgeois prigs in command.

Manson's endless diatribes to his followers were abrim
with Rousseauesque concepts. Had he lived in Revolutionary
France he would no doubt have joined in their attempted
fulfillment via the "National Razor." For there is only a
relatively short step from starry-eyed infatuation with a romantic dream to hideous cruelty in trying to make it come
true. We have probably been fortunate that so far the mild-
as-milk devotees of, say, the Hare Krishna cult have lacked
the power to disseminate their vegetarian ecstasies by other
than gentle persuasion. The same applies to any number of
currently innocuous visionaries, who often remain innocuous
only so long as they lack opportunity to be otherwise. Let it
be remembered that Nazism, too, sprang from the roots of
Germany's nineteenth-century romantic movement, epito-

---

* The earthy Danton became so irritated by Robespierre's constant harping on moral virtue that he burst out: "Virtue? Virtue be damned. Virtue
is what I practice with my wife every night." Robespierre, who was almost
certainly impotent, never forgave him for that jibe.

mized by bands of idealistic, unworldly young poets with flowing locks.

The Manson massacre in Benedict Canyon was an act of romantic nihilism, a fist shake at civilization at large, the attempt of a reeking, unwashed outsider to imprint his personality on the dry-cleaned exurbia that wouldn't recognize him. The establishment was baffled by the utter pointlessness of the mass butchery, but the counterculture understood—and perhaps shared—some of the frustration-bred hatred behind it. Hence the sniggering note of sympathy for Manson on the part of the underground press—a kind of sly editorial elbow nudge, a stage-whispered "See . . . *now* those mothers are paying attention."

Attention to what? Presumably to Guru Charlie's messianic gospel as preached through his rock ballads, which were painfully devoid of musical talent. Apparently it was his consistent failure to find a market for his songs that caused Manson to sic his slaughter squads on those deaf ears in Los Angeles. If they won't hear me, let them *feel* me!

The manic quest for recognition places Manson alongside some very unlikely companions in crime. For this mania is not necessarily ostentatious or even overt. Occasionally it can smolder as quietly as the grave. In the case of Miss Probert it was hardly noticeable.

Gertrude Levinia Probert was a genteel, rather prissy maiden lady living in a shabbily respectable rooming house on Chicago's South Side. She scraped by on a small annuity, barely enough to cover her basic requirements, including a quarter for the collection plate come Sunday. Her landlord described her as an ideal tenant: soft-spoken, polite, scrupulously clean, and given to early bedtime. Her fellow lodgers were fond of her, though they sometimes smiled over her one peculiarity: a Florence Nightingale complex. Miss Probert assured everyone that she was a highly qualified nurse ("with all my certificates"), who had ministered to numbers of sick celebrities.

The fact was that she had neither training nor certificates, nor had she—so far as could be checked—ever nursed anyone in her life. But Miss Probert's self-image as a Lady with the Lamp was the focal point of her existence. When the other lodgers—the only people she met socially—insisted on ignoring her claims, she set about convincing them. Her method was to poison them, one at a time, and then nurse them back to health. In the course of two years she poisoned five people—one of them fatally. The fatality was not premeditated; Miss Probert simply underestimated the toxic effects of hyoscine on some individual systems.

She reaped no visible advantage from her crimes, merely the hard work involved in attending elderly men and women seized with painful intestinal disorders. Her dosing, as a rule, was remarkably accurate—just enough to make her patients miserable, not so much that they would see a doctor. As her reputation as a nurse in residence grew with every "cure," Miss Probert took to bustling in and out of sickrooms wearing a starched cap and apron. Newcomers to the establishment believed she *was* a private nurse. Miss Probert radiated glory; she became almost attractive.

Then, unfortunately, a retired carpenter named Alex Wadrofsky died under her care. The resultant coroner's inquest ended Miss Probert's nursing career. She pleaded guilty to second-degree murder but showed no visible signs of remorse. Perhaps, in her romantic soul, the two years as Florence Nightingale's proxy were worth all the gray eternity to come.

4

They Come Younger Every Year

The victim of a fifteen-year-old mugger is as much mugged as the victim of a twenty-year-old mugger; the victim of a fourteen-year-old murderer or rapist is as dead or as raped as the victim of an older one.
—Sociologist Dr. Ernest van den Haag

Some of our neighborhood kids will shoot you for a buck or maybe just for laughs. It's got so I'm scared to walk my own turf after dark, and I'm pretty tough. But they're real monsters, some of them. And they come younger every year.
—Anonymous Chicago car thief

On the afternoon of September 19, 1974, an undersized, bespectacled student named George Vasil attempted to rape twelve-year-old Pamela Vasser. Finding himself impotent, he crushed the girl's skull with a rock, thrust a pointed branch into her vagina, then hid her body in the grass. Three months later a jury found George guilty of first-degree murder. The judge sentenced him to death in the electric chair. He had recently turned fifteen.

On April 11 of the same year, four boys, aged thirteen to fifteen, delivered groceries to Mrs. Mary Robertson. They had arranged beforehand to kill her, partly for her stereo set but mainly for the fun of it. Once inside the woman's apartment, they hacked her to death with her own kitchen knives. They took the stereo, a box of candy, and a wall poster. Six months later a judge pronounced the four guilty of "juvenile delinquency." They were sent to "training school" for terms that cannot be extended beyond a maximum of three years.

Seen in juxtaposition, these two examples convey a realistic picture of what passes for juvenile justice in the United States in the second half of the twentieth century.

The legal differences between them should have weighed in George Vasil's favor. His crime was unpremeditated, whereas the murder of Mrs. Robertson had been carefully planned. He was a borderline psychotic, while the four boys qualified as "dull-normal." He had committed no prior offenses; the four boys had all been through various scrapes with the law. But such details count for little in a system in which the nature of a deed appears quite unrelated to the sentence meted out. What matters, first and foremost, is *where* you do your killing.

Pamela Vasser was slain in the small Florida town of Fort Pierce. Her death horrified the entire community. Because of the "brutal and vicious nature" of his crime, Vasil was tried as an adult in a local circuit court with both the time and the inclination to heed the feelings in town.

Mary Robertson's murder occurred in New York City, which has long ceased being horrified at anything. Her four alleged killers were consequently arraigned in Juvenile Court, known in police parlance as "Kiddy Court." This court processes an unending stream of youthful murderers— some of them homicidal sadists—but does not call them defendants. They are "respondents," even though they may have had to be brought in handcuffed. The court conducts not trials but "adjudicatory hearings." It has no prosecutor, merely a "counselor." Neither the names of the accused nor the sentences they receive can be revealed publicly. In any case, regardless of their past records, they cannot be given more than three years of confinement, of which they usually serve less than eighteen months.

This maximum penalty even applies to cases like that of the group of youngsters who stuffed gasoline-soaked cotton wool into the rectums of drunken derelicts (as well as dogs and cats) and set them on fire. Such actions are lumped together with shoplifting, burglary, vandalism, prostitution, etc., under the label "juvenile delinquency" and treated with the same sort of legal medicine. And, since the court files are sealed after a hearing, it is virtually impossible for the public even to learn what exactly these kids have done, to whom, and how often.

There are nationwide about three thousand of these courts, through which pass well over one million boys and girls a year. Not all juvenile courts are as frantically pressured, packed, and overworked as the New York institutions, nor are they generally quite as disorganized, understaffed, and decrepit. But they all elicit similar sardonic grins from cops and delinquents alike—the grimace of people who know a sham when they see one.

The sham of our so-called juvenile-justice system is expressed in the sense of futility felt by those who run it. As one court official summed it up for me: "We are not allowed to punish, and we don't have the facilities to rehabilitate. So we neither punish nor rehabilitate. We merely irritate."

Dominated by this sense of futility, the courts play an elaborate game of make-believe. The first rule is that things must not be called by their correct names. Thus, jails become "reception centers" or "trade schools," guards become "counselors," imprisonment "supervision," and a judge's sentence a "program." My favorite piece of judicial jabberwocky came from an institution director who informed me that one of his charges had come under his care "after committing a series of self-destructive acts." These acts, I later discovered, consisted of gouging out a little girl's eye with a screwdriver, performing sodomy on a sixteen-month-old infant, and setting fire to a couple of synagogues. I have a hunch that this director will go far in the system. He knows his semantics.

The jargon is of vital importance because only by resolutely dubbing every spade a rose twig can the system survive, at least in its present form. This form only reflects the manner in which it functions—not to alleviate a crisis situation but to camouflage its existence; that is, to convey an impression of organized purpose by shuffling the components around, more or less randomly picking one up here and dropping another there in the vague hope that if you keep shuffling long enough the crisis will somehow go away. Or, alternatively, the components will become old enough to be handled by adult law enforcement.

The crisis, needless to add, shows no sign of going away. It grows worse every month, causing the shuffle to become a little more fumble-fingered with every new deal. The awful truth is that juvenile crime in general has risen by 1,600 percent in twenty years—an increase that for shock value beats every other statistic this country can offer. *More crimes are currently being committed by children under fifteen than by adults over twenty-five.* Nearly one third of *all* violent crimes are being perpetrated by the under-eighteen group, and the most violence-prone age level is fifteen. The FBI Index for 1974 listed 1,399 boys and girls under eighteen arrested for murder. Of this total, 470 were fifteen and under; 41 were under twelve. Please note that this includes only those arrests specifically involving homicide; cases of negligent manslaughter were not included. The overall arrests of youths under eighteen stood at 2.5 million.

Set against this tidal wave of young criminality is a juvenile-justice system that neither dispenses justice, or anything resembling it, nor is even a system. At best it might be described as a patchwork of semiautonomous bureaucracies in which no one has either final control or ultimate responsibility. The opportunities for buck-passing are limitless, and most bureaucratic energy is expended on interdepartmental warfare. Milton Luger, former director of the New York State Division for Youth, compared the setup to the plot of a Shakespearean tragedy: "Everybody stabs everybody to the left."

There is no long-range planning, no cohesive formula, not even a permanent set of principles. Juvenile law is administered according to periodic fads and regional foibles—hence the importance of geography in determining the disposition of any particular felony case. The system hasn't even made up its collective mind as to what constitutes a juvenile. In the majority of states it's anyone under eighteen, but, under certain circumstances, it can be sixteen in New York, seventeen in Illinois, fifteen in New Mexico, and thirteen in Georgia. We also have a federal Youth Corrections Act, apparently framed by legislators from another planet, which posits the age of twenty-two as the upper boundary of "youth."

Because the keynote of the system is not justice but expediency, juvenile courts are permitted to remand youngsters to adult courts for certain felonies, such as rape or murder. Not all rapes or murders—not by a long shot—but only the *vicious* ones elicit such treatment. When does a rape or murder become vicious in the eyes of the courts? When it stirs a community to enough anger to threaten repercussions for the authorities involved. Should the populace appear complacent or apathetic about the deed, well, then, the rape or murder remains within the grab bag marked "juvenile delinquency," to be dealt with in a half-hour hearing instead of a time- and money-consuming trial. Thus, we get the breathtaking disparity of sentences illustrated at the beginning of this chapter. We also get a brand of jurisprudence in which what you do and how you do it is less important than where and to whom.

Washington, D.C., as a rule, is a splendid place for youthful homicide, particularly when it happens during a purse-snatching—a hazard to which the natives have become more or less inured. But, as the killers of eighty-four-year-old Mrs. Werlich found out to their sorrow, you must be careful in your choice of targets.

The four boys, all black, spent the morning of January 13, 1976, looking for someone to rob. It had to be someone elderly; other than that, the target could be picked at random. First they tried an old-age home, but failed to gain entrance to the two rooms they knocked on. Back on the street, they spotted a black lady who looked ideal. Unfortunately, she turned out to be one of the boys' mother. Then, shortly after noon, they sighted their quarry emerging from a stately Victorian house near Dupont Circle. She was Gladys Hinckley Werlich, grande dame of Washington society and the first woman from the capital city ever to fly in an airplane—but the boys had no means of knowing that. They tackled her just as they would any other old lady with a snatchable purse; a running charge at full tilt was sufficient to send her sprawling to the pavement. Although the boys failed to get her purse, Mrs. Werlich cracked her skull and never recovered consciousness.

All this happened in broad daylight and was observed by several witnesses. Ten days later police nabbed three of the youngsters—two sixteen-year-olds and one aged twelve. D.C. Superior Court Judge McCardle, apparently because he did not consider the D.C. jail—the only place in which they could have been held—a fit place for teens, promptly released the two teenagers without bond. It was a routine spring, perfectly in tune with what is known as revolving-door justice and in keeping with juridical practice throughout the country. Only this time it backfired with a devastating bang.

Some two thousand Dupont Circle residents signed protest petitions against the judge's action and staged open-air demonstrations. Mrs. Werlich's son gave a press interview demanding the death penalty as a deterrent to crime. Telephone wires to the U.S. Attorney's office ran hot with indignant calls from prominent social and political figures. Irate locals with impeccable credentials inundated newspapers with letters castigating Judge McCardle. Community groups pasted furious pamphlets on the doors of the District Court.

Lo and behold! The youths too young to be locked up in jail were indicted and charged with first-degree murder in the case that—somehow—had ceased to be an act of juvenile delinquency. The fourth youth indicted, when caught, turned into an even worse embarrassment, for he was already free on personal bond after allegedly pulling a similar purse-snatching just two blocks away from Mrs. Werlich's home. On that occasion he had been released by the judge without cash bail, despite the fact that he had neither a fixed address nor a job. Subsequently, he had also consistently ignored the condition that he phone a bail agency every day. Now—after Mrs. Werlich's death—another judge revoked his bail and gave him six months for contempt of court, prior to his facing the first-degree-murder rap.

The boys had clearly been amiss in their selection of a victim. Had they instead picked on someone reasonably obscure, no murder charge of any degree would have arisen. This was demonstrated by the slaying of eighteen-year-old Michele Godbout in New York's Central Park. Michele was riding her bicycle when attacked by a youth identified as "Rodney L." The boy first seized her bicycle, then battered her to death with a golf club. The sequence is important: Rodney already had the bike when he decided to kill the girl so as not to leave an eyewitness. This—unlike the Washington case—constituted first-degree murder. Unlike the Washingtonians, however, New Yorkers neglected to manifest the required volume of outrage; it comes harder for them. Consequently, Rodney remained a juvenile delinquent and went to Family Court. There the judge (whose identity I am not allowed to disclose) gave him *up to* eighteen months in an unlocked rehabilitation center—a sentence that means Rodney will actually serve only six to eight months before being free to roam Central Park again.

New York's Family Court is unreal, a slice of Dante's Inferno staged by the Marx Brothers. Corridors, waiting rooms, and toilets are crammed like cattle cars and about as clean, the stench so thick that it appears visible, the din mind-numbing: parents screeching at the top of their lungs, attendants bellowing, children yelling greetings and obscenities across the rooms. I watched three kids performing an impromptu rock dance on a table. An attendant ordered them to get off. "Fuck you," the kiddies chorused and went on dancing. In one corner a small girl, her skin livid with red blotches, was vomiting from sheer terror. Her mother, busy shouting at a lawyer, threw a brief glance in her direction, then turned back to her shouting.

Only a portion of the youngsters there, I learned, were charged with felonies. Others were alcoholics, junkies, prostitutes of both sexes (some less than twelve years old), or borderline mental defectives. About one third were so-called status offenders or PINS: Persons In Need of Supervision. Their crimes wouldn't be crimes if committed by adults: running away from home, truancy, incorrigibility, or being beyond parental control. These last—the most pathetic of the lot—were tossed into this judicial meat grinder together with full-fledged juvenile gangsters, professional thieves, and murderers, and frequently ended up in the same institutions.

Reformers have labored for years trying to separate PINS from the mass of actual delinquents, at least to keep them out of jail. They have had little success so far. Separate institutions and separate procedures cost money. So the youth facilities, already overburdened, are loaded down with an additional quarter of a million status offenders a year, charged with "crimes" of which no adult could be guilty. Most of them spend no more than a couple of days in jail, but around forty thousand wind up with sentences of from four months to two years. Not only do they take up space, manpower, and resources that could be used for the benefit of real felons, but, by rubbing shoulders with them, they also frequently learn to imitate them.

Take the case of Juan M. The child of a Puerto Rican prostitute and drug addict, Juan was born with heroin-withdrawal symptoms. Shortly after his eleventh birthday his mother moved in with an unemployed waiter who alternately beat up and sodomized the boy. In order to get him out of the house, Juan's mother pronounced him "uncontrollable" and dumped him on a juvenile court. At the time his uncontrollability consisted mainly of bedwetting, but after a few months in an institution it began to assume more ominous proportions. Juan was small for his age and hence unable to hold his own in a fistfight. Juan responded to attacks or provocations by resorting to weapons—that is, by using anything that lay handy. Once aroused, he wouldn't or couldn't stop hammering at his opponent until dragged away. He frequently lost control of his bladder while fighting, and his dripping jeans infuriated him still further. When other kids called him "Juan Skunk" and the staff dubbed him "our maniac," Juan did his best to live up to the title. From fighting only in self-defense, he gradually turned aggressor and came to enjoy the terror he could spread with a weapon in his hand.

After seriously injuring another boy with a baseball bat, Juan was transferred to an upstate institution reserved for "violent incorrigibles," recidivists, and juvenile murderers. He learned to stay out of trouble there—at least long enough to be released at the age of thirteen. He also learned the rudiments of lock picking. Otherwise, he was a functional illiterate, incapable of reading and comprehending a simple sentence. Following his discharge, Juan carried out a string of burglaries that netted him enough to make him financially independent of his mother. He even acquired a follower of sorts—a twelve-year-old syphilitic. When in the course of burglarizing a hardware store they were surprised by an elderly, limping watchman, the younger boy fled, but Juan stood his ground. Grabbing the nearest weapon—a claw hammer—he swung at the watchman's head, knocking him unconscious. Then he frenziedly smashed the fallen man's skull and tried, unsuccessfully, to saw off his nose with a blunt pocketknife.

At the time of writing Juan is serving eighteen months in a nonsecure state facility. I heard the details of his case from a staff psychiatrist who termed him "a severely disturbed and antisocial adolescent." Not an altogether surprising analysis.

Juan M. is *not* typical of contemporary juvenile delinquents. He was unluckier than most. The significant feature of his brief career is that he spent more time in confinement when he had committed no crime than he will for his homicide conviction.

Kids who learn the ropes of the system can manipulate it to an extent that affords them something close to immunity from punishment. The three youths who killed New York taxi driver Morris Rotter in 1974 had a total of forty-two previous arrests behind them, including charges for robbery, grand larceny, burglary, and shoplifting. Two of them had been arrested for holding up a taxi driver just seventy-two hours earlier—only to be freed again to murder another. A fourteen-year-old who got himself shot while trying to rob a Brooklyn grocer had piled up twenty-one previous arrests for such diverse offenses as robbery, arson, assault, and auto theft.

One eighteen-year-old school dropout may even qualify for some future edition of the *Guinness Book of Records* courtesy of the D.C. Juvenile Court. On the evening of April 7, 1976, he and another teenager allegedly shot and killed economist Robert Bailey in the course of a Washington street robbery. Bailey had been on his way to a neighborhood-association meeting called to discuss street crime. Earlier the same evening the boys had robbed three persons; on their way home afterward they robbed a fourth. At the age of fifteen one of the youths had been consecutively convicted of armed robbery, shoplifting, grand larceny, and burglary. At sixteen he was released on "after care"—the juvenile version of parole. At seventeen he was charged with attempted robbery ("attempted" simply because his victim had no money to be robbed of). On that last charge, Superior Court Judge Draper released him without bond, conditional on his re-porting once a week to the D.C. Bail Agency—by telephone. Two months later, while a grand jury was still pondering whether or not to indict him, he held up Robert Bailey. Neither of his parents attended his murder hearing.

Such case histories are microcosms of the grotesque waste-land entitled the juvenile-justice system. Court of Appeals Judge Irving R. Kaufman called it "the failure of the reha-bilitative ideal." Criminologist Gerald Haslip attributed it to "too many decisions by too many mediocrities, based on too little knowledge, taken in too little time and put into practice with too little money." Actually, it is far more than that; it represents part—perhaps the saddest part—of the wreckage of the American Dream.

The entire concept of a separate jurisprudence for juveniles is of amazingly recent origin. Throughout most of history children from about the age of seven were tried in adult courts according to the standard laws of the period, receiving sentences which were usually—but not invariably—more lenient. After the anti-Catholic Gordon Riots tore London apart in 1780, two fourteen-year-old apprentices were among the twenty-one persons hanged by King George's government. The poet Selwyn observed that he had never before seen boys "weeping so piteously." The supposedly enlightened French Revolutionary Army of 1792 executed several of its drummer boys, aged sixteen and seventeen, after a regular court martial found them guilty of "looting by force." As a whole, capital punishment for children was rare, but lengthy imprisonment in adult institutions was taken for granted.* When Oscar Wilde served his stretch in Reading Jail, he found that nearly one third of his shaven, shackled, treadmill-walking fellow convicts were in their teens.

America's first juvenile court was established in 1899 (in Chicago), and it wasn't until 1925 that forty-six states had set aside special courts and procedures for children. With this progressive movement, however, went a much broader definition of delinquency than before. Until the emergence of separate institutions, youngsters went to court *only* when charged with acts that would also be considered criminal for an adult. Offenses like truancy, running away, and incorrigibility were dealt with in rough and ready fashion at home. Now these status offenders poured into the juvenile-law process, clogging its channels, mingling with genuine young criminals and—inevitably—copying them. Almost from

---

* Most of the exceptions were due to religious fanaticism. The Spanish Inquisition burned numbers of "young heretics." Calvin had a girl of nine burned at the stake in Geneva for "raising her hand against her mother." The Puritans of Massachusetts decreed the death penalty for "a stubborn or rebellious son."

the start, the system began to show unmistakable symptoms of strain, but very few people recognized them clearly enough to sound warnings.

On the contrary, reformers throughout the nation labored hard to further extend the legal definition of "juvenile," thereby pushing more and more offenders into the system that was simultaneously to confine, protect, and rehabilitate them. Their rationale was a form of benevolent social myopia that, under the circumstances, wrought more havoc than any amount of reactionary punitiveness. Most of the reformers were intellectuals from urban middle-class backgrounds, the end products of lengthy academic careers in good schools. They superimposed the duration of their own youth on the delinquents and firmly believed that no one was truly capable of "adult" misdeeds until the age of twenty-one or so. They ignored or rather misinterpreted history, which proves otherwise. England's "Black Prince" of Wales was sixteen when he won the battle of Crécy, Joan of Arc seventeen when she stormed Orléans, Alexander the Great nineteen when he began his conquest of the known world (an age at which he wouldn't have been allowed to buy a drink in today's California). Such examples were countered by the argument that the increase in the human life span since then must also have led to a prolongation of our formative period. And so it had —for the middle class. In the ghettos life remained pretty much as it had always been. And it was there that the explosions originated whose shock waves destroyed the dream structure of the reformers.

Nobody was prepared for the phenomenon that began to make itself felt here in the mid-1950s—a tide of roaming runaway youngsters that swelled to over one million a year by the 1970s. Simultaneously an epidemic of juvenile muggings, assaults, robberies, and murders spread out from the metropolitan ghetto areas, rendering first the adjoining districts, then entire cities, unsafe at any hour.

Unprepared as it was, the United States had no means of countering this visitation. There was, first of all, no central authority to lay down guidelines, only a totally fragmented crazy quilt of regional bodies, sometimes overlapping, often contradicting one another. There was utter confusion about the *nature* of the scourge. Like many bacterial diseases, it manifested different forms. The ghetto gangs were semi-literate, underprivileged youngsters, infected by the hopeless squalor of their surroundings. But most of the runaways and suburban delinquents came from comfortable bourgeois homes and were *over-* rather than underprivileged. Both groups were handled by the same judiciary, but what—if anything—was the connection between them?

Phoenix school psychologist William Hall ventured a sweeping answer: "Society seems to be flying apart. The kids just feel the vibrations much more than adults." The vibrations they caught most clearly were the palsied tremblings of the juvenile-justice system. The delinquents were the first to notice that the establishment had painted itself into a corner from which it could merely make feeble lunges in their direction.

The liberal reformers, proclaiming *Don't punish—rehabilitate*, had rendered it virtually toothless—at least so far as the tougher culprits were concerned. Although most of the reformers have now realized that their motto has become a joke, the alternatives still strike them as too repulsive. "If you can't rehabilitate a thirteen-, fourteen-, or fifteen-year-old," asks Charles Schinitsky of the New York Legal Aid Society, "who can you rehabilitate?" The melancholy answer seems to be: under current circumstances, hardly anyone.

From the vantage point of hindsight, it is easy to sneer at the idealists who turned out to have been wrong for all the right reasons. But no credit belongs to their opponents of the hit-'em-where-it-hurts school. For while the conservative diehards consistently advocated longer stretches in stronger jails, they were never willing to allocate the funds necessary to build, staff, and maintain them. If rose-tinted ignorance was the curse of the liberals, the fiscal Scroogeism of the conservatives—plus their gut-level aversion to any attempt at centralizing authority—contributed at least as much to the debacle. It was entirely their fault that the first comprehensive federal law to deal with juvenile crime was not passed until 1974. It authorized federal grants to develop community programs aimed at preventing delinquency. Toward this end, President Ford generously committed $25 million—less than his administration forked out to save a single big corporation from well-deserved bankruptcy. This at a time when, according to Senator Birch Bayh, juvenile crime was costing the U.S. $12 *billion* annually.

Facile optimism and cheapskate mini-measures were the main ingredients in the making of the tragedy. Theoretically, young delinquents were to have been rehabilitated by a carefully staged process that included expert counseling, the learning of useful trades, psychiatric treatment when necessary, and a thorough reorientation to society before their release. In practice, most juvenile centers were too overcrowded and understaffed to accomplish any of these aims. Their precarious control over their charges was not even sufficient to prevent gang-rapes. The "useful trades" turned out to be patently useless in the absence of available jobs. "In effect," one California counselor told me grimly, "our course in motor mechanics helped a lot of them become better car thieves."

Release procedures, far from being carefully regulated, grew in a wildly haphazard manner. Regardless of court verdicts, they are determined by parole boards or state administrators with the power to abort any sentence. Frequently their sole criterion is temporary expediency. They will release charges simply to alleviate overcrowding in their facilities, after a cursory glance at the offenders' behavioral records *while in confinement*. Prior criminal records may not enter the decision at all. They may not even be available, but may lie scattered around three or four different regional offices whose harried staffs have misfiled or mislaid them. As a result, a juvenile killer can be back on the prowl within ten months, while a warehouse thief serves three years.

One of the most important factors—and sometimes the only factor—involved in releases is the psychiatrist's assessment. This is rarely the work of a staff therapist, however, since few juvenile institutions can afford one. Goshen Center, New York State's high-security lockup for boys, for instance, has no full-time psychiatrist or psychologist, but tries to scrape along with part-timers. This occurs in a state so saturated with therapists that they're analyzing the psyches of basset hounds, and in a center reserved for murderers, repeat offenders, and kids too violent for other training schools.

Mental therapy was once to have been one of the keystones of the entire youth-rehabilitation program. It has become its bleakest fiasco as a result not only of the scarcity of clinicians and their chronic lack of time, but also of the dismal quality of so many. Unable to afford first-class practitioners, the system tends to attract highly motivated third-raters—therapists who are often more influenced by their patients than their patients are by them.

I met a representative specimen of their tribe in the person of . . . well, let's call him Sid. After four years in the system, Sid has come to identify with his patients to the point where he cultivates an Afro-style mop above his pale, *angst*-creased countenance and tries to give his native Bronx voice a Harlemese inflection. He wears scuffed sneakers, glasses mended with tape (to denote poverty), and an imitation Benin amulet around his neck. Not only does he manage to cram even more "dudes" and "motherfuckers" into his speech than do his patients, but he concludes every other sentence with a resounding "Right on." He hints that he, too, has a juvenile record (which is not true) and that the correction authorities dislike him (which is).

Altogether Sid seems far less concerned with "curing" his patients than with being accepted by them. In his conversations with me he revealed an odd blend of admiration for and fear toward his charges, plus the belief that any readjustment he might induce would probably work to their detriment. After all, they were returning to ghetto environments, where violent antisocial tendencies help rather than hinder survival.

The boys, I learned, feel equally ambivalent about Sid. They accept him strictly in the role of a potent, if rather eccentric, ally—a sympathetic clown who can be manipulated by those who know his weaknesses into helping them get out. They develop a remarkable knack for giving him the *right* answers (those he expects of them). Some of the repeat offenders, having gleaned as much of his psychiatric jargon as he has of their street talk, use it in the same calculated fashion. They laugh about him, but always with the awareness that he holds the key to their freedom. Listening to them made me realize the sheer farcicality of our compulsory jail therapy. It also explained why the rate of recidivism among juvenile offenders approaches 80 percent.

When the youth authorities are feeling particularly nonchalant, they don't even bother going through the pretense of rehabilitation. Even in a case where a juvenile court has handed down a verdict of guilty of murder, kidnapping, conspiracy, armed robbery, and auto theft, the youth authorities have reasoned that the juvenile offender was either beyond rehabilitation or not in need of it!

In February 1976, a big-mouthed, tiny-brained young drifter, Owen (not his real name), had recently been released from a juvenile institution. He had no money, but he did have ideas—mostly centering around the robberies he intended to pull.

Four days after he met Cathy (not her real name), a young runaway, Owen waylaid Mrs. Elizabeth Koetz, a middle-aged nurse, in the parking lot of a South San Francisco shopping center, taking her purse and forcing the woman into the trunk of her own car. He and his new friend discussed what to do with their prisoner as they drove north along Highway 101. In the wooded countryside near Willits, they made up their minds. First, Mrs. Koetz, wearing her white nurse's uniform, was forced to lie face down in the bushes bordering the highway. Then Owen shot her through the back of her head. The youngsters drove on, turning east through the scenic mountains of Trinity County, heading nowhere in particular, enjoying the ride. They had an elderly blue Mustang, a .22 pistol, and fifty-seven dollars from the dead woman's purse. Sufficient unto the day . . .

The joyride ended around five that morning, when a sheriff's deputy spotted their defective taillight and tried to stop them. The Mustang took off in a tire-screeching chase over the winding mountain road, with the sheriff's car in hot pursuit—just like prime-time television. Some twenty miles later, the Mustang hit an embankment and skidded to a halt. Owen and Cathy piled out, unhurt but shaken. "The girl was clinging to the guy," the chief deputy reported. "She seemed wild with fear." Naturally she did. This time *she* nearly got hurt, rather than some irrelevant nurse she didn't even know. Owen began to weep on cue. "I have something to tell you," he sniffed, dabbing at his eyes. Peck's Bad Boy, confessing another broken window, was ready for his spanking.

Owen, being nineteen, was slated for an adult murder trial. In contrast, Cathy went for a hearing in juvenile court. Since there was no question of her having been coerced into her little adventure, the court found her guilty of five felonies. But exactly twenty-five days after she reached juvenile prison, California's Youth Authority released her on parole.

"It's a shock," said District Attorney Duncan James. "The young lady was involved in a really terrible crime—she couldn't possibly be rehabilitated in twenty-five days." The youth authority, to be sure, claimed no such record. "We think," a spokesman announced loftily, "that a warm home climate would be a lot better for her than a state institution." And there the matter rested. The youth authority, cloaked in comfortable anonymity, is accountable to no one—with the possible exception of God.

It was hilariously coincidental that San Francisco Juvenile Court Judge Francis Mayer chose that very week to berate critics of the system. "You don't blame the medical profession just because people get sick," declared the judge. "The juvenile justice system has yet to be given full community support to get the job done." Apparently it hadn't occurred to the good judge that people may not be supporting the system because they don't believe in it—least of all in its ability to "get the job done." Besides, you would certainly blame the medical profession if you saw it administering a treatment that rendered patients progressively sicker by the year.

Nowhere is that sickness more evident than in the nation's classrooms. The Senate Subcommittee on Juvenile Delinquency called them "combat zones," and produced the casualty figures to prove it. The Subcommittee's report was published in 1974 and was based on a survey of 757 school districts. "The number of American students who died in the combat zones of our nation's schools between 1970 and 1973 exceeds the number of American soldiers killed in combat during the first three years of the Vietnam conflict," Senator Birch Bayh, the chairman, stated. The deaths numbered 355, and they included students shot down in playgrounds, stabbed or battered to death in corridors and washrooms, sniped at through classroom windows, pitched off roofs, and caught in the crossfire of hostile forces battling in schoolyards. They did not include the "hundred of thousands of students" wounded, maimed, or permanently crippled during nonlethal assaults or sexual attacks. Nor did they include the estimated 70,000 teachers in every section of the country who become victims of assaults each year—assaults that range from being struck in the face to being raped at gunpoint in front of their class.

What the report called "an even more ominous statistic" was that the number of weapons confiscated by school authorities at the end of the 1973 term had increased by 54 percent since 1970. These weapons included knives, clubs, pistols, and shotguns sawed off for easy concealment in a student's locker. A good proportion of this armament is intended for purely defensive purposes. As a thirteen-year-old put it, while pleading for the restitution of his ten-inch dagger: "If you don't gimme back that knife, I'm a dead kid. Like, I can't *survive* without it—all the others got theirs."

Up to this point we have always attempted to compare American conditions with those elsewhere, preferably those

in other Western industrialized societies. But here the com-
parisons stop. There are no parallels anywhere, neither in the
industrialized countries nor the Third World; nor, for that
matter, in any other period of human history. The United
States remains unique as the only nation ever to boast multi-
digit casualty reports in its school system.

Perhaps the ugliest facet of the entire juvenile-violence syndrome, both inside and outside the schools, is the growth of
street gangs. Former social worker Alex Norman, currently
with UCLA, was quoted as saying "You have a whole generation of kids who can't cope. It's such a monster now that no
one knows where to grab, the head or the tail." Some trained
observers of the scene have reached a rather different conclusion. The kids, they noticed, seem to be coping quite nicely.
It's the adults that can't.

As a New York police expert on youth gangs told *Newsday*:
"They kill whoever they have a mind to kill, and there isn't a
damn thing you can do about it." The song sounds familiar,
but it seems odd coming from someone speaking on behalf of
thirty-two thousand heavily armed men in blue who call themselves "New York's Finest." He might have been talking about
the Mafia instead of ragtail bunches of mutually hostile teenagers who, if they weren't so ludicrously incompetent with firearms, would have wiped each other out years ago.

The mayhem they create is truly ghastly—far worse even
than the ordinary citizen imagines. Dr. Walter B. Miller
of the Harvard Law School's Center for Criminal Justice
compiled a government-funded analysis of youth-gang activities in twelve American cities. In six of them, the gang problem was described as "extremely serious." They were New
York, Chicago, Los Angeles, Philadelphia, Detroit, and San
Francisco, where gangs committed 525 murders from 1972
through 1974. Dr. Miller wrote: "Probably the single most
significant development affecting gang-member violence during the present period is an extraordinary increase in the
availability and use of firearms. . . ." His report noted that
New York police found certain Bronx gangs possessed arsenals
of modern weapons, including rifles, automatics sawed-off

shotguns, handguns, homemade mortars, bazookas, Molotov cocktails, and pipe bombs. In conclusion, he stated: "Many urban communities are gripped with a sense of hopelessness that anything can be done to curb the unremitting menace of the gangs."

The menace, however, stems less from the lethal powers of the gangs than from the attitude of the communities confronting them—an attitude that can be described as a mélange of muddle-mindedness, inertia, and sheer blue funk. Youth gangs are not new, nor are they an American phenomenon. America is simply the only country that indulged in negotiations with them, conferring upon them the quasi-governmental status of warring powers and thereby helping them become permanent sores on the urban landscape.

Yet, where sufficient determination and appropriate resources are brought to bear on the problem, street gangs are probably the easiest of all criminal manifestations to control. I saw French, British, and Japanese police curb their respective gutter gangsters, effectively forestalling any chance of their developing monster proportions. London, for instance, suffered successive waves of youth mobs calling themselves Teddy Boys, Mods, Rockers, and Skinheads, any one of which might have grown into a full-fledged menace had it remained undisturbed. The point is that they didn't get the chance. I watched Scotland Yard * virtually wipe out the Skinheads in two years by applying what is known as "heat therapy." A London police spokesman described the process to me:

> They make it simpler for us by identifying themselves. The Teddies wore Edwardian togs, the Rockers motorcycle outfits, the Skinheads cropped their hair short. Something like uniforms. And, of course, that enabled us to pick them out every time. We grabbed them whenever there was a disturbance anywhere. Or even when there wasn't. You might say we harried them, all along the line. We wouldn't let them congregate or cluster in any particular area. We were always searching them

---

* Scotland Yard is a term embracing the entire London Metropolitan Police, uniformed and plainclothes. The famous detective branch is the CID (Criminal Investigation Department).

for illegal weapons, always moving them on, breaking up their numbers—because numbers make them dangerous. We only arrested them for criminal acts, but we kept *moving* them, even from premises like pubs and cafés. Now, it's no good doing that kind of thing a couple of times and then laying off. You have to keep it up, follow through all the time until the message sinks in. And we did just that.

Well, in due course they started shedding those uniforms that rendered them conspicuous. This may seem a minor thing, but it more or less finished the gangs. It took the—well, the *magic* out of the business. Made them just ordinary street hooligans without cohesion or glamor. You might say it destroyed their morale, like it would in an army that suddenly has to wear civvies. They lost most of their starch that way. We haven't had much trouble with them since.

No one would prescribe the exact same methods for other countries where conditions differ. In Japan, where parental control is stronger than in England, the police worked through the families of known gang members, but just as relentlessly and with equal success. The families got so tired of constant police visits that they took their roaming offspring in hand. What counts are not the methods but the principle behind them. The principle, briefly summarized, is the denial of legality status for street gangs per se. In other words, the denial of their right to exist.

This may sound like a radical innovation, but it was actually the way America's cities were kept moderately secure for more than a century. The principle was never formalized but was quite effectively enforced by cops on the beat, who habitually broke up potentially menacing bands of youngsters by ordering them to "move along and get out of here." It may not have been egalitarian or even entirely legal. But, insofar as it maintained the right of the majority to walk the streets in peace by nipping in the bud countless thousands of fights, muggings, thefts, and murders, it was truly democratic in spirit.

All this changed during the 1950s with the emergence of predominantly black and Puerto Rican ghetto gangs. Now the problem acquired a racial tinge and threw the entire concept of impromptu gang dispersal into disrepute. People flocked to see *West Side Story*, the fabulously successful musical whose semicomic villain was an "Officer Krupke" who kept butting his nose in every time the gang leaders were trying to hold socio-philosophical discussions. The play quite correctly portrayed the gangs as basically protective associations, formed to guard certain areas (turfs) against invasion by other gangs. The resultant brawls (rumbles) were relatively bloodless affairs, fought out with fists, clubs, auto radio aerials, and a few zip guns. They caused a lot of injuries but rarely corpses.

It was during this period that city and police officials conceived the disastrous idea of negotiating with the gangs. It might have been more benign than breaking them up, and was certainly cheaper in the short run, but it embodied an absolutely fatal concession. By recognizing the mobs as guardians of their turfs and thus helping them delineate their borders, the officials implicitly transferred the protective function from the police to whichever gang was strong enough to seize it as a prize. In effect, by their abdication of civic responsibility they took the first step toward the legalization of mob rule. All the horrors to come were a logical consequence of this step.

To be sure, the original ghetto gangs were to fade out during the 1960s, chiefly as a result of wholesale heroin addiction that rendered them incapable of any kind of organized action. But in the early 1970s the street gangs reappeared suddenly, and, like the secondary stage of syphilis, in a vastly more dangerous form.

Having abandoned the old clubs and zip guns together with the leather jackets, the mobs were now able to boast instead of huge quantities of high-grade firearms, together with caches of incendiary missiles manufactured in cellar workshops. Rumbles still occur, but most of the gangs have dropped their "protective" tasks and now operate primarily as criminal organizations. Extending their raids far beyond any turf confines, incorporating entire inner-city areas and occasionally spilling over into the suburbs, they no longer guard but rob, plunder, and murder on an organized scale.

Nevertheless, the turfs are still their rightful domains, tacitly ceded to them by cowering authorities intent on fiddling their budgets while Rome burns about their ears.

New York is a striking example of this mentality. According to Captain Francis J. Daly, commander of the Youth Aid Division (another Orwellian euphemism, inasmuch as this unit is mostly concerned with fighting juvenile crime), the city currently harbors 255 street gangs, with 8,000 verified members and 20,000 alleged ones. Their depredations have increased with their numbers. During 1974 they committed 1,187 criminal acts; in 1975 the score was 1,339.

Over the same period the city authorities saw fit to cut police budgets, so that now only seven intelligence officers have to do the work formerly tackled by thirty-five. Consequently, the number of youth gang members arrested dropped by 24 percent, despite the rise in gang crimes. If you stack up the financial costs of the crime increase against the money saved by the budget cuts, you get an idea of the kind of bargain achieved by the municipal Mr. Micawbers. But a photo published by *Time* magazine makes the point better than a thousand statistics. It shows three members of the Royal Javelins gang flaunting their automatic rifles on a rooftop overlooking the fire-scarred wastelands of the South Bronx, lords of all they survey. The picture could have been taken in war-torn Beirut. It could also have served as a cover illustration for a volume chronicling two decades of diplomatic palavers with street gangs.

Some five hundred murders notwithstanding, the powwows are still continuing at various levels. Indeed, they have reached such a degree of sophistication that the negotiating parties hold separate press conferences to convey their respective views to the media. Thus, we are treated to diatribes by New York's Dragons and Chicago's Blackstone Rangers informing us of how they are actually misunderstood civic-benefit societies persecuted by the cops. When, in the past, the Ku Klux Klan tried to stage similiar comedy acts, at least the Eastern press had the savvy to laugh about them. Nobody laughs at the gang spokesmen. On the contrary, publications have fallen over one another in order to run portraits of such benevolent associations as the Crazy Homicides, Death Makers, Killers, Skulls, Tomahawks, Crips, Errol Flynns, Savages, and so on, ad nauseam.

The pinnacle of absurdity was probably achieved in Detroit during the bleak and blood-soaked summer of 1976. Two youth gangs broke into a Sunday rock concert held in downtown Cobo Hall. They occupied the stage, blocked the exits, and proceeded to rob, beat, and sexually molest the captive audience. Although there were ten policemen on duty, their protection was, to put it delicately, unnoticeable. The following day the city administration recalled 450 cops who had been laid off as a result of budget cuts. Coleman Young, Detroit's first black mayor, slammed down an unprecedented 10:00 P.M. curfew on all youngsters under eighteen, accompanied by an urgent call to the police to stamp out gang activities. But simultaneously a gang representative held— yes, you guessed it—a press conference at the same Cobo Hall. After complaining of persecution and discrimination, he distributed a computer printout containing the names, addresses, and telephone numbers of twenty policemen—all black—and proceeded to assure reporters that his outfit knew the name of every black cop in the city. The spokesman was neither arrested nor questioned, possibly because this might have contravened his diplomatic status or the Geneva Convention or the United Nations Charter. Deputy Mayor Beckman, however, did have a comment. "We were amazed," he said. "We have no idea how they got hold of that printout, but we're sure looking into it right away." Lenny Bruce in his heyday couldn't have improvised it better.

The peculiar folly of officialdom's entering into quasi-formal negotiations with the likes of street gangs lies in the fact that every such contact helps to reinforce the power and legitimacy of the mobs. In the long run it thus accomplishes the very opposite of what the authorities are trying to achieve. Joining a gang is largely a quest for identity. Negotiating with a gang means bestowing official recognition on it—in effect providing its members with the self-image they crave, *reward-ing* them for having joined. The same applies to an even greater extent to the leadership. Most gangs don't have established leaders but merely temporary boss types for certain actions who must constantly reassert their dominance. By treating them as spokesmen, the authorities confirm their authority in the eyes of the rank and file and may even reinforce their positions to the point where they become genuine autocrats. Similarly, government agencies habitually hire gang leaders—at substantial wages—for effortless make-work jobs in community programs. These programs are usually run for the exclusive benefit of gang members—again, rewarding them while ignoring nondelinquent youngsters. Moreover, because the leadership types are invariably the toughest elements in the packs, these jobs appear as unmistakable bonuses for badness—a lesson that can't fail to sink in.

As a result, the lower echelons of some agencies are crawling with individuals boasting formidable police records. The only condition of their tenure seems to be that they not mug anyone while on duty—although this, too, has been known to happen. The Los Angeles County Department of Community Affairs employed a young man who had previously been arrested for airplane-hijacking threats, for assault, for carrying loaded firearms, and for driving around a local high school with a loudspeaker urging students to "off the pigs," while sporting a private police badge.

In December 1975, Los Angeles mayor Tom Bradley presented a handsome "Certificate of Appreciation" for "outstanding activities" to the Eighteenth Street Gang. These activities consisted solely of participating in a football game with the rival Diamond Street Gang. Every year thousands of boys' teams play football matches without warranting such honors. The only reason for the citation was that the Eighteenth Streeters ranked as possibly the most vicious youth gang in the country. Therefore, their willingness to play ball —albeit grudgingly—had to be rewarded. The mayor had placed a premium on violence; and while he may not have been conscious of this, you can rest assured that the other gangs were.

Some people within the law-enforcement process are aware of the self-defeating fatuity of these methods. What's more they know the remedies that *should* be applied. Occasionally they are even allowed to try them—but never for very long. Something always happens: Funds run out, manpower gets short, a political shuffle occurs, private interests intervene, or the whimsical breezes that govern our juvenile-justice system blow a new fad into the minds of the powers-that-be. The proposed remedies are then scuttled, the ship lurches off on another tack, and yet another good man fades into the shadows to fight frustration. One of them was Bill Melcher.

Readers of *Helter Skelter* may recall a brief mention of him in the book. Bill Melcher was the young deputy District Attorney who befriended "Squeaky" Fromme while she stood vigil outside the Los Angeles court where her master, Charles Manson, was being tried. Melcher's wife baked Christmas cookies for all the Manson girls. Later, when the police arrested Squeaky on an armed-robbery charge, Melcher fought hard to prove her innocent. "Clearing her," he said, "was my greatest satisfaction in three years as a prosecutor."

Melcher, then, is a long way removed from the conventional "tough gangbuster" image. But he knows his territory: the "battle zone" of unincorporated East Los Angeles. Eight square miles of crumbling, heat-baked, graffiti-smeared, bullet-scarred hovels called the barrios, it is a human nightmare where 140,000 people live in a permanent state of civil war and half the mothers have lost sons in gang feuds; where there are houses with every window shot out; where families sleep on the floor in a back room because every night the front of their home is raked with gunfire; where mothers—caught when a gunfight erupts in the neighborhood laundromat—push their babies into the washing machines to protect them from the bullets. It is a place where a giant, muddy-eyed eighteen-year-old can relate the following to an L.A. *Times* reporter as if it were an everyday occurrence:

Me and a friend was on reds that night, just cruising around when I saw this strange dude just walking alone down the street. I never saw him before, so I don't know what barrio he was from . . . but I went over and strangled him. Sure there were witnesses, because this dude was screaming and stuff. But nobody talks to cops. Why did I kill him? Because he was on our turf, man.

Because gangs mean chiefly the barrios and the barrios are almost entirely Chicano, Melcher was an excellent choice for the Juvenile Division's Gang Suppression Unit. Melcher's wife, Denise, is Mexican; he speaks fluent Spanish, cultivates a very macho mustache, and could pass for a dry-cleaned version of Zapata. More important, he had rapport with the population; he liked them and was liked in return. He told me: "Don't buy any of that nonsense about violence and lawlessness being Mexican character traits. If anything, the opposite is true. Those barrio people are *more* law-enforcement-oriented than the rest of us. The whole gang problem is caused by a very small group of little monsters—maybe one or two percent of the locals. But those two or three thousand, with the weapons they have and the terror they inspire, can turn the whole area into a hellhole.

"A murder is committed and the killer arrested. But nobody will testify against him in court—not even the victim's family. Why? Because they know the killer's friends are still out there in the streets and will murder *them* if they open their mouths. And that they'll get no protection from the law. Ordinary families can't fight gangs, not in the barrios or anywhere else. They have to go to work, attend to their children, sleep at night. But the gangs don't have to do any of these things. They have all the time in the world. They can watch you for weeks, and wait for just the right moment to burn down your house or shoot you or cripple your kids. So the ordinary, decent people keep their mouths shut. And we get no witnesses. But, believe me, they have the same values we hold. Only it's kind of hard to exercise them when you're lying flat on your living-room floor with bullets screaming overhead."

Melcher knew that the success of his Gang Suppression Unit depended on winning the confidence of the "silent ones," and that this in turn depended on a highly visible presence. In the barrios, the protective clout of the law is measured strictly according to rank. Uniformed cops count for little; detectives for more; a district attorney *in person* for a great deal. Melcher made a point of being there in person: talking to families, addressing community rallies, quizzing victims, trailing the movements of drifting gangs like a menacing shadow. Now and again he even talked to the members—not from a negotiating stance but simply to let them know that he was there, keeping an eye on them, ready to crack down. No junior gangster gained any prestige from conversing with him. He offered no rewards for good behavior but made it unmistakably clear that he wouldn't stand for any other. Moreover, he was always around, always turning up when least expected in an unnerving fashion.

Actually, presence was only a secondary purpose of the Unit. The main objective was to coordinate the activities of the District Attorney's Office with those of local law enforcement and promote the greatest possible cohesiveness of the two as a force pursuing one specific aim at a time—in this case, suppressing certain targeted gangs. In London, Paris, and Tokyo this method has always been taken for granted. In Los Angeles, where half a dozen departments are constantly kicking one another's shins, it was considered experimental.

Every straw in the wind suggested that the experiment was working. Barrio dwellers not only started to volunteer information but actually began contacting the D.A. on their own initiative. As gang activity took a nosedive, street shootings became scarcer, to the point where optimistic citizens began to replace their shattered, boarded-up windows with glass. In October 1975, Melcher made a hard-hitting speech before a Chicano audience at Rown Elementary School. Cheering wildly, the men and women of the barrio rushed the platform to fling their arms around him, hug him, pat his shoulders. Over and over they repeated, "Thank you, señor, but for God's sake be careful."

In the months that followed, Melcher and the assigned deputy sheriffs broke the back of the L'il Valley Gang, one of the most notorious in the area. As some of the members went to jail, the majority left the outfit when the applied heat began to scorch them. Somehow the cops were getting evidence that was previously unavailable. Sensing a cautious air of jubilation in the neighborhood, Melcher set his sights on the next target: the Geraghty Street Gang. Unfortunately, the Geraghty Street boys were to be saved—not by the bell, but by a departmental shuffle which put the Gang Suppression Unit out of business.

It would be pleasantly dramatic to reveal a nefarious political cabal behind this move, a stab in the back by venal superiors. Alas, I could find no signs of any such intrigue. The official justification—"personnel shortages"—seems to have been all the motivation involved, although perhaps the name Gang Suppression Unit sounded a little too *direct* for an organization accustomed to dealing in euphemisms. Under a more sonorously misleading title—say, "Community Street Associations Protective Division"—it might have survived a bit longer. As it was, after seven months in operation, the Unit closed shop in March 1976, with Melcher being transferred to other, unrelated functions. When I subsequently visited the barrios, things had returned to "normal": The newly glassed windows were boarded up once more; fresh bullet marks and new "placas" (gang signatures) marred the walls; and, as the locals informed me, the L'il Valley Gang was back on its turf.

5

Sisterhood of Cain

After thirty-five years with female offenders, the important thing I have learned is that we differ in degree, not in essence. We differ in quantity, not in quality.

—Prison warden Virginia McLaughlin

On the entire myth-shrouded stage of criminology, no figure stands so obscured by emotional bias, wishful thinking, folklore, and ignorance as the female murderer. In magnified form this distinction mirrors the attitude of a male-dominated society to women generally. For historical, sociological, and psychological reasons we find it exceedingly difficult to accept the idea of a woman killer as simply a woman who kills. Because she is a woman she must perforce murder from different motives and with different feelings from a man. Should it turn out that her sentiments and motives were exactly the same, her very femininity is likely to be called into question and her acts regarded as "unnatural" or deviant. Not even the worst male maniac is ever punished by being robbed of his sexual identity.

Women in our society bear a dichotomized image that virtually precludes any rational view of their homicidal aspects. On the one hand, they are the supposedly softer, gentler, more sensitive, and less bellicose species. Let them commit violence, however, and they somehow become "worse" than their masculine counterparts: more bloodthirsty, more vicious, more unscrupulous, "more deadly than the male." It is often women themselves, even the most astute of them, who propagate this canard. In her classic *Murder and Its Motives*, the late and brilliant F. Tennyson

Jesse could write: "The woman criminal is the panther of the underworld. She can follow relentlessly through the jungle day after day, she can wait her time, she can play with her victim and torture him in sheer wantonness, and she can pile cruelty upon the act of killing as does the panther, but never the lion."

Quite apart from the falseness of her animal analogy (all wild predators kill as swiftly as possible), she subsequently proceeded to demolish her own thesis by describing the careers of two English doctors who poisoned their victims with just that slow, relentless cruelty she held to be the prerogative of female murderers. Nevertheless, so firmly was the myth of the deadlier female embedded in her mind that she failed to notice this contradiction.

A variation on the same myth is being stoutly defended on the unlikeliest occasions—such as at the National Conference on Women and Crime, held in Washington, D.C., in February 1976. The keynote speech was given by Dr. Freda Adler, author of *Sisters in Crime*, one of the very few first-rate books on the subject. "Although males will commit by far the greater number of absolute offenses," Adler said, "females are surpassing them in rates of increase for almost every major crime. It is apparent," she continued, "that they are no longer willing to be second-class criminals, limited to 'feminine' crimes of shoplifting and prostitution, but that they are making their gains noticeable across the offense board."

These remarks apparently stung the feminists at the gathering on the raw. Karen DeCrow, president of the National Organization for Women (NOW), declared herself ". . . outraged by correlations between the women's movement and the increase in crime." And one Euphenseniar Foster of the Women's Bureau informed the press: "Adler is the one person who stands out who could be an advocate for what is really needed. But she's feeding everybody, including us, half-truths and making a killing out of her horrible book."

What was so "horrible" about the book? Simply Dr. Adler's deduction that technology and the women's liberation movement have equalized men's and women's capacity for violent crimes. As she summarized: "A frail woman with a pistol is just as threatening to a bank teller as a burly man, and a demure female bank executive has the same opportunity for embezzlement as her male counterpart."

Dr. Adler's sacrilege consisted of printing the opinions of scores of female criminals who showed themselves totally indifferent—and often hostile—toward the women's movement. Their basic leitmotif was voiced by a Chicago prison inmate who stated: "It's like what they say, you know, about mountains. You climb them because they're there. Well, that's the way it is with banks and department stores—that's where the money is. It's not a question of whether you're a man or a woman. It's a question of money. That's it. Money."

The inescapable truth is that a link *does* exist between women's liberation and the crime rate. But the link is of the same nature as that between, say, national prosperity and the consumption of luxury goods. Some human beings will commit crimes in whatever sphere of activity they engage in. As more such spheres are opened to women's participation, they will—as sure as God made little red apples—commit crimes in them. The only reason why so few women have defrauded stock investors is simply that they have had few opportunities of doing so. As more women get to work on docks and at airports, proportionately more of them will be found pilfering cargo.

The progression is both logical and predictable, but it contradicts the myth cherished by certain feminists who insist that equalization of the sexes *diminishes* crime.

Unfortunately, our female-crime statistics are inadequate as well as misleading. Depending on whether you take them absolutely or relatively, you can interpret them to support diametrically opposite conclusions. Thus, between 1960 and 1974 the overall number of female arrests shot up a steep 108 percent—a rise that seems to indicate a female crime wave. Nevertheless, the number of *serious* crimes committed by women is still only around 20 percent of the total crimes in this category—a very low figure when you consider that women comprise more than half of the country's population.

In crimes of violence the increase of arrests among women was 160 percent (compared to 144 percent among men), a rise that sounds drastic indeed. Yet, even so, only about one out of every nine violent offenders today is a female. When we attempt to deal specifically with murder, the analyzing process gets still more difficult—for here we run up against the astonishing disparity between the number of women arrested for murder and those convicted of it. In 1974 over 2,000 females were booked on homicide charges, but only about one in ten was actually tried and found guilty—a fact which does not mean that the other nine tenths were innocent. Rather, the strange imbalance seems largely due to juries' reluctance to condemn females (especially if they have children) for crimes of passion, as well as the tendency of many judges to twist themselves into legal knots trying to divine reasons for acquittal.

Frequently courts will drop murder charges against women providing they turn state's evidence—an invitation most of them accept with alacrity. This time-hallowed American tradition has freed thousands of lethal ladies, while sending their male confederates to prisons or death chambers. The law may stipulate that *all* the participants in a felony resulting in homicide are commonly guilty of murder. In practice, prosecutors are very often happy to let the woman in the case go scot-free—even though she may have been the instigator of the crime—if she will only help them nail the man.

During the spring of 1975 this practice was strikingly demonstrated in rural Delaware County, Iowa, by the events following the sheriff's office's receipt of a missing-husband report filed by Myra Miller, a farmer's wife, and Dennis Fisher, the hired hand. Myra, a tall, buxom nineteen-year-old mother of three, related how she and her husband had quarreled two weeks earlier. Then the farmhand said that he had driven his employer to Dubuque at his request. Since then, it seemed, nobody had laid eyes on him.

The sheriff promised to look into the matter, which proved unfortunate for the pair. For the deeper he looked, the fishier their tale came to appear. Young Howard Miller was an energetic and successful farmer with thriving crops and valuable property. Deeply rooted in his home county, he had no apparent reason to vanish from the scene. Nor had he contacted any of his numerous relatives living in Dubuque. During the next two months, moreover, Myra and Dennis aroused further suspicion by hastily auctioning off all of Miller's cattle and farm machinery—as if they were preparing to move somewhere else. In fact, when on April 23 both were arrested by the sheriff, they were already in the process of moving to a new home in West Plains, Missouri, and, according to the police, they each made a statement that night. The following morning police officers headed for the calf shed of the Miller farm. They dug up the dirt floor and— two feet down—found the decomposing body of Howard Miller, with bullet holes in the head and right shoulder.

The sheriff's department quoted Fisher's admission that he had shot his boss after Miller had threatened to kill his wife because of her relationship with the farmhand. Then, in order to get rid of the body, they together decided to bury it in the calf shed and arrange the story about Fisher driving Miller to Dubuque. The denouement of this rustic drama was rather different from what those unaccustomed to judicial corner-cutting might have expected. Dennis Fisher drew a life sentence after being convicted with the aid of Myra's evidence against him. Mrs. Miller, originally charged with murder, was allowed to plead guilty to the considerably lesser offense of conspiracy to obstruct justice.

Perhaps it is indicative of a new trend that we now occasionally get a turnabout of this traditional development. On certain rare occasions courts will allow the male to plea-bargain himself into a lighter sentence at the expense of his female partner. This happened in Orlando, Florida, during the trial of Frances Willis and Rodney Artegian for the murder of Mrs. Willis's husband.

Frances, a hatchet-faced woman with an immense bouffant hairdo, had gone to the police with a yarn about "hippie-type strangers" beating up and murdering James Willis on the night of September 25, 1975. Her story crumpled fast when detectives found that the dead man showed no marks of a beating and had obviously been shot while peacefully sleeping in his bed. They also discovered that his slumber had been induced by a can of beer spiked with Phencyclidine —a tranquilizer used on horses. Furthermore, as it became more and more clear that the Willis marriage had been bad, they were quick to note that Fran was the beneficiary of her husband's seventeen-thousand-dollar life-insurance policy.

Investigations led them to Artegian, a physically handi-capped restaurant cleaner, who, when confronted, confessed that Mrs. Willis had offered him five thousand dollars to kill her husband. Beyond this initial admission, his account be-came so muddled that it was never clearly established exactly who murdered James Willis. Both of them entered the bed-room where the drugged victim lay sleeping. Then, either Fran or Artegian fired a shot from a tiny two-round derringer into his head. In any case, since it had been established that Fran had drugged her husband's beer and that Artegian had later disposed of the murder weapon, they shared the guilt. Nevertheless, the fact that his evidence was necessary to seal the case against Mrs. Willis meant that, after testify-ing as a state's witness, Artegian was allowed to plead guilty to second-degree murder and was let off with a fifteen-year sentence. Fran, convicted of murder in the first degree, was sentenced to life imprisonment.

Although there have been a few others with similar end-ings, the Willis trial still stands as a courtroom curiosity. The above examples, however, convey an idea of the ambiv-alence that typifies the feminine homicide role. As one dis-trict attorney told me: "If all women were convicted of the killings they set in motion, our female murder rate would be double—maybe triple—what it is. An awful lot of them man-

age to use men as their murder weapon—someone else to pull
the trigger or thrust the knife on their behalf. And that's
damned hard to prove in a court of law; most juries won't
buy it. I don't care what they say about the sexual revolution,
murder by remote control is still the most common type of
feminine homicide—same as it was fifty or a hundred years
ago."

Occasionally this control can be uncanny—based not on
persuasion but on a dark, primordial form of sexual power
that goes beyond modern psychological concepts and conjures up the medieval specter of the succubus, the female
demon that shrivels a man's brain and robs him of free will.
There are no other terms to describe the case of the self-
proclaimed California witch who, had she lived a few centuries earlier, would certainly have been burned as one.

A blonde, Madonna-faced beauty, Marlene Olive was sixteen. Although she encrusted her luminous green eyes with
the makeup of an aging Balkan spy and wore enough garish
jewelry to blind motorists at night, her execrable taste
couldn't quite ruin her natural loveliness. She struck out all
the more since she lived in Terra Linda, the plushest resi-
dential section of San Rafael, a district of manicured lawns,
thoroughbred sports cars, and Gucci accessories. Marlene,
however, *wanted* to be different from her surroundings,
which she loathed almost as heartily as she loathed her
parents. Born in South America, she had been adopted by
wealthy oil-company executive James Olive and his wife,
Naomi, who couldn't have children of their own. Moving
to San Rafael with the family when Olive retired, Marlene
came to detest her new environment. From being the adored
little darling of a small Anglo community, the move made
her just another suburban kid among thousands. She responded with a smoldering hatred for her parents that went
far beyond ordinary resentment and bordered on the psychotic. Among her peers she boasted of being a witch. Claiming that her real mother (whom she never knew) had taught
her the black arts, she carried a deck of tarot cards, spouted

mystical gibberish of her own invention, and practiced casting spells on her high-school friends.

Marlene's knowledge of witchcraft was practically zero and her constant voodoo babble was on the same level as all the occult jargon currently tossed around by teeners, but she showed remarkable judgment in selecting a dull, tormented, friendless drug user named Charles David Riley as the target for her powers. Still virginal, and weighing 260 pounds, Riley sold dope to students more in order to gain popularity than to earn money. Marlene zeroed in on him as if guided by an invisible beacon.

Riley was four years older, but the impact of her attention sent him spinning. After a few months of daily intercourse with Marlene, Riley stopped overeating, dropped fifty pounds, lost his nervous twitches, and "felt just great." But he paid a terrible price for this new self. Within half a year he became, literally, Marlene's slave. She made him wear a feminine bracelet and convinced him that it gave her magic control of his mind, that she could summon him by "psychic command" wherever he was, that he had to do anything she ordered and bear everything she inflicted. Witchcraft served only as a trapping. It was an extreme instance of what the Germans called *Hörigkeit*, for which there is no equivalent English term: the complete sexual subjugation of one person by another.

Marlene sent Riley out to steal clothes and jewelry for her. She had an ample allowance but preferred stolen things as being "more gypsy." She bit his arms and neck until her teeth drew blood, and carved her initials on his back with a pocketknife. Knowing Riley's chronic shyness, she made him demonstrate his subservience in public. He had to crawl on his hands and knees and perform cunnilingus on her while the company watched. Sometimes she would urinate in his face. The more embarrassed he grew, the more Marlene seemed to relish these exhibitions. As one of her girl friends commented, somewhat naively: "I don't think she liked him much."

The Olives tried to break up the pair by having Riley arrested on the rather comical charge of contributing to Marlene's delinquency. Riley was released pending a hearing on the charge, and there the matter rested. Neither the Olives nor the other parents involved had more than the haziest notion of what went on beneath the gloss of their sun- and dollar-drenched luxury enclave.

The matter was still resting in June 1975, when James Olive—a man of the utmost punctiliousness—missed a string of important business conferences. Telephone calls were unanswered, so several days later Detective Sergeant Bart Stinson appeared at the Olive residence to make personal inquiries. The large green hedge-shielded house at the end of the elegant driveway lay in silence as well as considerable disorder. Only Marlene was at home, and she gave vague and contradictory answers to questions on the whereabouts of her parents. Consequently, Stinson took her along for further grilling. The net of inquiries spread out, but caught no leads until an anonymous phone call sent the squad cars racing to a popular barbecue spot in a glade above nearby San Pablo Bay. There, amid empty beer cans and smoked-down marijuana roaches, were the ashes of a mighty bonfire. And in the ashes the officers found charred bones and a handful of human teeth—all that remained of Mr. and Mrs. Olive.

The San Rafael police quickly identified the anonymous caller, recognizing her voice as that of one of Marlene's friends. A statuesque blonde of seventeen, she now produced the most stomach-turning account California had heard since the Manson massacre. When she repeated it at the trial the following November, the courtroom audience alternately gasped and tittered—the kind of response usually associated with porno movies.

The girl testified that she had visited the Olive home two days after the murders. There were still some bloodstains on the floor and walls, which she helped Marlene clean up. Her hostess regaled her with details of the double slaying: Naomi Olive battered to death with a claw hammer; James shot four times; their bodies wrapped in blankets and driven out to the barbecue pit, then doused in gasoline and burned to ashes; the bones stomped to fragments by the feet of two sturdy, energetic youngsters. "Nobody's ever going to find them," Marlene said gleefully, "and I'm going to inherit a lot of money. And when I get it, Chuck and I are going to South America, where I belong." Marlene, as always, did the talking, with Riley merely nodding and grunting "yeah" at intervals.

There were reefers all around, plus beer and cocaine. Then the trio settled down to a prolonged "sex bash" in the bed of the murdered mother.

A trial attorney interrupted the witness.

"You mean," he asked, "that you knew at the time you were having sex with this man that he had killed two persons and burned their bodies—and yet you went to bed with him and had sexual relations in the bed of the murdered woman?"

The blonde nodded, a little nervously. "Well, *she* was there. She told us what to do and how to do it. Sometimes she liked having sex while other people watched and sometimes she liked to watch other people having sex."

"Why did you do it?"

"She made me. She could make anybody do anything. She was a witch and could cast a spell on anybody."

The attorney persisted. "You are certain you did not willingly participate because you enjoyed it?"

"We-ell . . ." the girl said hesitantly, "I guess I enjoyed it at the time. But . . . but, we'd been smoking grass and my mind was blown. I didn't know what I was doing. And— like I told you—she had this power."

"This power" must have been highly potent, because the witness spent an entire day and a night with the pair, "not knowing what she was doing" all the while. But the following day she made the anonymous phone call to the cops.

Although after his arrest Riley at first admitted killing both parents, he later modified his confession to include only James Olive. The Marin County superior court room was jammed to bursting point with college kids for the occasion. Unfazed by the glowering looks of the bailiffs who muttered about this being "no rock concert," they waited in long, patient lines for a seat or even standing room.

Finally Riley was led in, his long dark sideburns and drooping mustache clashing pathetically with his pink and pudgy baby face. He proceeded to give the jury yet a third version of his confession. According to this variation, Marlene had ordered him to kill both her parents. But when he arrived at her house, armed with a loaded pistol and high on LSD, he stepped into the sewing room and saw Mrs. Olive already dead, a hammer protruding from her forehead.

"I started to freak out. I wanted to leave the house, but I couldn't until I removed that hammer . . . I started to pull it out . . . It took all my strength. I got blood all over me. The blood felt like it was burning my hands."

In a flat monotone, Riley went on to tell how Mr. Olive walked into the room, caught sight of his wife, and screamed, "Oh, my God, Naomi!" The father spotted Riley and allegedly came at him with a paring knife. Riley fired four shots at him. Marlene, he said, stopped him from shooting himself and gave him beer and sex instead. Following the killing he spent the entire day "spaced out" on marijuana, cocaine, more beer, and more sex. That night he took Marlene out to dinner, met some friends, and went on to a drive-in movie.

The jury found Riley guilty of both murders, and Judge E. Warren McGuire sentenced him to become the thirty-seventh man awaiting the judicial green light to the gas chamber on San Quentin's death row.

Marlene's defense was undertaken by the formidable Terence Hallinan of San Francisco in return for half of the estate that—providing she wasn't convicted—would pass into her possession. During her juvenile hearing she claimed that Riley had "held her captive" and, hence, she was unable to inform the police for ten days after the murders.

The judge pronounced her guilty of first-degree murder and imposed the maximum sentence: four to six years in the custody of the California Youth Authority. "There is little else I can do," he added. When she is released, Marlene will be no more than twenty-three, and most probably she will get out even sooner.

The Olive case raised the usual wails of editorial horror from newspapers that had avidly printed the piquancies of the trial testimony, plus the inevitable shoals of letters from readers who had just as avidly read them, demanding to know what this country/the world/youth/femininity/morality or Marin County were coming to. Actually, Marlene's crime fell squarely within a female murder tradition dating back to Babylon. It had no specifically "modern" aspects. It was domestic in setting, oblique in execution, motivated by the customary mixture of personal resentment and financial greed. Even her age and method had ancient lineage. Cleopatra, Lucrezia Borgia, and Marie de Brinvilliers were even younger when they started dabbling in homicide, and "witchcraft" is one of the oldest devices used by women to bend men to their wills.

Just as throughout history, most murders committed by women today still belong in the domestic category. The majority of victims are still their own children, husbands, or lovers. And it so happens that the less "liberated" the woman —the more economically and emotionally dependent she is on a man—the *more* likely she is to do him in.

Even the awesome Georgia grandma who, in the course of two years, wiped out three quarters of her family formed part of a long historical chain of similar female poisoners, with whom she also shared a peculiar fierce religiosity. "Grandma" conveys a misleading image of Janie Gibbs. Having married farmer Charles Gibbs at the age of fifteen, she was a mere thirty-four when her grandson was born. A smiling, bespectacled young matron, Janie was famous for religious zeal in the little Bible-belt town of Cordele. She taught Sunday school, served on every committee, and proved herself a tireless "witness for the Lord." When not engaged in her church work, she could generally be found in her kitchen, baking, frying, or broiling Southern country dishes. Some of these dishes had unfortunate effects on her husband, three sons, and infant grandson, but not before Janie had insured their lives for a total of thirty-one thousand dollars. When, one by one, they went into hideous convulsions and died, Grannie Gibbs collected the insurance—duly handing over one-tenth of the money to the Pleasant Grove Baptist Church, the tithe that, like other devout parishioners, she was accustomed to paying for the church's work. Although the insurance companies grew increasingly suspicious when Mr. Gibbs and his two robust younger sons succumbed within twenty-two months, it wasn't easy to get evidence of foul play. Janie Lou Gibbs was "agin them autopsies" and refused to have her "dear departed all cut open." It was only after her oldest son and infant grandson were similarly struck down that her daughter-in-law, exercising her option as next of kin, was able to authorize a post-mortem. The findings of these two autopsies led police to exhume the bodies of the other deceased family members. When the coroner found that in every case death had resulted from arsenic poisoning, Mrs. Gibbs—much to the shock of the local Baptist congregation— was arrested and charged on Christmas Eve, 1967.

Shortly after her arrest, Janie Lou admitted the poisonings, describing in detail how she had given her firstborn a hurried dose in his morning coffee before she dashed off to her Sunday-school class. Nevertheless, it was only in 1976, after Georgia authorities had spent eight years struggling over the issue of her sanity, that Mrs. Gibbs was finally declared sufficiently rational to stand trial for mass murder. For the five lives she had taken, the court gave her five consecutive life sentences— a sentence as theatrically impressive as it was legally meaningless.*

For all this, the widespread assumption that women are inclined to favor poison as a means of murder turns out to be a chimera. In America, at least, women kill with the same

---

* These Jovian sentences accomplish little except to express the judge's feelings on a case. Richard Speck, the killer of eight Chicago nurses, received eight consecutive prison terms of fifty to one hundred and fifty years each. Nevertheless, he became eligible for parole in September 1976—nine years after his conviction. He didn't get his parole then, but he may at some future hearing. The decision is entirely up to the parole board, which can—and frequently does—ignore the original sentence of the court.

implements as men: most frequently, by a wide margin, with guns; next, with knives; finally, with virtually every other practicable gadget from automobiles to high explosives. It was this popular but mythical association with poison that gave rise to the legend of female murderers being the more subtly cruel, preferring their victims to die in lingering agonies. As far as cruelty can be measured, this is patently untrue.

Both sexes contain a certain proportion of sadists whose deeds occasionally boggle the imagination. There is not the slightest indication that this proportion is larger among women or that they are in any way more ingenious in the torments they inflict. This myth is part and parcel of the demonization of womanhood that we inherited from certain medieval theologians who blamed the discomforts of their own sexual hangups on willful female cruelty. Equally false is the naively chivalrous belief that women—merely by virtue of being women—are constitutionally incapable of every conceivable monstrosity. We can quite safely assume that there is no deed so devilish that *some* human beings, regardless of sex, cannot be found who enjoy perpetrating it.

Yet there is no denying that sadistic cruelty in women continues to carry by far the greater shock impact for us, because it runs so contrary to our accepted image of feminine sensibilities. The long historical line of female fiends, stretching from the Roman empress Messalina to Nazi Germany's Ilse Koch, stands out in a darker shade of scarlet solely because the practitioners belonged to the supposedly gentler sex. The only reason why they are considered worse than male brutes who have committed equivalent atrocities is that their acts seem so out of keeping with the prevailing notion of woman's nature as purer and gentler. It is this basic misconception that creates most of our current difficulties in responding to female crime.

Always the least adaptable of institutions, the police and the courts are also having the hardest time learning to grapple with the new development. I can honestly say that, among all the people whom I interviewed on the subject of female criminality, the most bewildered were cops and judges. They showed two types of reaction, both equally ineffectual. One was to flatly deny the upsurge of female crime, regardless of facts and figures. Apparently those couldn't be true because they didn't want them to be—the hallowed response of the blinkered. The other was a stunned bemusement, expressed by the constantly repeated phrase "I don't know what's come over them . . ."

This bewilderment does not apply to the gun-moll breed of outlaw which is part of American folklore. We have always had ladies like Irene Schroeder, who turned a Boy Scout leader into a desperate triggerman and went to the electric chair with him. Or Juanita Spinelli, known as "Duchess," who commanded her own mob of holdup bandits and made history by becoming, in 1941, the first woman to be executed in California. Or Barbara Graham, the high-class San Francisco call girl who was sent to the gas chamber for having pistol-whipped an old woman to death during a robbery and was subsequently immortalized in *I Want to Live*, possibly the phoniest movie ever made about a murderess. All these female desperadoes and scores of others like them worked with or through male associates, thereby remaining within the traditional pattern of feminine crime participation.

What lies beyond the ken of most police officers are the outbursts of rabid violence staged by women, on their own accord, unconnected with any felony, and in response to the slightest of provocations. In other words, actions hitherto reserved for only the most vicious types of male bully.

A Washington, D.C. woman tried to muscle in at the head of a long line of shoppers at the cash register of the Southwest Mall Safeway store. When the clerk ordered her back to the end of the line and another man laughed in her face, she screamed, "I'll give you something to laugh about," pulled an ice pick from her red leather purse, and stabbed the man through the chest, behind his ear, and through the arm.

In Ozone Park, New York, Fred Pirone tried to stop three white teenage girls from beating up a smaller black girl. One of the girls hit him with a bottle, knocking him unconscious. All three then systematically stomped and kicked him to death.

In San Francisco, forty-four-year-old Lois Luipage—who had served three years for killing her husband—got into a barroom argument with another woman. Mrs. Luipage grabbed a beer bottle from the counter and smashed it over the head of her opponent, who produced a .38-caliber revolver from her umbrella and shot Luipage in the face, killing her instantly.

In Oxon Hill, Maryland, William Goosby called the police and reported that his girl friend had stabbed him. When the two officers went to his apartment, they found him bleeding and ordered the girl to leave; instead she yelled, "You're going to have to lock me up," and lunged at the cops with a butcher knife. One of the officers felled her with a bullet through the chest.

In Baltimore, seventeen-year-old Bonnie Gill, one of the heavily tattooed members of a local motorcycle gang, stepped out of her house to celebrate New Year's Eve cowboy fashion —by firing her six-gun at the sky. When an irritated neighbor ran over to stop her, Bonnie shot him dead.

This is but a random sampling of hundreds of similar cases erupting over the length and breadth of the United States like plague boils. Most of them appear quite unpremeditated: irrational explosions of pent-up fury that strike at the first target within reach. It is the root cause of this fury that puzzles the police and judiciary. Nor does it seem much clearer to those feminists who are willing to go beyond the surface rhetoric of the women's rights movement.

Speaking at an annual meeting of the American Association for the Advancement of Science, Dr. Florence Denmark, a New York sociologist, said: "The female offender, whether acting by herself or with others, is not typically the emancipated intellectual striving for civil liberties. Her crime is rarely an assertion of civil rights, or an unconscious attempt at achieving her own or others' rights. She may feel dominated by men or even wish to imitate men or obtain male

approval for her actions." Dr. Denmark went on to state that
the rise in female crime cannot be separated psychologically
from inner conflict and stress. "The fact that more women
than men are reported to be suffering from some sort of
mental illness suggests a powerful link between what women
are experiencing and what they are doing."

Such a link might serve as the only explanation for the
current pattern of violence unleashed by prostitutes on their
customers. Since antiquity whores have fleeced their clients,
stealing their money and sometimes feeding them knockout
drops to facilitate the maneuver. But only in contemporary
America have they begun to assault them wholesale. The
mysterious aspect of this behavior is that it naturally spoils
business, driving more and more patrons to the comparative
safety of massage parlors. Street prostitution, in consequence,
has grown considerably harder over the past few years—yet
the casualty rolls keep mounting.

In a single month in midtown Manhattan, one hooker
stabbed an Italian glass manufacturer to death outside the
Hilton Hotel; two others splashed acid on cartoonist Charles
Addams; three more of them mugged former West German
defense minister Franz Josef Strauss—a Bavarian built like a
wardrobe. A Chicago hooker gutted a naked client with a
straight razor because he made disparaging remarks about
her perfume. Linda Agurs stabbed a customer to death in a
Northwest Washington motel when he caught her going
through his pockets. Two Los Angeles prostitutes smashed a
man's skull with a tire iron when he refused to engage both
of them for the evening. "Paddy hustling," the ancient con
game in which sex is promised but larceny is delivered, has
taken on a violent hue. A Bostonian visiting San Francisco
was lured to a Chinese housing project near the North Beach
night-life center, relieved of his wallet by two teenage girls,
and shot dead when he protested. A vice-squad sweep conducted in the San Francisco Tenderloin revealed that 20
percent of the arrested ladies had a history of violent crimes
(as distinct from the usual records of drug and larceny offenses) and that the chances of a john's getting battered,

slashed, or otherwise injured by a prostitute now stood at one in seventeen.

Street prostitution is sleazy everywhere, yet it seems indicative of our singularly eroded *joie de vivre* that we should add mayhem to all the other risks connected with the trade. New York's "working girls," as they call themselves were possibly the first to substitute overt threats for enticement and habitual violence for stealthy theft. Since then the new style of hooking has swept the country, rendering the once urbane demimonde of New Orleans and San Francisco as lethal as their sisters from Manhattan's 18th Precinct.

Some sociologists blame racial antagonism for this trend, but this is largely disproven by the fact that white whores are today as violence-prone as blacks and Latins. Most cops name drug addiction. "Those broads don't have much brain to start with," a Chicago vice-squad man remarked to me. "Get 'em on dope—and that's what their pimps do—and they become real Frankensteins, ready to break heads for fifty lousy bucks."

But the root causes seem to be less specific, more part of a general malaise—as if the hustlers, having become drunk on the smell of cheap blood and having partaken of the cosmic anger permeating the land, had responded in their own hysterical fashion. One of the "working girls" I interviewed was neither black nor an addict, but she had just emerged from prison after jabbing a client through the throat with a broken Coke bottle for no apparent reason. When I asked her about it, she gave a bored and slightly irritated shrug. "Aw, I dunno. I had a fight with Harry that morning and I was feeling—well, kinda sore at everybody. And that greasy asshole kept making these sucking noises at me—you know, like you do to a dog—and he kept on and on with them. So I guess I let him have it."

Although the new trend in female criminality is now the subject of dozens of books and hundreds of social studies, our justice system has so far not caught up with it. As the judiciary remains mired in the 1950s, female criminals ironically benefit from the same brand of male chauvinism that keeps noncriminal women confined to minority roles in the courts. On the one hand we have far too few women judges, attorneys, and prosecutors—for that matter, bailiffs, prison guards, and cops. On the other hand, women still stand an excellent chance of avoiding prison for offenses that would send men behind bars for years. In California, for instance, where the male-female overall crime ratio is five to one, there are currently 17,000 men serving state prison terms as against 750 women—a ratio of roughly twenty-three to one.

Yes, Virginia, women do quite often go to prison for murder, but the brevity of their stay there is often breathtaking. In 1970, Texas motorcycle-gang queen Bonnie Paprskar pleaded guilty to murdering three people: two Fort Worth Mexicans and the young son of one of them. Apparently the two men had sold Bonnie's husband impure heroin, so Mrs. Paprskar ordered the execution-style slaying of both, with the killers throwing in the kid for good measure. Although the prosecution had intended to demand the death penalty, she succeeded in gaining a twenty-five-year term from the judge in exchange for her guilty plea. Exactly four years later, Bonnie was freed on parole.

It took the FBI nearly three years to catch one of the ladies on their "Ten Most Wanted" list. Marie Dean Arrington was finally apprehended in New Orleans after escaping from the women's prison in Lowell, Florida, in 1969. She had been sentenced to death for killing the secretary of a Florida attorney—a murder that was committed while Ms. Arrington was free on appeal of a twenty-year manslaughter sentence for killing her husband.

To be sure, such judicial leniency has a price. In order to qualify for it, female defendants must conform to the court's idea of how a "real woman" behaves at a trial. This stereotype has been perfected by generations of smart defense counsels and comes stamped with the imprimatur of countless screen and video dramas. The lady must appear conservatively garbed, must wear little makeup, and (lest reporters call her "stony-faced") must be "visibly upset"— that is to say, she should speak in a strained stage whisper while dabbing her eyes with a Kleenex at prescribed intervals. Copious tears are fine, providing they flow well.* She may sob, lose her memory, develop palpitations, or even faint whenever cross-examination gets tough, but she must *not* display wit (that's the judge's prerogative), and above all she must never show genuine anger. A surprising number of jurors assume that a woman capable of anger is capable of anything.

Inez Garcia, for one, very likely blew her own case by disregarding the above rules. Moreover, in the process of becoming a feminist *cause célèbre*, her trial once again proved that with certain types of friends supporting you to the hilt, you don't need enemies.

Garcia, a very pretty, illiterate, and rather primitive Cuban–Puerto Rican, was raped in a back alley of Soledad, California, on the night of March 19, 1974. One of her attackers, a three-hundred pound lout named Miguel Jiminez, stood guard while his seventeen-year-old buddy, Louis Castillo, worked her over. As soon as she was free, Inez ran to her house, loaded a .22 rifle, and went after her attackers. When she found them beating up her friend, Fred Medrano, for the second time that day, she shot and killed the hulking Jiminez; Castillo got away when her rifle jammed.

Inez Garcia had been in mental hospitals three times. By all the rules of the game, she should have been either acquitted on a diminished-capacity plea or, at the very most, convicted of manslaughter. This was precisely the course her defense attorney, the famous Charles Garry, attempted to steer. But Inez was doubly unfortunate. On the one hand, she had one of the most obtuse, somnolent, and prejudiced juries California could muster. On the other, she attracted the attention of the radical man-hating wing of the women's movement—the members of which, smelling a martyr in the making, did their damnedest to turn her into one.

---

* When Dovie Dean, a Ohio grandmother of eight, stood trial for feeding her husband rat poison, the newspapers couldn't get over the fact that she never cried. Even before she went to the electric chair in 1954, they had christened her "The Murderess Without Tears."

Gathering in swarms inside and outside the courtroom, they hooted, yelled, cursed, waved fists, and brandished placards. Insulting, irritating, and infuriating everybody connected with the trial, their self-styled Defense Committee succeeded in surrounding Inez and manipulating her already overwrought feelings so as to instill *their* attitudes into her. Undermining her confidence in her lawyer, they issued statements on her behalf and gave her a brand-new vocabulary that she used innocently but with devastating effects at the trial.

Goaded and prodded by this vociferous claque, Inez Garcia's courtroom demeanor turned into a judicial kamikaze flight. She talked tough and indulged in heavy-handed sarcasm. Once she even burst out in screaming fury, "I'm not sorry. I'm only sorry that I missed Louis!" On another occasion she shouted at the prosecutor: "I killed that motherfucker, so why don't you just find me guilty and put me in jail, you lousy pig!" Everybody who knew her could testify that this was totally out of character for Inez—a gentle, pious, somewhat inhibited woman. But, taking her at face value, the jury found her guilty of second-degree murder, and the judge, after referring to her as "Mexican," pronounced a sentence of five years to life. The shrieking ladies in the galleries had their martyr.

The Garcia case had an epilogue. The court of appeals later overturned her conviction, and her new trial had a different outcome. In the meantime, law student Nan Blitman interviewed some of the jurors who had decided Inez's fate. One of them, an elderly black man, opined that "A rapist is not trying to kill her. He's just trying to give her a good time . . . giving a girl a screw is not doing her bodily harm. . . . I told the women that when I leave here, I'll have less fear of raping a woman now than I did before. At least I know that if I get shot, she won't get away."

The one who got away clean was Louis Castillo—the alleged rapist. He was never charged with anything. Perhaps the authorities were likewise of the opinion that he had merely been trying to give little Inez a good time.

If female violence in general has found American law enforcement on the wrong foot, then one particular facet has caught it virtually flat on its face: political terrorism. As a Washington consultant on violence prevention put it: "You might say that women terrorists have passed the Equal Rights Amendment on their own bat. The rest of us will just have to live with that *fait accompli.*"

The politically motivated female terrorist has no precedent in this country; her advent is as much of a fearsome novelty today as the armed bootlegger was some fifty years ago. By the early 1970s it had become obvious that women were fighting in the forefront of various radical groups and that they had taken de facto command of several of them. The Weathermen changed their name to the Weather Underground, since fifteen of the organization's thirty-seven known members were women. The Symbionese Liberation Army—though figureheaded by Donald DeFreeze, alias "Field Marshal Cinque"—was actually run by the dynamic female trio of Patricia Soltysik, Nancy Ling Perry, and Camilla Hall, who perished with guns in their fists during the band's last desperate shootout with the authorities in Los Angeles.

In 1969 the National Commission on the Causes and Prevention of Violence issued a profile of the typical Presidential assassin. He was depicted as a rootless young man alienated from his parents, a failure in marriage, frequently unemployed, who resorted to murdering a public figure to give himself a sense of identity. Six years later, after two attempts on President Ford's life, the would-be assassins were found to fit the profile in all but one essential: They were both female.

Lynette "Squeaky" Fromme had joined the Manson clan out of a craving for group acceptance. She aimed at the President as the symbol of the powers that destroyed her "family." Sara Jane Moore represented the classic Dostoevskian identity quest: She was an FBI informer who grew to sympathize strongly with the radicals she informed on. Caught in an agonizing personality conflict, she tried to resolve it by striking an unequivocal blow at *the* establishment figure. Her dilemma reflected that of the numerous Czarist police spies who, after infiltrating Russia's revolutionary circles, became so entangled in their philosophy that they no longer knew which side they were really on. Some of them ended up assassinating the government officials paying them.

The rise of the American female terrorist is part of a development taking place around the world. And the amazing feature of this phenomenon is that it expresses itself most strongly in those countries in which women have hitherto played decidedly minor political roles: Japan and Germany. The Japanese "Red Army," perhaps the most malevolent of all revolutionary bodies, is currently led by Fusako Shigenobu, a former Meiji University co-ed who— among other atrocities—masterminded the slaughter of twenty-eight civilians at Israel's Lodt Airport in 1972.

All of West Germany's guerrilla groups use women in their assault squads. The deadliest of them, the Baader-Meinhof Anarchists, were dominated by their co-founder, journalist Ulrike Meinhof. Arrested in 1973, Ms. Meinhof was discovered hanged in her prison cell three years later— whether by her own hands or those of her jailers is still under investigation.

So far this country's woman guerrillas have not matched their overseas sisters in sheer ferocity. But their personalities have delivered stronger shocks to our justice system than have their bombs. Neither doped-up prostitutes nor cretinous motorcycle molls nor conventionally hard-boiled gang girls, these women fit none of the stereotypes to which the nation's law enforcers were trained to respond. Among the Weathermen, Bernardine Dohrn is a graduate of the Chicago University law school; Kathy Boudin, a *magna cum laude* graduate of Bryn Mawr, speaks fluent Russian and Spanish. Patricia Soltysik, the SLA's chief theorist, was an honor student and university scholarship winner. Most of the female terrorists came from upper-middle-class backgrounds, acquired excellent educations, and possessed skills that could have earned them satisfactory incomes. To render them even more puzzling to their opponents, the majority would be considered better-than-average-looking, and some could pass the All-American-Girl charm test.

Given all this, how is one to account for their becoming revolutionary terrorists? Chronologically, most of them began as students in the civil-rights movement and graduated into the political confrontations of the antiwar struggle. In the process, instead of shrinking back from the stench of tear gas, spilled blood, and jailhouse filth, they hardened into humorless and fearless fanatics. But there was more than political radicalism underlying this evolution. It is quite possible that politics was merely a catalyst which provided them with an excuse to rebel against the insufferable male condescension they experienced from their comrades and enemies alike. They were, in other words, enraged and humiliated by the degree of protective cover they enjoyed because of their femininity, by the assumption of the authorities that—because they were women—they were less of a threat. As psychiatrist Frederick J. Hacker surmised, "Only with weapons in their hands could these female group members fully believe in their own emancipation."

This was made even clearer by Beate Sturm, bomb thrower of the Baader-Meinhof organization: "One thing I found really great about the whole business, the feeling of being genuinely emancipated as women. There were several things we were better at than the men, where we felt stronger than them. For instance: we were much less scared than they."

6

The Syndicate Wars

There's nothing for you to worry about. We only kill each other.
—Benjamin "Bugsy" Siegel

Godfather, stay here with me and help me meet death. Perhaps if He sees you near me He will be frightened and leave me in peace. Or perhaps you can say a word, pull a few strings, eh?
—Mario Puzo, *The Godfather*

At 11:15 on Saturday night, March 4, 1944, history was made in the death chamber of Sing Sing prison. While everybody present was aware of this fact, most aware of all was the small middle-aged man with deep creases running from his nose to the corners of his mouth. Entering quickly, he first gave a sardonic flicker of a grin when he saw the newsmen dispatched to record his last moments on earth begin to scribble furiously. Then, making a sharp, sentrylike turn, in one final flamboyant gesture he hurled himself into the arms of the electric chair. Seconds later, 2,200 volts shot through his body, jerking it stiffly against the leather straps and filling the room with the faint, pervasive smell of singed hair.

The man in the chair was Lepke Buchalter, born Louis Bookhouse—the Brooklyn pushcart thief who, in a parody of the Great American Success Story, rose to command a mighty business enterprise called Murder, Inc. Buchalter made history on two accounts: He was the only wealthy person ever lawfully executed in the United States, and he was the sole member of the National Crime Syndicate's board of directors to suffer that fate. All the rest died either by each other's hands or of natural causes.

The Syndicate—also known as the Mob, the Outfit, the Combine, or the Commission—represents the distilled essence of organized crime in America. It has no counterpart anywhere, not because other nations necessarily enjoy higher ethical standards, but because nobody else could afford it. The Syndicate is the ultimate luxury indulged in by the world's richest society: the retort in which big crime coalesces with big business and big unionism for the purpose of milking the economy of sums so stupendous that they would have bankrupted any other country long ago.

In fairness, we should add that the Syndicate presides over the one segment of American life in which violence has actually decreased over the past decades. This segment, which happens to be the nation's biggest industry, is organized crime. More specifically, if we accept the recent Justice Department estimate that organized crime takes in fifty billion dollars a year, then, in terms of people killed per billion dollars earned, its performance has improved vastly since the time Lepke went to the chair. Its ratio today may even be better than that of certain legitimate industries, such as coal mining.

The Syndicate has come a long way since it arose in the spring of 1934 out of the bloody convulsions of the Maranzano war.* On the September afternoon in 1931 that saw Maranzano's assassination, some forty-three Mafiosi died nationwide—several of them slowly and hideously. One Sam Monaco had an iron pipe driven up his rectum; his partner Louis Russo was castrated before having his throat cut. It was the greatest massacre in underworld annals and filled a number of important people with the resolve that it must not happen again—at least not on such a scale.

The composition of the "hit squad" that stabbed and shot Maranzano in his Park Avenue real-estate office is of great significance. It reflected the alliances that were to create the Syndicate. Two of the men—Red Levine and Bugsy Siegel—were Jewish and worked for Meyer Lansky. Two—Albert Anastasia and Thomas Lucchese—were Italians in the em-

---

* Salvatore Maranzano, Manhattan Mafia chief, is credited with coining the term "La Cosa Nostra"—literally, "our thing"—which has since been used to denote the entire Mafia organization. Maranzano, however, applied it only to his own New York outfit, and in underworld parlance it still means strictly the East Coast branch.

ploy of Lucky Luciano. Together they represented those portions of the underworld toying with the idea of one great
corporation that would cover the country.

The brainchild of Lucky Luciano and Meyer Lansky, the
National Syndicate had its birth pangs during a week-long
gangster conference in New York City. The palaver ended
with the appointment of the Syndicate's first board of direc-
tors, which read like a *Who's Who* of American crime:
Charles "Lucky" Luciano, Meyer Lansky, Louis "Lepke"
Buchalter, Johnny Torrio, Dutch Schultz, Frank Costello,
Jacob Shapiro, Vito Genovese, Thomas Lucchese, and Abner
"Longy" Zwillman.

If to a great many people today the Syndicate is synony-
mous with the Mafia, it wasn't like that at the start, and
in certain respects it still isn't. The Mafia was, rather, a
separate all-Italian body, some of whose members sat on the
Syndicate's ethnically mixed board. Over the years, to be
sure, by a relentless process of attrition, the Mafiosi have
tended to edge out most of the others. Nevertheless, the
"Honored Society" still maintains a structure quite distinct
from the Syndicate, and its five thousand or so adherents
form merely a small fraction of the underworld denizens
controlled by the Combine.

The original principles upon which the Syndicate was
founded were those of a giant, multifaceted business corporation. The business was crime, and the primary function of
the Combine was to eliminate—or at least reduce—the constant intragang warfare that wasted lives and diminished
profits. The Syndicate did this by marking out territories
and allocating franchises guaranteeing unrestricted control
over activities such as gambling, prostitution, labor racketeer-
ing, and loansharking within each territory. At that stage
narcotics did not play a major role. The Combine acted as
a communications center, keeping the lines open between
the hundreds of franchise chieftains. It was also a kind of
appeals court that would adjudicate complaints of infringement or conflicting jurisdictional claims, and it could, if it
saw fit, punish the offenders.

This last item was possibly the most important, for if the Syndicate was to wield any power worth mentioning, it had to maintain its own enforcement squad, independent of the gunsels attached to the various territories. To this end, Meyer Lansky supposedly conceived the idea of a unit of professional killers that would have no function other than killing at the Syndicate's orders—a flying squad that could be sent to any part of the country at a moment's notice and would strike without knowing why, mostly without knowing their victims, except from photographs. Members of this elite unit were duly recruited from the bloodthirstiest thugs of the Italian and Jewish gangs infesting Brownsville and East New York. Their names, methods, and vocabulary were to become part of America's folklore, and the title that the newspapers invented for them—Murder, Inc.—may yet outlive the Syndicate. But for nearly ten years the troops (as the Syndicate called them) operated in complete secrecy, their existence unknown even to the rank-and-file mobsters. Their commander was changed at intervals, so as not to get them accustomed to one boss; first it was Bugsy Siegel, then Albert Anastasia, then Lepke Buchalter. Each added his own refinements. The troops abandoned those old and noisy gangster favorites, the submachine gun and pineapple grenade. Instead they adopted the ice pick, which was silent and easily concealed. Roughly a third of their victims died from having their lungs punctured with this lethal household instrument. The strangling noose was another silent favorite. But their No. 1 specialist, the hulking maniacal Pittsburgh Phil Strauss, carried no weapons at all. He used whatever tool was handy at the spot he had selected—anything from a steel bar to a fire ax, on one occasion a letter opener.

Buchalter developed a businesslike argot to serve as a code, particularly during telephone conversation. An assignment to kill was a "contract"; the actual murder a "hit"; the victim either a "mark" or a "bum." Contract prices ranged from $1,000 to $6,000 a hit, depending on the risks involved and the importance of the bum. Each killer also had an expense account and was covered by highly benevolent injury insurance and family-care funds. But the risks were delightfully minimal, thanks to the strategy worked out by Buchalter. This entailed the use of flying hit squads from coast to coast so that the hit men would always be outsiders without any visible connection to their victims.

As Pittsburgh Phil, who had a remarkably big mouth, bragged to an associate in Florida: "Hell, there isn't hardly any risk. Most of them pops are cinches. I can trail a bum two, three days without him getting wise. Till I find the right spot. He don't know me and I don't know him, except from a picture. And the cops run around blind. There's no motive, see? No connection. And I'm outa town next day."

Criminologists are still trying to assess the body count piled up by Murder, Inc., during its decade of anonymity. They face an impossible task, since the different hit squads worked independently, and only three out of an estimated dozen were ever uncovered. But we do know that the Brownsville and Ocean City, N.J., troops between them filled about 1,600 contracts—450 by Pittsburgh Phil's squad alone—and the nationwide total may have reached 9,000. In order to keep too many throttled and punctured corpses from being fished out of rivers and bays, the troops had their own carefully selected graveyards in deserted farms, quarries, and warehouses.

Although the Syndicate used its killers chiefly against franchise violators or outsiders trying to "dip their beaks," on occasion it also set them on colleagues. The obstreperous Dutch Schultz, for instance, was their first fellow director to become a bum. Schultz (whose real name was Arthur Flegenheimer) had tried to break the iron Mafia rule: *Never* harm top government officials. When Special Prosecutor Thomas E. Dewey began to investigate Schultz's New York rackets, the Dutchman demanded a contract for him. The Syndicate members pointed out the extreme unwisdom of such a move, whereupon the choleric Schultz bellowed, "If you guys are too yellow to go after Dewey, I'll get him myself and I'll get him in a week."

After Schultz had stormed out, the other directors held

a brief consultation. Their decision was summarized by Albert Anastasia, then commanding the troops: "Okay, I guess the Dutchman goes." The Dutchman "went" that night, riddled in the washroom of a Newark restaurant by a hit squad that included Mendy Weiss and Bug Workman. Not until six years later did Dewey learn that Murder, Inc., had once saved his life.

He learned it from the source to which we owe nearly all our knowledge of the assassin army: Kid Twist Reles. One of the outfit's ice-pick specialists, Reles was arrested in the summer of 1940. A shambling, heavy-browed thug who actually looked the part, Reles himself facing a possible hot seat, shrank back and, in return for a promise of immunity from prosecution, began to sing. He sang the scales all the way up to Lepke Buchalter. Reciting names, dates, and places, he detailed an endless list of killings with a kind of humorous gusto that acted like an icicle tracing your spine:

> So then they strangle him. Rudnick is laying there. . . . Then Abby grabs him by the feet and drags him over to the car. Pep and Happy grab the neck. They put him in the car. Somebody says, "Hey, that bum don't fit." So Abby pushes. He buckles it up to make it fit—he bent up the legs, like so. Just as they push the body in, it gives a little cough or something. With that Pep starts with the ice pick and begins punching away. And Mayone, he says, "Lemme hit this bastard one for good luck," and he hits him with the meat cleaver, some place on the head. . . .

Buchalter fought back with a batch of twelve contracts: eleven for possible witnesses, one for Kid Twist. But although he succeeded in getting eight of them, including Reles in his allegedly safe police hideout,* the eliminations came too late. Kid Twist had already sung half his song, and the tune was fatal for Lepke. He went to the chair, accompanied by Mendy Weiss and Louis Capone (no relation to Al). Three others, Pittsburgh Phil among them, went ten weeks later.

---

* Reles allegedly fell from the window of his heavily guarded room at the Half-Moon Hotel in Coney Island. Six policemen were in the room with him at all times, raising the question of whether only some or all six of them pushed him out. It may be indicative of the NYPD at that period that none of the cops in question was prosecuted—not even for dereliction of duty.

That, however, was all—six out of possibly ten times that many professional killers. Murder, Inc., had been uncovered and publicized, but that didn't mean it ceased to exist. In a considerably more modest fashion it is still functioning. Similarly, the Syndicate was to cut its losses, shed some of its directors, but keep its purpose intact. It was to repeat this process over and over in the years to come.

Lucky Luciano was sent to prison and, in 1946, deported to his native Italy. For the next eleven years things grew rather quiet around the Combine. The directors were busy consolidating their positions and feeling out new territories. They were getting older and—with some exceptions—wiser. They kept the killing rate low, although there were the inevitable rash spirits who had to be taught a lesson. One of them was their old pal Benjamin "Bugsy" Siegel, who became rash enough to try building up his Las Vegas gambling empire without cutting in the East Coast mob. Bugsy died in a hail of rifle bullets in the apartment of his lady friend, Virginia Hill, who, it is rumored, had set him up for execution. Before his wounds had stopped bleeding, two men strode into the office of Bugsy's luxurious Flamingo Hotel in Las Vegas and announced: "We're taking over."

Apart from such regrettable incidents, the Combine prospered in semi-peace. But in the hot summer of 1957 the Genovese-Costello war erupted with a ferocity and duration that most underworld watchers had believed were evils of the past. Like most wars, it was the result of a number of overlapping causes—some stemming from greed, some from fear, some from personal antagonisms. The ostensible cause was Vito Genovese's ambition to get himself proclaimed *capo di tutti capi* ("boss of bosses") among the Mafia families. Blocking his path was Frank Costello, who, although semi-retired and besieged by federal tax hounds, still packed enough prestige to challenge that title. Alone, the troubled Costello was no match for Genovese. But he had a mighty ally within the Syndicate in the person of Albert Anastasia. The former chief of Murder, Inc., was probably the most feared—certainly the most violent—of the Syndicate directors.

He might have stymied Genovese's ambition from the start if he, too, hadn't made a terrible enemy. Little Meyer Lansky detested the big, blustering Anastasia for reasons that were psychological as well as monetary. Anastasia was the antithesis of Lansky: a thunderer to a whisperer, an ostentatious blood spiller to an invisible stalker in the shadows, a rogue elephant to a cobra. At the start, most of the underworld bets were on Anastasia for a winner by knockout. It took a while before the spectators realized that the benignly smiling, always self-effacing Lansky was by far the deadlier of the two.

The war started with a bungled attempt by Genovese to have Costello assassinated. As if to reconfirm his title as Lord High Executioner of the Mafia, Anastasia retaliated with the execution of four Genovese henchmen. So it went, tit for tat, with the odds apparently favoring the Costello-Anastasia team. Standing on the sidelines, watching the slaughter and biding his time, was Lansky. When he stepped in, it was *he* who delivered the knockout punch. He delivered it in his own particular style—obliquely.

Enjoying a close working relationship with Cuban dictator Fulgencio Batista, Lansky had built up a flourishing network of tourist hotels and gambling casinos in Havana. For years Anastasia had been trying to muscle in on that highly lucrative field, but found himself rebuffed every time. Now Lansky calculated that the moment had come, and with Batista's active support he complained to the Syndicate and succeeded in substantiating his complaint that Anastasia was guilty of trying to nibble at his fellow director's franchise. When the remaining directors passed the inevitable death sentence on Anastasia, the contract was handed to a group of promising young newcomers who had the advantage of being unknown to their mark: a trio of brothers named Gallo led by one aptly called Crazy Joe.

On the morning of October 25, 1957, two men surprised Anastasia in his favorite barbershop, at the Park Sheraton Hotel. Wedged in the barber chair with a cloth draped over him, the Lord High Executioner made a massive and helpless target. Although their marksmanship was awful—out of ten bullets fired at close range, only half hit the big man— Anastasia died and Crazy Joe Gallo's rise began.

This murder should have ended the Syndicate war but didn't. For although the Mafiosi now recognized Genovese as "boss of bosses," he didn't reign long. In July 1958 the federal government indicted him on narcotics charges and sent him up for a fifteen-year stretch. He continued to wield considerable power even from federal prison, but his absence left the kind of leadership vacuum that invariably meant bloodshed. Over the next nine years it flowed in torrents.

Chicago, long known as the Combine's "Mad Dog town," got possibly the most unpleasant don in the country: Sam Giancana, called Momo by his intimates. Foul-mouthed, vulture-faced, and perpetually ill-tempered, Momo lacked the lethal finesse, the diplomatic smoothness favored by the New York directors. Impressed by such niceties as the stringing up of suspected informers on meat hooks and turning a blowtorch on them, the New Yorkers agreed that he was just the right man for Chicago.

Giancana possessed a certain disarming honesty. During World War II he avoided service by answering the draft board's questions regarding what he did for a living with "Me? I steal." The board promptly rejected him, describing him as "a constitutional psychopath." In 1960, however, the CIA did him the honor of recruiting him for the job of assassinating Fidel Castro. Momo mismanaged the operation, perhaps on purpose, and it quite likely cost him his life. In 1975 a Senate committee investigating CIA activities was considering calling Giancana to testify. But before they could do so, somebody shot him seven times in the basement kitchen of his fortress-style home in the Chicago suburb of Oak Park. CIA director William Colby immediately declared: "We had nothing to do with it." An unofficial spokesman for the Syndicate said the same.

Meanwhile, the factional strife in New York grew grimmer by the month. The Gallo and Profaci gangs went to war and fought each other to a bloody stalemate, leaving twenty-six of their men on the field. In the revamped Syndicate, Anastasia's erstwhile adjutant, Carlo Gambino, rose to a towering position. A short, bulb-nosed Brooklyn man with twinkling little eyes and immense savoir-faire hiding his ruthlessness, Gambino became the model for Mario Puzo's *Godfather*. The similarities went all the way to his courteously sinister verbal style, his imposing Long Island retreat in Massapequa, the tomato plants in his garden, and his habit of picking out fruit and vegetables at Italian neighborhood stores.*

But while Gambino ran his family with great aplomb and a minimum of overt violence, his was only one of five such units in New York, and he had little influence over the others. The most troubled of all was the outfit headed by Joe Colombo, of which a faction was the Gallo gang. Crazy Joe Gallo emerged from a prison stretch in a bitter and truculent mood. His older brother had died of cancer, and he complained loudly that Colombo wasn't giving him a fair share of the family profits. The real cause of the strife may have been that Colombo was too busy with other affairs to pay proper attention to his clan, for, to his misfortune, Joe Colombo had discovered civil rights.

Colombo organized a tumultuous crusade to "cleanse the good name of my fellow Italian-Americans." What he wished to cleanse it of was "the stain of underworld association cast upon us by the media and certain government bodies." He threw his formidable energies into the formation of the Italian-American Civil Rights League, which included Governor Rockefeller as an honorary member. Colombo revealed himself as a fine orator, à la Mussolini, denouncing the "conspiracy against me and all Italian-Americans" and predicting that "God's sting" would strike those "who get in our way." He led a vast crowd of demonstrators to the FBI office in

---

* Gambino lived up to his literary alter ego even in his demise. He died in bed of a heart attack in October 1976, aged seventy-four. His funeral was attended by hundreds of mourners and protected from reporters by a ring of hard-faced young men who told strangers: "The family requests they be left alone—so take a walk, huh."

New York City, directing operations from a loudspeaker van and joining in the rhythmic chant "Hi-dee-hi, ho-dee-ho, the FBI has got to go!"

It was all terribly un-Mafiosi, and the noisier the crusade became, the more the Syndicate disliked it. Colombo should have taken heed when Gambino discreetly withdrew his men from the League, but he was too absorbed in his own oratory to catch the rustling of danger. He claimed a hundred and fifty thousand members, appeared on television, gave press interviews, and declared that the Mafia was a figment of anti-Italian imagination. By then the directors of the Combine were looking around for a way—any way—to shut him up. They had a deeply rooted aversion to publicity that might attract investigation.

It *may* have been purely coincidental that the Gallo mob now swung into action against the League, but most observers agree that they were encouraged to do so by the Combine. The first ominous signs appeared when Gallo henchmen went around tearing down the posters announcing a gigantic rally on Italian-American Unity Day, June 28, 1971. As the date drew closer, the action grew rougher. League canvassers were beaten up and had their pamphlets burned. Colombo's boys called on Italian shopkeepers, ordering them to close their stores on Unity Day and to display posters announcing this. Then the Gallo mobsters called on the hapless merchants, removing the posters and threatening dire consequences if they *did* shut.

On the day of the rally Colombo was in great form, shaking hands with so many people that he seemed to possess three arms. Suddenly a bearded black man approached him, whipped out a pistol, and fired three shots at his head. As Colombo folded up, his bodyguards blazed away at the assassin. The crowd shrieked and scattered, trampling down some of the festive decorations. With two men lying in pools of their own blood, Unity Day—and the League—lay in shambles. Colombo miraculously survived his brain injury, but only as a speechless, motionless cripple in a wheelchair. His attacker was dead, riddled with bullets.

There is no absolute proof that Gallo arranged the assassination, but all available evidence points to it. The authorities, as much as the Mafia, were convinced that Crazy Joe had utilized his well-known prison friendships with black convicts to recruit a killer who wouldn't be ostensibly connected with him. It was a historical first—never before had a black man intervened in a Mafia feud. Some saw it as the handwriting on the wall.

In a way the use of black gunpower was characteristic of the new Joe Gallo, who continued to startle and dismay his Cosa Nostra brethren. If his black prison associations were not bad enough, what followed was worse. Crazy Joe was going highbrow—turning into an egghead—reading longhair books and using words nobody could understand. The general consensus was that now he'd really gone crazy.

Gallo had indeed developed a new lifestyle. He frequented literary and show-business parties in Greenwich Village, made friends with playwright Neil Simon and producer Hal Prince, drank with avant-garde authors and artists, and had plans for writing his autobiography—a project that must have given several hundred mobsters sleepless nights. The gunman with the domed forehead, long sideburns, and hooded reptilian eyes could be seen quaffing wine at Elaine's, surrounded by admiring literati. He not only read Camus and Hermann Hesse but loved quoting them. Similarly, he lost all interest in poker and became a formidable chess player instead. His new friends found him refreshing, remarkably intelligent, and quick on the uptake. Said one Village scribe: "Joe had little formal education but an instinctive grasp of language. He could absorb abstract ideas and apply them to practical issues better than any academician. He had a great sort of Feifferish sense of humor that made up for his fiendish temper. He'd stop halfway through an outburst and start laughing at himself. Also he bought all of us a helluva lot of drinks."

Nevertheless, Gallo continued to lead his gang and took all the precautions necessary to stay alive. He knew the Colombo mob was after him and rarely ventured out without

his hulking bodyguard, Pete "the Greek" Diapoulas. For
ten months he avoided all the traps laid for him, until,
shortly after his second marriage, he made a single slip. On
the evening of April 7, 1972, he celebrated his forty-third
birthday by taking a group of people on a nightclub spree.
They included his new wife, his bodyguard, and his sister.
Around 3:00 A.M. they were sitting in Umberto's Clam
House on Mulberry Street when four men burst in with
drawn automatics. Gallo had time to leap halfway out of
his chair before two slugs caught him. He dragged himself
out to the street, and was clutching a wall when a third
bullet finished him off. He fell on his back, his fingers
scrabbling in the blood on the pavement before they stiff-
ened.

The two leaders were down, but the Gallo-Colombo war
went on. The last brother, Al "Blasto" Gallo, took over
Joe's command. The place of the paralyzed Colombo was
filled by yet another Joe: Joseph Brancato. In the ensuing
clashes, around twenty men were killed—including four innocent outsiders. This last mishap occurred because the
Gallos had imported a hit expert from Las Vegas. He was
commissioned to wipe out four ranking Colombo torpedoes
while they were dining at the Neapolitan Noodle restaurant
in Manhattan. When he arrived, however, they had departed,
their places taken by four respectable businessmen. All four
became victims of mistaken identity.

Although the Syndicate could not halt these brushfire wars,
it did finally manage to contain them, thus preventing the
outbreak of an underworld war that would have decimated
the organized-crime scene. Compared to the nationwide
slaughters of two decades ago, the current conflicts are mere
skirmishes. "Just enough to weed out the saps," in the words
of Joe "The Baron" Barboza, who became a sap himself
by absorbing three shotgun blasts in San Francisco's Sunset
district in February 1976.

If the nature and purpose of the Combine had not changed
over the years, its composition certainly had. Nearly all the
old directors were gone, felled by one another, by sickness,

by senility, or by law enforcement. Only Meyer Lansky survived everybody and everything, including assassination attempts, federal investigations, stomach ulcers, cardiac failure, and open-heart surgery. Now in his seventies and reputedly worth three hundred million dollars, the wizened little man from Grodno continues as the Syndicate's policy maker and financial expert. Perhaps he owes his survival to his *differentness*. In a world of school dropouts, he graduated with honors from New York's P.S. 34. While his peers acquired stables of mistresses, he stuck by his wife, Thelma, who cooked the kind of food he liked. While others built their Xanadu mansions in the suburbs, he moved into the bourgeois comfort of a Miami Beach apartment and walked his small, ugly dog every night. Asked why he didn't keep a bodyguard, he replied, "So what's the police for?" While others postured and snarled, Lansky smiled like a Jewish uncle, shrugged his shoulders, and awaited his chance. Nobody who ran afoul of him died a natural death. But in all probability *he* will.

The secret of Lansky's endurance record may have been that he always moved one important moment ahead of the others. Every time the Mob decided to venture into a new field, he already had a foothold there and thus ranked as the indispensable expert. For, just like a mammoth business conglomerate, the Syndicate is constantly reaching out and diversifying while retaining a firm grip on its basic core.

This basic core remains organized crime. In his book, *Crime in America*, former U.S. Attorney General Ramsey Clark gave a masterly description of what this signifies:

> Organized crime supplies goods or services wanted by a large number of people—desperately needed cash, narcotics, prostitutes, the chance to gamble. These are its principal sources of income. They are consensual crimes for the most part, desired by the consuming public. This fact distinguishes the main activities of organized crime from most other crime. Few want to be mugged, have their assets embezzled or their cars stolen, but it is *public demand* [my italics] that creates the basis for the activities of organized crime.

Any number of reformers have suggested that these commodities should be legalized, to deprive the underworld of its main sources of revenue. But there are several economic as well as emotional reasons in the way of such a solution. Loansharking, for instance, has succeeded in building up its take to an estimated $600 million a year only by lending money at interest rates of 30 percent or more to cyclical businesses—businesses such as the garment industry, which can't raise loans from legitimate banks because they represent bad risks. To the underworld, the risks aren't bad at all— they will accept the borrower's body as collateral. If he doesn't pay up, he is liable to get his arms and legs broken.

Nor has the introduction of legalized gambling, such as lotteries and off-track betting, made any inroads into criminal profits. For whereas lottery and OTB offices demand cash, the local bookies and neighborhood numbers operators—the lower echelons of organized crime—give credit. Furthermore, they pay off right away, often within an hour of a win. Here the loanshark works in happy tandem with the bookmaker. If a bettor can't meet his debt to the bookie, he is steered to the shark, who advances the money at horrendous interest. Finally, not only do illegal gambling winnings have the advantage of being relatively easy to conceal from the IRS, but recent studies have indicated that the odds are actually better than those of the state-run games.

In prostitution we come up against the ancient Anglo-Saxon distaste for legitimate bordellos—a prejudice that is by no means exclusively Anglo.* No matter how many scathing proofs are offered against the fabulous hypocrisy of our present setup, there is no doubt that is how the grass-roots majority of folks want it. The fact that prostitution exists doesn't worry them unduly. What they can't abide is the idea of its being legitimated (the same posture that, incidently,

---

* Until 1946 France maintained one of the world's lowest VD figures by means of strictly supervised and controlled *maisons de tolérance*. Then a weird parliamentary alliance of right-wing Catholics, Socialists, and Communists voted to have them closed. Since then the VD rate has shot up to American levels, but no deputy so far has had the courage to demand that the brothels be reopened.

also characterizes their attitude toward homosexuality). In any case, legalization does not necessarily mean the end of Mob dominance. Most of Nevada's legitimate bawdyhouses are under Syndicate control.

The Combine has largely withdrawn from the retailing end of the narcotics trade. It seemed the take wasn't worth the heat. Today, most of the risky aspects of the business are handled by blacks, Cubans, and Puerto Ricans. But since the minority operators can't raise large amounts of cash, the Mob still finances the bulk purchases abroad and collects huge chunks of the net profits. And because of its grip on the import traffic from Europe, the Syndicate can regulate the market here to a considerable extent.

Over the past ten years the Mob has established a monopoly in cigarette smuggling by smashing up all freelance competitors. They buy truckloads of smokes in tobacco-producing states like North Carolina, where the cigarette tax is two cents a pack, and drive them into states like New York, where the tax slug is twenty-six cents. There, forged tax stamps are pasted on the cartons, which sell for four dollars— a dollar or more below the standard retail price, which leaves a fat profit for the bootleggers. As one of them told me proudly: "You see—*everybody* wins." Everybody, that is, except New York State, which loses around $110 million in tax revenue from the 44 million cartons of cigarettes bootlegged annually.

Pornography is also highly profitable. A Syndicate-run studio can churn out a hard-core movie for less than two hundred dollars, using nonunion "actors" at rock-bottom rates. The duplicates haul in multiple profits for years. Chopped into reels, most are sold to home-movie customers at twenty-five to fifty dollars a reel, depending on the action; the rest go into the peepshow theaters owned by the Mob. An added advantage of these theaters and porno shops is that they are legal. At the end of the year they file corporate tax returns showing the maximum possible profits—even if they stayed half empty most of the time. In this fashion, they act as hideouts for money the Mob actually makes from illicit operations.

Organized crime does not directly participate in felonies such as bank holdups and payroll heists. These are left to freelance bandits who are willing to risk their hides for what —by Syndicate standards—are laughable returns. The Syndicate, however, will play banker for them, exchanging "hot" money for safe currency and taking a cut that runs as high as 40 percent of the loot. And quite frequently the Mob will tip off the cops as to the identity of the robbers, earning the gratitude of the police and insuring their continued myopia with regard to its own activities. Above all, organized crime has no hand in the kind of offenses ordinary people fear most: muggings, street robberies and assaults, burglaries, and store holdups. Under certain circumstances it will even help to suppress them.

I gained some insight into this phenomenon during the years I lived in a portion of lower Manhattan then recognized as Mafialand. Most of the buildings and real estate in the area were Mob-owned, as were the cafés, taverns, night spots, and streetwalkers. You rubbed shoulders with Mafiosi every time you had a drink. Many of the old men playing dominoes at outdoor tables were Prohibition veterans who had "made their bones" under Joe "the Boss" Masseria and loved talking about it. I had a passing acquaintance with Crazy Joe Gallo during his Camus-quoting phase, and polite relations with a dozen or so minor Mob soldiers, their wives, and their black-shrouded mamas.

It was—as New Yorkers measure these things—a safe, well-run neighborhood. Shopkeepers paid their dues to a Mafia-front "benevolent association" and received real protection in return—there hadn't been a store robbery in years. We had two street killings, but on each occasion the victim was a hoodlum whose death resulted from internecine strife that didn't affect outsiders. Old ladies ran no danger of having their purses snatched—after all, you never knew whose mother someone might be. The houses were antique but, thanks in part to the absence of vandalism, were kept in

good repair. Garbage was collected with amazing prompt-
ness, car thefts were rare, and while nighttime strollers were
often propositioned, they were never assaulted. New York's
dreaded juvenile gangs, which the cops allegedly can't control, gave the area a wide berth. On the one occasion I saw
a bunch of them congregating in an alley, a car with three
men inside mounted the pavement and drove right through
them at full speed, scattering them in all directions.

After the Mafia sold its property and moved out, the
district deteriorated before our eyes. Garbage piled up in
stinking heaps, windows were smashed and buildings burned,
cars and apartments were ripped off wholesale, shopkeepers
were robbed blind. The streets became dangerous at night
and overrun with youth packs by day. After my apartment
was burgled twice in one month, I moved out myself, feeling
vaguely nostalgic about the Godfather.

I took with me some notions regarding the social implications of organized crime. One was that, although only a
small segment of the locals were involved in it, a great many
sympathized with the operators. They ignored the periodic
bloodshed as being none of their concern. My old street-
corner grocer said, "Sure, they shoot people here sometime,
but they don't do it lika those animals." What he meant
was that they killed only combatants—each other. Yet there
was a boiling lynch-mob fury against those the old man
called "animals": the drug addicts, the plundering juveniles,
the freelance muggers, the housebreakers and robbers.

People were acutely aware of the benefits they derived
from Mafia pull at City Hall and were quite willing to
allow the capos their rakeoff. When a notorious Mafia poli-
tician was indicted for taking bribes in return for contract
allocations, they voiced astonishment that anyone should
either doubt it or make a fuss about it. "Well, naturally he
takes bribes. Why else go into politics?" They refused to
believe that any large city in the world is run without the
help of crime organizations; indeed, they seemed to regard
such a state of affairs as somehow contrary to human nature.
It didn't even seem to have occurred to them that things

like regular garbage disposal, housing repair, decent street lighting, and police protection constituted their rights as taxpayers rather than favors graciously bestowed on them by the Honored Society. They were, above all, unconscious of the real price exacted by the racketeers—a price they would continue paying long after the favors had evaporated.

The rackets net the Syndicate a fabulous flow of cash (estimated as equivalent to the combined annual profits of the three or four largest industrial corporations in America) that must be utilized. Although between $200 million and $300 million has been tucked away in private Swiss bank accounts, beyond the reach of federal tax investigators, most of the colossal amount remaining finds an outlet in Mob participation in legitimate enterprises such as the record and film industry, real estate, banking, commercial sports, trucking, food processing, construction, cosmetics, and the hotel industry. And wherever the Mob gets a toehold, its peculiar practices enable it to transform this into a stranglehold.

They will corrupt city officials in order to get zoning laws altered in their favor, bribe government inspectors to pass shoddy materials supplied for public works, line the pockets of industrial and food supervisors to get them to overlook safety and health precautions, defy pollution controls, ignore building and fire regulations, eliminate competitors by violence or the threat of it, confound the balances of an open-market economy by rigging the mechanics to their advantage. My neighbors in Mafialand saw only the occasional gunshot victims claimed by the Mob feuds. They couldn't comprehend that children killed or maimed by defective school buildings, workers poisoned or crippled because of unenforced safety laws, families incinerated in firetraps, motorists slaughtered by illegally overloaded trucks are just as much victims of the Mafia as the sprawling hoodlum corpses in the gutter.

In this respect, they were no blinder than the millions of staunch and honest workingmen who watched—first enthusiastically, then apathetically—while the Mob took over their unions. They, too, counted small short-range gains and ignored immense long-term losses.

The gangsters entered the labor movement by courtesy of the blatantly illegal union-busting tactics of certain employers. Jimmy Hoffa recalled the savage struggles during the 1930s, when he was organizing the Teamsters: "They [the bosses] hired thugs who were out to get us, and, brother, your life was in your hands every day. There was only one way to survive—fight back. And we used to slug it out in the streets. . . . The police were no help. The police would beat your brains in for even talking union."

When employers used goon squads to break picket lines and beat organizers to a pulp, the cops turned a conveniently blind eye—when they didn't actively intervene against the labor forces. It seemed only logical for some embattled unions to bring in their own hired hoods. Lepke Buchalter became an "enforcer" for the garment cutters' union and later for the truckers. Albert Anastasia joined the New York longshoremen and ran his own local for years. The same development took place in other unions, including the United Mine Workers of Kentucky and Tennessee, who faced the most rabid opposition of all. There is no doubt that underworld minions helped to win the bloody labor wars of the 1920s and '30s. "If only," as one historian phrased it, "by demonstrating that *both* sides could play the game of cracking skulls and smashing jaws."

Rank-and-file union members at first relished the help of professional thugs. But as soon as their organizations were recognized and flourishing, they found themselves in the position of the sorcerer's apprentice: Having conjured up the dark spirits, they were unable to exorcise them. What was worse, the rotten apples in the union barrels contaminated others—especially in the top layers. Some union leadership became so interwoven with the Mob as to be virtually indistinguishable—a development for which the rank and file has paid dearly, if in a well-camouflaged manner. This is evident above all with regard to the pension funds to which all members had to contribute, which reached staggering amounts. As the funds swelled, so, mysteriously, did the small-print clauses precluding more and more workers from drawing on them. A worker could lose a quarter-century of contributions by being laid off one day before retirement age. Often workers were simply not paid their pensions— or not the full amount—even though they fulfilled all requirements. Going to court meant facing a battery of slick lawyers, delays, obstructions, and postponements that might drag on until the plaintiff was dead. Trying to rally fellow unionists became increasingly dangerous. "Troublemakers" were often found dead in ditches . . . or not found at all.

When the then Attorney General Robert Kennedy investigated the $1.4-billion Teamsters Pension Fund, he discovered that much of it had gone to purchase or build Las Vegas casinos, Florida hotels, California real estate, Midwestern country clubs, and some of the swank resorts in which Syndicate executives took their rest and recuperation—often accompanied by union leaders and politicians, but not by the poor saps who had faithfully coughed up their fourteen dollars a week in the delusion that they were safeguarding their old age. As a result of Kennedy's investigation, Jimmy Hoffa went to prison, then—ironically—fell victim to his underworld ties. When, after spending five years behind bars, he was sprung by President Nixon (whose election campaign the Teamsters supported to the tune of $250,000), Hoffa tried to recapture his power position in the union, but the Mob didn't want him back. When Jimmy persisted in his efforts, some "persons unknown" took him for that one-way ride from which only Lucky Luciano ever returned.* Hoffa's body was never found.

Even starker was the tragedy surrounding the pension fund of the United Mine Workers. In 1969 a union dissident named Joseph Yablonski challenged "Tough Tony" Boyle for the presidency of the UMW, charging that Boyle had

---

* Charles "Lucky" Luciano earned his nickname through being taken for a ride by members of the Legs Diamond gang, during which he was stabbed eight times with an ice pick and had his throat slashed. None of the injuries proved fatal, and Luciano walked home after being dumped on a Staten Island beach.

diverted large portions of the pension fund for his own use. Thanks to brazen ballot rigging, Yablonski lost the election, but the contest was too close for Boyle's comfort. He ordered the dangerous rival rubbed out. The three liquor-soaked goons, recruited for $5,200, murdered Yablonski's wife and young daughter along with him. In due course nine people—including Tony Boyle—drew from one to three life terms apiece for their parts in the conspiracy.

Recited case by case, these Mob murders give the impression of having involved a far greater number of victims than they actually did. Currently they amount to less than one percent of our homicide rate—a bagatelle compared to the corpses claimed by domestic violence. And the fact that most of these victims were themselves criminals helps to disguise the far graver menace lurking behind the modest casualty figures. The real threat stems from the continual upward and outward expansion of the Syndicate—its ceaseless burrowing into new areas of influence. Mob representatives have now infiltrated regions that were closed to their ilk only ten years ago: international oil conglomerates and Wall Street, to mention two. With that kind of financial power at their disposal, political power cannot be far away. Whether or not the Nixon administration accelerated the achievement of such power on a national scale is still open to dispute. Clearly the Mob has wielded considerable political influence for a long time. During the Nixon administration many of the characters frequenting the Oval Office espoused a moral philosophy alarmingly similar to that of the Syndicate. Herbert Kalmbach shaking down business corporations on behalf of his boss, Presidential pardons for racketeers following hefty contributions to the campaign kitty, payoffs and rakeoffs accompanying the dealings of Agnew, Mitchell, Dean, Ehrlichman, Colson, Haldeman, et al.—all bore unmistakable parallels to the ethics of the underworld. If nothing else, the men involved in Watergate have prepared the moral climate that the Godfather needs in order to make his entrance.

7

The Gay and the Dead

The killer, a pathological specimen, is an alarming offshoot of the degenerate breed which is constantly undermining the social fabric. Emotionally thwarted, he can only make contact with his fellow man by spilling his blood.
—Henry Miller, *The World of Sex*

The bodies started turning up on Christmas Day, 1972. They were found all along the Pacific coastline from the southern edges of Los Angeles to Newport Beach in Orange County. Some had obviously been thrown from speeding cars and lay in roadside ditches and on freeway shoulders. Others had been dismembered, the widely scattered pieces randomly stuffed into plastic bags and garbage bins. One plastic-wrapped head had come to rest on the conveyer belt of a recycling plant, while a hairy left leg was stuck in a junk heap behind a Sunset Beach saloon.

By July 1973 the tally had reached five, with one head and two sets of genitals missing. Only two of the bodies were identified: One was a young Marine from Camp Pendleton, the other a salesman out of Yorba Linda. All of them, however, had certain common denominators. They were young Caucasian males who had been sexually assaulted and either strangled or suffocated. Two had also been castrated. Since none of these murders has been solved to date, the police are still uncertain whether they were the work of one killer or of several unconnected killers.*

* The "trash bag murders" were considered solved when, in December 1977, a former aerospace worker named Patrick Kearney pleaded guilty to a total of 21 slayings. The bearded bespectacled 38-year-old Kearney, himself an avowed homosexual, refused to give a motive for his slaughter spree, and

Five unsolved slayings don't amount to much in a patch of Southern California that had several hundred of them. Nevertheless, they were of considerable significance in that they marked the beginning of a wave of homosexual murders that is now sweeping the United States and sending tremors through gay communities from coast to coast. These killings are distinguished by their exceptional brutality as well as by a ratio of unsolved cases matched only by the casualties of the Mafia wars.

"There are definite reasons for this," a Los Angeles homicide-division officer told me. "When you're dealing with a homosexual-type murder you're facing a whole bunch of different possibilities. The killer may be gay. Or he may be someone who *hates* gays. Or he may be killing just for the money and disguising the deed to *look* like a homosexual crime. So unless we can learn something about the background and associates of the victims, we're liable to get stalled. For that we need cooperation from the gay community. And they don't always—uh—cooperate."

The gays tell it the other way around. "The cops hate our guts. They don't give a shit how many of us get knocked off," said a homosexual journalist. "Their investigations were so slapdash you'd think they were after a shoplifter. They'll never solve these killings until some political pressure comes down from above—and that's pretty unlikely."

Both of my informants were right to an extent. Although male homosexuality "between consenting adults" has achieved a dubious degree of legality in some states, police harassment, shakedowns, and entrapment are still going strong in others. The attitude of the average uniformed cop

---

the court made no attempt to find one. Nor did the authorities proceed with another seven murder charges against Kearney, which might have upped his score to 28 killings and made him the biggest mass murderer in U.S. history. Kearney was given two concurrent life sentences and told by Superior Court Judge John Hews: "In all likelihood, you will spend the rest of your natural life in state prison." Note that word "likelihood," which illustrates the uncertainty of two—or any given number—of so-called "life sentences."

remains largely unchanged, ranging from indifferent contempt to an almost phobic aversion for "queers."

The gay community—an inchoate, shifting, transitional
mass—harbors a profound distrust for policemen, based on
generations of official persecution and unofficial squeeze. No
sudden ray of legal enlightenment can melt defensive postures formed in centuries of survival outside the law. Criminal codes may have mellowed, but widespread heterosexual
hostility and persistent prejudice continue to keep thousands
of part-time "deviates" hidden in their closets during the
day—closets that often contain a suburban wife and children
as well. For many bisexuals, secretiveness is vital and can be
obsessive. Their night contacts are made on a first-name or
false-name basis and consummated anonymously in motels
or cars or on lonely beaches. Anonymity is the shield that
protects the fabric of their lives and their careers. They
aren't likely to discard it for the benefit of the men with
badges, regardless of what they may know. For them fear
of exposure outweighs even the danger that their own skins
may be next in line.

But none of these circumstances played a part in the
mind-boggling horror that erupted into the news during
that same summer of 1973. It emanated from—of all places—
that bastion of Western squaredom, Houston, Texas. For
sheer monstrousness it surpassed anything Americans had
ever known. It was, in the phrase of one Eastern reporter,
"the pestilence at noonday, the face of the moon in darkness."

It began with a telephone call logged at police headquarters on the heat-heavy morning of August 8. The voice at the
other end was young, slurred, and illiterate: "Listen, ya
better come on over. Ah killed a guy here."

"Here" turned out to be a small ramshackle bungalow in
the suburb of Pasadena. When the squad car pulled up, two
teenage boys and a dazed girl were waiting in front. The
bungalow was sparsely furnished, and the half-empty rooms
smelled of a sweetish blend of blood, vomit, booze, marijuana, and acrylic paint; the policemen were to remember

that peculiar odor for years to come. On the floor lay a man with long sideburns, flies buzzing around six bullet holes in his face and chest. Against the wall stood a heavy rectangular plywood plank with handcuffs or nylon ropes dangling from each corner; next to it, a portable radio linked to a pair of dry cells, whose significance the officers missed at first. The cells gave the radio enough volume to drown out screams. At the far end hung a gaudy colored print of Jesus, captioned LOVE.

The house and gadgets, police learned, belonged to the dead man, a thirty-three-year-old electrician named Dean Corll. One of the boys, Elmer Wayne Henley, Jr., acne-plastered, hazy-eyed, sporting a hairline mustache admitted that he had shot him. Why? Well, it seemed that Corll liked to "have fun" with young boys, procured for him by Henley. But that morning Corll had threatened Henley, so Henley had to shoot him in self-defense—that is, he had to because he knew that Corll sometimes killed those young boys. Several of those he'd already killed lay buried in a rented boat shed. Yes, Henley knew where it was; leastwise he *thought* he knew.

In the sticky afternoon heat a small column of cars headed for the Southeast Boat Storage, ten miles south of downtown Houston. They carried homicide detectives, four prison trusties to do the digging, and the handcuffed Henley as a guide. The interior of the empty boat shed was like an oven; the searchers dripped sweat before they had raised a shovel. Once they started to dig, it seemed as if they were excavating successive layers of a nightmare. First came a few objects: boys' sneakers, rags of T-shirts and socks, belts, a pocketknife, a mildewed comic book. Then came the stench —an overwhelming blast of foulness from the earth that turned the men sickly white and made them fight nausea. And then came the bodies.

Some were skeletons, others in various stages of soggy decomposition; some had been only a few days or a week in the ground. They were encased in clear plastic bags, each in its own little shroud. As one plastic bag after another was first uncovered, then hauled out by the prison trusties, you could see how the contents had died. There were bullet holes in the skulls of some, strangling cords wound around the necks of others—their mouths wide open as if screaming in silence. One boy's chest had caved in from a tremendous kick or blow; another seemed to have been clawed or chewed to shreds. Some were castrated, their sex organs stuffed into the bags with them.

There were more, and more, and still more bodies—all boys between thirteen and eighteen, all white, most of them fair-haired. After the eighth sack, the trusties had to be let out to breathe fresh air—two of them retching, one sobbing uncontrollably. The detectives took over the digging. Among them was Karl Siebeneicher, whose fifteen-year-old cousin had been missing from home for weeks. He found him in the tenth bag.

Outside it was growing dark. Fire engines arrived from Houston and played floodlights on the scene. TV crews and reporters had gathered in droves and were relaying the body count to one another: "They just found two more—does that make twelve or thirteen?" And still the digging went on; all through the muggy night and the next day the body count climbed. As the men reached the bottom layers of the pit they had to don face masks and work in short shifts because the stench and the sight had become nearly unbearable. The sacks had disintegrated, and the surrounding soil was a glutinous bog of decay, sprinkled with limbs, skulls, and bones. After the twenty-seventh body, the digging ceased. Very likely there were more, but the Houston police decided to call off the search. There was no point in digging further: Texas had already broken the American homicide record for this century.

Meanwhile, cops and reporters became acquainted with Wayne Henley. The pimple-cheeked seventeen-year-old babbled incessantly. Sometimes he complained about "gittin' all dizzy," but his great terror was of being left alone—especially in the dark. The detectives gentled him along, putting up with his blurred whining as well as sudden bursts of snotty arrogance. They felt that a confession was on the way, and they were right. But when it came it left even the veterans among them feeling oddly helpless in the face of something that none could quite conceive, despite the evidence all around.

Henley had met Dean Corll two years earlier and had been more or less living off him ever since. His main task was to keep the electrician supplied with boys. His secondary chore was occasionally to help him kill them. In return he received money, the use of a car, food, liquor, and a lot of drugs. The third person in the trio was a tall, fine-featured boy named David Owen Brooks, who enjoyed the same privileges and had similar duties. Between them the two lads brought a steady trickle of youngsters into Corll's often-changed abodes. ". . . Wanna come to a party, man? A real cool party? Sure, climb in, we're jist drivin' there."

The party kicked off with moonshine liquor, rounds of reefers, and sniffing sessions of acrylic paint (which Corll stole on his job at the Houston Power Company). It ended when the visitor passed out. On awakening he found himself stripped naked, gagged, and spread-eagled on the plywood plank, his arms and legs secured by handcuffs and nylon ropes. The floor was neatly covered with plastic sheeting to catch blood and excrement; the radio was kept going full blast.

What followed then lasted from ten minutes to half a day, depending on Corll's mood and spare time. In conclusion, he usually shot or strangled the boy, alone or with his young assistants. Henley wasn't sure exactly how many he'd helped kill—maybe six or eight. Brooks, he said, had accounted for four. Altogether Henley guessed there might have been about thirty victims—an estimate that left a few unfound.

Henley was mildly troubled by these activities. He slept badly, always kept a light on, and drank huge quantities of beer, which rendered his naturally thick speech almost unintelligible. Otherwise, his mother and brothers noted nothing unusual about him. In private, so to speak, he was heterosexual, and it was one of his girl friends who brought the horror to an end.

Rhonda, aged fifteen, ran away from home after a row with her father. Henley didn't know what to do with her and conceived the harebrained idea of taking her to Corll's bungalow in Pasadena. Although he also brought a boy named Tim Kerley along, when they arrived at Corll's, around three in the morning, the electrician was livid about having a "dame" intruding on his masculine pleasures. Appearing to calm down after a while, he finally produced a can of acrylic paint for his guests and sat watching as they took turns "huffing" deeply.

Having sniffed paint, drunk hooch, and smoked grass until he nodded off, Henley was later to come to only to find that this time *he* was staked out on the board, with Corll snapping handcuffs on his wrists and muttering, "Kill you all . . . kill the goddamn lot of you . . ." Talking fast and desperately, Henley pleaded for his life, promising he'd help torture and kill the others. Finally, Corll smiled and unlocked the cuffs. "Okay, Wayne. You work on the chick. I'll take the guy."

Tearing off his clothes, Corll mounted the bound and gagged Kerley. At that moment Henley grabbed the electrician's pistol from the table and fired six shots into him. Then he freed the others and rang the police. The three went outside to wait, Rhonda still giggling to herself and mouthing, "Bang-bang-bang."

This was the gist of the confession Henley initially made but later retracted. It revolved around a central figure of nearly incomprehensible evil—a phantom scores of people knew but nobody seemed to have noticed. Who—or what— was this creature, Corll?

He bore an uncanny resemblance to Robert Musil's *Man Without Qualities*, perhaps the finest study of a sex murderer in literature. There was no color or substance to him, no sharply etched characteristic anyone could recall. He was nondescriptness personified: a tall, chunky individual with a perfect crowd face, wearing conventional, slightly shabby clothes. A neighbor said, "Dean Corll? He was vanilla. You

know—kind of sweet and blah." He had a lady friend whom
he dated occasionally. She thought he "had respect" because
he never demanded sex from her. People vaguely remembered
his good temper and helpfulness. Corll was always fixing wires
or mending switches for them and never charged a dime.
But mostly folks didn't notice him. "Hell, he hardly ever
opened his mouth," said one of his fellow workers. "I went
to a party with him, and he just sat there like a clam. Only
time he talked was to some dumb kids." To his neighbors,
Corll's sole eccentricity seems to have been his desire to
mix with teenagers and be accepted by them. People thought
it slightly odd that a man in his thirties should be continually
hanging around boys, lavishing presents on them, and clown-
ing to keep them amused. Nobody dreamed that he had a
sexual motivation, for in the traditionally redneck view of
life that predominated in the patchwork of decrepit homes,
back-yard industries, and storefronts that made up the
"Heights" neighborhood where he hunted, a homosexual
meant a "faggot," and there was nothing remotely effeminate
about Corll. Had he worn a beard or longish hair, he would
have been regarded with intense suspicion. As it was, he
blended perfectly with the locals, sharing their partiality for
beer, hellfire religion, and white supremacy. Although he
frequently changed addresses, he definitely "belonged" in the
Heights. Even when he finally moved out to Pasadena, the
Heights remained the pond from which he fished his victims.
One or twice neighbors heard commotions in his house—
moans, muffled screams, and dull knocking, like a head bang-
ing frantically against wood—but decided it was "some drunk
having a ball."

All this doesn't explain the core of this satanic conundrum: How could a man murder twenty-seven or more
children from a closely knit community in the course of two
years without attracting *some* police attention? The answer
lies in the peculiarly anemic state of the Houston constabulary. Despite its great wealth and garish opulence, the Texas
metropolis ran a cut-rate police department. In 1973 it employed just 2,200 officers for a population of 1.3 million

(Detroit, also considered underpoliced, had 5,400 for 1.5 million people). Underpaid, badly trained, woefully undisciplined, and atrociously led, this skeleton force had no hope of controlling a town that size, and apparently wasn't meant to. Instead, citizens were encouraged to "carry protection" in the form of handguns. One result of this rugged frontier philosophy was a homicide score that boomed to over 300 a year—for a time the highest per-capita murder rate in the country. The other was the absence of certain frills—such as police searches for missing persons—taken for granted in more effete regions.

Had the Houston cops made even cursory efforts to find the dozens of Heights boys reported missing, they would have come upon the tracks of Henley and Brooks, who worked with minimal concealment. But despite the fact that there were always detectives available to staff a totally redundant antisubversive unit, no such effort was possible because of the manpower shortage. Agitated parents were informed that their sons had probably run off and "joined those hippies in California." The police couldn't do a thing, and anyway, they were bound to turn up again. Most of them did . . . in the plastic sacks beneath Corll's boat shed. Tragically, most of the parents knew full well that their kids *hadn't* run away, that something had happened to them. The blue-collar folks concerned had neither the money to hire their own investigators nor the clout to get police action. Faced with the indifference of the powers that governed America's "City of the Future" like a nineteenth-century bargain basement, they were quite simply helpless.

Henley and Brooks went to trial in the glare of worldwide publicity, the court packed with reporters from every part of the globe. From the way certain members of the Houston establishment behaved you might have thought it was the journalists who had slaughtered the kids. They gave the impression that the whole affair was a conspiracy hatched by the international news media against the fair name of Houston. The local cops reacted in their own particular fashion: by cracking down indiscriminately on all gays.

The trials revealed little about the accused and even less about the dead Corll, whose presence loomed over the proceedings like a malevolent shadow. No one tackled the question of what could have driven such a bland, amiable *manqué* to commit mass murder. Nor did anyone ask how the two youngsters in the dock could have been led to help him in such a bewilderingly nonchalant manner. Sometimes they had participated in the killings; sometimes stood guard or watched; sometimes walked out as casually as you might walk out on a boring parlor game. Neither of them had any idea—or had given much thought to—why Corll would pay some boys for sex, treat others like a kid brother, and rape, torture, and butcher a third lot. All they knew was that the man's appetite for victims had been increasing at such a pace that he would have liked them to deliver to him "about one kid a day." The deepest insight Brooks came up with was "Well, I guess the Corll who did the killing just wasn't the same guy folks knew the rest of the time."

The jury found Henley guilty of six murders, declaring a seventh—the shooting of Corll—"justifiable homicide." He was sentenced to a total of 594 years in prison—a sentence that might possibly keep him confined until middle age. Brooks drew one life sentence. Thus ended the murder case without parallel in American history.*

---

* It does have a striking parallel in Germany. Fifty years earlier Fritz Haarmann, the "Werewolf of Hanover," proved an even greater embarrassment to that city than Corll did to Houston. Between 1919 and 1924 Haarmann murdered forty to fifty young boys, mostly by ripping out their throats with his teeth during intercourse. Since, apart from what he earned as a paid informer for the Hanover police, he derived his main income from hawking meat and old clothes on the black market, he was able to add not simply their clothing but many of his victims themselves, chopped into unrecognizable portions, to his stock. The skulls he tossed into the Leine River, from which children kept fishing them out. He, too, had a junior partner: a pretty, ice-cold parasite named Hans Grans, whom Haarmann adored, pampered, and frequently took beatings from. Together they haunted the area around Hanover's railroad station, then swarming with waifs and runaways. Haarmann befriended the handsomer boys, taking them home to his fetid garret, from which they rarely emerged in one piece. After his arrest in June 1924, the walls of this room were found caked with blood. Haarmann was tried for twenty-four murders, although he remembered twice that many and waxed tearfully sentimental about them. "I have a very sensitive nature," he told the judge in his girlish voice. "Perhaps I

The most chilling aspect of the homosexual murder syndrome is the disproportionately large number of juveniles involved. As criminologist Lawrence Quinn pointed out:

> It doesn't mean that inverts have a greater tendency toward child murder than anyone else. Merely that the potential victims are more accessible. Let me explain this: The same species of sadistic pedophiliacs who kill small girls if they are heterosexuals will murder young boys if they happen to be homosexual. But whereas girl children are usually better watched and instilled with at least a modicum of caution, this is often entirely lacking in boys. I'm not only talking about sheltered kids with good homes. The most vulnerable are probably those considered street-wise. They frequently encourage homosexual advances for what they think they'll get out of it, then end up in situations from which they cannot escape.

This vulnerability was spotlighted by a special investigation conducted by the Los Angeles police in October 1976. It revealed that around thirty thousand children—predominantly boys aged six to seventeen—were subjected to "sexual exploitation" in the L.A. County area alone. According to Captain William J. Riddle, commander of the LAPD's Juvenile Division, "They fell victim to every conceivable sex crime, including acts of sadomasochism."

Several hundred of these boys were prostitutes, working in houses or on street beats, but in both cases controlled by professional pimps. Riddle estimated that a twelve-year-old can earn up to a thousand dollars a day, of which the pimp takes six hundred or more. The boys are also used in highly explicit 8-mm porno films, sold at the going rate of a hundred dollars a reel. "These films have become very sophisticated," said Riddle. "In fact, they are sold by different age groups—if you want a film featuring ten-year-olds,

---

have two souls." He was beheaded in 1925, his brain preserved at Göttingen University.

Haarmann's Germany was a country defeated in war, torn by uprisings, utterly impoverished by a collapsed currency. Hanover was bankrupt, starving and freezing, its demoralized police unable to keep track of the hordes of homeless kids roaming the streets. These factors at least partly explained Haarmann's long immunity from arrest. None of them can be applied to Houston, Texas.

you ask for it—and by the different perversions customers prefer."

While the boys are exploited by the pimps, they are also protected from extreme physical harm. This does not apply to the multitude of juvenile freelancers known as "chickens." Sergeant Jackie Howell of the Abused Child Unit in Los Angeles described them as "kids without a point of reference, trading sex for friendship, a hamburger and maybe a movie— pathetic kids looking for a little affection." But their pursuers, called "chicken hawks," contain the potentially most dangerous element of the gay subculture, especially since their victims have little or no inkling of the risks they run.

The majority come from one-parent homes more or less devoid of authority or emotional support. Used to fending for themselves, they often acquire a veneer of gutter finesse that deems it sharp to provide a stranger with sexual gratification in return for cash or narcotics. Very few of them have homoerotic tendencies themselves—they are sex objects in the truest sense. And because so many of them *think* they know the score, they wind up as small crumpled corpses in some lonely dumping ground.

Nonetheless, a surprising number of murders committed by gays have no sexual motivation at all—at least not in the sense you might expect. Their perpetrators are often transvestite prostitutes who have joined their female colleagues in the widespread practice of robbing clients instead of servicing them. These male whores in "drag," having become an integral part of America's metropolitan night scene, now pose a peculiar set of dangers to their customers as well as to themselves.

The bulk of their patrons are homosexuals, who run the same risks as any straight john. But many transvestites will also hook heterosexuals—particularly drunks—and reveal their true sex at the last possible moment. Quite frequently this pays off—some clients will go through with the deal in a spirit of adventure, tickled by the intriguing "differentness" of the situation. Others, however, react with maniacal fury to the deception, and then the outcome is anybody's guess.

It can entail a badly battered or dead hooker as well as the reverse.

The latter was the case in a murder trial that had Seattle newspapers in a quandary—unable to decide whether to refer to the defendant as "he" and "him" or "she" and "her." The accused was a tall honey-colored youth with melting brown eyes, charged with stabbing a man fatally on—of all days—Friday, February 13, 1976. The young man's name was Oaland Graham, but he was better known around Seattle's miniature scarlet strip along downtown Pike Street as Jackie. Wearing falsies underneath a clinging sweater, a bouffant wig, and skin-tight pink slacks. Jackie had piled up a score of arrests for prostitution, plus one for grand larceny.

Around two in the morning, he/she had sashayed into a Pike Street all-nighter and approached a husky shipfitter named Brad Lee Bass. The customer mistook Jackie for a girl and, on that basis, came to a fifty-dollar misunderstanding with him. But outside, in the white neon glare, Bass saw the light and tried to back away from the deal. Several people watched Jackie suddenly wade into the man, kicking, flaying, and swearing, until his wig was knocked off in the scuffle. This indignity, which clearly revealed his true sex, apparently sent him over the edge. Someone slipped him a knife, and moments later Bass collapsed on the pavement with a fatal stab wound in his chest.

Graham faced the court wearing a demure pants suit and insisting on being called "Ms." He was convicted of second-degree murder. The one thing brought out by this sleazy little street drama was the latent hysteria of so many transvestites—a lethal hair-trigger touchiness stemming from what must be the ultimate sense of insecurity. Since they frequently combine this with considerable physical strength, plus drug habits or alcoholism, they become walking booby traps liable to explode at the slightest jar. As a muscular Chicago cabdriver admitted to me: "I'd rather fight an armed pimp any day than a t.v."

In recent years the nationwide drug culture has united straight and lavender underworld types in curious alliances formed for the sole purpose of exploiting homosexual "fat cats." Strong-arm thugs team up with male hustlers and bisexual procurers in order to seduce, blackmail, steal, or rob, as the opportunity presents itself. What renders these partnerships extremely dangerous is their improvised, ad hoc character and the resulting streak of emotional instability that often prevents the collaborators from following pre-arranged plans. Dozens of their victims have died because at a crucial moment one of the partners went haywire. This was what happened in the worst sex-and-homicide scandal ever to rock Philadelphia's high society.

People who knew him called John S. Knight III a Renaissance man—a rare blending of wealth, breeding, scholarship, artistic talent, and physical prowess. He was considerably more than just heir to the nation's largest newspaper chain, Knight-Ridder Inc., which owns the Philadelphia *Daily News*. An honor graduate of Harvard and Oxford, art connoisseur, dynamic advertising salesman, first-rate reporter and administrator, he could have carved out several brilliant careers for himself even without family connections.

His colleagues at the *Daily News*, where he worked as special-projects director, knew the thirty-year-old Knight as a courteous, charming, somewhat reserved young executive with a taste for Saville Row suits, hunting, weightlifting, and his own gourmet cooking. His other tastes were so carefully concealed that their revelation came as a bombshell.

Knight inhabited three different worlds—or closets—and managed to keep them very nearly watertight. The first was the world of wealth and social position that was his as grandson of press patriarch John Shively Knight, where he passed as solidly heterosexual, if rather fastidious. The second was the creative world of painters and writers, in which he moved as an equal and was generally considered "ambidextrous." The third was the sweet-gamy underworld of boy hustlers, Spruce Street pickups, gay bars, and sex boutiques, which regarded him as a rich and delightfully generous queer. Which of these worlds reflected the "real" Knight no one can say. Perhaps, in true Renaissance tradition, all three.

Knight's luxury apartment in Rittenhouse Square, the elegant heart of Philadelphia, was a bachelor's dream pad, crammed with art treasures, books, exotic weaponry, and sporting gear. It was there he took his young boy friends to be dined, wined, photographed, and eventually bedded. He liked the poor-waif types: doe-eyed, delicately featured, and not overbright—in fact, the more infantile the better. Among them was twenty-year-old Felix Melendez, a half–Puerto Rican product of the South Philly slums—boyish and underprivileged enough to become a favorite. What Knight didn't know was that the blue-eyed and lisping Felix ran with a team of toughs preying exclusively on homosexuals.

On the evening of December 7, 1975, Knight was entertaining house guests—his former Harvard roommate, Dr. John McKinnon, and his wife—belonging to World No. 1. Host and guests had a long conversational nightcap and retired about 2:30 A.M. At five that morning Mrs. McKinnon was roused naked from her bed by three intruders. They were waving handguns and knives in wild excitement, shouting confused orders. Mrs. McKinnon had to help them search the apartment and was stabbed before she succeeded in fleeing downstairs. The whole scene was so chaotic that only with the arrival of the police was it discovered that John Knight had been murdered. Tied up with belts and socks, he was lying on the floor of his bedroom, a gag deep in his throat and five knife wounds in his back and chest. Judging by his bruises, he had put up a fierce struggle before being overpowered. The officers also found something else: a trove of homoerotic pornography, including dozens of Polaroid shots of naked boys and tape recordings of the sound effects of masculine lovemaking.

Mrs. McKinnon described at least one of the intruders as "definitely homosexual," and, in consequence, the most concentrated police heat Philadelphia had ever known began to scorch the gay community. There were wails of "persecution" from various gay journals, which would have screamed just as loudly if the cops *hadn't* investigated with all possible vigor. Anyway, the methods employed showed commendably fast results. Within four days Chief Inspector Joe Golden announced that warrants had been issued for three South Philadelphia suspects. One of them was Felix Melendez. The others were identified as Steven Maleno, a twenty-five-year-old known for his habit of stealing from his homosexual lovers, and an older man, Salvatore Soli, a mustachioed, tattooed car thief, who also had a record for armed robbery.

Maleno gave himself up a few hours later. Then the body of Felix Melendez was found shot dead in the wooded area surrounding a New Jersey country club. Soli's mother went on television, pleading, "Salvi, please come home . . . let me hear from you so I'll know you aren't dead like the other boy." Police did not hear from "Salvi," but a panicky go-go dancer in Miami, Florida, rang the local cops and told them she was holed up with Soli, who had shaved his mustache and dyed his hair strawberry blond. Both were returned to Philadelphia.

The girl was one of those abstruse child-women who seem to be scampering around the edges of every other felony murder—not actually participating, but always in the know and hollering for help only after the corpses are cold and the air gets hot. This one, it turned out, had attended the palaver that decided Knight's fate. According to her, Melendez suggested that he knew "just the person to take for money. A rich guy—his name is John."

The trio set forth with only a Saturday-night robbery in mind. But things got fouled up very quickly. Knight refused to let Melendez in, and Felix had to scream, "I love you, John—I love you," in the hallway until Knight opened the door. Then all three piled in and jumped on top of their victim. Knight fought hard, and it took their combined strength to tie him up and gag him. The raid became a shambles when robbers discovered that there were guests in the apartment. Later that night, when the girl met up with Soli and Maleno, she heard only that Melendez had "gone berserk." Apparently she didn't ask many questions.

They fled to New Jersey, with the men showing off some

rings and gold coins they had taken from Knight's apartment. Reaching a stretch of secluded woodland, Maleno and Melendez got out of the car and disappeared into the darkness. The go-go girl remembered hearing three shots, after which Maleno returned alone and told her: "You didn't see a damned thing." Then they split up, with Soli and the girl heading for the Florida sunshine. Their car broke down en route, and they had to make it to Miami by Greyhound bus. Three days later, she got up the nerve to call the police.

In court, the two men claimed that the dead Melendez had stabbed Knight. The jury thought otherwise and found Salvatore Soli guilty of the murder. In fact, the slaying was almost certainly unpremeditated—the byproduct of a hopelessly bungled rip-off worthy of the primitives who performed it. John Knight's separate worlds had suddenly and fatally overlapped, destroying him in the process.

No community has been as deeply affected by the current murder cycle as America's gay capital, San Francisco. The shock impact stemmed less from the number of killings than from the circumstances surrounding them. San Francisco has long prided itself on being a haven of tolerance, a live-and-let-live metropolis par excellence. The city's estimated 120,000-plus male and female homosexuals (out of a total population of barely 710,000) have achieved the nearest thing to complete social recognition this country has yet to offer. They wield considerable political and economic power, and in the area known as Castro Village gay subculture has developed to a level where it can no longer be called *sub*—it is the dominant texture.

Compared with Los Angeles, for instance, San Francisco's gays have suffered a minimum of police pressure, and have consequently tended to cooperate with the law to a far greater extent. On the surface at least, it seemed as if the Golden Gate city would provide America with a working model of sexual coexistence. Then—starting in 1975—came a series of atrocious homosexual murders that had the police stumped and the gay minority feeling outraged, disillusioned, and grimly apprehensive. At the time of this writing, despite all the leads supplied by gay citizens who went to unheard-of-lengths to assist the investigators, the seventeen worst of them remain unsolved.

The killings fell into three categories, each typifying a specific brand of homosexual mayhem. Five were mutilation murders of Tenderloin drag queens, apparently perpetrated by one or more slashers with a psychotic hatred for transvestite prostitutes—an inverted Jack-the-Ripper syndrome. Six others were stabbings of white middle-class men picked up in Castro Village bars by a sinister cartoonist the police nicknamed "Black Doodler." He always made contact with his victims by sketching their portraits and had intercourse with them before using his knife. Stanford psychology professor Philip Zimbardo believes that this man is driven by an "attraction-repulsion complex." As Zimbardo explained: "It's highly likely that he is someone who may be attracted to the homosexual experience on one level but, at another level, feels a powerful moral outrage toward it."

The six murders in the third category had a setting most gays prefer to give a wide berth: the so-called S&M scene. "S&M" stands for sadomasochism and has become a fairly widespread form of sex play in hetero circles. Among gays— particularly San Francisco gays—it has become a costumed and highly stylized ritual reminiscent of the preening, strutting, and crowing ceremonies of certain bird species. Only a small percentage of homosexuals "get off" on pain, but those that do literally take their lives in their hands in order to indulge their taste.

In San Francisco their stomping ground is Folsom Street, south of Market—a stark, gritty thoroughfare lying amid looming warehouses and sprinkled with little bars called Ramrod, Folsom Prison, No Name, Fe-Be's. There the "hunks" gather after dark. Some are bikers, some look like bikers, other still are looking *for* bikers, and it takes a practiced eye to distinguish them. The universal garb is macho black leather—even though it's often vinyl. Each Easy Rider, whether he actually rides or not, comes loaded down with enough metal to stock a hardware store: chains and bracelets, enormous bunches of keys, tools carried in gun holsters, nail-studded belts around their waists, and outsize imitation Iron Crosses—sometimes accompanied by holy medals and a Virgin Mary or two—at their necks.

The keys aren't meant to unlock anything but to denote status. "Masters"—meaning sadists—wear them on the left hip, "slaves" on the right. Both are apt to display handcuffs in their belts, but only the masochists show little yellow handkerchiefs peeping from their hip pockets. So they meet, circle each other like wary gunfighters, and eye their identification symbols. Verbal contact consists mainly of monosyllabic grunts. With metal jangling, bikes revving, and jukeboxes blaring all around, not much could be heard in any case. A glance is usually sufficient to separate whippers from whippees, which is what counts. They have a drink, which in Folsom Street means beer, and then they're off to their special brand of pleasure, which can be a bamboo cane in a cockroach-run hotel or a private torture chamber in a plush suburban pad.

All six casualties of this cruelty cult were "closet slaves" who wore straight clothes during the day and donned their leathers only at night. One of them—a smooth young lawyer named George Gilbert—owned an apartment in San Francisco's swankest high-rise. He had an abiding passion for being bound, gagged, and whipped to the point of orgasm. When his body was found, he had seven jagged stab wounds in his stomach.

"Knowing that these guys were passive masochists who liked flirting with danger doesn't help us much," said a police investigator. "When they're out to get their rocks off, they'll pick up anybody anywhere—in a bar, a bath house, a dark alley—particularly when it's getting late and they're beginning to feel desperate because they haven't found a trick earlier. Sure, they know the risks they are taking in their neighborhood. But, I don't know—sometimes I get the feeling there's a kind of death wish involved."

Sometimes that does seem the only explanation for the

compulsive longing that drives these vinyl sheep toward their slaughter pen. In his *Midnight Cowboy*, James Leo Herlihy has given us the description of one such who, sooner or later, is bound to meet his butcher:

> "Now with Marvin, I think I'm doing extremely well. Initially —I mean before he met me, he looked upon himself as something about the size and value of a worm. But he couldn't bear such an exalted position, it was too burdensome, he just couldn't wear the mantle, he was desperate. And now, in just a few short months, I've reduced him to the point where he's just a sort of an underfed maggot, and he's delighted with the progress we've made. . . . But this won't last, I'm afraid. Marvin's too ambitious. Ultimately, he'll want me to step on him entirely, just lower my heel, so to speak, and grind him out of existence altogether. However, I haven't actually signed on for that. . . . Besides, Marvin can't afford to be murdered, not on his salary. I suppose if he's lucky, somebody might lose control some day and do the thing for free. But not me. I know my work."

As mentioned earlier, a great many straights also practice S&M, but minus the fancy dress and with considerably more caution. With them it usually occurs in reasonably secure circumstances—between lovers or between "reputable" call girls and their clients. Hardly any straight pain-seekers are reckless or desperate enough to search for tormentors in the back alleys of a warehouse district. It takes a highly developed self-destructive streak to attempt that.

"It could be regarded as the ultimate outgrowth of what is essentially a hothouse culture," said gay psychologist and counselor Stan Heilig. "Homosexuals have been forced to provide their own social and economic structure, which is held together from the inside because of pressure from without. This makes for a ghetto climate within the structure and fosters the kind of aberrations of which the leather cult represents an extreme—the *reductio ad absurdum* of symbolized masculinity."

Perhaps it is the absence of strong outside pressures that accounts for the remarkably low homicide rate among lesbians as compared with male homosexuals. Criminologists have not been able to explain why female inverts—who are prone to the same passions as their male counterparts—so rarely end up murdering each other. To be sure, there is plenty of violence—brawls, beatings, slashings, assaults—in the lesbian world, but hardly ever does it have fatal consequences. And, at least in our time, there has occurred among lesbians nothing resembling the systematized mass murders of male gays.* Some lesbian sex roles, like the relationship between "bull dykes" and other "fems," entail a certain amount of physical bullying but seldom the theatrical cruelty of the leather boys.

When lesbians kill, their victims are almost always straights and the reasons nonsexual. The most spectacular lesbian homicide in recent years occurred during a prison break in April 1974 that had all the earmarks of dozens of such breaks staged by male convicts. Three young women—Brenda Spencer, 24, Lucille Smith, 25, and Essie Mae Willock, 20—escaped from the Kentucky Correctional Institution near Louisville after battering one guard with a broomstick and spraying another with Mace. Although the girls were serving time for relatively minor felonies, they were known as "hard cases," and set about proving it the moment they got out.

The trio first captured a pickup truck and forced the driver to strip and run off naked. Then they broke into a house, where they changed their clothes and stole two pistols. They drove to Brinkley, in southeastern Arkansas, held up a grocery, and took the contents of the cash register plus all the cans of beer in the little store. When police officer Morris Greenwalt stopped their speeding truck about twenty miles away, on Interstate 40, a single shot hit him the moment he stepped from his car. Then two of the women jumped out, tore the service revolver from his holster, and emptied seven shots into him.

* One lesbian, however, piled up the possibly most gruesome murder record in history. Transylvanian Countess Elizabeth Bathory (1555–1615) tortured and killed between 200 and 650 young peasant girls in her castle at Csejthe, sometimes bathing in their blood. She was tried by a Royal Hungarian court in 1611 and walled up in her bedchamber, where she died after four years.

Two hours later they descended on a lone farmhouse, catching a family at supper. Squads of Arkansas state troopers, who were following on their heels, surrounded the building. One of the girls yelled, "Stand off or we'll kill everybody in here!" They held guns to the heads of the farmer and the grandmother, but the troopers merely backed some distance away and maintained their ring.

The stalemate continued through half the night, the girls growing progressively drunker, fingering their weapons and cursing, while police spotlights played on the windows. Finally, their nerves gave way. They tossed out their guns and filed through the door with their hands in the air.

In court the trio looked younger than their actual ages. Small, round-featured, and long-haired, they seemed quite unlike the popular image of "convict dykes." But they put up a brave and noisy front. The three alternately barked like dogs and screamed for heroin, although none was an addict. They held hands, kissed one another on the lips, and grinned at the newsmen: "Yeah, we're lesbians." Brenda Spencer and Lucille Smith received life sentences for the killing of Morris Greenwalt. Essie Mae Willock got off with eleven years.

The reason why the lesbian world has produced few of the dangerous grotesqueries of male homosexual society may be that it was never a genuine outlaw culture. Lesbians have always enjoyed a privileged—almost accepted—position. Why this was so remains one of the mysteries of modern jurisprudence. The fact is that legislators somehow left them out of the numerous statutes framed against male deviates— possibly because most Victorian politicians didn't know they existed, at least not in any appreciable numbers. Whatever the reason, this oversight rendered female homosexuals immune to legal persecution. They did not live under the constant threat of blackmail and the unceasing fear of exposure, imprisonment, and subsequent loss of livelihood. In consequence, their community, by and large, didn't develop the paranoid overtones of the male set. They were less closely knit; therefore, less inclined toward collective hysteria, less haunted by the feeling of being outcasts. Even the minority of virulent man-haters among them were untinged by self-hatred, which is the emotion most likely to engender violence in its ultimate form.

8

Ghettocide

There is a danger that U. S. society is dividing
into those who can buy the new life-style and those
who are left. A lot of people will simply be relegated
to those empty holes, the urban cores.
   —Rand Corporation demographer Peter Morrison

Coming back here was just like the war hadn't
stopped. People keep getting killed all around you.
Except the pay is worse and you're never due
for no R and R.
   —Vietnam veteran Jefferson Aldridge

The man's scream and the firecracker pop of the shot rang
out almost simultaneously along the leprous tenements of
Chicago's Woodlawn section. The man, bent double, raced
frantically across the street and crawled under a parked car.
His pursuer, clutching a revolver, followed more slowly and
lost sight of his prey in the darkness. A young girl darted
out from a doorway and pointed at the car. "There he is—
under there," she yelled. The gunman waved his thanks.
Then he kneeled down and emptied his weapon into the
wounded man's face. The girl gave a shrill, childlike giggle
and scampered around the next corner, the gunman melted
into the night.

By the time a police squad car and an ambulance had
arrived, the victim—half his skull blown away—had long ago
stopped twitching. A crowd gathered, hooting, jeering, and
jostling, playfully hurling bottles at the ambulance. They
laughed uproariously whenever the attendants ducked. The
patrolmen made no attempt to find witnesses among the
spectators, and none came forward. The corpse was loaded
into the ambulance and whisked away, leaving the gutter
stained red.

The bloodstains on the curb, which remained visible until the rain washed them off, lasted longer than any official interest in the victim or his slayer. To the Chicago Police Department the incident meant merely another statistical digit—one more ghetto murder among hundreds. Neither the law nor the ghetto dwellers felt greatly concerned over whether or not it was solved.

The exact location of the killing is irrelevant; it could have occurred in the corresponding areas of any of twenty cities, taken the same course, and reached the same denouement. The significance lay in the fact that all the participants, except two policemen, were black, and that all displayed an identical degree of callousness. For therein lies the germ of the sickness that is turning ever-larger regions of urban America into canyons of fear: a silent agreement between the establishment and its stepchildren that murder doesn't matter very much, At least not so long as they commit it only among themselves.

This agreement, though never formulated and hardly ever discussed, is one of the oldest social compacts in the nation, dating back to the very first enclaves set aside for underprivileged minorities. The basic text runs something like this: You will live in the most dismal, crowded, and dilapidated portions of town, receive the worst conceivable health care, sanitation services, and educational facilities, and suffer the highest disease, accident, and infant-mortality rates in the country. In return, we will allow you to assault, rape, maim, and kill one another with a minimum of interference on our part. This will be so in order to induce you to work hard, long, and cheerfully so that you or your children might one day move out of your enclave into a better one—thus making room for the next batch of underprivileged.

In a brutal fashion the compact proved eminently effective throughout most of American history. For, while it contained precious little comfort, it included a realizable hope. It defined ghetto existence as essentially transient—a form of purgatory through which one generation of underdogs would pass before the next one attained the nirvana of middle-class comfort elsewhere. You could work your way out, providing you expended enough energy. Work was the key that lowered the invisible barriers that hemmed you in.

Strangely enough this was a luxury concept of upward mobility, possible only in a nation with immense growing space and a continually expanding economy. Sometime during the 1950s, however, it had quite obviously begun to fail. The economy was still expanding, but automation and other factors were eliminating those millions of unskilled jobs that the ghetto inhabitants needed to make their escape. The gates slammed shut, leaving behind them a ghetto population far more handicapped than any of their predecessors. The vast majority of them were black, and the triple bind of color prejudice, lack of education, and shrinking job markets was to prove an insurmountable hurdle. From a transitory stage the ghetto environment became a permanent hell, with no relief in sight.

Furthermore, hell was bursting at the seams. Floods of newcomers, streams of people even poorer and less able to cope than those already inside, kept pouring in. Blacks from the rural South, Puerto Ricans, Mexicans increased the pressure on the available acreage while bringing nothing except a high birthrate. Since the underprivileged could no longer rise out of the ghetto, they spilled over its edges, expanding its borders and immediately transforming each overrun territory into yet another ghetto. With every added square mile the claustrophobic rage inside them mounted, the prisons grew, while remaining prisons. Meanwhile, in response to the infection of larger and larger city areas with ghetto blight, more and more of the middle class fled to the suburbs. New York constitutes the prime example of this urban disease. Fifteen years ago, the desolation known as the South Bronx lay separated from the other called Harlem by the prosperous East Side of Manhattan. Today the South Bronx forms the northernmost spearhead of a chain of festering slums that begin at Spanish Harlem, run into Harlem proper, stretch across the river to become the South Bronx, and inexorably creep north toward Westchester.

As the ghettos burst open like rotting sacks, their jungle violence engulfed the adjoining districts and beyond. For, although the optimistic note had vanished from the compact, the part about the semi-toleration of mayhem still holds true to an astonishing degree. The result is a homicide rate so hideously out of scale with the rest of the country that we have to classify it with a specially coined term: ghettocide. In round figures, it means that a black male ghetto dweller is ten times as likely to get murdered as a white man, a black female five times as likely to get raped as a white woman, and either of them four times as likely to get assaulted as a white.

Statisticians frequently point out that well over half of our killings are perpetrated by blacks, but they do not quite so frequently add that nine times out of ten their victims are likewise black. Among young black males today, homicide is the second leading cause of death. Roughly 20 percent of *all* deaths in that age group stem from criminal violence—a ratio unmatched anywhere else in the Western Hemisphere.* Furthermore, the rate of intraracial murder is rising much faster than our overall homicide toll.

The newspapers of both races tend to skirt the psychic impact of this black-on-black carnage, albeit for different reasons. The white press knows that its readers worry about black crime only when it affects *them*. Black papers prefer to dodge the issue because they consider it "too sensitive"; they fear it may cause further stigmatization of their race. Together they have created what resembles a conspiracy of semi-silence surrounding one of the most explosive problems of our time. They are chiefly responsible for the wondrous ignorance of most whites concerning the terror haunting black communities—terror far starker than what they suffer.

Not many Detroit whites—and hardly any outside Michigan—are aware that the ghastliest kidnap tragedy in the

---

* The only comparable percentage exists among youths in the slum sections of Bangkok, Thailand, a country whose overall murder rate is proportionally three times that of the U.S.A.

city's annals was an all-black affair. It took place in December 1973 and cost the lives of two little boys, one of whom was familiar to millions of TV watchers. They were the 699th and 700th homicides in Detroit that year. Eight-year-old Gerald Craft, possessor of an irresistible urchin grin, became anonymously famous by gobbling huge helpings of fried chicken in a television commercial. On the afternoon of Saturday, December 1, he was playing football with six-year-old Keith Arnold outside the home of his grandmother. Then both boys disappeared and were never again seen alive.

The following day a hoarse telephone voice demanded fifty-three thousand dollars for the return of the children. The police were unsure just why the criminals believed the boys' families could raise that kind of cash. They prepared— and bungled—a stakeout. A fake package of ransom money was dropped at the spot indicated, where two men in another car picked it up. But the tailing police vehicles didn't move fast enough, and the kidnappers' car got away. Two days later the small bodies of Keith and Gerald were found in an open field at Romulus, near Detroit's Metropolitan Airport. Each of them had been shot twice.

The Detroit *News* posted a reward of five thousand dollars and set up a special "Secret Witness" phone number for informants. All the tips that led to the breaking of the case came via this channel. Within a week the police rounded up three men and a teenage girl. Classical products of the Detroit slums—the men—Geary Gilmore, Bryon Smith, and Jerome Holloway—were all twenty-one years old, drug addicts, and semiliterate. The girl, as usually happens, made a statement that clinched their conviction for kidnapping and first-degree murder. All three went to prison with mandatory life sentences.

The three slayers exactly fit the stereotype whites hold of the perpetrators of "black violence." Actually, they were nothing of the kind. They planned the murders as part of a felony for profit whereas the overwhelming majority of intra-black mayhem is senseless, purposeless, unpremeditated, and rooted in badly bruised egos. As Dr. Alvin F. Poussaint, author of *Why Blacks Kill Blacks*, pointed out: "You have a release of anger that's being directed against each other. . . . A lot of black killings are struggles over self esteem; who's going to have the last word, who put who down, that sort of thing."

In the worst of New York's three Harlem precincts—the 28th—roughly one out of every five hundred residents ends up a homicide victim. The overall American ratio, by comparison, is one in every ten thousand; the English ratio is one in every two hundred thousand. More than a third of these ghetto killings occur during bar fights, street brawls, arguments at parties or family gatherings. The reasons are often so ludicrously trivial that they wouldn't have caused more than a raised eyebrow anywhere outside the pressure-cooker atmosphere of the ghetto.

In a tavern on West 120th Street, two old drinking buddies were arguing about whose turn it was to buy the next round. One called the other a "tightwad." The man pulled a "Saturday-night special" from his hip pocket and pumped five slugs into his friend; the sixth shot misfired. The same night, on the same street, two teenage boys pushed a nine-year-old off a sixth-floor rooftop because "he spit out near us." Two blocks away, at a family dinner at which nothing stronger than coffee was drunk, three men were discussing cars. One of them, a garage mechanic and the father of four children, told his brother-in-law, "You don't know nothing about cars anyway." The brother-in-law picked up a carving knife and jabbed it into the mechanic's eye, piercing his brain and killing him instantly. Seconds later the entire apartment became a battlefield, with seven people brandishing knives, hurling bottles, and throwing plates. Apart from the secondary consequences of one penniless widow and four fatherless children, the results were: One man was dead, another had a cracked skull, and a small child was permanently disfigured by deep gashes in her face.

Blacks number only about 12 percent of the national population, but they form 52 percent of our homicide victims. Most of them are killed ostensibly for reasons as paltry as those mentioned above—"ostensibly" because the actual causes are rather different. Chicago author and television personality Vernon Jarrett put his finger on the situation when he told an interviewer:

> The kind of crimes we are now seeing are something wholly new in the black community. We used to take pride, talking among ourselves, that blacks didn't commit the kind of sick, psychotic murders that we saw white people doing. We had to watch out for what blacks did to each other; we knew whites didn't care. There used to be a strict black code of morality: "It doesn't matter how poor you are, there is no excuse for doing damage to another black person." But this old ethic has been knocked away. The new ethic is "Do anything you damn please; do the worst things that whites do." What is wrong with the black community is just what's wrong in the rest of the country at large. These problems just break out first in the black community. Whites try to ignore what's happening in black areas but these troubles eventually break out to threaten the whole society, just like narcotics did.

What is happening is that a number of refinements infused into ghetto life over the past decades have dramatically increased both the level of desperation and the means of venting it. Together with mass unemployment, which has ceased to be a short-term, "cyclical" phenomenon, came the influx of hard drugs. Slum dwellers have always sought solace in alcohol, which—however detrimental—was at least cheap. The new soporifics are illegal and therefore vastly more expensive, giving addiction to them an added razor edge.

Simultaneously, an avalanche of armaments poured into the ghetto areas, ranging from millions of the shoddy bargain pistols called "Saturday-night specials" to sophisticated hardware like automatic rifles, machine guns, and bazookas. Along with them arrived tens of thousands of jobless, uprooted Vietnam veterans—men who had been trained not only in the use and maintenance of these weapons but also in the killer mentality essential for their utilization. To make matters still more drastic, a large proportion of these vets also brought home full-fledged heroin habits.

Thus, the technical basis for a bloodbath was assembled.

It dovetailed with just the right psychological and political stimuli to bring it about. One of them was television—a device Marshall McLuhan quite rightly rated alongside Gutenberg's printing press in revolutionary potential. For while the ghetto is a sealed world that prevents outsiders from looking in, television enables its residents to look *out* at endlessly tantalizing vistas of possessions and lifestyles enjoyed by others and unobtainable by them. The video box turned every ghetto denizen into a hungry kid with his nose glued to a candy-store window.

During the civil-rights surge of the 1960s there was a flare of wild hope, which flickered for a brief moment but then quickly burned to ashes in the dismal reaction that followed. The only legacy left by that shining glimpse of Camelot was a handful of disastrous judicial sops thrown at black politicians to give them *something* to show their constituents. The total effect of these sops—bail "reforms," eased parole regulations, reduced sentences, and furloughs for major offenders—benefited no one except black criminals. It lessened their risks, put more of them back on the streets, and weakened protection for their victims without in any way helping to diminish the social causes of their criminality. The people penalized were precisely those trying to survive in ghettos without resorting to violence.

Moreover, as if to insure that their numbers should dwindle, the entertainment industry launched its wave of "blaxploitation" movies. It is difficult to convey the sheer godawfulness of these kitsch concoctions to a person who hasn't seen one. Churned out on paper-doll budgets, populated by comic-strip characters, plotted for a grasp of retarded twelve-year-olds, they voice a ceaseless strident hymn in praise of violence—*black* violence. The featured ideal is the flip, detached mass murderer; the climax is an orgiastic massacre. Although the victims come disguised as dope pushers, crooked politicians, Mafiosi, or loansharks, their nomenclature is quite irrelevant: They are targets, clay pigeons, created for the express purpose of being mown down, blown up, groin-slashed, knifed, incinerated, and throttled by the "mean street brother" or his female equivalent, the "tough mama." A good proportion of the casualties—sometimes most of them—are white, and audiences roar loudest when the paleface baddy gets it in the guts and kicks off convulsively, pumping gore. But the most important thing is that the disher-outer of wholesale death is black and that he or she never show the slightest spark of compassion, emotion, or even undue interest. That's cool, man.

Aimed exclusively at street audiences, ignored by reviewers, often grossing twelve times their production costs, these humanoid cartoon cacophonies of bangs, groans, screams, musical burpings, and speech-balloon dialogue elicit a powerful sense of identification among their intended audiences—especially the young. Dr. Alvin Poussaint has described how black youngsters in Brooklyn drastically increased their use of cocaine after the movie *Super Fly* glamorized the drug, and how practically the entire student body of a Los Angeles high school started wearing gold coke-spoon necklaces after the West Coast debut of the film.

Stimulating dope habits is a minor sin of these cinematic time bombs. According to Police Commander Joe DiLeonardi, head of the Chicago homicide section, his department investigated a series of unrelated murders and robbery-murders in which the methods and language used by the slayers were exact copies from recent blaxploitation films. In a number of killings the murderer announced himself by snarling, "Nigger Charlie is here," following the words he had heard on the screen.

There has not been, as yet, an imitation of Pam Grier's little subtlety in *Foxy Brown* in which she presents a pickle jar containing one baddy's genitals to another baddy . . . but give us time. Meanwhile we have the case of a Los Angeles black who tried to perform one of *Shaft's* casual acrobatics by tying a rope to a rooftop chimney and attempting to swing from it into an open window. He smashed into the wall instead and fell to the ground, sustaining multiple fractures of his spine and pelvis.

An uninitiated observer might conclude that all these

paeans to black mayhem are Goebbelslike propaganda efforts aimed at preparing ghetto minds for a forthcoming holocaust of the honkies. But if you consider that they are, in fact, made by white entrepreneurs with no motivation other than box-office bucks, you have to admit that there exists a border-land where plain greed merges with lunacy. You may also have to concede that Lenin had a definite point in stating "When we come to hang the world's second-last capitalist, the last capitalist will sell us the rope."

The violence spawned by this conglomeration of factors has vented itself largely within the ghettos—so far. The reason is proximity: Since most of the outbursts are unpremeditated, the logical victim is someone living nearby. But even when it reaches out beyond the ghetto confines, the likeliest targets are people inhabiting adjoining areas—in many instances those who have just emerged from ghettos themselves. Among them the fear of violence is probably greater than in any other demographic group.

Trinidad, in the northeast sector of Washington, D.C., is haunted by this fear. A lower-middle-class neighborhood on the hilly west side of the Anacostia River, Trinidad consists mostly of family homes owned by their occupants and has few local criminals. But across Florida Avenue runs the H Street corridor, still scarred and scorched by the 1968 riots that left most of its stores blackened shells, and from there death creeps into Trinidad—the mindless amok death that is the trademark of the ghetto.

Six times in two years it struck within a one-block radius of a particular shop on Florida Avenue. On the night of February 7, 1976, it struck the shop itself. The Berkley Farms Fish & Poultry Market was a black family enterprise. The Tillmans were hard workers, and Samuel Tillman, Jr., stood behind the counter from eight in the morning till midnight. At 12:30 A.M., Sunday morning a neighborhood boy panted into the fire station opposite shouting, "There's something wrong over there. There's blood all over the place."

When the police reached the scene they found three men

sprawled in a heap next to the frozen-food counter. All three
had been shot in the head and hideously chopped up with a
heavy knife. They were young Sam Tillman, his cousin and
employee Raymond Washington, and a customer named
Charles Scott. They also found a fourth man, still alive but
only just. Benjamin Washington, a cousin of the dead man
who was also employed at the store, had somehow survived
a rain of blows with a machete and a meat cleaver that
smashed into his skull and chest. The killers left him for
dead, but he recovered sufficiently to identify them.

There were three of them—two men and a teenage boy.
Entering shortly before closing time, one of them aimed a
gun at the staff and made them lie face down on the floor
while the others ransacked the premises. Then, one by one,
the men on the floor were shot, stabbed, and hacked. Washington tried to flee, but the teenager slashed him down with
his machete and kept on slashing until he thought he'd killed
him.

Acting on Washington's description, Metropolitan police
surrounded a dilapidated brick building and dragged a man
from his bed at gunpoint. All the tenants of the house were
on welfare, and the place seemed to be held upright by layers
of dirt. A second man and a fifteen-year-old boy were hauled
in within days.

At the trial, Samuel Tillman, Sr., aged seventy-two and
hard of hearing, sat among the spectators like a lost soul.
His deafness saved him from the grisly details of the
slaughter, but his pouched eyes kept staring at the man in
the dock. "I don't know," he murmured over and over, "I
just don't know." He had been robbed three times himself
while he was running the store, but he couldn't comprehend
the massacre. "They always just took the money and got out
fast as they could. That's all they did. Why'd they have to
butcher my boy?" He shook his head with the thin fuzz of
gray hair and repeated, "I just don't know."

For a few weeks the old man kept the Berkley Market
going on his own. Then he sold it and faded into retirement.
Another black business, another piece of hope, had joined

thousands like it in succumbing to black violence. Inevitably they are replaced by the white chain stores, the big corporations with lots of muscle whose managements live elsewhere, who employ armed guards and replace the sales staff as fast as it gets "wasted." Thus, the ghetto underdogs slip down another rung on the ladder, constantly increasing their economic impotence by their reaction to it. As one black grocer, whose shop got torched during the Watts riot, commented, "It's just like cannibals tearing at their own flesh."

Considerable anger against the "cannibals" is now boiling among black elected officials throughout the nation. Unfortunately, little of it is filtering down to street level. There the political rhetoric remains mired in the inane tub thumpers' logic that turns every ghetto thug, rapist, or killer into a political martyr simply because he happens to be poor. What these howling prophets of "Third World Revolution" have forgotten—or perhaps never learned—is that every successful revolutionary movement, from the sans-culottes to the Viet Cong, first dealt swiftly and mercilessly with those among their ranks who injured their own kind. No such development is discernible in the embattled ghettos.

"The problem is ours," declared Joseph B. Williams, administrative judge of New York City's Family Court, at a Harlem community meeting. "The solution needs to be ours." Clarence Guillemet, director of the Dixon Research Center, a black crime-fighting group in New Orleans, announced: "There is a greater acceptance of the black police officer now than there used to be. The black officer used to be a low-level informant. Now he's involved to a higher degree, he's not just an informer or a door-shaker. He can relate better."

Inspectors Rotea Gilford and Earl Sanders, two black homicide detectives on the San Francisco force, could have told him differently. They were investigating the strangulation murders of five young black women over a two-year period starting in 1974 in the Bay View–Hunters Point area, a predominantly black neighborhood. All five had been stripped, sexually assaulted, and strangled with their own pantyhose. The investigators got nowhere, partly because the killer left no clues, but mainly because they received no cooperation from the public. "I know we could break these murders, but the people won't come forward," said Sanders. "They are not walking in off the street and helping us. Once we've found them, they'll tell us what they know. But it's like pulling teeth."

On the same weekend that Jessie May Rose, one of the victims, was throttled, a local woman went night fishing in the bay. She heard a loud commotion—a girl screaming for help—and then saw her running away with a man at her heels. The man caught the yelling girl, dragged her into a van, and drove off. We don't know whether this particular girl was Rose or her attacker the mass strangler. But we do know that neither the fishing lady nor anyone else called the police or breathed a word about the incident. The information surfaced days later, purely by accident.

In January 1974, when Coleman Young gave his inaugural address as the first black mayor of Detroit, he declared: "I issue a warning now to all dope pushers, rip-off artists, and muggers. It is time to leave Detroit. Hit the road!" It didn't quite work out that way. The dope pushers, rip-off artists, and muggers stayed and multiplied. They multiplied so copiously that they dominated the face and character of the city, expanding their old East Side stomping grounds to embrace most of Detroit. The folks who hit the road were the tax-paying middle class, whose departure further impoverished the place. Of course they were merely following the example set by Henry Ford, who made his money in Detroit and then decamped to Dearborn, whence he disseminated phony rustic virtues and the even phonier *Protocols of the Elders of Zion*.

Granted, the exodus from Detroit (which lost 8.4 percent of its population and now has fewer inhabitants than in 1925) began well before Mayor Young took office. Granted, he and all other urban officials are battling the consequences of police indifference combined with police brutality toward black citizens. Granted, there are far too few minority officers in the nation's police forces; granted, the prevalence of poverty, inferior education, gruesome housing, governmental neglect, and a tragic sense of uninvolvement with the country at large. All these causes still don't validate the suicidal lethargy of black communities in tackling the rats gnawing at *their* vitals. It is one thing to know that the white establishment cares little about depredations inside the ghetto; it's quite another to demonstrate that the inhabitants care just as little themselves.

A variety of black anticrime groups have indeed been formed in such cities as Chicago, Philadelphia, New Orleans, and Memphis. They range from regular citizen street patrols to teenage intelligence networks collecting information on dope pushers. But their overall effect has been minimal, both legally and psychologically. Participants can't match the glamor of the pimps and pushers in their Borsalino hats and platform shoes, cane-swinging and swaggering as if the ghetto streets belonged to them—which they do. So what if they slash a few hundred black bodies in the process and poison a million more—not a fraction of the energy and determination used by the pushers in fighting one another has been expended on fighting *them*. The heroin war currently gripping Harlem is being watched from the sidelines by a population as passively unembroiled as if the struggle were taking place in Hollywood.

Basically, the contest is between two types of heroin and their respective dealers, both of them black or Hispanic. The first group is the old guard with Mafia connections, pushing heroin obtained via Mafia channels. The second bunch are young upstarts working independently and importing their supplies from Mexico and the "Golden Triangle" of Thailand, Burma, and Laos. The Turkish stuff is by far the superior product, nearly 90 percent pure and therefore capable of being retailed in an extremely diluted form. The Mexican and Far Eastern drug doesn't stretch nearly so well. But whereas the Turkish-French connection lies in white hands, the Mexican-Asian pipeline is black and Hispanic all the way, and so independent of the whims of Mafia bosses.

Harlem is the distribution center for heroin dealers throughout New York, the source on which the city's estimated 100,000–250,000 users depend for their shots. Control of this center means control of a fabulously profitable trade. The wholesale price of one kilo (2.2 pounds) of heroin ranges from $40,000 to $70,000, depending on purity. This kilo can be diluted or "cut" into 76,000 or more two-grain "bags," sold to addicts for around $8 each. This means a profit of about $500,000 from a single kilo. According to the NYPD's Narcotics Division, some five tons—or 4,500 kilos— of heroin were smuggled into the city during 1975. Such a quantity brings in $2.5–3 *billion* for the dealers—enough money to meet all of Harlem's housing, schooling, and health needs, if it ever found its way into the hands of people willing to use it for such purposes.

This kind of cash is worth any number of corpses. Thus, the old guard of dope racketeers are grimly defending their profits against the newcomers, known as "cowboys." The old dealers have the advantages of wider experience, bigger bankrolls, political contacts, and larger numbers of muscle men. But the upstarts are lean and ravenous as wolves in winter, driven by a searing hunger for wealth that makes them take risks the established fat cats wouldn't consider. Their torpedoes are Southern country boys—not very street-wise but crazily reckless and incredibly brutal. Above all, their gunmen are unknown in Harlem, which enables them to strike with numbing surprise. Again and again in the past hungry lightweights have pulverized satiated heavies who just wished to hold what they had. It may happen once more. So far the score is roughly even. Of the thirty-six or so distributors and importers who were shot, strangled, drowned in the Passaic River, had their throats cut, or simply disappeared, about half belonged to each faction.

If the cowboys win, they will make Harlem's heroin traffic an all-black business for the first time since the trade began. Their denser admirers will undoubtedly consider this a triumph, but it would be hard to imagine a more melancholy victory. Harlem would benefit no more than Brooklyn benefited from the riches of the Mafia. The only possible result would be a further increase in the addiction rate—meaning yet more theft, robbery, and murder. The concern of the white city fathers over such a development was shown by their initial reaction to the heroin war. In June 1975, just as the struggle got under way, they trimmed the Police Narcotics Division from 450 men to 312. Most of the dismissed officers were blacks and Puerto Ricans—the only ones who could effectively infiltrate the new drug rings.

If the city is not doing much about the dope pestilence, Harlemites themselves are doing less, to wit, practically nothing. Leather-lunged black militants, after years of thundering against social evils from street corners, have yet to take any action against the worst of them. Apparently it hasn't occurred to them that at least part of the solution lies in their own hands. Quite possibly an armed, disciplined, and strongly motivated body like the Black Muslims could chase the pushers out of the district; certainly they could make drug dealing exceedingly difficult. Yet the crusading Nation of Islam keeps coexisting with the heroin hustlers, and quite a number of its members indulge in occasional jolts themselves.

Farther north, across the Harlem River, the inhabitants of the South Bronx are drawing attention to their plight by burning down the neighborhood. What's more, they're doing it in cahoots with their absentee landlords, which makes it the most original firebug operation in history. But, whereas the landlords and realtors have definite aims in view, the locals know little beyond the fact that they want *out*.

These five square miles of territory have been described as "perhaps the closest that men have yet come to creating hell on earth." The fires of this hell have been burning for ten years at a steadily increasing pace. Now they flare at a rate of thirty-three a day, even hitting a record forty outbreaks during one summer afternoon. Nearly all of them are arson jobs, set for a variety of reasons. Sometimes they are ignited on whispered orders from the owners; sometimes for looting purposes; sometimes as gestures of protest; and sometimes purely for entertainment. Occasionally a few families or kids or oldsters or derelict winos burn right along with the houses, but that isn't intentional.

As a slum, the South Bronx represents something special: an exhibition piece demonstrating the ultimate stage of urban decay. Harlem at least stands more or less intact, but the South Bronx resembles nothing so much as the bomb-blasted ruins of Berlin and Hamburg after World War II. From the air you can see the tenement blocks gashed by huge brownish patches indicating where buildings once stood. At street level you notice that many of the blocks are burned-out shells—uninhabited, stripped of every pipe, beam, or fitting that could be sold. There is even the characteristic smell of a blitzed city: burned wood and paintwork mingling with the odor of hundreds of thousands of loose bricks lying in heaps wherever you look. You can look up and down entire blocks without spotting an unsmashed window. Every other front door seems to hang on broken hinges. All around you stretch the rubble lots, forming a landscape of their own— a fantasy built of tangled wire, splintered boards, charred scraps of furniture, rusty bedsprings, and greenish puddles, populated by rats. The rats of the South Bronx are special too. They behave not exactly as if they already owned the place, but as if they didn't quite own it *yet*—like impatient new tenants badgering the old ones to hurry up and get out so that they can finally move in and take over.

At any time of the day or night, there are pillars of white smoke rising skyward, denoting fresh fires. The burning buildings are mostly, but not always, empty skeletons. Aided by the circumstance that one fifth of the homes are without water, packed tenements catch ablaze as well. Yet even when the fire trucks arrive as lifesavers, they are often greeted with fusillades of bricks and bottles, occasionally with shots from the rooftops. Then the firemen, black and white, go to work with such expressions of concentrated loathing and disgust as you'll rarely see on human faces.

Too many people, it seems, stand to profit from fires: the

owners of abandoned houses, out to collect fire insurance; the dudes actually starting the fires and getting paid for it by the owners; the looters; the tenement dwellers, who *may* collect the relocation allowances that the city gives fire victims, and possibly get a somewhat better home out of the deal as well; finally, certain real-estate developers who would love to see the whole district cleared of its unpalatable populace so that they can rebuild it into a nice middle-class neighborhood fifteen minutes from midtown Manhattan and featuring rents the unpalatables can't afford. There have been charges that some firemen themselves are kindling fires whenever new budget cuts threaten their jobs.*

Slowly but steadily, the South Bronx *is* becoming emptier. About 40,000 of its 400,000 residents have already moved out and with every new fire people in adjacent blocks pack up and go, knowing that their turn may be next. Most of them head northward, biting into the upper Bronx, turning a once-prosperous region into a replica of the stone jungle they left behind. For, regardless of where they migrate, they carry their afflictions along with them: About 40 percent live on welfare; 30 percent of those able to work have no jobs; perhaps 25 percent can't read or write, in English or any other language; and a conservatively estimated 35,000 are drug addicts.

Roughly 80 percent of the inhabitants are black, Puerto Rican, Cuban, or belong to other groups termed "Hispanic." The rest are ethnic whites, mostly Jewish or Italian, surviving in small scattered pockets like islanders amid rising swampwater. The pall of doom hanging over these enclaves is so thick you'd swear you can feel it. In winter the streets empty of white faces around five o'clock, because it grows dark then. Old people store garbage in their apartments for days because they are afraid to take it outside. Some never go to bed without moving a heavy chest against the front door. Many have abandoned their bedrooms and sleep in

---

* A curious parallel existed in Constantinople during the declining years of the Turkish Empire. There the term "fireman" could denote either a person who extinguished fires or one who started them, and the two jobs were frequently interchangeable.

the foyer in order to be near the door and a chance of escape in case "they" break in through a rear window. "They" are the Puerto Ricans and blacks who ambush, battle, and murder each other on a scale reminiscent of the tribal warfare of New Guinea headhunters—the difference being that whereas headhunters spare the elderly, in the South Bronx the old are prime targets. As one sixteen-year-old killer explained, "They can't fight and they can't run, and some is even too scared to holler."

One sure indication that the city has written off the South Bronx is the shortage of policemen. The 41st Precinct, covering half the area, ranks as the most violent in New York and musters 364 uniformed officers. This works out at one cop per 469 residents. The ratio for the metropolis as a whole is one policeman to 243 people. This means that the residents most in need of protection are actually getting little more than half the police power allocated to other regions.

"Protection" is a rather optimistic term when applied to the South Bronx. A good part of the time policemen there are busy protecting *themselves* against various forms of attack, including mass assaults on their station houses. Their role could be compared to that of a garrison force in hostile territory, trying to keep a lid on things as best they can. Their quarters blend well with the universal squalor surrounding them. The 41st Precinct house on Simpson Street, nicknamed "Fort Apache," is a dark, dank cavern built seventy years ago, its windows covered by thick slabs of concrete. In his book, *Fort Apache*, police captain Tom Walker described his first visit to the locker room:

> It was in the basement; more correctly, it should have been called a swamp. To reach my locker, I had to wade through half a foot of putrid, mosquito-infested water. Raw sewage poured into the room, and several large, menacing rodents sought neutral corners only when I began to growl at them. Across from the locker room, a door had a sign above it that read LUNCH ROOM.

As the torched-out southerners swarm into the upper Bronx, they dislodge the residents already there. The struggle isn't difficult, merely tragic, for the people in their path are mainly the descendants of Jewish immigrants who had escaped the slums of lower Manhattan. They had prospered, and for about one lifetime the Bronx's Grand Concourse reigned as the Champs-Élysées of New York's manufacturing set. Today, the trash-reeking streets just a few blocks away become no man's land, gang territory, as soon as the sun goes down. The bourgeoisie are departing as fast as they can. Left behind are the elderly trying to live on Social Security while clinging to their familiar apartments, their memories, and what remains of their dignity. Their chief role now is to provide prey for the ghetto predators. About twenty-two were murdered and about six hundred of them were beaten and robbed during 1976.

"The end will come when all the old, white middle-class people are finally dead and gone, and the problem will be passed on," Detective Donald Gaffney told the Washington Post. "These are the last of the vulnerable around here, and when they're gone, this neighborhood will go the same way the South Bronx went. The whole place will fall to ruin."

The process resembles a demented game of musical chairs, but one in which more and more of the players are leaving the circle and sitting down elsewhere.

Since 1970 New York has lost half a million people and 300,000 jobs to this form of urban attrition, which is pushing the city into bankruptcy. The city fathers look on with the kind of resigned fatalism with which the Chinese once viewed the Yellow River floods that drowned a few million peasants at irregular intervals. *The gods gave and the gods take away* . . . and the gods are presumably burning down the South Bronx.

Illegal immigrants, slipping into the United States at a rate of more than one million a year, are simultaneously among the main causes and the main victims of this galloping "ghettofication." They are causes inasmuch as they place immense pressure on the job and housing market; victims inasmuch as their helplessness invites physical attack and economic exploitation in equal degrees. Coming from the

Philippines, from Taiwan and Hong Kong, from Central and
South America, from the Caribbean countries, there are about
eight million "illegals" in the country. They fill the bottom—
the rock bottom—of the economic barrel.

Easily the poorest among them are also the most numerous: the Mexicans. They have the easiest access to the U.S.,
although "easy" in their case is a strictly relative term. Most
of them come through the "corridor": the five-and-a-half-mile
stretch of California frontier that runs from the San Ysidro–
Tijuana port of entry to the Pacific Ocean. It is bleak and
lonely terrain, with a few scattered farmhouses, sprawling
asparagus fields, narrow dirt roads, and to the east the steep
Otay Mesa, gashed with overgrown canyons and gorges and
swarming with jackrabbits and rattlesnakes. There are plenty
of hiding places, and the chain-link fence separating Mexico
and the United States has enough holes to admit an army
battalion.

The main obstacle is the Border Patrol, equipped with
four-wheel-drive vehicles, walkie-talkies, and "starlight" tele-
scopes that can pick up moving figures in semi-darkness at
four hundred yards. But the Border Patrol is so short of manpower that they consider themselves successful if they catch
a quarter of the illegals crossing over in any given month. "It
can be damned frustrating," a patrolman told me. "They
come over in groups of twenty to a hundred. And often we
stop one group and have to watch a bigger group get past
because we just don't have the agents to handle both. Talk
about the boy with his finger in the dike. . . . Only we don't
have a dike here. It's a sieve."

The Border Patrol is a minor worry for the illegals. If they
get caught, they merely get taken back to Mexico. The real
predators don't wear uniforms. They are the border bandits—
the young Chicano thugs from San Diego and Los Angeles
who prowl the corridor at night. Primarily they're after loot,
the pitiful possessions and small sums of money the illegals
carry. But they are also indulging a perverse fratricidal hatred
for their victims. They call them *pollos* (chickens) or "Tijuana boys" and blame them for most of the misery in the

barrios. Above all they hate them for being even poorer and more ignorant than themselves.

The crossings are carefully organized, but underneath the guise of organization often lies a trap. The aliens pay a "coyote" or "arranger" so much per head on the Mexican side. The coyote furnishes transportation and a "mule": the driver and guide who take them across. Frequently the coyote is paid double, once by the aliens and again by the grower who wants to employ the aliens at starvation wages. The mule, too, often collects double rates. He is paid by the coyote and, in many cases, by the bandits for leading his charges into their hands.

The hoodlums don't merely rob their fellow-Mexicans, they delight in pistol-whipping them, in breaking their bones, and occasionally in knifing them. In the winter of 1975 they waylaid a group of five aliens, including a young peasant couple. The thugs stripped all of them naked, then took turns raping the seventeen-year-old wife. When her husband protested, they tied him up, placed a shotgun between his legs, and blew off his testicles. The man bled to death during the night.

Between 1975 and 1976 there were 251 robberies, 7 rapes, and 7 murders in that small belt of borderland, and these totals include only the fraction of incidents that are reported. "These are the same young thugs who make up the youth gangs in the barrios," said Manuel Prida, a Mexican-American social worker in East Los Angeles. "And they continue hounding the illegals after they've made it into the country. The gangs stake out their territories in the barrios, and naturally those *pollos* don't know about these turfs. So they blunder in and the gang members shoot them. Or firebomb the hovels they live in. Well, after a while the 'Tijuana boys' also get guns and start shooting back. So we have a feud that goes on and on—more people killed, more houses bombed— all that waste among people who can't afford waste. Maybe one feud gets settled, then the next batch of illegals arrive and the whole shit starts over again."

The basis of all this bloodshed is not some territorial im-

perative but poverty and hopelessness. With every fresh
swarm of illegals, the position of the native Chicanos gets
a little worse. The swarms keep coming because even the
grimmest American poverty is plush compared with Mexican
conditions. "Maybe they have only a rusty water tap in their
American house and only cold water. In their Mexican village they have no taps at all. If your water has come from
one communal well, a tap in your house is luxury," Prida
explained.

Leonel Castillo, controller of Houston, Texas, whose Span-
ish-speaking residents have more than tripled since 1900,
sympathizes with the plight of the illegals, but adds: "All
our successes in dealing with poverty and other problems are
wiped out by the new arrivals. The bottom of the barrel is
always filling up."

The people benefiting from this influx are the produce
growers of California's Imperial and San Joaquin Valleys.
Some of them pay coyotes in Mexico fifteen dollars a head
for illegals delivered straight to their farms. It's a bargain
price, for these modern peons provide the cheapest, most
docile work force a rancher could dream of. Once on the
farms, they are effectively isolated. The threat of arrest and
deportation keeps them confined. They can't read newspapers, and they know nothing of agricultural labor laws.
They'll toil ten, twelve hours a day for a pittance and their
keep, while the season lasts.

In the cities the illegals can move freely but are possibly
even worse off. The clothing sweatshops pay them around
twenty dollars a week for piecework, rising to perhaps fifty
dollars as their skill improves. On this they must house and
feed themselves. How is their business.

As the poverty pressure in the barrios—the Mexican ghettos—mounts, so does the possession of firearms. This is a
uniquely American phenomenon, a local application of
Goering's famous "Guns before butter" dictum that keeps
the level of armaments in our slums rising to keep up with
the unemployment figures. A man may not be able to
obtain a job, a pair of shoes, or even a balanced diet, but

he can always, by one means or another, get hold of a pistol. In many cases he has to if he wishes to stay alive, for the barrio feuds that usually erupt among teenagers quickly embroil their elders. Thus, the same brutalization process that has already engulfed Harlem is at work in East Los Angeles.

"There used to be a time when even the toughest gang kids had three strict 'no-nos,' " said Lieutenant Hayden Finley of the Juvenile Bureau. "First, never hurt a mother. Second, don't hurt little kids. Third, never kill a father figure, especially a very old man. But now they've got no rules. None at all."

The favorite style of warfare today is to shoot up a house with the entire family inside. Chances are you'll hit *someone*—it doesn't matter much who. A thirteen-year-old Chicana named Dolores gave me a description of what this mode of attack feels like on the receiving end.

My small sister heard them coming about ten o'clock, I think. We just had time to duck into the back room. We all lay down on the floor. My mother grabbed my baby brother out of his cradle and lay on top of him. They started shooting and they shot out all the windows and they shot holes in the door. The vase with the flowers got smashed and the picture of my grandfather in his uniform and all the dishes on the table. I could hear the bullets hitting in the walls and I got down real low on the floor, as low as I could. I tried not breathing, but I couldn't do it. Not for very long.

After a while it got quiet. My father told us not to move and he crawled into the front room and looked out. Then he waved to us that they'd gone, so I looked out too. All the neighbors were looking out through the curtains. There was nobody in the street any more, just a lot of glass and stuff. The neighbors were shouting. Then I saw that my mother had blood all over her and one of her ears was hanging down, like dangling. She didn't cry at all. But my father, he cried. I'd never seen him cry. He was always laughing. At the hospital they couldn't put my mother's ear back on again. She only has one ear now, but she keeps her hair over the place.

My older brother, Largo, said he knew the guys who had been shooting. They were from another barrio. One of them was called Ray, I think. Now we sleep in the cellar every night. I don't like it. But my brother said he and some fellows will go look for that Ray and shoot *him*. Maybe then my father will laugh again.

9

No Rhyme and Little Reason

---

*Me and Wayne, we was going to cut off his little
finger and send it home to his mama, and write a note
saying, "This is all that's left of your little baby."*
—Georgia death-row inmate Carl Isaacs

Kenneth Bryant, aged seventeen, an alcoholic since the age
of eight, was very drunk when he walked into the 7-11 store
on Richmond Highway in Groveton, Virginia. Drunkenness
for him didn't mean lurching and mumbling; rather, it meant
a dull, nagging, incoherent rage, like a toothache of the
psyche, that simultaneously drove him on and muffled him
against reason—what little he had.

He was the only customer in the store on that hot August
night in 1976. As he took a can of grapefruit juice from the
shelf, the night manager, James Cox, came up and said something to him. Bryant looked at him, his young pudding face
expressionless. Then he groped beneath his shirt, drew out a
small pistol, and shot Cox in the chest. The manager ran
toward the back of the store, and Bryant shot him again. Cox
slipped in his own blood, fell down, scrambled up, and was
running when the third bullet hit him. He staggered to the
washroom, slamming the door behind him. Bryant fired twice
more, the slugs ripping through the wood. The manager slid
to the floor and died.

The boy knocked both cash registers from the counter with
a wild sweep of his arm. Cramming thirty dollars into his
pockets and shielding his face, he walked out. Next to the
store he saw a gas station, attended by a small Lebanese man
named Younes. "I thought maybe he'd recognize me," Bryant testified later, "so I pulled my gun. I figured if I pulled
a gun on him, I might as well take his money. I said, 'Give
me your money and turn around. If you say anything, I'll

kill you.' Then I shot him in the back and took about $70 off him. I tried to shoot him again, but there wasn't any more bullets."

Younes survived because Bryant hadn't bothered to check his ammunition. Even when sober, he rarely bothered about details. Early that morning he roused his half brother, at whose home he was staying, and told him he needed a ride to the bus station because he was "in a bit of trouble." Bryant didn't offer any further information, but the half brother knew him only too well. He dropped him off at the Greyhound stop, then telephoned the police. At noon that day detectives arrested Bryant as he was standing in line at the downtown bus terminal in Washington, D.C., waiting for a bus to take him home to Kentucky.

Five months later, Kenneth Bryant came up for trial on charges of murder, robbery, and malicious wounding. His court-appointed attorney had spruced him up as much as possible. The boy's lank hair was brushed over his face in a youthful cowlick; his stance was straight, and his clothes clean. Nevertheless, even the Virginia jury had difficulty understanding the hoarse Southern drawl he seemed to have stolen from the pages of *Tobacco Road*. Moreover, there was his record, a chronicle of society's failure not merely to rehabilitate Bryant but to make any impression on him at all.

Born in a dreary western Kentucky factory town, he was one of six children whose father had an extensive rap sheet. In winter his mother worked at stripping tobacco, while the old man supposedly looked after the brood. One day she returned home to find her husband and the three youngest boys sniffing glue and drinking whiskey. Kenneth was then seven. At nine he was booked on his first breaking-and-entering charge. While on probation he stole—and promptly cracked up—two cars. Between his ninth and sixteenth birthdays he was convicted of thirty-one offenses in his home town, ranging from habitual truancy to carrying concealed weapons. Meanwhile, his father and two older brothers were continually in and out of prison, sometimes sharing the same institutions. The Department of Human Resources considered a foster home for him, but somehow never got around to finding one. It would, in any case, have been a difficult task.

When Bryant left school for good at the age of thirteen, he was a heavily tattooed alcoholic who viewed every fresh stretch behind bars with philosophical detachment. "I'll pull my time" was his standard refrain. The remarkable feature is that he never learned *anything*—not even the basic skills of criminality. He remained as incompetent at burglary, car theft, and shooting as he was at respectable occupations. Prison psychiatrists found his IQ "average," but they may have been stretching a point. His muscular development was far above average. He frequently described himself as a weightlifter, and most people believed him. In 1974, after his sixth spell in a detention center, the youth authorities reported that he had "matured a great deal." Perhaps they were referring to his physique.

Eighteen months later Bryant was back in court—this time, at his own request, charged as an adult. His attorney summarized the predicament everybody felt: "In my opinion there's no benefit in sending him to prison, but there's also no benefit in sending him to a juvenile institution. . . . I don't think we have an institution that's geared for such an individual."

After serving nine months for car theft, Bryant went to Virginia to live with his half brother. This young man had tried to help several members of the family in the past and was willing to make an attempt with Kenneth. He put him to work at a produce stall he owned and kept a sharp eye on his drinking. But on the evening of August 16 his pregnant wife went into labor and he had to take her to the hospital. Kenneth took the opportunity to go on a minor binge, putting away most of a pint of Jim Beam and a dozen beers. And, as he phrased it, "When I get drunk I get mad and stuff."

He arrived home at midnight and decided he needed some grapefruit juice to mix with the whiskey he found in the house. Before going to the 7-11 store one block away, he

took his sister-in-law's small nickel-plated gun, allegedly because the neighborhood kids didn't like him and he was
afraid of being jumped. The store manager, he also alleged,
accused him of shoplifting. Then Kenneth "got mad and
stuff" and the manager—married just two weeks—lay dead.
In a letter from jail to a buddy who was also incarcerated,
Bryant wrote: "Did it come as a surprise to you that I killed
a guy and I probably would have killed two, but I ran out
of bullets? He [Cox] messed with the wrong person."

His court-appointed lawyer put up a gallant fight. He
referred to the murder as "a drunken caper," and declared
that his client was too intoxicated to know what he was
doing. "Kenny is a seventeen-year-old, mixed-up boy—a
seventeen-year-old alcoholic with a father and two older
brothers in and out of jail. . . ." Maybe it was that "Kenny"
that raised the hackles of the jury . . . Kenny with his gunny
and presumably with his rubber ducky. Anyway, they fixed
his sentence at life plus seventy years—a sentence that will
make Kenneth all of thirty-two before he becomes eligible
for parole.

The most disconcerting aspect of this case is that Bryant's
attorney was probably right: The murder *was* a drunken
caper and Kenneth probably was not fully aware of what
he was doing. Moreover, the jury quite possibly even believed him but pretended otherwise because they felt duty-
bound to put the boy away for the maximum stretch in
order to preserve humanity from him. The jurors may have
sensed a truth that the law will not—perhaps cannot—
recognize: that a person who persistently blunders into situations where he is liable to kill is far more dangerous than
another who kills once with cold premeditation. For the
deliberate slayer will, in all likelihood, not kill again, but
the blunderer is apt to claim victims so long as he remains
free to follow his muddled urges.

Bryant, multiplied by fifty thousand, typifies the basic
nature of the terror stalking America's streets today: the
woolly-brained, hopelessly inept youngster, barely in touch
with reality, whose violence is totally arbitrary and unfocused

because he can't connect cause and effect. Although it happens that Kenneth is white and that many others of his ilk are black, they all share certain characteristics that have nothing whatsoever to do with their pigmentation: They are practically unemployable, even in boom periods; they will abandon any job program organized for their benefit because work—or workmanlike crime, for that matter—demands application; they cannot be reached by any method now at our disposal, because they are either too drunk, too stoned, or too dumb to respond; and they cannot be deterred because their utter lack of imagination renders them nearly immune to fear.

They hardly ever plan to murder, not even when they habitually pack loaded firearms. But their actions are such that, on any given day, the question of whether or not they will murder someone is left entirely to chance. They may go on for years without harming a soul, or stage a massacre on the very first job they pull. But they will always remain firmly convinced of their innocence, because they hadn't *intended* to kill anyone.

Their favorite form of crime is the street holdup, which can be instigated on the spur of the moment and requires no preparation. This is a primitive, clumsy, and not very profitable style of robbery, but there is virtually no protection against it. And it epitomizes the bone-deep fear that empties our streets at night and is decimating our cities. Someone who may or may not have a gun walks up behind you and says, "Give me your money." He may shoot you if you don't give him the money; he may shoot you if you do; he may not shoot you either way; or, finally, he may have nothing to shoot you with. The rub is that you never know, and once it has happened, you'll never be quite the same again.

Allen Burnett, Billy Mabry, and Aaron Freeman didn't know either. The three teenagers, in high spirits and singing snatches of familiar tunes, were strolling up Bedford Avenue in Brooklyn on a cold November afternoon in 1976 when a voice behind them said, "Gimme money." There were three young men behind them, one holding what looked like a toy pistol. When Burnett answered, "I don't have any money," the man with the gun fired once and the seventeen-year-old fell, mortally wounded by a bullet in his skull.

Two days later Leo Hermel, a middle-aged garment cutter, was walking along Kosciusko Street, two blocks away from the murder scene, when two youths emerged from a doorway. Blocking his path, one of them pointed a large revolver at him and mumbled, "We want your wallet, man." When the garment cutter growled in reply, "Go to hell," the pair stared at him blankly for a moment. Then the gunman shouted, "Go to hell yourself," and both ran away.

Leo Hermel was foolish and lived; Jesse Lampe of Chicago was wise and died. When a man stuck a pistol in his ribs and demanded cash, Lampe handed over not only his wallet but his wristwatch as well. The robber pocketed both, then shot him in the stomach and fled. The Kenneth Bryants—whatever their names—deal out death with the randomness of a roulette wheel. Because they are extraordinarily stupid, they often get caught. But, like the street slayer of San Francisco philanthropist Edwin Golden, they may turn out to be only fifteen and therefore safe from any legal consequences worth mentioning. Even if they are considered legally liable adults and serve the seven-year stretch that is the average murderers do today, it will probably make little impression on them, because they have only the haziest concept of time in relation to their lives. They weren't going anywhere before prison, and they won't be going anywhere afterwards, so what difference does it make? They are living negations of the rehabilitation principle, because there is nothing to rehabilitate them *for*.

There is a female equivalent of the Kenneth Bryants. To be sure, she is somewhat rarer—but only to the extent that women are less prone to commit deeds of violence. Otherwise her profile is exactly the same. Occasionally several of them gather in one place—by accident or design—and then the consequences can be as irrationally hideous as anything perpetrated by their spiritual brothers.

During January 1976 a group of them—all young and

variously "deprived" women between eighteen and twenty-
five—attended the Job Corps Training Center in Excelsior
Springs, Missouri. Having signed up for the government-
sponsored courses in nursing, food services, and welding,
they lived in the school facility, but often dropped in on a
friend of theirs in nearby St. Joseph who occupied a ground-
floor apartment in a shabby two-story house and was more
than happy to share her place with her Job Corps pals and
their boy friends.

On the evening of January 7 three of them—two trainee
nursing assistants and a food-service apprentice—came visiting. The four women and several men who ambled in and
out at intervals launched into a two-day party with the aid of
large quantities of beer, wine, gin, vodka, and marijuana. At
some stage of the festivities—nobody could remember just
when—the others developed a gradually increasing hostility
against plump, brunette Sandra Beam. Although the causes
were as fuzzy as the girls' thought processes, they apparently
stemmed from Sandra's relations with black men, which the
others resented—none more virulently than Eileen (not her
real name), who was later found "mildly mentally retarded."

Deciding to get Sandra drunk, the girls forced her to down
successive glasses of vodka and gin. When she became sick,
Eileen and another girl I'll call Irma (not her actual name)
grabbed her by the hair and—after they had laced the liquor
with shampoo and silver polish—poured more spirits into her.
Sandra vomited, and Eileen hit her, calling her a "whore
and a nigger-lover." From then on, goaded by mutual en-
couragement and the helplessness of the victim, collective
sadism acquired a momentum of its own.

Over the next forty-four hours the girls took turns inflicting
obscene torments and humiliations on Sandra, interspersed
with time off for resting and boozing. They cut off portions
of her hair, beat her with their fists, a belt, and a paddle,
dumped her into a bathtub of cold water and rammed a
bar of soap into her mouth, shaved her pubic hair with a
blunt razor, daubed her face and body with spray paint and

nail polish, and used rubbing alcohol to douche her vagina,
pouring the rest of the liquid down her throat.

All this time various young men came and went—joining
the party for a few hours, then going to work or to sleep
before reappearing. Although the men didn't participate in
the tortures, none of them helped the girl, either. One of them
tied Sandra to a chair overnight (she had passed out) and
removed all sharp objects from the room, in case, as he put
it, "she came to and got violent."

Finally, after the party had gone on for nearly two days,
St. Joseph police headquarters received a phone call from a
woman saying that "something happened" at the house on
South Fifteenth Street. When two squad cars reached the
address, the officers found a human shape wrapped in a
blanket. It was Sandra, half her hair gone, her feet painted
black, her face stained red, her entire body swollen, bruised,
and crusted with blood, her nose broken, and several of her
teeth knocked out. Death, the pathologist decided, was due
"to a blow on the head and internal burns of a type associated with having consumed rubbing alcohol as well as
ethyl alcohol."

In court the partying ladies seemed vaguely astonished,
like artificially inseminated cows. They were variously charged
with second degree murder and manslaughter. In the case
of Eileen, the jury recommended life imprisonment. None
of the male visitors stood trial. Failure to render aid to a
fellow creature does not constitute a felony, except in certain
uncivilized societies, such as the South African Hottentots
and the Eskimos prior to Christianity.

Lawmen tend to speak scathingly about the public's failure
to prevent senseless horrors of this kind. But on numerous
occasions the legal apparatus helps in bringing them about.
Sometimes it does so through misapplied leniency, more
often by culpable negligence. There is no doubt, for instance,
that the Hardin family would be alive today if the Colorado
prison system had operated with even a modicum of competence.

When Richard Turner was sent to the penitentiary at

Canon City, the psychiatrist described him as the "classic rapist." A big, long-haired, ham-fisted oaf, the twenty-three-year-old ranch hand had a reputation for being rather dim-witted but harmless when sober. After a few drinks, however, he developed a manic sexual appetite that went far beyond the range of normality. Lunging at all females within reach and picking fights with their escorts until thrown out, he became the kind of insufferable barroom nuisance familiar to every tavern patron. Needless to say, Turner—suffering from the common delusion that he could "hold his liquor"— insisted on drinking. The upshot of one such binge was a charge of raping two teenage girls under revolting circumstances. Turner pleaded guilty with the usual rider of I-didn't-know-what-I-was-doing.

In Canon City, Turner was classified as "extremely dangerous and liable to commit rape again when not in a controlled setting." On three separate occasions the Colorado Parole Board turned down his appeals, basing their decisions on psychiatric findings. But confinement worked in Turner's favor, since it kept him off liquor and thus in his usual sober state of amiable dumbness. By chance he also became a material witness in a prison stabbing, enabling him to ask for a transfer to another institution since his life was allegedly in danger at the penitentiary.

He was transferred to the Fremont County Jail—a much more relaxed place, which operated a work-release program. At the same time, by an incredible piece of bureaucratic sloppiness, Turner's records and parole-board reports were not passed on to Sheriff Jack Vernetti, the man in charge of the county jail, who therefore had no idea of the type of prisoner he was boarding. All he saw was a lumbering yokel who kept his nose clean. When John Hardin offered to employ Turner on a work-release basis, the sheriff agreed without hesitation.

Hardin was a farmer and happy family man who also worked as a part-time guard at the Canon City prison, where he first met Turner. Lacking any qualifications to be a prison guard, Hardin was, moreover, a person who unfortunately believed in his knack for "knowing people," sizing them up on the basis of little more than the look in their eyes and the way they shook hands. (Every con artist in the world cultivates a firm gaze and "manly" hand clasp as part of his stock in trade.) Having been convinced by Turner that the two battered victims of his assaults had actually been willing partners and, hence, that *he* had been the victim of a frame-up, Hardin let him help with the haying at the Hardin ranch in the foothills of the Rocky Mountains. In this way he not only brought the "classic rapist" into contact with his attractive wife and two young daughters, but also put him in the vicinity of a gun case containing seven rifles, shotguns, and pistols, plus hundreds of rounds of ammunition. Finally, as if to stretch his luck to the limit, he even took him drinking. Thus, on the night of August 26, 1976, when the Hardins, another couple, and Turner arrived at Gab's lounge bar in Penrose, a little township about ten miles from the Hardin homestead, the evening began its inevitable Greek-tragedy course toward disaster.

As the liquor went to his head, the grinning Turner grew increasingly unmanageable and aggressive. He stalked around the bar bellowing and swearing, pawing the waitresses, strangers, and the wife of Turner's friend, rubbing himself against any female he could get hold of. The other couple left in disgust, but the rancher-guard didn't seem to notice that he had lost control over his charge. Instead of immediately calling the sheriff, he tried to turn the matter into a joke, half wrestling Turner away from the women and buying him more drinks. Around midnight he managed to bundle him into his van and, much to everybody's relief, they drove off. The glow of the van's taillights heading in the direction of the Hardin farm was to be the last people saw of them.

The next morning Sheriff Vernetti found what remained of the Hardin family. The parents lay bludgeoned to death in the carport; Mrs. Hardin was naked. The two young girls were sprawled in their rooms, also stripped and with their heads smashed, and in the nursery the searchers came upon three-year-old Jimmy, his skull beaten to pulp. The three females had been sexually assaulted—either before or after death. All five people were also riddled with pistol shots. They had been massacred in what could only have been an outburst of berserk frenzy, perpetrated by someone who had suppressed his violence for a long time. Hardin's gun case was empty, and his pickup truck was gone, as was Turner.

Now the State of Colorado swung into a massive effort to track down the "mad-dog killer" before he killed more. Hundreds of men and four spotter planes swarmed out over Fremont County in one of those dramatic Stetson-hatted manhunts that would have been more impressive if it hadn't become necessary in the first place by such egregious bungling. Every cop and civilian within earshot of a radio was alerted for a yellow truck driven by a maniac armed with at least six guns.

Meanwhile, the inhabitants of every one of the small settlements sprinkled about the back-country area were placed in the gravest danger. Although early reports indicated that the truck was heading north, in the direction of Wyoming, the lawmen picked up the trail too late to prevent another assault. Near Willard, Colorado, the escape car stopped at a lonely farmstead. Turner leaped out and held up the two women and the thirteen-year-old girl inside. He tied the adults to chairs and dragged the girl into the barn, where he raped her. But, for reasons as unaccountable as most of his acts, he left all three alive.

Four hours later the pursuit cars came upon the yellow pickup, halted in a rural back lane with engine trouble. A farmer, obviously trying to render first aid, was tinkering under the hood. When police bullhorns blared, he jumped back with his hands in the air. As the officers cautiously closed in, they heard a single shot from the truck. When they peered inside, Turner lay across the steering wheel, dead from the bullet he had fired at his temple. The hunt was over.

In the aftermath, Governor Lamm promptly suspended Colorado's work-release program until all prisoners involved could be "thoroughly investigated." It was the same old comedy routine, performed year in and year out. Theatrically irate government officials, one wary eye on the voters, demand "thorough screenings" of release programs—*after* some sensational bloodbath has spotlighted their inadequacies. Knowing full well that such screenings are beyond the capabilities of our current prison system, they go through the motions of action, secure in the belief that after a bit of stage thunder the public will forget about this particular crop of corpses until the next one comes up, when the whole act will be repeated.

The officials are not entirely at fault. Some of them are mortally sick of this macabre charade. But at regular intervals the powers that be foist upon them yet another "rehabilitation" program. A scheme is borrowed from, say, Sweden and expected to work equally well here despite the fact that it invariably entails selection and supervision measures for which America's understaffed, overstrained, mismanaged, and corrupt penal system has neither the personnel nor the facilities. If such programs somehow never rehabilitate a soul but fertilize graveyards instead, this does not mean that they are unworkable per se, merely that they can't work under the conditions prevailing *here*.

To illustrate this, let us hark back to the case of Kenneth Bryant for a moment. While awaiting his murder trial, Bryant was lodged in the Fairfax County Jail—precisely the type of penal institution that supervises work-release programs. He was allowed to choose his cellmate and picked a slightly built youngster, a good head shorter than himself. During the night Kenneth raped the boy, hitting him in the face when he resisted and pushing his head into a foam rubber pillow when he tried to yell. When the county sheriff was questioned about the incident, he said by way of explanation, "I tried assigning everyone to partners and had more confusion and fights in that time than I did before or after." So naturally, in order to avoid "confusion and fights," he let his charges select their nocturnal rape objects. After being sentenced on the rape charge (he got one year for his

little prank), Bryant was led from the Juvenile Court with
two sheriff's deputies holding his arms. As they walked past
the bench on which the victim was sitting, Bryant managed
in passing to give him a shattering kick in the ribs—a kick his
two husky guardians were apparently unable or unwilling to
prevent.

The above is a fairly mild sample of the control our
county jails exercise over their inmates. It is illustrative also
in that the people running them are the very same who
conduct the screening processes that decide who will hit the
streets while still serving a sentence.

Further up the ladder we have establishments like the
Lorton Reformatory complex in Washington, D.C. No
county hoosegow, this. Lorton is a federal penitentiary holding some of the nation's most dangerous criminals. In 1971
Lorton launched its Resocialization Furlough program—a
scheme originally tried in Denmark—in which inmates who
had completed half of their minimum sentence would be
allowed out into the world for periods of up to seventy-two
hours. Under the regulations, a convict serving a minimum
twenty-year sentence was not to be considered eligible for the
program until he had completed 80 percent of his stretch.
So much for the regulations; let us now consider the reality.

In September 1976, John Irby—a convicted murderer—
was arrested for running a drug-sales operation while on
furlough from Lorton. One week later, D.C. police arrested
Elroy Lewis for carrying a loaded pistol without a license.
Lewis, convicted of murdering a liquor-store owner during a
holdup, had begun his twenty-years-to-life sentence in 1968,
so he had served only 40 percent of his minimum time when
the Lorton administration placed him on furlough. Even
so, he had served considerably longer than Charlie James,
who was nabbed while driving a car with a loaded handgun
under the seat. Although James had just begun a life term
for homicide in 1969, he had to wait only two years to gain
admission to Lorton's work-release program. Accordingly, we
must conclude that the .44 Magnum he had with him in the

car was a tool of trade—just as, presumably, were the surgical face masks police found alongside the gun.

Please note that none of the convicts concerned had been released on parole. Officially they were still serving their sentences and were thus safely in custody—a semantic nicety that helped to spare the unwary public some anxiety and the Lorton authorities some embarrassing questions. The same deceptiveness applies to the status of residents in so-called halfway houses. Although control over their activities is—to put it mildly—rudimentary, prisoners living in such residences are presumed to be doing their time. In fact, supervision amounts to little more than having them check in and out at prescribed hours.* Outside the premises they're on their own.

The regulations state that prisoners granted the privilege of halfway-house living must be carefully screened and judged "well advanced toward complete rehabilitation." We can only assume that the Lorton administration believed this about Arthur Byrd and Reginald Lewis. In July 1975 both were living in the institution's halfway house on Thirteenth Street, N.W. On the thirtieth of that month they held up, bound, and gagged a lay preacher named Mary Louise Brown, eighty-four-year-old Arthur Holland, Wilhelmina Rogers, and eight-year-old Tawnya Smaw in an apartment on Columbia Road. After robbing the place they killed all four—including the child—by execution-style shots in the head.

In fairness it must be stated that every Lorton program is a political football kicked merrily back and forth among the D.C. Department of Corrections, the Justice Department, the Attorney General, and the Washington City Council—each of them exerting authority while disclaiming responsibility. With everyone passing the buck and the buck stopping nowhere, it is not hard to see why a scheme tested successfully in Denmark develops certain flaws when transplanted here.

---

* A New Jersey halfway-house inmate shot a man dead, chopped him into pieces, scattered them around Harlem and lower Manhattan, had his suit cleaned, and reported back to his residence in spotless condition and on the dot.

·But this is nothing compared to the measures applied to some of those the law declares to be sexual psychopaths. One such case was that of James Ruzicka, an apparitionlike creature who received the label in a Seattle court in 1973. He was twenty-three years of age and had been in and out of juvenile centers and prisons since he turned nine. He first practiced bestiality as a boy, then graduated to molesting little girls, and finally was convicted of raping two young women at knifepoint. He was the product of a traumatic childhood combined with the effects of LSD, cocaine, mescaline, and heroin. Almost six feet tall, stooped and thin, with a wild tangle of hair, a drooping mustache, his eyes two blurs behind thick glasses, he bore not the slightest resemblance to the popular conception of a rapist. He rather looked like the breed of youngster who might drink some guru's bathwater in search of spiritual bliss. Only his maggot complexion and tight-lipped jailhouse argot revealed his background.

After pronouncing Ruzicka a sexual psychopath, Superior Court Judge David Soukup suspended his ten-year prison sentence on condition that he join a sexual-offender program at Western State Hospital near Tacoma. Although the hospital had security wards for dangerous cases, the special program entailed increasing measures of trust for the inmates. Progressing rapidly, Ruzicka soon achieved a kind of trusty position in which he escorted other members to their work places—areas within the hospital grounds but outside the maximum-security region. After nine months of program participation, he walked out of the hospital and vanished.

During the next four weeks, sixteen-year-old Nancy Kinghammer and fourteen-year-old Penny Haddenham disappeared from their homes in West Seattle. They found Penny first. She was hanging by a rope from a tree in a patch of woodland bordering the West Seattle Expressway. Medical examiners discovered that she had first been raped and throttled, then strung up.

Nancy turned up a month later, buried half naked under a pile of garbage in a vacant lot used as a dumping ground.

Wrapped in towels, the body was too decomposed for the manner of her death to be established with any certainty.

The girls had lived less than a mile apart in an area of West Seattle where, as the homicide men discovered, Ruzicka had stayed after fleeing the hospital. His former wife had put him up initially. Her new husband hadn't minded his predecessor's visiting for a while. Taking thirty-nine dollars and a few items along with him, Ruzicka had left suddenly and without saying good-bye.

Next the Seattle police learned that, under a different name, Ruzicka was already in custody in Beaverton, Oregon. He had raped a thirteen-year-old girl there, claiming afterward that she had been more than willing. "I asked her if she wanted to ball, and she didn't say 'no.' So I figured she wouldn't mind. . . ." He had offered the same tale about all his victims, and always appeared hugely surprised when the survivors called the cops.*

Having been convicted for rape in Oregon, it was only later, during his time in jail, that Ruzicka confided to a cellmate that he had raped and killed two girls in Seattle. The police also found that a knife he had lost on the scene and the towels wrapped around Nancy's body had come from the home of his obliging ex-wife. Consequently, in August 1975 Ruzicka went on trial before the Washington Superior Court for double homicide. Found guilty on both counts, he was sentenced to two consecutive life terms—to be served after completing his ten-year stretch in Oregon.

Ruzicka's crimes had no rationale anyone could perceive, perhaps not even himself. He had raped five females and killed two of them, but he had also let three others go—one while he was on the run and had logical reasons for eliminating witnesses. Yet, so ambivalent is the legal definition of "sexual psychopath" that there was no question of his pleading innocent by reason of insanity. Psychiatrist Clarence

---

* A common reaction among rapists. As a type they seem to have an astonishing capacity for self-delusion, for accepting as genuine the things their victims might say in order to avoid being killed.

Nessling, who studied his case, advanced the nearest thing to a plausible explanation of his behavior:

> Ruzicka was the loser type *in extremis*. He felt totally isolated, partly because of his awful childhood, partly because of physical defects, like his eyesight. In jail they called him "Mr. Magoo." His self-esteem was about zero. He spent years searching for his father, and when he finally thought he'd found him the man denied it furiously—didn't want to have anything to do with him.
>
> He couldn't relate to women in any fashion except by rape. That was his way of making contact. Using a knife to make them submit, then forgetting about the knife so he could imagine they'd actually wanted him. If the two dead girls had said something that hit home on his colossal inferiority complex, he would very likely have reacted by murdering them. The effect would have been like jabbing a needle into an open sore.

The loser image is perhaps the most lethal tag our society can pin on a person. It seems to have turned thousands of people into walking time bombs, ready to explode in the hands of whoever touches their trigger. In the case of John Wayne Wilson, this was done by his female alter ego—another loser by predestination, named Roseann Quinn.

Although he perpetrated one of America's most publicized murders, Wilson's name remains virtually unknown. He was the shadowy Godot figure who stalks the final pages of *Looking for Mr. Goodbar*—a novel that topped the best-seller list because it evoked the very essence of the two-o'clock-in-the-morning terrors haunting liberated but alienated big-city women.*

Wilson never raped anyone in his life, nor did he have the faintest inclination to do so. Men paid him twenty dollars a throw for sex, and he could attract women as often as he desired one—which wasn't too often. A tall, fair, cleanly profiled boy from rural Indiana, he had drifted into New York City as he drifted everywhere—on a current of alcohol and acid that muffled the sharp edges of his existence and made day-to-day living bearable for him. At twenty-four,

---

*Two women writers dug out the minutiae of this case and produced two versions of the same event. Novelist Judith Rossner created *Mr. Goodbar*, while reporter Lacey Fosburgh presented the facts in the New York *Times*.

he had spent time in mental hospitals and received a lot of medication but no therapy to speak of. This was because doctors couldn't pinpoint what was wrong with him. It might have been everything or nothing, depending on how you viewed it. Wrapped in passivity as in a straitjacket, unable to hold jobs or maintain human relationships, Wilson was utterly ineffective at whatever he did. Even his bisexuality was largely passive—as he lay still while his partners used him. Every routine task was a challenge to him—a challenge from which he shrank because he was convinced he couldn't meet it. His sole aim was to place narcotic pillows between himself and the threatening reality around him.

In New York, Wilson made his one serious attempt at self-assertion He got married. Like everything else he attempted, it didn't work. Within four months he was drinking harder than ever and tripping on LSD again. But now he developed a new and strangely unfocused aggressiveness—a rabid-dog temper that snapped in all directions and snarled at the world instead of whining. Something in his mind was crouching in a corner, teeth bared. He was in that condition when he met Roseann Quinn.

She was slightly deformed, a skin-and-bones redhead with glasses and a disfigured hip that made her walk with a limp. As if she were being flayed by a relentless whip, she seemed driven to seek constant reassurance that her handicap didn't matter—when at every moment she *knew* it did. She sought reassurance from men, from having them desire her malformed body—and only her body. She prowled the neighborhood bars for men, taking them back to her disheveled little pad, which always smelled faintly of rancid grease and marijuana smoke. She picked up three, four lovers a week, but there were never enough; there was never enough reassurance.

Her cold promiscuity clashed with the remnants of a Catholic conscience—a childhood leftover she thought she had shed. The conflict produced guilt; the guilt, in turn, produced a dangerous craving for punishment. Roseann began to select types who would punish her—anyone who

looked brutal or drunk or weird enough to promise a beating.
If they didn't volunteer violence, she would bait them until
they obliged. Night after night neighbors heard the sounds
of blows and her sobbing shrieks and tried not to listen. In
the morning Roseann would appear alone, makeup daubed
over her blackened eyes and bruised features, and make her
way to the Bronx school for the deaf where she taught underprivileged children who adored her.

She lived on Manhattan's West Seventy-second Street, a
permanent wind tunnel where the gusts are always blowing
millions of dirty paper scraps as if trying to camouflage the
flaking ugliness of the buildings. On winter nights, with
whiffs of steam fluttering from the sewer gratings and junkies
huddling in doorways, it presents a Doré landscape of urban
melancholia. New Year's Eve, 1973, was such a night.

Tweed's Bar was crowded. The narrow, draft-ridden room
was crammed with people who hadn't been invited to anyone's party. At midnight there were some thin cheers that
didn't take—perhaps because few felt very optimistic about
the new year or nostalgic about the old. Tweed's that night
was a convention of the lonely. Roseann sat by herself at the
bar, her glowing red hair—her best feature—spilling over her
shoulders. A few feet away and also alone sat John Wayne
Wilson. Sometime during the night the two met, talked in
random snatches over the howling jukebox, and went home
together. Three hours later, Roseann was dead, New York's
first homicide victim for 1973.

She died horribly. When the police found her sprawled
on the rumpled sheets of her bed, the entire room was
splashed with blood, the pillows drenched with it. She had
been choked by hand as well as strangled with her panties,
which were still knotted tightly around her neck. There were
eleven gaping knife wounds in her thin body; her face had
been pounded beyond recognition; her breasts and thighs
had been bitten and clawed; a red candle had been shoved
deep into her vagina. The final blows seemed to have been
inflicted with a small metal statuette that rested across her
face, hiding the smashed lips and nose.

The newspapers described her injuries in salivating detail, but they were wrong about one particular: Roseann had not been raped. When Wilson was arrested in Indianapolis six days later, he gave two different versions of what happened that night.

The first version—the one he gave to the homicide detectives—was the one used in *Mr. Goodbar*. In it he said that they had made love, but immediately afterward the girl had ordered him out of her apartment—she had literally pushed him out of bed and told him to get lost, scratching his bare back in her hurry to be rid of him.

He gave a different account to his lawyer. According to this second version, he had been drinking hard that day, and when the moment came he found himself impotent. Roseann sneered at him, poking savage female fun at his limpness exposed in the candlelight.

Whichever story was true, she touched off an explosion of rage in him. He throttled the girl, hammered her with his fists, ripped her apart with a kitchen knife, and finally used the candle she had lit by the bedside to inflict the last gesture of contempt on her. Regardless which version was accurate, both showed the uncanny efficiency of Roseann's urge for self-destruction. As for Wilson, the prison psychiatrists diagnosed him as schizophrenic, with both homicidal and suicidal tendencies. Strangely enough, none of the psychiatrists who had examined him before had discovered any such traits. In the end it didn't matter much anyway, for Wilson never stood trial. He hanged himself in his cell, using sheets obligingly supplied by a prison guard.

No scientific study has yet established a correlation between the loser image and our homicide rate. But policemen, watching the bewildering increase of so-called motiveless murders, have an uneasy awareness of such a connection. "I can't give it to you in concrete terms because we haven't any statistics on the subject," said Homicide Lieutenant Rick Latham. "It's only a gut-level feeling, the kind you get when you've been a cop for nineteen years come Easter. But I believe a lot of people nowadays commit murder to leave some sort of imprint on the world. Like they feel they're bits of nothing . . . zeroes . . . invisible. So they go and kill somebody just to make a mark, to have attention paid to them for once, to show that they can make *some* difference. To prove that they *exist*, if you follow me. Prove it to others—or maybe just to themselves."

We don't know what Norma Jean Armistead was trying to prove, because nobody ever asked her. A mousy, middle-aged obstetrical nurse working at the Los Angeles Kaiser Hospital, she could have passed for one of Lieutenant Latham's "invisibles" before she committed what must be the eeriest crime of our century.

In October 1974 Armistead created a "paper pregnancy" for herself by filing the appropriate records at her hospital. A pregnancy at age forty-four struck some people as rather unusual—though not unusual enough to cause more than raised eyebrows. About the time her fake pregnancy should have been due to culminate, Armistead zeroed in on a genuinely pregnant woman: twenty-eight-year-old Kathryn Viramontes.

Visiting the unmarried mother-to-be in her Van Nuys apartment on May 15, 1975, just before she was scheduled to give birth, the nurse cut the woman's throat from ear to ear, then opened her abdomen, performing a makeshift but remarkably skillful Caesarean section that removed the nearly full-term baby alive. Bundling up the infant, Armistead proceeded to a hospital, where she checked herself in as a patient, claiming that she had given birth to the boy at home. At this point, inevitably, her scheme collapsed and she was arrested.

A Superior Court jury found her legally sane and guilty of first-degree murder. When she heard the verdict, nurse Armistead wept quietly. Whether she wept for the dead mother, the living child, or herself, only those in tune with the echoes of her mind could have told.

10

The Politics of Homicide

There have been an increasing criminalization of politics and a politicalization of criminals. It's reached the point where there are no criminals in San Quentin any more. They're all freedom fighters.
—Frederick J. Hacker,
Professor of Psychiatry and Law

We must firmly understand that government "intelligence" dogs are sick, the deranged scum of humanity, worldwide terrorists, butchers of poor people, enforcers for the rich parasites who have no love or concern for the American people or poor people throughout the world. The assassinations of Martin Luther King and numerous others, and the COINTELPRO and Phoenix programs were created by the same degenerate minds to help keep the rich people in control.
—*Tug*, publication of the New
World Liberation Front

The most remarkable thing about political murders in America is that there are so few of them. Considering the blood-curdling trumpets sounded by left and right extremists, considering the torrent of printed and shouted exhortations to violence flooding the country, considering the plethora of available weaponry, it seems downright astonishing that the United States has so far escaped the sort of guerrilla struggles waged in Ulster, Argentina, and the Philippines. "Few," of course, is a relative term. America today has many more politically motivated slayings than, say, twenty years ago. But, compared with the 100 percent rise in other forms of homicide over the same period, political killings have lagged far behind the general trend.

This is not, as some pundits like to think, because such mayhem is somehow "un-American." Far from it. The U.S. has an old and grim tradition of political murder going back to the Jayhawkers of "Bleeding Kansas" on the eve of the Civil War. There was, however, a difference between terrorist groups here and abroad. In America even the most virulent of them—the Golden Circle, the original Ku Klux Klan, the Molly Maguires—tended to be localized in their activities and limited in their aims. By and large they wished only to alter certain conditions in one particular region. Their target was not the country's existing social order but a few strictly circumscribed aspects of it. There were no native American equivalents of the Russian Narodniki, the Japanese Black Dragon Society, the Irish Republican Army—organizations dedicated to using force to bring about a general upheaval. It is significant that out of America's four Presidential assassins, only one—John Wilkes Booth—actually belonged to a political organization. The others were freelance terrorists or lunatics or both.*

The sole exception to this rule were the anarchists—the American wing of an international movement, established here in the 1880s. It would take pages to explain how this "daydream of desperate romantics," this most humanitarian of all activist creeds, became the philosophical lever for the starkest forms of violence. In any case, the anarchists were not alone in exhibiting this curious evolution. At various stages such a tendency is equally visible in Christianity and Buddhism. Anarchism espoused what its theorists called the "propaganda of the deed," a nebulous term that could be interpreted to mean anything. As historian Barbara Tuchman wrote: "Down in the lower depths of society, lonely men were listening. They heard echoes of the tirades and the trumpets and caught a glimpse of the shining millennium that promised a life without hunger and without a boss.

---

* Leon Czolgosz, the killer of McKinley, called himself an anarchist but had been rejected by the movement. Lee Harvey Oswald was a self-styled Marxist but not a member of any party. Charles Guiteau, who murdered Garfield, was a disappointed office-seeker without any ideology.

Suddenly one of them, with a sense of injury or a sense of mission, would rise up, go out and kill—and sacrifice his own life on the altar of the Idea."

In the eighteen years from 1894 to 1912 the anarchists accounted for an Italian king, an Austrian empress, one American and one French president, two Spanish prime ministers, and scores of grand dukes, governors, cabinet ministers, and assorted government officials in a dozen countries. During the Chicago Haymarket Square riot of 1886 they hurled a bomb that tore seven policemen to shreds. They produced—in the deformed German bookbinder Johann Most—the most formidable revolutionary terrorist America had known. But they never managed to plant roots in the United States. Throughout their history the anarchists remained a microscopic foreign splinter in the American tree, with no influence extending beyond a tiny group of urban immigrants.

Just how badly they were out of tune with national sentiment was shown by anarchist Alexander Berkman's attempt to assassinate industrialist Henry Clay Frick during the bloody Homestead Steel strike of 1892. Frick had been one of the least loved figures in Pennsylvania before the attempt. Overnight he became a hero and near-martyr, even to people who opposed his hidebound antiunionism. The idealistic Berkman became the villain of the day.

Eventually, it was not the hated government but the Marxists who demolished the anarchists. An unbridgeable gulf loomed between the followers of Marx, who believed in an omnipotent state, and the anarchists, who believed in no state at all. Marxist discipline and organization won hands down and virtually eliminated the anarchists from the ranks of the radical left, at least in this country.

But today, with orthodox Marxism declining in credibility among Americans, the anarchists are beginning to reassert themselves—though under different labels. There is something about their intensely individualistic, libertarian creed that appeals strongly to the dozens of minuscule bodies that make up what passes for a revolutionary movement.

It may appear strange that today's terrorists should feel inspired by those discredited anarchists of the past rather than by their Marxist foes. Americans love winners, and anarchism lost everywhere while Marxism captured one third of the globe. But the attraction is logical. Our revolutionaries were shaped by the student and hippie dreams of the 1960s, which were essentially revivals of nineteenth-century romanticism. They couldn't hack the regimentation of the Communists, their Victorian priggishness about sex and their puritanical distaste for the drug scene. To a Marxist functionary of either Maoist or Moscow persuasion, the very thought of revolutionaries blowing grass or imbibing acid is anathema.

Most important, the Marxists believe only in coordinated mass action: strikes, riots, and armed risings. They despise individual terror methods as "romantic self-indulgence." And the whole point for America's political slayers lies in the assertion of their individualism—in the idea of a *personal* blow against the system.

People like the Tullers, for instance, could never have worked within a Marxist apparatus. They epitomized the go-it-alone character of this country's terrorists, their isolation from the mainstream as well as their pathetic muddleheadedness.

Before a federal prosecutor named him "probably the most dangerous man in the United States," gaunt, slope-shouldered Charles A. Tuller was a Department of Commerce employee making twenty-six thousand dollars a year. A Don Quixote type in wire-rim glasses, with a history of psychiatric troubles, Tuller greened into a "middle-class revolutionary" at the age of forty-six. In an amazing reversal of the usual process, he tutored his two sons in the doctrines of class warfare. Until then the boys—Bryce, nineteen, and Jonathan, seventeen—had been fanatical only about baseball. But in 1972 the Tuller trio and a fourth man set out to demolish capitalism by robbing a bank in Arlington, Virginia. Everything went haywire from the start. Neither accomplished revolutionaries nor bank robbers, they seemed to careen out of control into big-time crime like a snowball rolling down a hill. Having shot and killed the teller and a policeman in their attempt to rob the bank, they then fled empty-handed. Getting as far as Houston, where they unintentionally murdered an Eastern Airlines ticket agent, the four skyjacked an airliner to Cuba, where they found asylum.

Stuck in exile with three murder charges, one attempted-robbery charge, and a skyjacking charge on their records, yet with absolutely nothing to show for it, the Tullers had, by their third year there, become nearly as sick of Cuba as Cuba was of them. Although they knew the FBI was waiting for them, Tuller and his sons decided to come home. It doesn't say much for U.S. Customs that the three had no trouble slipping into Miami with clumsily faked drivers' licenses for identification. Once here, they needed money. After robbing a supermarket in Virginia, they sent Bryce to hold up a store in North Carolina. This was to be their final blunder, for Bryce was disarmed by the store manager and handed over to the cops. Three days later Charles Tuller and his younger son walked into the FBI office in Washington and gave themselves up. "I couldn't stand it without my boy," said Tuller wearily. "I had to see him again."

Subsequently, the three saw a lot of one another in various courtrooms. Beginning with a sentence of ten years for felonious assault, they successively collected heavier sentences with each subsequent trial: fifteen years for attempted robbery, two life terms apiece for double murder, one hundred years for air piracy and kidnapping. In the droll fashion of contemporary justice, only the century sentence—unless reversed, of course—could actually keep them imprisoned for life. Still, the judges probably enjoyed handing down those farcical stretches—and some newspaper readers still take them seriously.

But the courts failed to fathom the nature of the propellant that drove this mild, highly intelligent man to charge windmills, taking along the sons whom he loved more than life. Tuller somewhat feebly quoted Thomas Paine's advocacy of armed force against George III. One psychiatrist described him as a "unique thinker who held genuine concern for the underprivileged and believed the country was going to hell and was rife with corruption." Two more depicted the entire trio as "schizoid personalities."

None of this explains what compelled their rampage. Finding this explanation is highly important insofar as it might shed light on the motivations of other political terrorists. The Tullers, we must remember, did not act from any personal grievance. *They* had not been deprived, victimized, or maltreated by society. They were, however, frustrated to a degree difficult to imagine for the socially better adjusted or less deeply concerned.

Part of this was due to their inability to influence large numbers of ordinary people, to make them share their own burning sense of outrage over some inequity. Psychologist Hugh Dunbar wrote that this can result in "a feeling of total impotence as well as isolation. In turn this produces a sense of defiance, the determination to act alone, to perform some spectacular deed that will *make* the uncaring masses sit up and listen. I am certain that if Tuller had been an accomplished speaker or writer—if he had been capable of arousing a big audience—he wouldn't have touched a gun."

This frustration also obsessed Sara Jane Moore, who tried to assassinate President Ford, but it is fairly rare among the middle-aged. It is widespread among youth, however, particularly among college students experiencing the crisis of American intellectual life: the vacuum created by the absence of common values and moral yardsticks. They may, for instance, learn from a newspaper that a shortage of funds has forced the government to cut several million people off food stamps and, on the same page, read that a movie producer is boasting of investing $24 million in a rehash of *King Kong*. Seen in juxtaposition, such contradictions make their social conscience boil. How, they ask, can society allow this person to squander sums on his cinematic zilch that could have provided free milk for every ghetto baby in the country?

But in venting their feelings to others they find that very

few share their concern—at least with anything approaching their own intensity. The majority thoroughly enjoy *King Kong* while remaining quite undisturbed by the idea of its wasted revenues. The common moral values are missing— what strikes a few as a horrendous social crime leaves the multitude indifferent or even amused. The outraged few find themselves isolated in their anger, unable to articulate it in words that would stir an echo in the general public.

To make matters worse, the few have freedom of expression. They can't blame establishment muzzles for their failure to stir the majority. They *know* they are out of step with the masses, lone voices in the crowd, and that knowledge is one of the harshest blows a free society can inflict. It robs them of their comforting self-image as gagged prophets and exposes to a strong light all their naked ineffectuality. Much of the convulsive obscenity of our so-called underground press is undoubtedly due to the fact that it *isn't* underground. It can freely compete for public attention and thus reveal how pitifully little it gets. The rage of its writers is sparked at least partly by the government's refusal to play the genuine oppressor—to consider them worth suppressing. Pinpricks do not a martyr's crown make.

Thus, we get the wryly comic spectacle of self-proclaimed revolutionaries haranguing media conferences about "Amerikka's Fascist dictatorship" while demonstrating the fiction of that statement by the very act of delivering it—not to mention their patent ignorance of the meaning of fascism.

This impression is not lost on the revolutionaries, most of whom are perceptive enough to see the basic contradiction of such postures. They therefore edge toward goading the establishment into some kind of reaction—into anything that might validate their claim to be engaged in mortal combat with tyranny. The goading may take the most infantile forms, such as the spitting and pie-throwing antics of the Yippies— practices that, incidentally, do not prevent their journal, the *Yipster Times*, from being readily available on newsstands. It may, however, also take the form of gunfire and high explosives. At this point the authorities really *do* react, and

frequently in a very ham-handed manner—using sledgeham-
mers to swat flies. When this happens it elicits one of two
responses from the revolutionaries—responses that serve to
separate the hot-air spouters from the Jacobins. The former
raise a tremendous cry of "Foul!" followed by an emotional
appeal for legal rights that they previously had sworn didn't
exist in this police state. The Constitution, once denounced
as a pious fraud, suddenly becomes their shield and bulwark.

In contrast, a small, granite core of dissidents respond by
actually submerging and turning into bona fide terrorists.
They are made doubly dangerous by being aware of their
isolation—by no longer pinning hopes on mass sympathy for
their cause. Almost unconsciously they develop an elitist attitude that distances them still further from the common
herd they claim to serve. After a period of underground
existence, this begins to affect their language. Their communications to the public take on a strange, stilted tone.
Sounding like a cross between a computer manual and a
Peking wall poster, they become virtually unintelligible to
the very people they are addressing. The subterranean atmosphere in which they live magnifies minor issues out of all
proportion and sets them wrangling among themselves like
medieval scholastics over points of political doctrine. This
causes them to splinter into ever-smaller factions, each claiming to be "purer" than the others and each tending to amplify
their rhetorical militancy in direct relation to the decline in
the numbers of militants available to give it substance.

This was, in fact, the fate of America's most successful
guerrilla body: the Weather Underground Organization
(WUO). Its members originally belonged to the radical
Students for a Democratic Society (SDS) but broke away
in 1969 to avoid infiltration by police informants. Very ably
commanded by a Central Committee of five, the Weather
people spent seven years planting bombs in the Pentagon,
the Capitol, and twenty-five other "symbols of American
imperialism," launching a magazine and a booklet entitled
Prairie Fire, and dodging the FBI with considerable aplomb.
They even starred in a documentary film about their under-

cover life, shot in "safe houses" ringed by highly efficient security screens.*

So far the Weather people have killed nobody but themselves. Three of their number died when a Greenwich Village bomb factory blew up—a common mishap for clandestine munitions makers. Otherwise, their explosions were carefully timed for the early-morning hours and the police warned beforehand, so as to avoid injuries. But the factionalism endemic to such circles got to them as well. In January 1977, Bernardine Dohrn, one of the five leaders, issued a manifesto denouncing the other four in true Peking style. The Central Committee, it appeared, had been guilty of mortal sins against ideological purity. It had "denied aid and support" to the Black Liberation Army, the SLA, and other less competent fugitive groups, and had instead helped Abbie Hoffman, who didn't need it nearly so much and wasn't nearly so risky. "That is," Ms. Dohrn charged, "our security and our safety were placed above that of Black and Third World organizations." The Committee Four had also perpetrated the "crime of spontaneity," which is Peking wall jargon for harboring original ideas not contained in the party doctrine.

The denunciation seemed to augur an irrevocable split and probably spelled the end of the WUO's seven-year career. Nonetheless, the amoebalike ability of such underground groups to survive partitions, with each severed portion continuing an active life of its own, makes it unwise to predict their imminent demise. Such caution is made still more mandatory by the playful ease with which identities can be changed in this country. Sara Jane Moore (whose real name is Kahn) did it five times. Jane Alpert, who jumped bail on bombing charges in New York in 1970, obtained Social Security cards under assumed names in three states. A Massachusetts bank even gave her a car loan. A society with eight million illegal aliens floating in limbo—many of them speak-

* The movie, titled *Underground*, was the work of filmmakers Emile de Antonio, Mary Lampson, and Haskell Wexler, and took several months to complete. It speaks volumes for the oppressiveness of "Police State Amerikka" that none of the makers were prosecuted for their efforts, even though Mr. de Antonio publicized it in the Los Angeles *Times*.

ing no English—provides few obstacles to an intelligent fugitive's shedding his or her skin as often as required.

The foundation stone for an edifice of phony documentation is a genuine birth certificate—that is, someone else's genuine certificate. You can find just what you need by scanning the death certificates at a county recorder's office. You select a child that died in infancy within a few years of your own date of birth. You then send—as it is perfectly legal to do—for a copy of the child's birth certificate and, presto, it becomes yours. The best feature of your acquisition is the fact that birth and death certificates are not cross-referenced anywhere. Thus, no one has a means of knowing that Joe Smith, aged twenty-seven, actually died at the age of two. On the strength of that certificate you can obtain, in not much more than a month, any other identification you may need: Social Security number, baptismal record, driver's license, passport, etc.

All this makes a joke of the assertion that the U.S. resembles an authoritarian state—or even a well-organized one. In recent years certain credit-card companies have exerted pressure for the introduction of national identity cards, a measure that would make life difficult for credit swindlers and political fugitives alike. But since the credit corporations are already notorious as America's foremost privacy invaders, their scheme has little chance of success.

As a rule, the underground militants of the New Left have tried to avoid bloodshed by striking at property rather than people. The notable exception was the mini-squad of fanatics with a seven-headed cobra as an emblem and the rather convoluted title of Symbionese Liberation Army (SLA). Ostensibly led by ex-convict Donald DeFreeze, the SLA's real chiefs were three mordacious young women (see Chapter 5). DeFreeze was largely an embarrassment with delusions of grandeur, indicated by his self-bestowed pseudonym of "Field Marshal Cinque" (shades of Uganda's Idi Amin, another ersatz Field Marshal). Trotsky, who commanded a Red Army of three million, never rose above Commissar.

The SLA had a talent for psychodrama that kept them in

the media spotlight for twenty-two months. Their kidnapping and conversion of Patty Hearst, their costumed theatrics, and their final, nationally televised shootout in Los Angeles* provided the public with a Roman circus of thrills, surpassed only by the Manson horrors. But the SLA's political impact was virtually nil, despite the ideological earnestness of its leaders.

Their guerrilla tactics were ferociously adolescent. They assassinated progressive black educator Dr. Marcus Foster, gunned down a housewife during a bank robbery, shot their way out of a store after one of them got caught shoplifting a pair of socks, and eventually died fighting in their last stronghold because they failed to take the elementary precaution of posting sentries outside. For the revolutionary left, the SLA was a setback, useful only in providing a handful of symbolic martyrs.

The radical right, by contrast, has been relatively dormant in the last decade. They shot their bolts during the 1960s in a last-ditch attempt to stop—or at least cripple—the civil-rights movement. Their major "accomplishment"—the sniper slaying of Dr. Martin Luther King, Jr., in 1968—also became their worst debacle. The nationwide wave of grief and revulsion that followed temporarily smothered the baying of the far right.

Temporarily . . . for their terroristic *potential* is far greater than anything on the left. True, their publicists are utterly devoid of propagandistic skill (the pamphlets concocted by the American National Socialists, for instance, must have sent Dr. Goebbels spinning in his urn). But because they are inherently nonrevolutionary and reactionary, they may draw upon allies and resources far eclipsing anything the left-wingers could hope for. In certain areas, particularly the rural South, those include law-enforcement officials. The old, un-

---

* Some journalists accused the police SWAT teams of overreacting on that occasion because they replied to automatic-weapons fire with everything in their arsenal. According to this odd combat morality, you're only allowed to hit back at the enemy with the same amount of lead he's throwing at you.

holy alliance between redneck sheriffs and the Ku Klux Klan is still functioning, though less overtly than before.

In June 1964 this partnership perpetrated the most sickening tragedy of the Southern vote-registration drive. That month three civil-rights campaigners—Michael Schwerner, James Chaney, and Andy Goodman—were arrested for "speeding" in Neshoba County, Mississippi. Then they vanished. It took twenty-five thousand dollars in federal reward money to locate their bodies, which had been buried with a bulldozer. Their killers, it turned out, were a mixed bunch of local Klansmen—two of them sporting sheriff badges. The slaughter backfired badly. It made the name of Mississippi an insult and the three young men—two white and one black —symbols of interracial brotherhood. But the combination that killed them remains a silently potent threat.

We stand in very real danger that frustrated cops and right-wing vigilantes will coalesce into a lethal partnership here as they have elsewhere. In Brazil such an alliance spawned the infamous "death squads," which have murdered —sorry, "executed"—nearly a thousand people designated "enemies of society." With vigilantism already in the air, it might require only the admixture of a few score police to produce a powerful terror organization—made all the more brutal by the delusion that it is "upholding the law."

Sometimes it seems as if certain dissidents were trying to bring about just such a development. A New York police sergeant, so furious that he didn't trust himself to speak, showed me the January 1972 issue of the Black Panther news sheet *Right On!* It showed pictures of eleven dead policemen, along with the following text: "Victories for the people in New York alone saw the assassination of 14 pigs. Malcolm X's birthday was celebrated with the assassination of two pigs Piagentini and Jones." The same edition also featured a cartoon showing a cop as a rifle target, with the caption "Power to the Shooters."

This was six years ago. Since then the Panthers have apparently transformed themselves into a benevolent association that mainly provides breakfasts for needy children. With their erstwhile leader, Huey Newton, in flight from a murder charge, their philosophical godfather, Eldridge Cleaver, has discovered the virtues of men's fashion designing, American capitalism, and of Jesus Christ—in that order. But despite this metamorphosis, it isn't altogether easy to forget the time the Panther newspaper published a photo of Robert Kennedy lying in his blood over the caption "Death for another pig." Or the Panther street-corner orator I heard refer to Schwerner and Goodman (who died for black rights in Mississippi) as "a couple of New York Jew boys who'd run away from their mothers."

Officers Waverly Jones and Joseph Piagentini were not slain by the Black Panthers as such but by a splinter outfit calling itself the Black Liberation Army. The Panther press merely did the cheering. Although Jones was black, Piagentini white, in reality, as a writer in the New York police magazine *Spring 3100* observed, "They were killed because of their color, which was neither white nor black, but blue."

The BLA has so far been the only faction in this country to unleash a systematic murder campaign against the police. They killed cops as a matter of policy and—despite their readings of Chairman Mao—had virtually no other aims. It was a desperate, suicidal venture, for, whatever else America's police forces may lack, they possess tremendous esprit de corps and have always displayed the most relentless determination in avenging fallen comrades. Neither the anarchists nor the Mafia had ever attempted such a direct confrontation with the police, which may be one reason why they lasted so much longer.

On the night of May 21, 1971, the radio-car team of Jones and Piagentini answered a call in a Harlem housing development. The brawl in question was over by the time they arrived. As they walked back to their car, two black youths silently fell in behind them. Suddenly the pair whipped out pistols and began firing, keeping it up until the policemen collapsed on the ground. Then they bent over them, dragged out the cops' service revolvers, and emptied these, too, into their bodies.

The NYPD did not at first connect this motiveless attack with another that had occurred two nights earlier. On that evening, a radio car had been machine-gunned from another vehicle on 106th Street; two officers were badly injured. The link between the two incidents was established only by the BLA's own messages delivered to the New York *Times* office. The first was accompanied by the number plate of the machine-gunners' car and began: "Here are the license plates sort [sic] after by the fascist state pig police. We sent them in order to exhibit the potential power of oppressed peoples to acquire revolutionary justice. . . ." It was in this message that they first identified themselves as the previously unknown "Black Liberation Army." When, three days later, a second message arrived claiming credit for the double murder as well, it became a byword among law officers. With two officers crippled for life and two killed outright within three nights, it now appeared that this was intended to be merely a start.

Somewhere in New York—and, as it turned out, not only in New York—lurked a group of men dedicated to exterminating cops. Three months later, with the New York assaults still unresolved, the killers struck at the other side of the continent—in California. On August 29, three young black men walked into the police station in suburban Ingleside. Casually approaching the duty sergeant's desk, one of them produced a shotgun from under his coat, pushed the muzzle through the speaking hole in the glass partition, and blasted the unsuspecting sergeant out of his chair. The other two opened fire at random, wounding a woman clerk. Then the trio dashed out, squeezed through an opening previously cut in the freeway fence, and fled in two waiting getaway cars.

In January 1972 it was New York's turn once again. Patrolmen Gregory Foster and Rocco Laurie—another black-and-white radio-car team—were walking around the corner of Avenue B and Eleventh Street when three black men, who had just passed them walking in the other direction, pulled guns from their pockets and started firing from behind at the blue backs. Even after the patrolmen had gone down, the three kept pumping slugs into them, riddling them like sieves. Foster was hit eight times, Laurie six. As before, the assassins grabbed their prostrate victims' service weapons. One was seen performing a kind of war dance over the fallen bodies. Then the three vanished down the street. A day later the inevitable message arrived: "This is the start of our spring offensive. There is more to come. We also dealt with the pigs in Brooklyn. We remember Attica." The note was signed, "The George Jackson Squad of the B. L. A."

For a brief moment it seemed as if the conspirators posed a genuine threat to the country's law-enforcement apparatus. Appearances proved deceptive, for the BLA was not an "army"—not even in the underground sense of the Irish Republican Army. The 200–300 men and women involved were deeply embittered, well armed, and fanatically brave. But they had neither effective leadership and discipline nor long-range strategy. Their organization was haphazard, their planning methods amateurish. They got stoned on grass, which didn't help their timing any. Worst of all, they ignored Mao Tse-tung's dictum that guerrillas must blend with the population "like fish in the sea of the people" until the moment they struck at the enemy. Their enemy, obviously, was the police. Yet the "army" constantly struck at civilians as well: They held up banks, robbed stores, conducted dope deals, and stole cars—felonies for which their idols, the Red Chinese partisans, would have executed them on the spot.

Their organization began to unravel in a series of attacks bungled through sheer negligence. In San Francisco they tried to machine-gun a lone radio patrolman from a car, only to have their weapon jam. In the subsequent chase, three of the four assailants were killed or captured. In St. Louis they opened fire on two cops who tried to give them a traffic ticket. One policeman was riddled, but the other fired back. Within minutes the four BLA men became locked in a hopeless gunfight, with squad cars converging on the scene from all directions. As a consequence, one was killed, two captured, and one escaped. On the New Jersey Turnpike they shot and killed one state trooper but had one man killed and a woman "soldier" wounded by the return fire—all in addition to wrecking their car.

Within two months the BLA's proclaimed "spring offensive" lay in shambles, with their own casualties far higher than the police's. Even more destructive was the fact that they had blown their cover. They were no longer anonymous shadows but fugitives with faces on post-office walls and fingerprints in police files. Their fatal weakness was their background: Nearly all BLA members had criminal records and thus could be traced through the legal machinery once their identities became known.

The commanders were tracked down and arrested. Added to the others captured or slain, this spelled the practical elimination of the BLA's leadership corps. The trials, encompassing a dizzying multitude of charges in a number of states, dragged on for the next three years. Although the killers of Jones and Piagentini were ultimately convicted, other trials ended in hung juries or acquittals that enraged police officers while confirming radicals in their suspicions of police frame-ups and harassment.

Accordingly, the disintegration of the BLA left police and black radicals in an equally embittered state. Most law officers believed that the courts, in order to avoid a further exacerbation of ghetto unrest, had deliberately downplayed the seriousness of a nationwide murder plot against them. The radicals felt, conversely, that the courts had ignored the element of justifiable revenge behind the movement: the memory of countless frame-ups, beatings, insults, and inhumane degradations inflicted on black prisoners.

There were a number of other loose threads tangling up the entire issue. Several BLA members were convicted of felonies ostensibly unconnected with politics. But were they really unconnected? Is a revolutionary who holds up a store a political activist or an ordinary robber? This point has far more than merely legalistic importance—it causes a split in the moral attitudes of large segments of the American public.

On one side there stands what urbanologist Edward Banfield described as "the idea that disadvantaged groups have a kind of quasi right to have their offenses against the law extenuated, or even have them regarded as political acts reflecting a morality 'higher' than obedience to the law." This view is obviously shared by no less a person than Representative John Conyers, chairman of the House subcommittee on crime. "Stealing," wrote the Michigan Democrat, "has always been a means of redistributing the wealth. I'll grant you it has been a risky and inefficient technique, but who can deny that it has paid off for some practitioners?"

On the other side there are ranged those who firmly believe that crime and revolutionary politics don't mix, that in order to pursue one you must abandon the other. This is the attitude of most liberals sympathetic toward the underprivileged. Surprisingly, orthodox Communists think likewise— though for different reasons. For them, any pairing of crime with revolutionary activism is anarchist heresy. They base this on unhappy experiences in the Russian and Chinese civil wars, when both sides engaged in impromptu banditry on occasions. More specifically, as Red Army general Michael Borodin put it:

> We found that banditry undermined the fighting power and morale of our partisan units. It was too easy, too pleasant, compared to facing an armed enemy. After a time elements that indulged in such depredations succumbed to them. They became bandits, pure and simple, and finally had to be liquidated by our better disciplined forces lest they contaminate the entire army with their anti-social bacilli.

In any case, Representative Conyers is wrong about theft being a means of "redistributing the wealth." Wealth has been redistributed by revolution, by taxation, by confiscation, but *never* by larceny, grand or petty. Ancient Rome, medieval France, and Victorian England had theft rates that would stagger the modern imagination, with slum children trained in the craft from babyhood, without accomplishing even an infinitesimal redistribution of worldly goods.

There is no doubt that criminal entanglements of every kind have sabotaged black activism more effectively than establishment resistance. You don't have to reach as low as the ideological yahooism of Eldridge Cleaver—a self-confessed rapist who professed to believe that the black man's body, specifically his genitals, was a weapon in the class-race war, which wasn't so much a belief as an obscenity. But again and again skillful and promising black militants on the road to success were destroyed by their own inability to banish their criminal background.

Typical of their breed was Adam Rogers, a handsome, muscular six-footer who battled his way into municipal prominence in San Francisco before he was thirty. At one time Rogers was assistant director of the Economic Opportunity Council and a commissioner on the Hunters Point Model Cities commission, as well as coordinator of a security-guard program protecting redevelopment sites. He had a foothold on the career ladder of local politics, and his climb upward need not have been handicapped by his extremely murky past. Other wardheelers have ascended to great heights with far grimier records.

But Rogers, for all his street know-how, couldn't learn when to change methods. Instead of utilizing pull, he stuck to strong-arm tactics, alienating his colleagues and his patrons alike. In 1973 he was naive enough to beat up two poverty-program officials in an effort to reinforce his demands for a seventy-five-thousand-dollar contract. Subsequently indicted on their complaint, he pleaded guilty to attempted extortion and battery—in consequence losing his Hunters Point sinecure.

Having finally reemerged with the Housing Authority and begun to move up again, Rogers once more reverted to his old ways—a mistake that was to be his last. In December 1975 Rogers arranged—or was suspected of arranging—a robbery at the home of a woman drug dealer. The lady, however, lured him to her apartment, where her henchmen overpowered him and tied him to a chair. Then she injected him with repeated solutions of heroin, garlic, Clorox, and lye. When, just before he became incoherent, Rogers pleaded to be allowed to "die with dignity," the lady just laughed. She and her pals slowly strangled their victim with an extension cord, letting him gasp for a while before smashing his skull with a hammer. His body was stuffed head first into a sleeping bag and dumped in Candlestick Park.

There has always been a paranoid susceptibility to conspiratorial interpretations of events within America's political thinking. Fifty years ago millions of folks believed that Al Smith was running for president merely to install the Pope in the White House. Thirty years ago a like number were convinced that Henry Wallace, given half a chance, would turn the country into a Soviet colony. Today, however, the conspiratorialists have increased to the point where they could quite possibly elect a President of their own—that is, if they could all believe in the same conspiracy. Luckily, they do not. The far-out fringes of the right and left cherish opposing concepts: the former's nightmare about a Black-Jewish-Commie-Atheist-Pornographers-Faggot cabal and the latter's fantasies regarding a Military-Bankers-CIA-Fascist-Zionist-Mafia complot. The more rational middle doesn't hold with such comprehensive conspiracies. Instead, they feel themselves surrounded by a multiplicity of smaller plots, ranging from artificially created oil shortages to the suppression of news items concerning the origin of UFOs.

Much of this thinking may reflect a form of national shell-shock. America has had its four most popular leaders mown down in mid-career, has been militarily defeated by a midget Asiatic power, has seen a Vice-President narrowly avoid joining a former Attorney General in jail, and has been assured by a ruling President on television that he was *not* a crook. It would take more than ordinary imperturbability to absorb such blows without some neurotic mass reaction.

Partly, however, it is due to a certain native innocence and a dangerous tendency toward untrammeled hero-worship. The revelations concerning the wormy side of the FBI, for instance, would not have been so crushing if the Bureau hadn't represented a slice of popular mythology. An entire generation imbibed the Hoover mystique through a dozen fictitious serials, scores of motion pictures, piles of pulp magazines, and an endless stream of promotion material featured on break-fast-food boxtops. It would have been unthinkable for the chiefs of the Sûreté Nationale or the CID to publicize themselves and their outfits like high-pressure evangelists. Consequently, their fall from grace would not have resulted in any noticeable traumas.

As it was, the whole ballyhoo merely served to keep J. Edgar Hoover in charge of the Bureau for a record forty-six years and turn him into a cult figure. It did not help make the FBI one iota more efficient as a crime-stopper, and in fact may have made it less so. For the boxtop halo around his head served to maintain Mr. Hoover in control long after the idiosyncrasies of dotage should have led to his retirement. This artificial extension of his tenure was a significant factor in the FBI's decline from an effective law-enforcement body to the point where it wasted huge amounts of time and money pursuing plots generated by its own agents.

This was done through COINTELPRO or "Counter-Intelligence Program," according to which FBI infiltrators were to instigate and organize violent acts by subversive organizations, which the Bureau would then either "uncover" and squash or—where it was more politic to do so—allow to proceed. The program was nothing but a warmed-up version of the ancient *agent provocateur* game that the secret police of the Russian Czars played with such gusto. And, like the Czarist minions before them, the FBI learned that the game was self-defeating—it made the Bureau resemble a dog perpetually chasing its own tail.

In May 1976 FBI Director Clarence Kelley issued a public apology for these tactics during a lecture at Westminster College in Fulton, Missouri. "Many of the activities being condemned were, considering the times in which they occurred—the violent sixties—good-faith efforts to prevent bloodshed and wanton destruction of property," Kelley said. "Nevertheless, they were wrongful uses of power."

What these activities mainly achieved was to supply fuel for the conspiratorialists. Having learned that the late Mr. Hoover harbored a phobic dislike for Dr. Martin Luther

King, Jr., it became easy for his detractors to deduce that he had masterminded King's assassination. Because the FBI had cooperated very halfheartedly with the Warren Commission's investigation into the death of John F. Kennedy, the next step was to make the Bureau responsible for it. In the same way, since the FBI's undercover operations were so entangled that one hand frequently didn't know what the other was doing, people began to see the Bureau's hand behind *every* assault on prominent figures. In short, it produced a hot-house atmosphere in which science-fiction fantasies luxuriated, fertilized by the Bureau's mania for deception.

Suspicion flourished not only about the murders of President Kennedy and Dr. King—whose assassins had been "invisible"—but also regarding Robert Kennedy and George Wallace, whose assailants struck in clear view. True, Sirhan Sirhan had shot Robert Kennedy in the midst of eyewitnesses —but who set him up for the deed? At least two learned professors have suggested in all seriousness that the shrimpish Palestinian had been hypnotically programmed, à la *The Manchurian Candidate*, to draw attention by firing at Kennedy while another gunman did the actual killing. Which only serves to confirm the French philosopher Pascal's contention that virtually any belief can be sustained if the believer is willing to encrust it with enough assumptions.*

Similarly, Arthur Bremer, the grinning, dog-food-eating crackpot who shot and paralyzed Governor George Wallace in 1972, has been linked to—hold it, not the FBI, but Nixon's White House "plumbers." I can best describe this link by quoting directly from one of the prime conspiracy journals, the *Berkeley Barb:* "One report suggests that a major television network possessed a photograph tying Bremer in with the 'plumbers,' but refused to publicize it for fear of then-

---

* Further proof was offered by another professor, a luminary of Northwestern University, who published a book entitled *The Hoax of the Twentieth Century*. In it he declared that the genocide of Jews by the Nazis was merely a figment of Zionist propaganda, notwithstanding the intact gas chambers, the mountains of documentation, the evidence of two million survivors, and testimony from three camp commandants and several hundred former guards.

President Nixon's reaction. Those who feel the 'plumbers' were involved point to the potential threat Wallace presented to Nixon's conservative electoral support as a motive."

Note the carefully contrived nebulousness of this statement. The hints and suggestions reveal absolutely nothing but do it with that knowing we're-on-to-them air that is the *prana* of conspiratorialists. Making piles of bricks with two wisps of straw is child's play for them. According to one of his assistants, former New Orleans D.A. Jim Garrison used to discover linkages between conspirators simply through establishing their propinquity—from the fact that they happened to be living not far from one another.

Perhaps the greatest damage done by this two-sided game of obfuscation is the manner in which it helps to obscure the seed of the unrest of which it is a symptom. This seed could be given the single word *hope*: hope raised to inordinate heights by the minstrels of Camelot and dashed by those who followed them; hope curdled and gone sour in the stomach of millions, fermenting into hate.

Eric Hoffer spotlighted this process in his definitive study of political fanaticism, *The True Believer:*

> Misery does not automatically generate discontent, nor is the intensity of discontent directly proportionate to the degree of misery.
>
> Discontent is likely to be highest when misery is bearable; when conditions have so improved that an ideal state seems almost within reach. A grievance is most poignant when almost redressed. . . . It is not actual suffering but the taste of better things which excites people to revolt.

11

While of Unsound Mind

The principle is, that the sole end for which mankind are warranted, individually or collectively, in interfering with the liberty of action of any of their number is self-protection. That is, the only purpose for which power can be rightfully exercised over any member of a civilized community, against his will, is to prevent harm to others. His own good, either physical or moral, is not a sufficient warrant.
> —John Stuart Mill, *On Liberty*

A basic underlying difficulty continues to be a lack of adequate medical knowledge to properly diagnose mental illness. Very little really is known about the human mind.
> —U.S. District Judge Gerald Gesell

"Insane" is an expression we psychiatrists don't use until we get to court. Insanity is a question of public opinion.
> —Dr. Karl Menninger

On Palm Sunday morning, 1976, Melissa Norris was preparing her baby son for church. A tiny, tense nineteen-year-old, she was visiting her friend, Joyce Pope, in Gaithersburg, Maryland, before going to the service. She massaged little Demiko's belly with olive oil and had the baby chortling when she suddenly stared wide-eyed at his skin and began slapping him with her open palm.

The slaps became harder, rougher, and now the mother started babbling in an unnaturally deep voice: "Don't you know I can see you, Devil? Oh, I see you—don't you know I'm God?" She dug her fingernails in the child's navel, making him scream. "Don't you know this is God's property? Don't

249

you know you can't stay in God's property? Oh, what is this evilness I see? Jesus Christ will get you." As her voice rose to shrieking pitch, she slammed both her fists into the baby with all her force and screeched, "Jesus—in the name of Jesus I rebuke you . . . I rebuke you . . . the blood of Jesus is upon you . . ." She rained blows on the child's head and stomach, then hooked a finger in his mouth and lifted him clear off the table, howling snatches of the exorcism ritual practiced by the Christian Tabernacle Church, to which she belonged. ". . . Satan, filthy demon . . . the Lord God rebukes you . . ."

Her friend stood by, horrified but too frightened to intervene, while Norris grabbed the boy by the throat and shook him like a rag doll, until he finally hung limp, his head flopping to one side. Gradually the mother calmed down, and her friend called an ambulance. It was too late. Little Demiko died en route to the hospital. The autopsy revealed a brain hemorrhage brought on by the "severe trauma" of repeated head blows.

Five months later, Melissa Norris stood before Montgomery County Circuit Court Judge John Mitchell, charged with murder. She pleaded not guilty by reason of insanity, and on the face of it had excellent grounds for her plea. The diminutive woman, less than five feet tall but remarkably strong, had a history of violence dating back to her childhood. She herself claimed to have set the fire in which her mother and younger brother burned to death. She had attempted to strangle one schoolmate, and threatened another with a broken bottle. Once, under the influence of LSD, she had choked her grandmother so badly that the old lady called the police. In 1974 she joined a sect of Holy Rollers that believed in exorcising devils. During Norris's pregnancy she underwent exorcism and had several demons extracted from her body. This, however, did not prevent her from twice trying to throttle her baby. Witnesses remembered her acting strangely for days prior to the murder. She had thrown away all her clothes—allegedly on God's command—and informed people that she was Jesus Christ reborn.

For most courts outside the United States, Melissa Norris would have presented no great legal problem. Either she was guilty of murder and would go to prison, or she was insane and would be confined to a mental institution. There appeared to be no logical third alternative. But in America the marriage between psychiatry and law—between the most inexact of sciences and one demanding considerable exactitude —frequently results in judicial paralysis. At times it has made our courtrooms resemble vestibules of Alice's Wonderland. Lewis Carroll could hardly have improved on the proceedings in Montgomery County.

For a start, judge, prosecutor, and defense agreed that Norris had indeed been of unsound mind when she killed her infant. But expert opinion was divided on her *current* condition. One psychiatrist consulted by the court classified her as a "hysterical personality of the dissociative type" with a "100-to-one chance" of committing further violence.

Dr. Edward Acle of Springfield Hospital testified that Norris was psychotic from the time she arrived at Springfield shortly after the murder in April until "a few days before our evaluation on May 19." At that point doctors who had seen her decided that "she did not need any more psychiatric treatment in a hospital setting." It was, Dr. Acle admitted, "a very quick recovery."

A third psychiatrist, Dr. Brian Crowley, stated, "This case is a deep and vexing mystery to me. I think predictions as to this lady's future are extremely difficult . . . since there is some possibility that whatever produced this mysterious condition . . . may produce it in the future. As of today, I would not sign a commitment certificate."

This expert testimony couched in all the scientific precision of an astrology column, presented Judge Mitchell with a dilemma. He had already accepted the accused's insanity plea, so he could not sentence her for murder. On the other hand, it appeared that she was not certifiably insane *at that moment,* and so could not be sent to an asylum. The judge delivered what seemed to him the only possible verdict: He ordered the prisoner released. Melissa Norris, having committed infanticide in front of an eyewitness, left the court a free woman. Furthermore, as a result of her trial she was no longer required to undergo psychiatric treatment.

But, faithfully adhering to the logic of Wonderland, the law's wrath fell on the eyewitness. Although she hadn't laid a finger on the child, the hapless Joyce Pope was solemnly declared guilty of child abuse. She was sentenced to two concurrent seven-year prison terms, of which all but eighteen months was suspended. As a kind of absurd footnote, the judge ordered her—the witness—to undergo psychiatric treatment while on probation. Melissa Norris had no such obligation.

The wheel of justice had turned full circle. And State's Attorney Lawrence Beck had received an answer to the question he had posed rhetorically during his court plea: "Must we really wait for another incident of violence to determine that this defendant is a danger to society?" The answer was yes. What's more, if such an incident recurred in the future, the result would quite likely be the same. For one of the main characteristics of the quandary we have built into our legal system is its permanence. It doesn't wear out or even thin with repetition.

Consider the career of one Garrett Trapnell, the personable son of a prominent Southern family. In a period of about eighteen years Mr. Trapnell was charged with a multitude of serious crimes ranging from armed robbery to airline hijacking. On each and every occasion he managed to convince the courts and the psychiatrists that he had been insane when he committed the crime but wasn't insane any more. By sticking to this ploy he avoided not only prison sentences but also any appreciable stretch in mental hospitals.

The blame for these absurdities rests less with the psychiatrists than with the role we have thrust upon them. The role is that of a forensic expert, akin to a forensic pathologist but with one essential difference. The pathologist, concerned with the flesh-and-blood evidence of the body, is required to testify only on what has already happened to that body.

The psychiatrist, who deals with the intangibles of the human mind, is expected to predict its future workings as well.

Adding to the immensity of this task is the fact that most psychiatrists are quite untrained for it. Forensic psychiatry is that sub-branch of the profession dealing with the legal aspects of mental disorders. This means that in addition to his medical education a forensic psychiatrist should spend at least a year studying the mechanics of the law, the rules of evidence, and a modicum of criminology. Only a handful of Americans, however, have received any such training—probably not enough to meet the needs of a single state.

Consequently, most psychiatrists consulted by the legal system are ordinary practitioners, completely out of their element in judicial matters. They resemble qualified riflemen called upon to act as ballistics experts. The average psychiatrist rarely sees a patient who doesn't come to him voluntarily. A voluntary patient seeks help and offers cooperation and a considerable degree of frankness in order to get it. But a criminal doesn't want help; he wants *out*. And once he acquires a smattering of the procedures involved, psychiatrists become sitting ducks for him. Providing he isn't assigned to the same individual each time, he can hoodwink them a dozen times over because with each session his knowledge of the "right" phrases grows.

While forensic psychiatrists possess a certain cognizance of criminal behavior patterns, even the veterans among them privately claim very little skill in forecasting future violence. In fact, I noticed that the greater their experience, the stronger their tendency to hedge their bets. Dr. Harvey Bluestone, formerly Director of Psychiatric Services in New York's Sing Sing Prison, gave a singularly mirthless laugh when I raised the question. He said, "No way. I can only go by past records, same as a policeman or any intelligent human being. If the record shows a man has assaulted fifty people, chances are he'll assault a fifty-first. But a psychiatrist's expertise at predicting this is no better than a probation officer's or a social worker's or that of the secretary who types the report.

"The trouble is that psychiatrists allow themselves to be misused. That, as professionals, they are given to making grandiose promises they can't deliver. Why? Because of the fees. Because there's money involved. Take a big case—a murder case with big financial or prestige stakes. Well, the defense attorney and the prosecution will each hire a psychiatrist. And each psychiatrist will look at the same set of facts and come to a different conclusion. And invariably the psychiatrist comes to the conclusion favoring the side that pays him. That may sound pretty harsh, but that's the way it goes. So you'll have one expert pronouncing a defendant sane and the other pronouncing him insane—and both basing their pronouncements on the same facts. The reason for this is, of course, our adversary trial procedure. Each expert winds up being in the employ of the prosecution or the defense—and the court winds up with two conflicting diagnoses."

The adversary trial concept, which allows virtually no "neutral" opinions, offers powerful temptations to psychiatrists. Other experts are more or less bound by the concrete frameworks of their fields, but mental tests can be interpreted so broadly that two testers may reach diametrically opposite conclusions without fudging their data or consciously acting in bad faith. Thus, one psychiatrist, testifying for the defense at a D.C. Superior Court murder trial, told the jury that in his opinion *any* person who committed a major criminal act was legally insane. In reply, psychoanalyst Dr. Ernest van den Haag commented that in *his* opinion the psychiatrist was legally insane.

Even if we scrapped the adversary system in our courts and used psychiatrists only as impartial advisers, their testimony would be of little help to the judicial system—at least in the trial stages of a case. Their science is, and perhaps must be, far too opaque to produce the clear-cut judgments required. Under cross-examination—simply by being forced to say black or white when the real answer is an indeterminate shade of gray—they will always be driven into pronouncements they can't validate and frequently didn't mean in the first place.

The term "insane," for instance, is not part of their vocabulary, yet they are constantly made to use it because vital portions of our legal code hinge upon its application. Our earliest legal test of insanity, the English M'Naghten Rule, asked only if the defendant knew "the nature and quality of his act" and was able to distinguish right from wrong.* In 1954 this was expanded by the Durham Rule of the D.C. Circuit Court of Appeals, and was further refined in 1962 in the Model Penal Code of 1962, which bases the test on a defendant's lack of "substantial capacity either to appreciate the criminality of his conduct or to conform his conduct to the requirements of the law." This added the notion of "irresistible impulse" to the criteria, with the result that a person may be found innocent by reason of insanity if he was unable to control his acts, even though he knew that they were wrong.

These standards appear flexible enough but are very difficult to apply in a court of law. Strictly speaking, almost impossible. How do you prove that an impulse was "irresistible"? Above all, how do you prove it when psychiatrists use one terminology and the legal system uses another? As Chicago law professor Franklin Zimring observed: "If your psychiatric labels aren't clear and the legal standards that you use to feed them into decisions are foggy, fog times fog equals fog squared." Proof is so difficult to supply that only about 3 percent of insanity pleas are accepted by juries. Nearly all the horrendous mass murderers in recent years were pronounced legally sane, even though some of them ate their victims. Just because a person hears voices commanding him to kill does not mean that jurors will accept these commands as "irresistible."

Occasionally judges won't, either. In New York's celebrated "Son of Sam" case, Judge John Starkey told a newspaper reporter that he wouldn't accept a guilty plea from the accused, David Berkowitz, if the suspect kept insisting

---

* M'Naghten, who believed himself persecuted by Sir Robert Peel, mistakenly shot and killed Peel's secretary. He was acquitted on grounds of insanity in the famous ruling formulated by the English High Court in 1843.

he had been driven to murder by demons.* Berkowitz claimed that he had shot all of his six victims on the commands of demons and monsters and that he had unsuccessfully tried to fight these apparitions: "I tried to burn them alive and shoot them, you know, shoot them in the yards. But they just wouldn't die. . . ."

An insanity plea also contains a Catch-22 situation, which explains why it is rarely used except in homicide cases. An accused acquitted on grounds of insanity cannot be held on criminal charges, but he or she can be committed to an institution and may be held longer than the prison term following conviction would have been. *May* . . . Here we enter a jungle of uncertainties where all signposts are obscured and incarceration or freedom becomes a matter of luck as much as anything else. The average stay of defendants committed to institutions is four years. But if they were originally found unfit to stand trial, the state may decide to try them on the original charge after doctors declare that they have regained mental competence. Whether the authorities actually do so depends on their alertness, on the time, money, and effort required, and on how aroused the public had been over their crime.

There are so many variables involved that the worst mass killer in Arizona history came within an inch of release after just four years in confinement. John Gilbert Freeman, a balding, beetle-browed upholsterer, had been through several minor scrapes with the law during his forty-one years. Most people merely considered him a foul-mouthed boor with a hair-trigger temper; some guessed that he was also a pathological liar; but nobody noticed signs of mental aberration in him, despite his habit of reacting to any interruption of his work with streams of four-letter invective.

In May 1971, Freeman's wife walked out of their Phoenix home, taking their two children along and telling the police that she "couldn't stand that man any more." From that moment, Freeman became obsessed with the belief that a

---

* Judge Starkey stepped down as trial judge of the case because of criticism over his discussing it with the New York *Post* reporter.

former fellow worker, who had deserted his own family, had run off with his wife. There wasn't a shred of evidence to support this, but Freeman began flying around the country, trying to catch the two together. He also took to visiting Novella Bentley, the man's deserted wife, trying to pump her for information on her husband's whereabouts.

In his coarse way, Freeman was perfectly amiable whenever he called at the ramshackle East Polk Street house of Mrs. Bentley, frequently playing parlor games with the children. Then, on September 2, the upholsterer flew to Los Angeles, allegedly to see a famous psychic who would reveal to him where his wife and children were hiding. He never saw a psychic, but was arrested on a child-molesting charge. The following day he was released on bond and caught the evening plane back to Phoenix.

About eleven o'clock that night, with a thunderstorm looming over the humid city, Freeman went to the East Polk Street house for the last time. He carried two .38-caliber revolvers, which he had bought in a pawnshop a few hours earlier. The house was filled with people: Mrs. Bentley, her daughter, her son-in-law, and four small children sleeping in a back room. Freeman opened fire on the three adults in the living room, emptying both revolvers into their bodies and the walls. Then, using a fork from the kitchen to extract a jammed cartridge, he reloaded. The children in the back had slept right through the fusillade. They were still sleeping soundly when Freeman walked in and, one by one, blew their brains out. With seven people lying dead around him, Freeman had established Arizona's one-man homicide record.

The police caught him just as he was leaving the house. Freeman dropped his revolvers, the barrels still hot, and surrendered peacefully. He remained silent until his arraignment five days later, when he shouted at the gathered newsmen: "It wasn't me! I didn't kill them! They were murdered by Communists!" Even before the preliminary hearing, court-appointed psychiatrists judged him legally incompetent to stand trial. Freeman was committed to the Arizona State Mental Hospital in Phoenix.

Early in 1975, a hospital panel decided that Freeman had regained his sanity. Their finding contradicted another medical board's conclusion that he was "an explosive and abrasive personality and a danger to society." But that was a minor point. The essential thing was that the state had never formally indicted him on any charge whatsoever, and now—four years later—it was technically too late to do so.

Freeman's attorneys immediately filed legal briefs in an attempt to gain complete freedom for him. The authorities in turn launched a series of dubious maneuvers to try—somehow—to hang on to him. Lost in the maze of legalistic hairsplitting was the only consideration that *should* have counted: Can a delusionary killer of seven people be permitted to walk free under any circumstances?

The State Supreme Court pondered the matter and finally ruled that Freeman could still be indicted because the original competency decision meant that the government couldn't have indicted him within the required 120 days after commission of the crime. The court machinery creaked into action, gathered witnesses, empaneled a jury, and proceeded to prove all over again what had already been established—that, apparently because he suspected their father and husband of sleeping with his wife, John Gilbert Freeman had slain seven people. The accused was found guilty. After sentencing him to seven consecutive life terms, Judge C. Kimball Rose ordered Freeman back to the state hospital that had already declared him sane for further mental examinations.

The above explains some of the reluctance of jurors to accept insanity pleas in murder cases—not because they really doubt the derangement of the accused, but because they may be too thoroughly convinced of it. No one could seriously question of lunacy of John Linley Frazier, the first of the Santa Cruz mass slayers. Frazier was convinced that the Biblical Revelation to John was addressed specifically to him and that God had chosen him to preserve the world's ecology. In October 1970 he bound and shot a prominent local eye surgeon, his wife, his two young sons, and his secretary, dumped their bodies in the swimming pool, then set the house on fire. Later Frazier explained that he had wiped out the family because they were "destroying the natural environment." A California jury found him legally sane—undoubtedly because they couldn't face the risk of having him turned loose four years hence.

If there is one group about which the public harbors greater misconceptions than about psychiatrists, it is their patients. This stems partly from folklore, partly from the media—both of which project melodramatic images of "mad killers." In reality, the homicide rate among the mentally ill is *lower* than that of the rest of the population. Alcohol is an infinitely bigger cause of murder than mental illness, which in the vast majority of cases tends to render sufferers helpless rather than aggressive.

It is true, though, that mass murderers (with the exception of professional hit men) are nearly always mentally deranged. Most of them can be classified as either paranoid or sexually sadistic, but within these broad and fuzzy definitions lie a multitude of nuances and subdefinitions. One form of paranoia, for instance, is the persecution complex. The victim may imagine that the U.S. Mail is conspiring to isolate him from the world. He finds fresh proof of this plot every time the postman doesn't bring him any mail. In textbook language, he is characterized by "persistent, unalterable, systematized, logically constructed delusions." His reaction to these delusions can vary widely. He may simply write endless streams of letters to newspapers; he may attack postmen or blow up post offices; or—and this is one of the insidious features of his disease—he may assault people or objects he somehow *associates* with the U.S. Mail.

An example of paranoia is the case of Frederick Cowan, a moving-company worker of Neanderthal looks and mentality. Cowan, who lived in New Rochelle, New York, weighed 250 pounds, was covered with swastika and skull tattoos, fervently admired Hitler, and believed that Jews and blacks were at the root of his and the world's troubles. In February

1977 he went on a rifle rampage at his company's office, killing five people and wounding five others before finally turning the gun on himself.

The most commonly diagnosed mental illness among murderers is paranoid schizophrenia. Persons suffering from this disorder experience visual or auditory hallucinations—they see things and hear voices. They tend to be withdrawn and suspicious. Their disease has an irregular pattern: Acute psychotic stages are interspersed with remissions, during which the symptoms may vanish completely. In those intervals the sufferers are, to all intents and purposes, rational. The dangers inherent in their condition depend entirely on what their hallucinations tell them. They may be ordered to eat nothing but green apples, or they may be commanded to go out and kill.

Herbert William Mullin, the second of the Santa Cruz multicides, was a classic paranoid schizophrenic. A trim, neatly dressed, soft-spoken young man in his mid-twenties, Mullin killed thirteen people between October 1972 and February 1973. He came from a staunchly Catholic and military background (his father was a retired Marine colonel) and always retained intense pride in his appearance. There was an uptight, sleek, and lethal quality about him—a distinct air of menace highly unusual among mass slayers. Mullin's dark eyes positively crackled with hatred when he was approached by bearded longhairs or anyone needing a wash. At several stages of his life he had practiced homosexuality.

Mullin referred to his victims as "sacrifices." He sacrificed them for the sake of humanity, in order to prevent earthquakes. He shared his concern over earthquakes with a good many other locals, for Santa Cruz lies near the San Andreas fault, a geological quake center. His killing spree coincided with a rash of predictions by assorted California psychics that a cataclysmic earthquake—dwarfing the famous San Francisco disaster of 1906—was due to occur in January 1973.

Mullin believed that he could ward off this catastrophe by piling up sufficient sacrifices—by eliminating a handful to save thousands. This theory was whispered to him by his voices and strengthened by confused interpretations of the Bible, his favorite part being the story of Jonah, "who saved the lives of his shipmates by jumping overboard and drowning." Somehow Mullin ignored the great fish.

His murders were almost totally indiscriminate and frequently committed on the spur of the moment. His victims included a priest whom he stabbed during confession, four young campers whom he shot outside their tent, two families that he massacred in their homes, and an old man whom he shot dead in his back yard. This final killing took place one morning when Mullin was supposed to take a load of firewood to his parents' house. When he awoke, he said, he received a "clear telepathic message" from his father: "Before you deliver a stick of that wood, I want you to kill me somebody." Mullin did so dutifully, in broad daylight, and so publicly that his capture was inevitable. The squad cars hunted him down while he was en route to his parents with the promised load of wood.

At his trial, the defense enlisted the aid of two outstanding psychiatrists: Dr. Donald Lunde of Stanford University and David Marlowe of UCSC at Santa Cruz. Both testified that Mullin was a paranoid-type schizophrenic "who doesn't appreciate the enormity of the evil and does not regard his acts as base and anti-social." But Marlowe made a tactical error in noting that the same diagnosis had been made by five different doctors at the five hospitals to which Mullin had committed himself voluntarily. The jury knew that all these hospitals had seen fit to release him, and they weren't interested in the legalistic fine points that had caused them to do so. The jurors were local people, folks who would have to live alongside Mullin if a sixth hospital let him go. So, contrary to logic and in the face of all evidence, they found him sane and guilty of eleven counts of murder. In this paradoxical fashion does psychiatric evidence boomerang in American courts.

It does so to an even greater extent in the case of sexually sadistic murderers—mainly because we still don't know (and few doctors pretend to know) what sadism is and what causes it. All we know are the outward manifestations, which can be nightmarish.* Like paranoia, traces of sadism exist in millions of quite harmless people who become sexually aroused by inflicting pain and/or humiliation on their partners. There are only degrees of difference—but 179 degrees— between them and the sadistic psychopaths who torture, mutilate, sometimes cannibalize their victims in order to reach sexual climax.

Sadism has an astonishing number of shadings and variations. You even get long-distance practitioners like Dr. Neill Cream, one of the ogres haunting Victorian London, who fed strychnine pills to prostitutes and relished his mental visions of their death agonies hours after leaving them. But the "ideal" combination of pain and humiliation is achieved by rape. Virtually all multiple rapists are sadistic (though not every sadist is a rapist), and rape-slayings are by far the most common form of sadistic murder.

During the seventeen-month period ending in September 1974, New York City experienced the most gruesome series of rape-murders in its history. There were some particularly macabre twists to this chain: Most of the nine victims were elderly, and eight of them lived in the same decaying hotel as their destroyer; the one exception resided next door. The hostelry boasting the plush title of Park Plaza Hotel, on West Seventy-seventh Street, stood as a crumbling symptom of the cancer gnawing Manhattan. Once an elegant, well-groomed establishment, the Park Plaza had become "a hovel with an awning" housing senior citizens in various stages of quiet desperation, together with hordes of what used to be termed "undesirables." It was in character for the place to employ someone like Calvin Jackson as a porter. Jackson

---

* The term "sadism," derived from the Marquis de Sade, was coined in the 1880s by the Viennese neurologist Richard von Krafft-Ebing. He also formulated the word "masochism," from the name of the novelist Sacher-Masoch, who specialized in that theme. Although Krafft-Ebing produced the first scientific case studies of this perversion, his explanations were patently wrong. He believed it to be an abnormal extension of masculine aggressiveness, ignoring the long historical cavalcade of female sadists.

was twenty-six, an ex-convict and a former junkie unable to hold a job anywhere else. But the Park Plaza gave him a peeling, roach-infested hole (which he shared with a girl friend) and let him work for his keep. Even after getting arrested for stealing a TV set from one of the hotel rooms, Jackson kept right on portering. He was cheap labor.

The first five murders on the premises passed almost unnoticed. The women—ranging in age from seventy-one to eighty-nine—lay in their oven-hot rooms for days before being found. By then their bodies had so deteriorated that the medical examiners made a rough stab at "chronic alcoholism" and let it go at that. Somehow they never noticed the strangulation marks on their throats, or the fact that, either before or after death, all had been raped.

The next three slayings were obvious enough. Seventy-nine-year-old Mrs. Yetta Vishnefsky was tied up with her stockings and had a knife protruding from her back. Kate Lewinsohn, sixty-five, had a fractured skull, and Winifred Miller was set on fire in her bed. But police investigations led nowhere. As a 4th Homicide Zone detective told me, "That place was wall-to-wall drug addicts, alcoholics, prostitutes, and pimps, and the rest old-age pensioners too scared to open their mouths."

Only when Jackson struck outside his home ground, in the adjoining apartment house, did the cops locate an eyewitness who had seen him climbing the fire escape. His last victim, sixty-nine-year-old Mrs. Pauline Spanierman, was raped, strangled, and battered to death in her twelfth-floor apartment. But now the police had a description of Jackson. They arrested him in the street a few blocks from the hotel. That evening he confessed, not only to the Spanierman slaying but to the eight others as well—five of which weren't even on the homicide list.

Jackson's trial centered around the insanity issue and little else. At the start the prosecution played his taped confessions to the court. In a whispered, whiny, spine-chilling monotone Jackson recited his deeds, murder by murder. They all sounded curiously alike, except that each time a different human being died:

> . . . I told her I wasn't going to kill her. Then I strangled her with my hands. I made sure she was dead by forcing her face down into a pillow. Then I sat in the room for an hour, watching to make certain she was dead. I sat there and I looked at her all the time. . . . When I came in the room, she was scared and she offered me some sex. She offered me money, too, and she talked to me for a long while. I guess she was hoping I'd leave, like that I might just be satisfied having sex with her. . . . She put her foot in my chest and tried to kick me away. That's when I bit her on the chest. Then I smothered her with a pillow, and she began peeing on her nightgown. . . .

It went on for seven hours: the pleas for mercy, the futile attempts to alternately cajole and bribe, the intercourse before or after the killing (Jackson couldn't always remember which came first), the petty thefts of cash or portable radios. And after seven hours there still was no explanation—no reason why a thief, living with a common-law wife, should rape and murder women who could be his grandmothers. Only a few incoherent stammers: "Well, I guess I kinda broke wild there, you know . . ." The court didn't know. Nobody knew—not even the psychiatrists, who, in an attempt to disguise that fact, unleashed torrents of trade jargon on the assembly.

They were, as usual, divided. Two psychiatrists testified that the defendant was sane at the time of the killings. Two more opined that he was mentally unfit to stand trial. Donald Tucker, one of Jackson's court-appointed attorneys, did his best to translate their opinions into English meaningful to the jury. "Is this a sane man?" he demanded. "He went to the refrigerator in nearly every apartment. He prepared a meal and ate it as he watched the body. He stayed for hours. Now I ask you—is this a legally sane man?"

The jurors thought so—they found Jackson guilty of all nine murders. Supreme Court Justice Aloysious Melia added his own touch of fantasy by giving him *two* life prison terms per killing—eighteen life terms all told. Which in practice meant that the defendant would not be eligible for parole until he was fifty-six.

Currently, there are reform moves afoot aimed at eliminating psychiatric evidence from murder trials. The reformers would make insanity arguments admissible only *after* the defendant has been convicted, primarily as aids (not directives) for the judge in sentencing. This would rob psychiatrists of nearly all the weight they now carry in court. It would also rid them of the temptation to color their testimony for the benefit of whichever side employs them. Some of the most ardent advocates of such reforms are psychiatrists sickened by what they consider nothing less than the prostitution of their profession.

Among them is Dr. Lee Coleman, a youngish, bearded Berkeley practitioner campaigning for a total divorce of psychiatry and law. "That doesn't mean I favor eliminating sanity assessments altogether," he told me. "Only I don't think psychiatrists should make them. Who should? Ordinary people. Eyewitnesses, police officers, next-door neighbors, the defendant himself . . . anyone actually involved in the case. Not experts attempting *post hoc* explanations of what supposedly went on in someone else's mind six months or two years earlier. In other words, you would develop testimony on the insanity issue just as you would on any other point. But let's throw out the idea that there are certain people— in this case psychiatrists—who have an expertise on this matter which, in fact, cannot be demonstrated."

Most reformers favor somewhat less radical changes, but all agree that psychiatric findings should not be superimposed on a court decision. Explaining one reform bill to a press interviewer, Paul Summit, counsel for the Senate Judiciary Committee, stated: "Whereas now a judge has no choice except to turn such a defendant over to doctors who may release him at their discretion, under the new bill a judge could, for instance, sentence the defendant to a term of fifteen years but add something like, 'In light of the medical evidence I've heard, I am ordering you to such and

such mental hospital.' That way the judge maintains some
measure of control over the case."

The proposed bill in question was modeled after a law
that has governed Swedish trial procedures for the past
twenty-five years. But in America it ran into furious opposition—not so much from psychiatrists as from groups
like the American Civil Liberties Union. "They had to go
all the way to Sweden to find a law that fitted their concept,
and it's just another example of trying to take away the
rights of the community and give it to some judge" was
the comment of Charles Morgan, the ACLU's Washington
director. "Those jurors aren't stupid. Matter of fact, they're
probably smarter than the lawyers and the psychiatrists. They
know who's lying and who's telling the truth, and they can
tell it from just listening to the defendant and looking at
him, and listening to the psychiatrists and looking at them."

I can only assume that Mr. Morgan was joking. Otherwise,
the suspicion arises that he has never seen a jury in action—
at least not during an insanity trial. For the fact is that most
psychiatric testimony is totally incomprehensible to jurors—
as it is to most mortals. This has nothing to do with
"stupidity," merely with the fabulous Esperanto employed
by psychiatrists on the stand. What, for example, is a juror
to make of the statement delivered by Dr. Emilia Salanga,
one of the experts testifying on the sanity of Calvin Jackson:
"There are problems in concept formation which may lead
to misinterpretation of reality, even to hallucinations wherein
an individual perceives a nonexistent stimulus—or it could
be in the form of delusion, which is a false belief that cannot be corrected by reason."

Psychiatrists are generally not to blame for their bewildering impact in courtrooms. The concepts of their profession
simply don't mesh with the terms imposed by the judiciary,
and our attempts to make them fit are fundamentally as
futile as forcing wrongly shaped pieces into a jigsaw puzzle.*

---

* The psychiatrists' inability to agree on an accused person's sanity is responsible for confessed double murderer Gregory Shaddy walking the streets
as a free man at the time of this writing. Shaddy, 18, was raised in the

A tragic example of this disjuncture in standards is provided by the case of former Eagle Scout, altar boy, and Marine Charles Whitman. Tall, fair, crew-cut, and superbly athletic, Whitman was also a straight-A student at the University of Texas in Austin. In short, he was virtually a ringer for the *Reader's Digest* image of the all-American boy. He was, that is, until the morning of August 1, 1966, when he took a rifle, a shotgun, a revolver, two pistols, and seven hundred rounds of ammunition to the observation deck of the college tower and started shooting. At that point he had already stabbed his mother to death, followed by his wife (a former Queen of the Fair of Needville, Texas), and the receptionist at the observation deck. During the next few hours he added outstanding marksmanship to the other qualities he had displayed at the school. He shot and killed fourteen people and wounded thirty more before being finally blasted to pieces by policemen charging up the stairs. Apart from his arsenal, he was found to have carried a bottle of spray deodorant, which he used in the intervals between bursts of firing.

It turned out that Whitman had been seeing the college psychiatrist prior to his rampage. He had told him that he adored his mother and his wife and that he hated his father "with a mortal passion." He also confided—four months before his rampage—that he kept thinking of "climbing that tower with a deer rifle and shooting people." The doctor maintained that this was "a fairly common fantasy

---

wealthy Westside section of Wichita, Kansas. On the night of July 24, 1975, he hacked and stabbed both his parents to death and stuffed their bodies into a bedroom closet. His first trial ended in a hung jury; the second acquitted him on grounds of insanity. In March, 1978, a panel at the Larned state security hospital, where Shaddy had been confined, decided that he was now cured and not dangerous to anyone. Shaddy was released and consequently became entitled to his share of the estate left by the parents he had slaughtered—estimated at over $400,000. Commented Clinical Director George W. Getz: "I really don't know whether he was originally insane. The jury found that he was. . . . I really feel sorry for juries because of all the damn fool things psychiatrists say." According to *Time* magazine, the prosecution in the case believes that Shaddy had managed to hoodwink the psychiatrists as well as the jury.

among students on this campus." Which, as an impromptu survey later revealed, was quite correct.

Had Whitman been taken alive, the psychiatrist would certainly have been asked to testify on his sanity. What would he have told the court? Would he have said that Whitman had been under severe nervous tension since his parents separated, that he suffered splitting headaches, that he worried about his grades, that he found it difficult to control his hostility? These conditions also applied to dozens of other students visiting the doctor—as, apparently, did the fantasy of sniping from the college tower, as did Whitman's hatred of his father, as did his marital frictions. Were all these students insane, then? More important, were they all potential killers? Inasmuch as they all displayed similar symptoms, why was it that only one of them actually killed? And why this particular one? Furthermore, why did he kill his beloved mother, wife, and fifteen total strangers, and not the father he professed to hate?

Given time for prolonged treatment, assisted by medication, the doctor *might* have been able to stabilize Whitman to a point where he would not have been dangerous *at that time*. But to predict his future behavior and to classify it according to recognized legal categories would have been as impossible for any psychiatrist as it is for a physician to predict cancer. He knows the conditions under which cancer frequently occurs, and he can warn of their presence. Beyond that, any forecast falls within the realm of guesswork—as would any psychiatric pronouncement on the "irresistibility" of the impulse that drove Whitman to his deed.

These diagnostic weaknesses, combined with the decrepitude of our custodial facilities, are the reason for the increasing reluctance of juries to accept *any* insanity plea. Thus, in 1972, a Maryland handyman named Richard Hilliard Jackson received ten years imprisonment for killing his little stepson. He served twenty-three months before being paroled to a halfway-house in Riverdale. But the authorities there couldn't cope with Jackson's drinking problems . . . so they released him!

In July 1977, Jackson was back in court on another murder charge. He had beaten and strangled an old woman to death. A psychiatric report claimed that on the date of the woman's murder, "the defendant was, in all likelihood, suffering from an acute psychotic state, characterized by agitation, paranoia and suicidal ideas, which was partly due to acute alcoholic intoxication but also due to his basic paranoid personality . . ." The jury nevertheless found him sane and guilty, possibly because they feared a repetition of the halfway-house farce that could dump a deranged killer back in their midst within a couple of years.

In the fall of 1969, a University of California research assistant from India named Prosenjit Poddar told his psychologist that he intended to kill Tatiana Tarasoff, a girl student who had rejected his love. The psychologist promptly informed the campus authorities, urging that Poddar be detained because of "severe paranoiac schizophrenic reaction." The police picked up Poddar and questioned him, but released him when he appeared quite rational. The psychologist's superior, moreover, ordered the officers to return the warning letter written by his subordinate and to *destroy all copies of it*.

On October 27 the Indian caught the girl on the front porch of her home and stabbed her twenty-two times with a bread knife. He was convicted of second-degree murder, which, with that whimsicality peculiar to our justice system, was reduced to manslaughter (meaning that, on second thought, the court became persuaded that the bread knife had accidentally slipped into Tatiana twenty-two times). Four years later Poddar was deported back to India. But in California the case had a momentous aftermath.

Tatiana Tarasoff's parents sued the university for two hundred thousand dollars, claiming that the authorities should have taken more strenuous measures to prevent the murder of their daughter. The lawsuit itself will probably roll around the court system till doomsday, but it produced a historical ruling by the California Supreme Court: In July 1976 the justices decided that a psychotherapist who knows that a patient intends to harm another person has a legal obligation to warn the intended victim. This may be taken for granted by the unlearned laity, but it assuredly is not in the psychiatric profession. Poddar's therapist, while writing to the police, never bothered to inform Miss Tarasoff that her life might be in danger, and his superior even took it upon himself to eradicate all traces of the original warning. As a result, Tatiana became a sacrificial lamb on the altar of psychiatric hubris—she was not even sufficiently fore-warned to run when her killer came for her.

The court decision, which struck most of the public as eminently sensible, caused a concerted howl of rage in psychiatric circles. Their god-priest status was being tampered with by secular hands! Suddenly Freud's couch became equivalent to the confessional box. The ruling, the doctors claimed, interfered with the confidentiality between patient and therapist. They declared that patients would now hide their homicidal tendencies—thus making it impossible to cure them. The medicos ignored the fact that the law already obliged them, for similar reasons, to report certain cases, such as gunshot wounds. They likewise ignored the detail that the ruling applied only when the life of a specific person was threatened—a far cry from having to divulge random fantasies.

The court decision may have dented some psychiatric *amour-propre*. But, as Justice Mathew O. Tobriner aptly wrote: "The protective privilege ends where the public peril begins."

The public peril, unfortunately, does not begin with troubled patients voicing violent thoughts. All too frequently it starts when the medical authorities ignore them. Whether this happens through the supercilious callousness of some therapists or by official decree, the resultant tragedies are equally unforgivable because they were so avoidable. Perhaps no sadder register exists than the long list of demented men and women who literally begged for help and were shrugged off.

The list is particularly lengthy in California, which boasted the nation's finest mental health system until Governor Ronald Reagan decided to practice some fiscal conservatism on it. After his election in 1966, Reagan proclaimed that mental patients should be "restored to community care"—a heartwarming euphemism for dumping them on their counties or on their families, neither of which could cope with them. The Reagan administration, which suspected the entire mental-health system of being vaguely "leftist," closed down five state hospitals and was prevented from closing the rest only by a protest bill passed in the legislature over the governor's veto. Still, it managed to reduce the number of inmates from twenty-two thousand to seven thousand by the simple expedient of tightening requirements for any hospitalization of more than three days.

The army of discharged patients were to receive treatment of sorts in community health centers operated by the counties. But there Reagan had reckoned without his fellow conservatives in Washington. Federal funds already allocated for the construction and staffing of these centers were cut off in 1972. Consequently, most of the projected centers were never built. The existing few were reduced to little more than dispensaries for tranquilizers, providing no "treatment" worth mentioning. San Mateo County, for instance, had twenty beds available for over four hundred patients in the area.

Not many families could afford the hundred dollars a day charged by private hospitals. The vast majority of ex-patients were herded into slum sections that quickly became known as "psycho ghettos." They filled hideous little hotels and boardinghouses, some of which you could smell from across the street. One of the side effects of the Reagan administration was the steadily swelling stream of babbling, screaming, or silently wall-eyed derelicts wandering around California cities. Most of them were merely pitiful and harmless; a few of them were not. These few gave the state a taste of horror such as it had never known.

In Santa Cruz County three former mental patients accounted for the murders of twenty-three people in less than a year. One of them was Herb Mullin, the slayer of thirteen discussed earlier in this chapter. Between 1969 and 1972 Mullin voluntarily committed himself to five mental hospitals. Each time the doctors diagnosed him as schizophrenic, twice as paranoid and highly dangerous. *"His personality profile indicates strong aggressive impulses which are tenuously controlled by denial and a passive stance. He has lately had insomnia and fearful fantasies. . . ."* Five times the doctors prescribed medication and turned him out. His sister commented naively: "They have such a funny way of treating people in mental hospitals. They keep releasing them."

While Mullin achieved fame as one of America's top multicides, others, caught in a similar plight, rated no more than a few paragraphs in the local press. Gloria Ladd committed herself to Napa Hospital after trying to kill her two small sons. She was given a measure of therapy and sent home. Later she succeeded in killing both her children, but failed at suicide.

Michael Butcher, driven frantic by the "voices" gibbering inside his head, pleaded with the authorities at Mendocino Hospital to let him stay. The doctors sent him home to San Francisco. Several months later, he shot and killed a stranger he saw jogging along the beach.

The mother of Kenneth Russell as well as her neighbors begged the doctors at Atascadero Hospital to keep the boy "until you're quite certain he's been cured." The doctors were far from certain, but Kenneth was discharged just the same. Three weeks later he was back in confinement—after having killed his closest friend.

In July, 1977, Michael Lowe rang the El Cajon police and informed them that he had bought a shotgun and was going to kill his estranged wife Cecilia. When the officers arrived to pick him up, he explained that he didn't really want to shoot his wife, he just wanted to talk to someone. The cops delivered him to the Community Mental Health Clinic, where Lowe was held for forty-eight hours, then released. As a local Mental Health spokesman put it: "If a person is not gravely disabled or a danger to himself or others—out he goes. It's a violation of his civil rights to keep him." One month later Lowe broke into his mother-in-law's house, where Cecilia was staying, shot his wife dead while she was trying to call the police, then fired a bullet through his own brain.

"It wasn't just the budget-cutting of the Reaganites that produced this crisis," said Dr. Nathan Schaub. "It's a combination of economic, legal and sociological factors, all interacting to produce a terrible quandary in the mental hygiene field. There is the Lanterman-Petris-Short Act—the Bill of Rights for mental patients. A good, humane law—only it's loaded like a time bomb. You see, the Act states that an individual can be detained only if he is a danger to himself or to others, or so gravely disturbed that he is unable to care for himself. Fine—but how do doctors decide on that 'danger' part?

"We may know that a patient is not dangerous *now*, while he's under treatment." The doctor rapped the table for emphasis. "Once he's outside, he may stop taking the phenothiazines we prescribe. He may discontinue treatment as an outpatient. Pressures build up: frictions with the everyday world. He's bombarded with input from television, newspapers, radios; his system gets overloaded and suddenly—bang—something may happen. Or nothing. It's the prediction game all over again. But a prognosis, unfortunately, is not a prophecy."

Dr. Schaub had put his finger on the unenviable position psychiatrists now occupy within the justice system. They must diagnose retrospectively *and* projectively—that is, judge a person's mental condition at the time of a certain deed—often years earlier—as well as guess whether he is liable to commit another in the future. Moreover, this unique chore is demanded of a science barely a century old—historically still in the toddling stage.

Some psychiatrists, as we have seen, are demanding that their profession be separated from the legal apparatus and to hell with the lost fees. But others are still busily fortifying the legend of their special, near-magical role in the process of law enforcement—a role that the media have already inflated to ridiculous proportions.

A psychiatrist helping an attorney analyze prospective jurors or a cop pick potential criminals or a judge fathom a criminal's motivation can contribute no more than these professionals can themselves, and often considerably less, if he lacks their experience. A psychiatrist's value in crime detection depends entirely on his ability to think like a detective or a criminal—in other words, to think outside his sphere rather than within it. His specialized training hardly matters at all.

Yet whenever a city experiences a series of patterned murders or other outrages, the police will ask psychiatrists and psychologists for a "personality profile" of the culprit. This has by now become an American tradition, and the cops pander to it—not because they expect practical results, but because the media love it and the public derives comfort from it. It's a ritual akin to the witch doctor tossing sand in order to insure victory in battle—it does no harm and sometimes it scares the enemy a little. The resultant profiles are usually not so much wrong as irrelevant—that is, they're ambiguously obvious pieces of theorizing, unconnected with the nitty-gritty, of fingering one deadly needle in an urban haystack. As a veteran of the Manhattan Homicide Task Force put it to me: "I've never known a behavioral scientist who was worth half a good stool pigeon."

The trouble with mentally deranged criminals is that they're nearly always loners and hence impervious to informers. So far there has been only one instance of such an individual inspiring a psycho-profile that actually helped to nail him. This was the work of a New York psychiatrist, James A. Brussel, who gave an astonishingly accurate description of the maniac nicknamed the "Mad Bomber." From 1940 to 1956 New York was plagued by someone planting homemade explosives in public places and writing letters to newspapers afterward. Although the Bomber never killed anyone, sometimes he came perilously close, and New Yorkers were getting jittery.

Working only with the clues the police could give him, Dr. Brussel came up with an almost uncanny portrait of the man: polite, quiet, methodical, of foreign, probably Slavic, extraction, middle-aged, symmetrically built, unmarried, lives alone, has no friends, conservative dresser. Finally he added the punch line: "When you catch him he'll be wearing a double-breasted suit. And it will be buttoned!"

When detectives arrested the Bomber he was wearing a double-breasted blue suit—buttoned. His name was George Metesky, his parentage Polish, and he held a paranoid grudge against the Consolidated Edison Company, which he believed owed him compensation.

Brussel's profile was a masterpiece, but it remained a solitary one. Since then the panels of experts have failed to accomplish anything comparable. In the case of the Boston Strangler, their efforts were ludicrous. In 1962 and 1963, the Boston region had thirteen spectacularly horrible sex slayings. The victims were bound, gagged, blindfolded, throttled, and frequently arranged in grotesquely obscene postures—sometimes with ribbon bows tied around their necks. In most cases the killer ejaculated on their bodies. The earlier victims were women between fifty-five and eighty-five years old. Later they tended to be girls in their twenties.

The conclusion drawn by most psychiatrists indicated two different murderers: one who strangled older women; another who was probably a homosexual and went after girls. None of the experts hit on the truth—namely, that the age pattern was purely accidental. The Strangler knocked on doors and murdered any female he happened to find alone. The panel ventured that both these men hated their mothers, had respectable backgrounds, lived alone, possibly were schoolteachers, were sexually inhibited, and killed in sudden outbursts of rage. All of which couldn't have been much more wrong.

Albert DeSalvo, the Boston Strangler, worshipped his mother and loathed his father. He had a slum background that was anything but "respectable." He lived with his German wife and their two children. He was a construction worker. He never killed in outbursts of rage but always with cool premeditation—carefully scouting out the territory first and desisting if he scented danger. He was oversexed to the point of mania; all his marital problems were due to his wife's reluctance to have intercourse as often as he desired—four or five times a day. He hated women because they excited him unbearably and never gave him as much sex as he needed. The only features the scientists named correctly were his physical strength and his persuasiveness. He always talked his way into apartments; there were never any signs of forced entry. These deductions were so obvious that any patrolman—or, for that matter, most cabdrivers—could have made them.*

Nine out of ten of the profiles concocted are equally vapid. They play at blindman's buff, groping in all directions in the hope of touching a sleeve. Occasionally they do, but not firmly enough to seize it, for the behaviorists producing them must necessarily deal in generalities and types. But policemen can't arrest a type. They require hard data: names, faces, fingerprints, locations, times, dates. None of which the psychiatrists can offer.

Instead of becoming involved in the process of crime detection, psychiatrists could fulfill a considerably more useful function in crime prevention—not in consulting rooms and hospitals, but at the street level, where most crime originates. A few—a mere handful—are doing this, but it takes a bigger than average share of idealism, courage, and dedication to weather the brickbats hurled by their colleagues and the frustrations supplied by their clients.

---

* DeSalvo was never tried for any of the thirteen stranglings to which he confessed in minute detail. He was already confined in Bridgewater State Hospital on various sex charges when he made his confessions. Since he had received a promise of immunity beforehand, he couldn't be charged with murder. Instead, he drew a life sentence for armed assault. In 1967 he escaped briefly, in order, as he explained, to draw attention to the lack of mental treatment in prison. In November 1973 he was killed by fellow inmates. The trials of the three convicts charged with his stabbing ended in hung juries. Technically, therefore, no one was ever convicted for any murder connected with the Boston Strangler.

Dr. Joel Fort takes both with equanimity and a certain quiet glee—the earmarks of the professional outsider. Among his proudest testimonials is a memorandum written about him in 1969 by John Ehrlichman, one of the Watergate worthies, when the Nixon government was seeking a director for its national drug-abuse program: "Fort can't be relied on to be a team player . . . do not use him in any White House or Executive Department agency . . . incorruptible."

A husky man with a bald pate, bushy mustache, and firmly incisive manner, Fort is pioneering an omnifarious field he calls social and health problem-solving. Considered a leading authority on mind-altering substances and a fervent antidrug crusader, he has branched out into a personalized, unstructured, unsubsidized, unofficial, and decidedly unprofitable program of aiding people with problems ranging from drug addiction, homosexuality, and obesity to crime, compulsive gambling, suicidal tendencies, and violence. One of his agencies is the National Center for Solving Special Social and Health Problems, known among San Franciscans as Fort Help. Occupying a remarkably ugly building in one of the sleaziest sections of town, Fort Help looks unorthodox enough to convey an image of its founder. Large, bare, with multicolored walls and a random scattering of settees, staffed by scruffily relaxed young volunteers of all four sexes, the place bears absolutely no resemblance to a mental-health clinic.

"That's because it isn't one," Dr. Fort explained. "At least not in the conventional sense. We don't call the people who come here 'patients,' either. We're trying to get away from the usual sickness labels. They're 'guests' and the staff members are 'helpers.' And what we attempt, basically, is to establish a link of mutual trust between helpers and those being helped. Not on the paternalistic therapist-patient pattern, but as between two equal adults.

"The important thing, the main thing, is that we're available. To anyone at all, with any kind of problem," he added. "They don't have to be *sick*—just troubled. One of the reasons why I moved away from psychiatry is because I found it of little relevance to the major problems of our society. For instance, I can't tell you how much violence we have prevented, because that's something we can't check out. But I know that we've provided alternatives for a lot of people who felt themselves on the verge of violence.

"What kind of alternatives?" Fort stroked his mustache. "That depends on the individual. We have no hard and fast rules. The guests choose their own alternatives—we merely suggest them. First, we make them *aware* of their anger or their violent impulses. Secondly, we try to get at the root causes—what it is that makes them feel that way. Then we suggest alternative methods of dealing with these impulses, ways that don't hurt other people. Maybe a change of job or work environment. Or just energy expenditure: athletics, bowling, tennis, boxing. Then you have people who can be helped by role-playing in psychodramas that allow them to ventilate their anger. There are innumerable possibilities.

"But we must try and detect violence and circumvent it *before* it explodes. That's the crux of the matter. To give people—or the people near to them—a chance of voicing their feelings, letting out some of the pressures building up inside them. What we really need"—Fort heaved one of his rare sighs—"and what we don't have is a twenty-four-hour violence hot line. A telephone staffed round the clock, like in suicide prevention. It would even be possible to do this nationally from one central place and telephone number that's kept permanently manned. Just a hundred trained people could serve the whole country." *

You have to see Fort Help in action to appreciate the novelty of its methods. There is no hierarchy among the staff and as little compartmentalization as possible. The helpers "specialize in being generalists"—all of them trying to help with any problem. If they can't help directly, they'll find an outsider who can. They offer what Dr. Fort calls a "smorgas-

* Since this interview took place, Fort Help has launched a shoestring operation called Violence Prevention Line. The service is manned by volunteers, but only functions from 6:00 to 9:00 P.M. daily and not at all on Sundays.

bord approach" to health care. This includes methadone maintenance, hypnosis, psychotherapy, Gestalt therapy, sensitivity encounters, group therapy, transactional analysis, crisis intervention, and a whole slew of enterprises termed self-help programs. They deal with from four hundred to five hundred people a week, face to face, and with hundreds of anonymous—often desperate—voices on the telephone. They are accessible. Not in stingily allocated bureaucratic doses, but on a drop-in-any-time basis. It doesn't take much imagination to visualize the difference a nationwide network of such Forts might make to our rate of urban violence.

"What I've been trying to do," said the doctor, "is to evolve a new profession that really has no name as yet. It could be thought of as social pathology or social problem-solving. I've tried to integrate academic and practical knowledge, social and psychological techniques into a new discipline. I think it's been more successful than the traditional methods in meeting problems like crime. And I *know* it's more relevant."

12

Have Gun, Will Use

Willie Poinsette was forty-eight years old and had a record of twenty-one previous arrests when, on April 8, 1973, he was charged with robbery and possession of a gun, both felonies. If convicted of these charges he would have faced up to thirty-two years in prison. Two days later in Criminal Court, Mr. Poinsette pleaded guilty to petty larceny and was sentenced to two months in city jail.
—New York *Times*, February 11, 1975

They won't take the Gun from my Hands until They pry it from my cold, dead Fingers.
—Popular American bumper sticker

However you slice it and whichever way you turn it, America's rate of violent death is linked with the number of firearms loose in the country. Although people do away with one another and with themselves by a variety of means, the favorite choice—by a vast margin—is the gun.

Since the start of this century, roughly 850,000 American civilians have been killed by bullets. This total is larger than all the military casualties suffered by the United States in all the big and little wars it ever fought, from the Revolution to Vietnam. It constitutes a record no other industrialized nation can even approach.

Only a portion of these deaths were due to homicide. Out of the approximately 27,000 men, women, and children who yearly perish by gunfire, some 12,000 are murdered, about the same number commit suicide, and around 3,000 die in gun accidents—often so monumentally daft as to defy belief. The gun is far and away our top murder utensil. Accord-

280

ing to FBI records, about 68 percent of all homicides are perpetrated with firearms—54 percent with handguns, the rest with shotguns and rifles. Machine guns don't seem to make the statistics.

There is a quite unmistakable correlation between gun ownership and the murder rate. Areas with the highest proportion of gun owners also boast the highest homicide ratios; those with the fewest gun owners have the lowest. The South, described by one writer as "that part of the United States lying below the Smith & Wesson line," has firearms in over half of its homes and a murder rate of 12.9 per 100,000 people. The Northeast, with guns in fewer than one third of its homes, has a murder ratio of 7.3 per 100,000.

Such figures, which could be extended to fill the rest of this book, all add up to the same conclusion: that Americans use guns to decimate themselves on a horrific scale. So do Thais, Mexicans, Nicaraguans, and other "undeveloped" people, but none in America's industrialized peer group. The U.S. gun-murder rate per 100,000 population is almost two hundred times greater than that of Japan or the Netherlands, one hundred times greater than that of England or West Germany, twenty times greater than that of Canada, Australia, or Italy . . . and so on throughout the industrialized world.

In only one country does the prevalence of firearms *not* match the national murder rate. That is Switzerland, which is by far the most heavily armed nation in Europe but which nevertheless has one of the lowest homicide ratios anywhere. Under the country's unique militia system, every one of its 700,000 trained citizens takes his carbine or submachine gun home with him, ready for instant mobilization. There is hardly a case on record of these weapons being used for private shootouts—a fact that speaks volumes for the Swiss temperament.

All other industrialized nations abroad control private firearms possession by means of licensing; Japan has a total prohibition on them. Their citizens do not regard this as an infringement of liberty. As one Norwegian businessman summarized their attitude: "Well, I need a license to drive a car. Why not to carry a gun?"

But in America gun control looms as the most combustible issue since slavery. No other controversy—not even abortion or school busing—stirs partisan fury to quite the degree of white heat as the subject of gun possession. This is because here the question carries deeply rooted psychological, political, ethnic, emotional, even sexual implications not present anywhere else. Unless you are familiar with these connotations, you can no more judge America's gun-control dilemma than you can decide on the issues involved in the partition of Ireland or the survival of Israel without knowledge of their historical backgrounds.

On only one point do all parties agree: "Gun control," as currently practiced in the United States, is an unholy mess, a malodorous mélange of three kinds of law: nonexistent, unenforceable, and semi-ignored. It's entirely a matter of taste which particular variety is the worst.

We have, for a start, only a vague notion of how many firearms the country contains, though we know that the total is fabulous. Estimates range between 40 million and 60 million, about 35 million of them being handguns. Another 2.5 million handguns are manufactured each year, and yet another 650,000 are imported from abroad. Around half a million pistols and revolvers are stolen each year and go on the underworld market, where they retail for as little as ten dollars.

Attempting to control this avalanche of hardware are hundreds of state, county, and municipal bodies with different sets of regulations. The local authorities neatly negate each other—for every restricted zone there's an adjoining territory with a wide-open gun market. In 1974 in New York City, for instance, where the stringent Sullivan Law applies, 95 percent of the 2,048 handguns seized by the police during crime arrests had been purchased out of town.

Finally, there is, of course, the Treasury Department's Bureau of Alcohol, Tobacco and Firearms. The triple title of the federal agency speaks for itself. It means that with 1,674 agents, the Bureau is supposed to enforce federal gun controls as well as those on alcohol and tobacco. It couldn't be done even if the agents worked at full capacity, which they don't.

We also have the Firearms Transactions Record—a federally required form to which all gun purchases are subject. On this form the buyer must swear that he or she is over twenty-one, a resident of the state, and neither a drug addict, an ex-convict, a former mental patient, nor dishonorably discharged from the Armed Forces. Since nobody checks on the truth of this declaration, it has never stopped anyone in the prohibited categories from buying weapons. All they have to do is lie. Herb Mullin, the Santa Cruz mass murderer who had been through two arrests and five mental hospitals, simply put "No" on the form when he purchased the pistol with which he killed ten people.

In April 1976 an eighteen-year-old Baltimore youth opened fire on pedestrians from the upper floor of a West Lombard Street house. He shot a policeman dead and wounded six other people before surrendering to massed SWAT units. The gamin-faced, tousled hysteric, who looked even younger than his years, babbled that he had fought with his girl friend and felt nobody loved him. "So I wanted to die and take some others with me." In his apartment police found a weapons cache of two high-powered rifles, two shotguns, four revolvers, three automatics and nine hundred rounds of ammunition—all purchased in local stores.

Random sniping sprees of this type are breaking out so frequently in U.S. cities that urban police forces now train special sharpshooter teams, equipped with bulletproof vests, to deal with them. Sniping is nearly always caused by what psychiatrist Harold Visotsky termed "the frozen violence in our society": the kind of festering cumulative anger that builds up silently in certain people over months and years and flares into raging violence at a pinprick as minute as the spark that sets off the detonator that explodes the cordite charge that sends a shell howling into the landscape.

Undoubtedly, of course, if a gun weren't within reach,

some other form of weapon would be. But since a gun is, statistically, five times as lethal as a knife and can kill at long distance, the death score in the wake of such outbursts would be one fifth or less in a society with no accessible firearms. There is also the fatal psychological oddity that a large proportion of violence-prone men (not women) have a special affinity for guns. They tend to collect them, hoard them, fondle them as misers caress money. Some, like the maniacal Hitler-worshipper and mass slayer Fred Cowan, even talk to them. In almost every firearms rampage the gunman was found to possess a multiplicity of weapons, often small arsenals. Cowan spent most of his modest income on shooting irons and displayed that much-quoted poster in his attic den: *They won't take the gun from my hands until they pry it from my cold, dead fingers.* Which, in due course, they did.

The link between certain pathological characters and firearms is a fact written in the blood of their victims. Sometimes this proclivity can backfire, literally. This is what happened to William Ernest Thoresen III, who spiritually belonged in the seventeenth-century England of "Regency Bucks" even though contemporary journalists tried to see him as a symbol of the American consumer ethic. Bill Thoresen was the son of the president of Chicago's Great Western Steel Corporation, a scion of America's industrial aristocracy. Tall, athletic, and superficially charming, he had the kind of bland handsomeness that quite often hides a berserk bent. In Thoresen's case it wasn't all that hidden.

At twenty he had been repeatedly arrested for assault and battery as well as shoplifting. He stole nearly one million dollars' worth of stocks and bonds from the basement vault of his father's North Shore mansion, returning them only after the old man agreed not to press larceny charges. He stole cars, trailers, and boats, simply for the hell of it; he pretended to be a drug pusher. Finally, after he somehow talked his younger brother Richard into making him the beneficiary of his will, in 1965 Richard was found dead in his car with a bullet hole in his skull, leaving the authorities undecided whether to call it suicide or murder.

Thoresen also collected arms, not by the rack but by the truckload. His collection included literally scores of revolvers, pistols, automatic rifles, and shotguns, as well as machine guns, mortars, land mines, grenades, an antitank cannon, and several bazookas. When after years of litigation, the authorities finally confiscated most of his armory, a U.S. Attorney quipped: "That guy has so many munitions, I don't know whether the government should prosecute him or negotiate with him."

Thoresen married a strikingly beautiful Chicago schoolteacher named Louise, who at first participated in his capers. She went car-stealing and shoplifting with him until their son was born. Later she explained that this "made life exciting for me." But, with motherhood, the excitement wore thin and, particularly after he began periodically beating her up, Louise began to see her husband in a different and more frightening light—not as a madcap playboy and adventurer but as an obviously disturbed and potentially dangerous individual.

On the morning of June 10, 1970, Bill Thoresen, having imbibed some LSD, once again beat up Louise and, according to her testimony, boasted that he had hired an assassin to kill his brother and subsequently killed the murderer himself. By then she knew enough about her spouse to believe him. When he advanced on her again, she took a revolver from the dresser and shot him dead.

Her murder trial was one of those screaming front-page affairs that luridly spotlight a tree or two but leave the woods in darkness. Louise was acquitted on grounds of self-defense and faded into comfortable obscurity. The death of Richard Thoresen remains a mystery. So does his grotesque older brother's lifelong immunity from any serious prosecution or even investigation—boons conferred on him by a society that apparently never saw further than his billfold.

By now the American public is painfully aware of the havoc wrought by the stupendous pile of armaments in circulation. According to both Harris and Gallup polls, two thirds of all citizens want registration of firearms and licensing of their owners. In other words, they favor a procedure long established with regard to motor-vehicle and dog ownership. On several occasions, especially after the shooting of the Kennedys, Martin Luther King, Jr., and George Wallace, Congress seemed to be girding itself for some decisive gun legislation—*seemed* to. For, when it came to the crunch, the proposed measures were either dropped, sidetracked, unraveled, or emasculated to the point of impotence.

The reason for this is that gun control is opposed by a substantial minority of voters, and this minority is wholly dedicated, fiercely determined, well financed and organized. It thus packs vastly greater political clout than the wishy-washy majority does. Its opposition takes different guises and bases itself on various premises, but its members' underlying fear is that licensing would lead to a gradual restriction of private gun ownership, perhaps to complete prohibition. In this they are quite probably right—there already exists a sizable ground swell in favor of taking all handguns out of the holsters of private citizens.

The gun-control opponents—"antis" for short—field two main organizations: the National Rifle Association (NRA), with over a million members, and the younger, more aggressive Citizens' Committee for the Right to Keep and Bear Arms, with a membership of about fifty thousand. Together these two bodies, backed by the grim resolution of millions of grassroots gunslingers, muster enough leverage to stymie control legislation where it counts, at the Washington level, though not always locally.

Their antagonists—the pros—have branded the NRA as nothing but a pressure group for the gun industry. And certainly the $1-billion-a-year firearms and ammunition business has lavished money on anti-control propaganda and political inducements of every sort, including some savage Congressional arm-twisting. But money alone couldn't rally the almost frenzied emotional support commanded by the NRA —support stemming from fears and resentments far beyond the issue of licensed weaponry. For a sample of these concerns, herewith portions of a letter sent to *Psychology Today*

magazine in response to a fairly mild advocacy for gun controls. The writer, incidentally, identified herself as one of the
Daughters of the American Revolution:

> Slaughter will continue with bricks, brooms, broken bottles,
> etc., even if all guns are banned. Don't try to convince Ameri-
> cans that criminals won't have guns just because there is a law
> against them. The NRA is protecting the right of the Constitu-
> tion. A group of anti-Americans keeps prayers from schools,
> now it is guns; will the press and flag be next? Would not anti-
> democratic countries want the U. S. A. unarmed so taking over
> would be elementary? . . .

In this slightly cracked nutshell you'll find most of the
extraneous matter that has wrapped itself around the gun
control controversy. Somehow school prayers, the flag, and
freedom of the press pop into the argument, pro-controllers
are equated with anti-Americans, and the nation's security
from foreign takeover is made to depend on privately owned
gats—God help us if it does. The lady's tone, however, was
moderate compared to the missives fired by the more rabid
antis.

When Marvin Helfgott, a West Los Angeles pharmacist,
launched the Coalition for Handgun Control in 1974, he
didn't know what he was getting into. He soon found out.
He and his family were showered with obscene hate mail.
One letter greeted him as "Dear Filthy Cur Dog"; another
was signed "Adolf Hitler." Helfgott's pharmacy was blasted
with BB shot; they were bombarded with abusive telephone
calls; the windows of their home were smashed; and hand-
bills demanding a boycott of their business appeared in the
neighborhood. The Helfgotts eventually joined the less vulnerable National Gun Control Center, based in Washington,
D.C.

Obviously firearms control touches a raw nerve and triggers
reactions no amount of gun-lobby financing could induce
by itself. To large numbers of Americans, this is a gut issue,
reaching deeper even than suggested by the NRA's most successful slogan, *When Guns are Outlawed, Only Outlaws will
have Guns.* Representative Steve Symms, Idaho Republican

and a member of the Citizens' Committee, may have touched the core in a quote printed in the organization's newsletter: "We believe that Americans should have the right to own guns because traditionally justice has always come from the ballot box, the jury box, but, if those failed, the cartridge box."

This statement may be of dubious historical accuracy, but it certainly expresses what so many rod devotees feel. When other means turn sour, justice resides in the crook of their trigger fingers. And in order to keep their fingers on the trigger, they are willing to go to virtually any lengths, including poison-pen letters, the harassment of families, and the use of awe-inspiring lies. At a Senate judiciary committee hearing held in Annapolis in 1976, one NRA representative—while keeping a straight face—told listeners: "There are just as many people being killed by being hit with baseball bats as with handguns."

From such traits pro-controllers have conjured up *their* image of the American gun devotee: an Archie Bunkerish troglodyte who identifies his "piece" with his penis and thinks of arms registration as akin to castration.* This is their gravest mistake, because it ignores one of the prime factors in America's private armament race—a factor that has nothing to do with "frontier mentality" but plenty with feeble law enforcement. The presence of a pistol in the drawer is often directly connected to the absence of a cop on the beat. After every assassination and every act of terrorism, there is a renewed stampede to buy firearms by perfectly innocuous men and women who feel abandoned by society's protective apparatus. In this paradoxical fashion, killings committed by privately owned guns stimulate sales of yet more private guns.

In his best-selling *Crime in America,* former Attorney General Ramsey Clark delivered what he obviously con-

---

* This theme originated in Sigmund Freud's *General Introduction to Psychoanalysis,* in which he stated that guns may symbolize the penis in dreams—but so may church steeples, snakes, sticks, pencils, knives, and a dozen other objects.

sidered a decisive argument against private firearms: "A state in which a citizen needs a gun to defend himself from crime has failed to perform its first purpose. There is anarchy, not order under law—a jungle where each relies on himself for survival. The wrong people survive because the calculating killer or the uninhibited psychotic more often wields the faster gun."

This is perfectly true—except that in parts of this country such anarchy already exists. It has been produced not by lack of law but by what practically amounts to the same thing: unwillingness to enforce it.

During a summer weekend in 1975, a small rural commune in southern Michigan was invaded by a pack of bikers from Detroit. There were nineteen of them, all with knives in their belts and skull emblems on their jackets. They had lots of fun—roaring full tilt at pedestrians and swerving at the last moment, relieving themselves on doorsteps, yelling obscenities at little girls, breaking down fences and plundering fruit trees, and deliberately running over the commune's pet beagle. One man who protested was beaten insensible by three of the heroes.

The sheriff was called and came—but only to explain that this was outside his jurisdiction. The state troopers came and declared that for weighty legal reasons they couldn't do anything either. The beaten man could file charges, of course, but that was a civil matter—in other words, none of *their* business. Meanwhile, they suggested, why not try the sheriff again? The commune people tried, but the bikers had cut the telephone wire.

On Sunday evening the bikers thundered off. They hadn't committed a really serious crime—even the beaten protester would be as good as new as soon as his nose and jaw mended. But the commune had, in Yeats's words, "changed, changed utterly." As one of the members, a bearded and gentle vegetarian, said to me: "Next time those fellows come to visit us, there'll be two revolvers and a repeating rifle in the house. And if they start on that nonsense again, so help me, we'll blow their stinking heads off."

There was nothing redneck about these people. Nor about Marcia Blackman, who got her gun the same year and used it the next. A husky brunette in her mid-thirties, Marcia left New York in order to find "peace and quiet" in San Francisco. She opened a diminutive soap-and-body-oils shop on Polk Street, but the peace and quiet failed to materialize.

Polk Gulch is a lavender patch, gay from curb to curb, with a dangerous sprinkling of hawks preying on the chickens. They swoop down from all over the Bay Area in search of easy marks and count the local retailers among them. During Marcia's first season in business, five stores on her block were held up—the gunmen sauntering in and out like faintly bored customers. Some were caught, lectured in court, then sprung on probation or appeal or suspended sentences. A few weeks later they were back on their Polk Street hunting grounds, grinning at the shopkeepers.

Inevitably, Marcia's turn came. The bandit didn't get much money, but the aftermath left her with an acid taste of fury. She looked at volumes of mug shots, drove around the neighborhood in a squad car, and listened to cops waxing negative as only cops can: "Even if we catch him, he'll get off. His lawyer will see to that. He'll grow a mustache or something, and you won't be able to identify him. It'll just be your word against his, lady. You'll see—he'll beat the rap."

"So what am I supposed to do?" she asked. "Sit and get robbed?"

"Get a gun, lady," the law advised. "And use it."

So Marcia Blackman, a New York liberal, bought a .38 revolver. She sewed a special pocket under her embroidered apron and kept the gun there, ready for the next bandit.

He arrived on January 14, 1976. "An average-looking white guy," she told me, "except for his eyes. They were kind of vacant—a dope addict's eyes. And the moment he entered I *knew* this was another holdup. Don't ask me how—I just knew. So I wasn't really surprised when he pulled a pistol out of his belt. From then on all I saw was that gun pointing at me. I wondered if it was a toy, and the guy must have read my thoughts because he clicked it—you know, cocked it—and said, 'Yeah, it's for real.' Then he said, 'I know you've been through this before. So gimme the money.' And I wondered how he knew I'd been robbed before. Maybe he was a friend of the guy that did it."

Marcia took all the bills in the till—forty-one dollars—and held them out with her right hand. With her left (she is left-handed) she clasped the revolver under her apron. The man shook his head impatiently. "Come on, you've got more than that. Hand it over—all of it." She explained that she'd just made a bank deposit, this was all she had. The gunman kept shaking his head, but he reached for the cash. In that split second Marcia accomplished a perfect Wild West draw and pulled the trigger. The bullet hit him in the chest, and he staggered back, still waving his weapon. Marcia took careful aim and shot him again. The gunman collapsed on the floor, his body blocking the doorway. Marcia ran from behind the counter, grabbed the pistol from him, climbed over him and made the street, a gun in each fist. Pedestrians carefully backed away from her.

The bandit was dead when the police arrived. He turned out to be Shannon Kolenda, a.k.a. James Tavanini, a Berkeley heroin addict with a hundred-dollar-a-day habit. His pistol had been stolen in another holdup. According to police records, Mr. Kolenda had already beaten one murder charge. Marcia received a load of fan mail after the episode, including several proposals of marriage. The mail as well as the shooting left her unruffled but quite determined to repeat the performance, if necessary. "The one thing I can't stand is the feeling of being a helpless victim," she said. "Anyone who walks in here to rob me is gonna walk out dead."

The authorities ruled the slaying "justifiable homicide" on the ground that Ms. Blackman was defending her cash register. They feel rather benevolently toward those who fight for their property. When Conrad Simmonds, a Bronx variety-store owner, shot and killed a burglar in December 1975, District Attorney Mario Merola called him "one of our most outstanding citizens, who doesn't sit by and let himself be ripped off."

It's a different matter when they're merely defending their bodies. In September 1976 an intruder broke into the fifteenth-floor apartment of Denise Dozier of Chicago. Her friend Angela Winslow was visiting her at the time. The man raped Miss Winslow, beat her viciously, and finally threw her out a window. Miss Dozier produced a pistol, rather too late, and shot the man, who escaped wounded. Angela Winslow survived; her fall was broken by the building's canopy. But the police promptly arrested her hostess on charges of failing to have the proper city and state registration for her gun and with discharging a firearm in a confined area.

Bodily defense, as distinct from property, doesn't rate very highly in Chicago. Fred Thomas, a small, bespectacled newsstand operator, carried a can of disabling spray in his pocket for just that purpose. When he was assaulted by a man who smashed his glasses and knocked his teeth out, he squirted his attacker's face and drove him off. The cops weren't worried about the assailant. But disabling spray is illegal. So they confiscated Thomas's can and locked him up, after explaining that they couldn't do a thing about his attacker since Thomas didn't know his name.

As Thomas told columnist Mike Royko: "Next time I'll handle it myself. I'll let him punch me until he has a heart attack."

The same month a New York bus driver was stabbed in the back by one of three youths who had refused to pay the fare. Spurting blood, the driver pulled a gun and shot one of the boys in the leg. By now you'll have guessed the punch line—it was the driver who landed in trouble. His gun permit was in order, but the New York City Transit Authority's rules forbid the carrying of firearms.

This chapter is headed by a vignette of U.S. justice à la mode that explains more about the rush for private weaponry than reams of NRA propaganda. It is fear and fury that turns homes into arsenals, not antediluvian twaddle about frontier traditions;* fear and fury that mock the efforts of handgun abolitionists who keep quoting the weaponless examples of Japan and England. But Japan and England have police forces that *protect*, as well as judges who imprison armed criminals for their first offense—not their twenty-first.

People like Ramsey Clark lack comprehension of the cosmic rage engendered among millions by the image of a hogtied, unresponsive judiciary that neither shields them from violence nor exacts retribution. Clark was an honest, intelligent, and enlightened official, but because of this lack he made as woeful an Attorney General as some of his corrupt, reactionary successors. He reasoned that poverty, illiteracy, and drug addiction were the roots of America's violence and that they should be tackled first—at the expense of penal measures. But alleviation of these evils is a long and slow process, whereas violence is immediate. People being threatened now aren't willing to wait for projected social reforms to take effect. They want an immediate antidote to the moronic viciousness that will plunge a knife into a man for the price of a bus fare. They read that in New York 80 percent of defendants accused of homicide plead guilty to a reduced charge and are freed on probation. They learn that nationwide the justice system achieves *one* conviction for every fifty serious crimes—and convictions aren't tantamount to prison sentences by a long shot. They absorb all this and go out to buy guns. And if the Sullivan Law says they mustn't have guns, then *tant pis* for the Sullivan Law.

During Ramsey Clark's term of office the journal *Black Panther* announced to its readers, "The only way we can do this is to pick up the gun. We are gonna walk all across this motherfucking government and say Stick 'em up, motherfuckers—this is a hold up; we come to get everything that belongs to us." This announcement, made in the pre-break-

* Australia, which is historically much closer to a frontier tradition than the U.S. and has a similar melting-pot makeup, shows one seventh of the proportionate private-handgun ownership of America—thanks mainly to an efficient, hard-hitting system of law enforcement.

fast-dispensing period of the Panthers, must have been worth several thousand gun sales on both sides of the race fence. Mr. Clark, who never allowed unpleasant facts to get in the way of his principles, ignored that straw in the wind—just as he ignored most others.

But it sparked off a curious legislative campaign against the so-called Saturday-night specials. This is a generic term denoting several brands of shoddy bargain handguns, mostly imported and selling at around fourteen dollars brand-new. The special is hideously erratic and notorious for hitting by-standers, rather than its intended target, but its cheapness makes it *the* ghetto gun. In this capacity it kills ten times more black and brown people than whites, though luckily it misfires frequently—hammer and firing pin being so far out of alignment that they can't discharge the bullet.

The special became the lightning rod for legislators wishing to demonstrate that they too were concerned about the homicide rate. The specials made ideal scapegoats. Since most of them were of foreign—Spanish or Belgian—manufacture, they cut into the profits of the native armaments industry. Accordingly, these cheapies were branded as America's top murder tools, responsible for an overwhelming proportion of armed felonies. Even Nebraska Senator Roman Hruska, one of the gun lobby's most strident spokesmen, declared, "I am for banning Saturday-night specials, but only providing we get the right definition and limitations of the term."

Ah, but there lay the rub. It proved quite impossible to work out a definition that would include only the alien models. The Bureau of Alcohol, Tobacco and Firearms, which undertook the task, had to define the special as "a gun of .32 caliber or less with a barrel not more than three inches long, and retailing for less than $50." This included so many U.S.-made models that the gun industry suddenly lost its enthusiasm for a ban. On top of this, a two-year study conducted by the Police Foundation "revealed" what every homicide dick could have revealed without undue study-ing—that the specials are used to commit crimes no more often than higher-priced brand-name weapons. Indeed, they are actually used less often, because professional bandits won't touch them.

The ban-the-special projects sank with nary a ripple. The only people who might conceivably have benefited from such a ban were ghetto inhabitants, whose representatives protested loudest against it. At least the removal of specials from the domestic scene might have lowered the rate of family killings in poverty areas by a percentage point or two.

Firearms control in America is locked in a stalemate similar to the trench warfare of World War I. When the smoke clears after each thunderous barrage, the lines are shown to have hardly shifted at all. The pro-controllers score local successes, but in Congress—the decisive area—the antis doggedly hold on to the status quo.

By and large, with some notable exceptions, the two sides correspond to the divisions between liberals and conservatives, and both show the inconsistencies that come with their labels. The liberals, while favoring laissez faire in matters like homosexuality, pornography, abortion, and marijuana, are gung-ho for banning private handguns. The conservatives, who urge the suppression of what they consider temptations to commit moral iniquities in other areas, demand complete freedom for gun toters.

Each camp accuses the other of "ignoring majority rule," while in truth both of them do so whenever it suits their tactics. Conservatives deny the validity of umpteen opinion polls showing hefty majorities in favor of stricter gun regulations. Liberals, with equal nonchalance, disregard every poll that reveals rising popular demand for restoring the death penalty. In order to reduce the appalling scale of gun mayhem in this country, both sides will have to surrender some cherished ground.

Handgun interdiction is practically impossible at this stage. The task of confiscating between thirty-five and forty million weapons would be quite beyond the capabilities of any government agency. But guns and their owners *can* be registered and licensed, and retailers obligated by law to report thefts of firearms (which they are not at present). Gun owners can also be made to pass proficiency tests in the handling of their weapons, exactly as you have to pass a driving test for your automobile license. The NRA could offer the necessary instruction in accordance with their avowed ideal of turning every citizen into a marksman or -woman. If nothing else, such lessons would at least prevent a couple of thousand folks from yearly blowing their brains out while loading, cleaning, or playing with their pieces. Moreover, just as you are fined today for improper parking, so also could penalties be levied for improper storage of a gun—particularly within reach of children.

We may not be able to deprive criminals of their gats, but we could render their use distinctly unprofitable. This would require mandatory prison sentences, *without probation*, for anyone—including juveniles—convicted of a gun felony. In this respect, the mere carrying of a gun in the course of a crime would have to count as equivalent to its use. Mandatory sentences may be anathema to the American Civil Liberties Union, but certainly no more so than gun registration is for the NRA.

The above measures would not, by themselves, greatly reduce the number of firearms casualties. But they would bring about a psychological climate that could do so in the long run. They would eliminate much of the fatal sang-froid with which we treat weapons—the constant waving around of shooting irons, the games-playing, the nonchalance with which petty thieves and pilferers pack a pistol along with their screwdrivers, the automatics left in the glove compartments of parental cars while their teenage kids are driving them.

At the current rate of increase, there will be a gun for every man, woman, and child in this country in the near future. It will, accordingly, take *some* change of attitude to prevent *Homo americanus* from going the way of the buffalo, the sea otter, and the passenger pigeon.

13

Chamber of Horrors

After I cut off my mother's head I cut out her larynx
and put it down the garbage disposal. This seemed
only appropriate, as much as she'd bitched and
screamed and yelled at me over so many years.
                                    —Edmund Emil Kemper III

In May 1973, the then Governor of Georgia—Jimmy Carter
—dispatched two special agents to help rural Seminole
County with a murder case that seemed beyond its capabilities as well as its comprehension. During the night of
May 14, six members of the Alday family had been slaughtered. In the sparsely settled, heavily inbred county, the
Aldays and their legion of relatives accounted for nearly
a third of the population. The shock of their killing left
the neighborhood numb. It was the worst anyone could
remember.

Like most others in Seminole County, the Aldays were
farmers, growing peanuts and corn on the family's five-
hundred-acre spread. One brother, Jerry, lived in a large
trailer home with his wife, and several times a week his
father and three younger brothers spent the evening there,
discussing farm affairs. On the morning after one such
family gathering, another brother found their remains.

The father and four sons were lying in different rooms of
the trailer—all shot through the head. Mary Alday, Jerry's
young wife, was discovered in a forest patch some distance
away. She had been stripped, hideously beaten, raped,
sodomized, and finally shot. Her car was missing, but another—a green Chevrolet—stood abandoned nearby. Its
owner, a college student named Richard Miller, turned out

297

to be the seventh victim. His body was found buried in the scrub a week later.

The hijackers of Miller's car were identified as escaped convicts from a Maryland correction camp. State troopers hunted them into the wild hills of West Virginia, tracked them with bloodhounds, and captured them when they dropped from exhaustion. The morning after the funeral of the six Aldays, their killers arrived at the Seminole courthouse in Donalsonville.

The scene there could have come from one of the 1930s lynch epics produced by Warner Brothers: the little brick courthouse on the dusty Southern town square, the rows of state police nervously fingering their guns, the huge buzzing crowd of overalled Georgia rustics—half of them kin to the victims—staring with a concentrated hatred that seemed to fog the air. Only the four prisoners struck a wrong note: three whites and one black, all ridiculously puny. Loaded with wrist and ankle chains and shuffling along among the hulking marshals, they resembled kids being dragged forcibly to school.

The three whites came from one family. Wayne Coleman, ginger-haired, tattooed, with most of his teeth missing, had been doing time for robbery; Carl Isaacs, mustached and delicately featured, for burglary. When they walked out of the minimum-security camp, their fifteen-year-old brother, Billy Isaacs, joined them for the ride. The black man, George Dungee, was the oldest and smallest of the group. He wore tremendously thick glasses that kept sliding from his nose and gave him the look of a disoriented mole. George had been serving a stretch for nonsupport of an illegitimate child. He was one month away from release when, for reasons he couldn't explain, he joined the others in their escape.

Once it became clear that there wasn't going to be a lynching, the trial ran smoothly. Young Billy turned state's evidence and supplied the details of their murder spree. The four had abducted Miller and his car, killed Miller, then driven to Georgia. They were in the process of robbing the

Alday trailer home when, one by one, the family members arrived, only to be shot down by Carl and Wayne—all except Mary. They took turns raping and sodomizing and beating her within sight of where her husband was lying in his blood. Then they dragged her outside, where George Dungee waited in the car. When George bleated, "Hey, what about me, fellers?" they handed Mary over to him. He raped her, then walked her into the wood and shot two bullets into her back. After that, they drove through three states, holding up a store in Virginia but not killing anyone else.

Why had they killed those seven? The accused didn't know and didn't care a great deal. Carl Isaacs of the girlishly delicate features remembered, "Me and Wayne, we was going to cut off Miller's little finger and send it home to his mama, and write a note saying, 'This is all that's left of your little baby.'" Only they never got around to it.

Wayne Coleman, skull-faced and gap-toothed, talked about his urge to kill. "I'd like to kill about a thousand more people. That's why I need to get out of here, so I can do something to ease this hate that's in me. When I kill, I feel a release."

The court sentenced the three men to death in the electric chair. The boy Billy received one hundred years in prison, a penalty as senseless as his crimes—more so, because the crimes were real, while the sentence was fictitious.

At the time of this writing, four years after their conviction, the trio are still dodging fate in the death row of Georgia's Reidsville prison. The interminable suspense— will we burn or won't we?—might be considered more "cruel and unusual" than the death penalty per se. Torture by hope is a uniquely American practice in our day. The last foreigners to use it were the clerics of the Spanish Inquisition. And yet it's hard to find sympathy for those three men.

"They weren't just remorseless—they didn't seem to feel *anything*," said a prison official. "No fear, no regrets; nothing. To them killing all those people meant less than running over a dog. Maybe now they're thinking about it—I don't know. But when they were caught it was like they were dead inside."

Psychologists describe such individuals as "sociopathic." In *The Mind of the Murderer*, Dr. Manfred Guttmacher observed that sociopaths usually have cruel fathers and hysterical mothers, and that their antisocial attitudes can be traced back to "brutal, rejecting, inconsistent, and capriciously affectionate parents." In retaliation, the sociopath inflicts cruelty on others and feels no guilt in doing so. Their adolescence, according to Guttmacher, is characterized by delinquency and frequent running away from home.

In contrast to Dungee, whose main problems were feeble-mindedness and drinking, all these points fit the white men of the murder trio, but they also apply to vast numbers of humans who never hurt a soul. Childhood traumas alone can't account for sociopathic behavior, and its other ingredients remain largely a mystery. Plenty of sociopaths have come from relatively happy home backgrounds.

Psychiatrists now use the term "sociopath" (or "antisocial personality") rather than the blunter word "psychopath" for no reason other than that it is less blunt. It delineates exactly the same personality disorder, which they can identify and render harmless through sedation but cannot cure. It is not a mental illness but rather a character defect so severe that it amounts to a lobotomy of the moral sense or conscience or whatever it is that gives us empathy with our fellow creatures. Dr. Joel Fort probably offered the most succinct definition: "A morality that is not operating by any recognized or accepted moral code, but operating entirely according to expediency to what one feels like doing at the moment or that which will give the individual the most gratification or pleasure. It includes an absence of conscience."

Sociopathic behavior is not necessarily violent. It can just as well manifest itself in passing rubber checks, insurance frauds, or thefts from friends and relatives. The difference between the sociopath and the common crook is that the former believes in his (or her) absolute *right* to obtain anything by any means he chooses, whereas the latter knows that he's doing wrong and accepts the consequences. The peculiar coldbloodedness of sociopathic killers, rapists, and torturers is due to their unquenchable sense of righteousness—the ingrained conviction that their deed is justified because *they* wish to commit it.

It is this conviction, untroubled by qualms, that also makes them astonishingly successful liars—an attribute publicist William F. Buckley discovered to his sorrow after he helped to spring one of them from death row. His name was Edgar Herbert Smith, and he had been sentenced to die for the 1957 bludgeon murder of a fifteen-year-old New Jersey girl. Smith spent fourteen years on death row at Trenton State Prison in New Jersey. He never ceased to protest his innocence and, in 1964, started to correspond with Buckley, to whom he wrote 2,900 pages (by his count) of letters. Buckley came to believe that Smith had not received a fair trial. A great many other people came to believe likewise after Smith—with assistance from Buckley—authored three near-brilliant books in his cell. The first, *Brief Against Death*, made him a national figure: the battered but unbowed victim of a hideous miscarriage of justice. Buckley's newspaper columns helped to boost Smith's sales as well as his image.

In 1971, after a "trial" that wasn't a trial but one of the grubbiest strokes of judicial bargaining ever perpetrated, Smith achieved his release. The judge who released him was himself convinced of Smith's guilt but equally convinced of his total rehabilitation. After all, Smith was now the author of two best-sellers, a member of Mensa, and, incidentally, the holder of the world's record for death-row residence. As he emerged from prison, Buckley's car was waiting for him and whisked him to New York, where—in front of the TV cameras—he once again assured viewers of his blamelessness in the killing of the New Jersey girl.

Five years later, Edgar Smith made the news again. He was wanted in San Diego, California, for assault, kidnapping, and attempted murder. In October 1976 he forced a young woman named Lefteriya Ozbun into his car at knifepoint, claiming that he wanted her money. When the woman, with a week's salary in her purse, fought desperately, Smith plunged the knife into her. She kept fighting, smashed her foot through the windshield, wrestled the door open, and tumbled out of the car onto the freeway. Smith stepped on the gas and screeched off.

Six days after this episode, Smith tried to ring his old patron Buckley from Las Vegas. The columnist was out of town, so the fugitive left a telephone number where he could be reached. Buckley turned this information over to the FBI. That afternoon the Feds arrested Smith in his hotel room.

Then came the bombshell. Extradited to San Diego, Smith not only admitted the assault on Ms. Ozbun, he also confessed that he had battered the New Jersey teenager to death twenty years earlier—first hitting her with a baseball bat when she rejected his advances, then crushing her skull with a large rock. "For the first time in my life, I recognized that the devil I had been looking at the last forty-three years was me," he announced. "I recognized what I am, and I admitted it."

But apart from an acute embarrassment for Mr. Buckley, what, exactly, *was* Smith? He could pass as a classic example of a sociopath: a creature bent on following his impulses, undisturbed by moral scruples, and only slightly disturbed by fear of the consequences. A person of outstanding intelligence, he had an impediment in his reasoning powers that made him act like a cretin. His motivation was apparently sexual the first time and financial the second, but on each occasion the inhibiting factors that might have been expected, given his IQ, were totally absent. Had they never developed or had they atrophied? Over the next fifteen years or so, prison psychiatrists will have a chance to fathom the mystery of Smith's character, but the odds are they will gain no greater insights than they have from others of his ilk.

There may be a correlation between the mounting pressures and complexities of our age and the prevalence of sociopathic crime. Journalists call this the Time of the Crazies, but few of the perpetrators about whom we have been talking can be said to be "crazy," even by the medical definition. "Evil" is perhaps more appropriate, although it would be worth a psychologist's diploma to use that word. The confusing aspect of our current sociopathic crime wave is that so many of its horrors seem money-motivated and therefore "rational." Killing for cash makes sense to us. There's a reassuringly old-fashioned touch to it, until we measure the mounds of victims against the sums involved. Then we realize that emotions other than greed must have been at work. If there is one basic difference between the murder boom of the early 1930s and the current one, it is the staggering quantity of death dealt out for minimal gains. Forty years ago, one or two victims in the course of a bank robbery were considered the peak of criminal ruthlessness. Today we are not surprised to find a roomful of corpses left in the wake of a hundred-dollar corner-grocery holdup. The difference is more than one of degree. It reflects a difference in attitude toward the taking of life that is, in turn, producing a critical imbalance in our social environment—while society has grown more reluctant to take the life of an offender, criminals have become more casual in their killings. As a result, while the proportionate number of murderers in our midst may not have increased over the past four decades, the number of their victims has skyrocketed.

Hundreds—perhaps thousands—of killings superficially classified as robbery murders are committed for reasons other than robbery. For the sociopath, robbery is often only an excuse he gives himself. First and foremost, he wants to *kill*, and will do so regardless of whether or not he meets resistance. Even elimination of witnesses may be merely a secondary consideration. It's the killing that counts.

For instance, the police view of one homicidal psychopath, who also staged robberies, was that he was primarily an armed holdup man with a tendency to gun down his victims.

The man, Roger (not his real name), an avowed homosexual who worked as a bar bouncer, was captured immediately after robbing a taxi driver one summer night in 1975. Under interrogation he admitted to a killing ten nights earlier and to seriously wounding someone the month before. Then, out of the blue, he confessed to three completely unrelated murders of which nobody had suspected him.

Earlier that year he had fired five bullets into the head of a hotel worker in the course of another robbery. Why? Roger asked him for his wallet and was told to screw himself. "I don't take that kind of talk," said Roger.

His third murder lacked even that much motivation. One evening in 1972 he had picked up a young woman in a bar. They had a few drinks, then took a drive to a deserted area outside town. En route they started arguing about a marijuana joint Roger insisted on smoking. She got mad at him for that, he said, and he got mad, too. Roger took the jack handle of the car and slammed her over the head with it. She lay still, but after a while she began to move. Roger hit her again and kept on doing so until he was sure she was dead.

No ostensible reason emerged for Roger's fourth slaying: the strangling of a young hotel porter. The victim wasn't robbed, because he had nothing worth stealing. But there could be little doubt at that point in Roger's admissions that he killed because he liked it—he had a disconcerting habit of chortling quietly to himself whenever he talked about murder.

All of this makes the particulars of his accommodation behind bars incomprehensible to anyone not familiar with the way certain county jails are run. Roger was lodged in a cell with two other homosexuals in on murder charges. As a fourth inmate, the jail authorities shoved in an eighteen-year-old youth half their size and neither gay nor homicidal. Were the jailers aware of what they were doing by delivering the youngster to those three? In any event, the boy was dead two days later—stabbed nine times during a night assault. Roger pleaded guilty to that slaying as well, claiming "frustration" as his motive. After all, he informed the court, he'd been locked up for eight damned months.

Yet, as sociopathic killers go, even Roger was an also-ran. The scores of victims piled up by others of his mentality can read like battle reports.

None of America's celebrated outlaw teams came near the body count achieved by two utterly obscure drifters of the Southwest during three weeks in 1973. Here again robbery seemed to be the motive, but in all likelihood was merely a stalking-horse. The satanic thoroughness with which this pair butchered their way through two states pointed at homicidal urges far stronger than their craving for cash.

Willie Steelman, aged twenty-eight, was a Californian; Doug Gretzler, twenty-two, a New Yorker. They looked incongruously mismatched. The curly-headed Steelman, with his wattled chin, was perpetually pouting, while the bespectacled Gretzler wore his blond hair shoulder length and his mouth set like a rat trap. Steelman had been a patient at Stockton Mental Hospital and was out on probation. Virtually nothing was known about Gretzler.

Their rampage began in Phoenix, Arizona, when the pair overpowered their two partners in a dope distribution scheme, details of which remain obscure. They trussed up and gagged the two, Mike Adshade and Ken Unrein, then threw them in the back of Unrein's van and drove to a trailer home in Apache Junction. The young man and woman living in the trailer were found ten days later— their heads shattered beyond recognition by shotgun blasts fired at close range. With their original captives still in the van, Steelman and Gretzler turned west toward California. They drove to the scrub-sheltered banks of Little John Creek, a quiet fishing spot south of Sacramento. There the prisoners were stripped naked and dragged out of the van. Unrein was strangled with a piece of rope; Adshade had his throat slit from ear to ear with a hunting knife.

It was as if these four preliminary murders had produced a catharsis in the pair, transforming them into amok runners whose movements were indicated by the trail of corpses they left behind. Retracing their path, one lawman wondered aloud: "What were they trying to do—depopulate the state?" Steelman and Gretzler drove back to Arizona, where they picked up two hitchhikers in the desert near Phoenix and killed them within an hour. Moving on to Tucson, they broke into the apartment of Michael and Patricia Sandberg, both University of Arizona students, and shot them dead. Then, returning to California in the new Datsun sedan they had stolen from the Sandbergs, they plunged still deeper into the morass of blood. On the night of November 6, 1973, a violent rainstorm hit the small, scattered town of Victor in the San Joaquin Valley. Apparently arriving together with the first thunderclaps, the Datsun stopped outside the brand new, ranch-style, redwood home of Walter Parkin—a virtual monument to California-style house-and-garden exurbia, with its Scandinavian furniture and swimming pool in the rear. The owners of a prosperous little grocery store, Walter and Joanne Parkin went with the image of their home: a young, hard-working, successful couple with two pretty children, and a social life that involved them with the entire community. Their house was usually filled with people, and the night of the thunderstorm—their last night—was no exception.

The Parkins went bowling that night with a couple of neighbors, Dick and Wanda Earl. Left at home were the two couples' four children, including eighteen-year-old Debbie Earl, and Debbie's boy friend, Mark Lang, who had been invited to keep her company. At some point Steelman and Gretzler forced their way into the house, and when the parents returned from their game they walked into a death trap. The two killers were holding their children at gunpoint.

Since there was little cash in the house, one of the intruders accompanied Parkin to his grocery, made him take four thousand dollars from the safe, then herded him back home. At some point, all seven adults were tied with nylon cords, gagged with torn sheeting, and made to squat in a large walk-in closet. The two young children, Lisa and Bobby, remained fast asleep in their bedroom. This is how they were found the next morning, except that they were all dead, each shot twice—once in the head, once in the chest. It was cool, systematic slaughter, and the killers must have taken their time about it. Perhaps they savored those moments: that glorious surge of power when the last frantic seconds of your victim's life are measured by the slowly increasing pressure of your trigger finger—when the helpless being before you has heard the shots and knows what's coming but can do nothing, absolutely *nothing*, to stop you. It was something to look back on, to relish retrospectively in those years to come.

The manhunt that followed lasted only sixty hours. Steelman and Gretzler were already wanted on kidnapping charges in Arizona. They had been seen in Victor and were traced to a seedy hotel in downtown Sacramento. Gretzler was arrested in his room; Steelman was smoked out of the apartment of a newly acquired girl friend with tear-gas bombs. Both of them talked, and the search for the scattered bodies of their victims began. The tally kept mounting: nine in Victor; two, three, four in Arizona; another two in California; two more in the Arizona desert. There were seventeen people in all, plus another three "possibles" that the police never bothered to try to pin on the pair. Were there still more somewhere? We don't know and aren't likely to find out.

Over the next few years the two men kept collecting life and death sentences, despite the obvious contradiction. First they received life imprisonment for the massacre in Victor, then death in the gas chamber for the slaying of the Sandbergs. Meanwhile, with a dozen more charges remaining as yet untried, they have joined the legion of Americans suspended in the iron-barred limbos of death row—waiting, waiting, waiting, while society tries to make up its splintered mind about what to do with them.

Those who interviewed Steelman and Gretzler behind bars found them distressingly "normal" in the colloquial sense. They seemed quiet, of middling intelligence (not very bright), and with no comprehension of the enormities they had perpetrated. It was just something that happened, man, something in the past, ancient history. What the hell did it matter *why* they'd done it? What mattered was the way they were being treated *now*—all the things they had to do without.

This is a characteristic shared by most sociopaths: their total disregard of the Newtonian principle of action and reaction, of the connection between their deeds and the consequences of those acts. This emotional blind spot can lead to almost comical outbursts of indignation the moment anyone hurts them *back*. In 1959 the dwarfish, bowlegged Charles Starkweather, by profession a garbage man in Lincoln, Nebraska, went on the warpath against humanity. He killed eleven people, including both parents of his teenaged sweetheart; then he rammed the hot barrel of his rifle down the throat of her two-year-old sister, choking her to death. Afterward Chuck and his lady love sat watching TV amid the corpses, holding hands and munching hamburgers. Two days later, a sheriff ended the spree by shooting out the rear window of Starkweather's car during a 115-mph chase. Chuck tumbled out, one hand in the air, the other clutching his ear, which had been nicked by a flying glass splinter. "You bastards shot me," he sobbed. "Look at me—I'm bleedin'!"

Starkweather was the last person executed in Nebraska to date, but in October 1975 the prairie state made headlines again with what may have been—if this is possible—an even worse massacre. The scene was the tiny plains community of Sutherland, population 850. Sutherland had two taverns and one maniac, who frequented them both. His name was Erwin Simants, and he was known as the quietest man in town. A casual laborer, Simants rarely spoke a word but drank every cent he earned. He was a little feebleminded, but few people noticed it—or noticed him at all. He got into trouble with the law once, for public drunkenness, and a neighbor paid the fifty-dollar fine to save him from jail.

The neighbor, James Kellie, lived in semi-retirement with his wife, children, and grandchildren—six persons inhabiting a small white frame house next to the similar house in which Simants lodged with his brother-in-law and sister. Three weeks after Kellie had done his neighborly deed, Simants took his brother-in-law's rifle and dropped in on his benefactor. He then shot the entire family, starting with the sixty-six-year-old James and ending with his ten-year-old granddaughter, Florence. Subsequently, he went home and left a scrawled note by way of an explanation: "Don't cry. It was the only way." He was arrested the following morning while trying to get back into the place.

The national headlines came during the pretrial proceedings, when U.S. District Judge Hugh Stuart issued a gag order forbidding newsmen to reveal the contents of confessions made by Simants soon after his arrest. The media took this as contrary to the First Amendment, "which does not allow one branch of the government, the judiciary, to dictate to the press. . . ." Judge Stuart countered that this was the only way he could insure a fair trial for the defendant. Otherwise it would be impossible to empanel an impartial jury, for the confession described how Simants had not only raped little Florence after she was dead but had attempted intercourse with her dead grandmother as well.

Whether the gag order contravened the First Amendment is debatable. It was certainly superfluous. The entire trial hinged on the issue of Simants's sanity, which would have been just as dubious had he never raped anyone. The jurors, as is usual in such cases, found him sane and guilty. Judge Stuart sentenced him to death in the electric chair— in effect to an indeterminate series of successively postponed execution dates.

In Sutherland, Nebraska, they still talk about *their* murders. In Santa Cruz, California, you rarely hear the word mentioned. This isn't because Santa Cruz is such a big place or the locals taciturn—which, by God, they aren't. Nor is it because the town is embarrassed about being dubbed "murder capital of the world." It's simply because the murders occurred in the past—last month or last year being "the past" thereabouts—and Santa Cruz is very much into "right now." If you admit to a past, you're admitting to growing older and may wind up *old*. And old age, to a large segment of the residents of Santa Cruz, is a social disease—only dirtier.

Santa Cruz has been called California *in extremis,* and therein lies its particular charm and its special curse. It consists of two cultures that won't blend—harmoniously or otherwise—and that give the area a strangely split personality that many people find irresistible. Lying sixty miles south of San Francisco, surrounded by wild mountains and blessed with a balmy oasis climate, Santa Cruz snoozed along as an idyllic tourist and retirement haven until 1965. Then, descending upon twenty-five thousand locals, came the spectacularly beautiful new campus of the University of California with its twelve thousand students. From a largely Baptist, staunchly conservative—even John Birchist—hicksville, Santa Cruz blossomed into the New Jerusalem of the counterculture. To be sure, the natives had asked for the college. They visualized formal junior and senior proms, campus-queen contests, a rah-rah football team, and lots of business-administration graduates spreading corporate paychecks around the community. What they got were braless, barefoot students, acid parties, head shops, and heavy infusions of crabs, rapes, gonorrhea, hepatitis, and rip-offs.

The main distributors of these blessings, however, were not the students but the so-called UTEs—a term derived from a local news sheet's fulminations against the "Undesirable Transient Element," and meaning anyone poor, mobile, and not born in Santa Cruz. Nobody counted the UTEs, but there were thousands of them. They came from the East Village, Haight-Ashbury, and points between—including jails and mental institutions. Having left places turned foul and finding one where the weather was kind, the living cheap, and the vibes good, they stayed on. "Where else," a female UTE told me, "can you go for a year and not work and never notice?"

The natives, on the other hand, noticed quite clearly. Most of the UTEs were pure parasites, scrounging, panhandling, or stealing their sustenance from the middle-class cornucopia of the collegians. Some peddled drugs, some ran hot-car operations, and some squatted in mountain vacation cabins that didn't belong to them. Since they dressed and talked like the students and mingled with them, there was no way of distinguishing them. What good did it do to brand them "hippie trash" when you couldn't tell a drifting meth junkie from a resident philosophy major?

Although the natives did all the complaining, it was mostly the students who got ripped off. They were a trusting lot, by and large, equipped with that beguiling innocence granted only to the prosperous young. "I'll never forget meeting my first pair of genuine speed freaks," one graduate reminisced. "The guy wore a ring on his big toe and his old lady—she was about fifteen, I guess—had green snakes tattooed around both her nipples. They were looking for a place to crash, so my roommates and I took them to ours. Next morning they'd gone and they'd taken my typewriter and a portable radio and two cameras. Funny thing was, none of us said anything about it. Today I'd swear like hell. . . ."

What made the students ideal victims was not so much tolerance as a complete lack of standards. Since everybody was "doing their own thing" and one "thing" was as good as another, they had no means of differentiating between originality and lunacy, between a nonconformist and a raving psychotic. Since every brand of hogwash was equally respected, and "I'm okay, you're okay" was an imperative, no borderline was recognized between the bizarre and the deranged. Intellectually, there wasn't such a great difference between a flab-chinned lady psychic twittering that "a thousand people who get together and heighten their vibrations can prevent an earthquake from happening" and Herb Mullin's claim of achieving the same result with a few human sacrifices.

Everything and everybody not belonging to the establishment was taken at face value. No one shrank from Chaucer's "smyler with the knyf under the cloke," providing he smiled. "They made life too comfortable for the killers," said a county cop. "In most places those creeps would have moved on pretty fast. Here they felt at home."

The murders began in the fall of 1970, and three years later District Attorney Peter Chang could describe his fief as a "murder capital." When the paranoid John Linley Frazier was caught, after exterminating the Ohta family, the county thought it had closed its file on multicides. Then came Herbert Mullin with his thirteen "sacrifices" to push Santa Cruz way above the U.S. homicide norm. To the consternation of the natives, both of them turned out to be local boys.*

And still the murders went on. Five, then six young women were missing—mostly after thumbing rides on Ashby Avenue near the campus. Some were seen again, but not in one piece: The bleached skull of Mary Ann Pesce lay in a wooded mountain ravine; the torso of Cynthia Schall, minus arms and legs, was washed up on a Monterey beach; the bodies of Rosalind Thorpe and Alice Liu—their heads and both of Alice's hands missing—were uncovered by road workers in Alameda County. Occasionally unidentifiable scraps turned up: a woman's hand without fingers, a female pelvic bone, one breast . . .

Lieutenant Charles Sherer was put in charge of a police detail with the sole task of solving the riddle of the vanishing hitchhikers. They checked out hundreds of leads and got nowhere. But they did come to recognize that a creature worse than Frazier or Mullin was on the loose: someone fascinated by dead female bodies.

* For details on Frazier and Mullin see Chapter 11.

In fact, he lived and drank and horseplayed right under their noses. So huge and grotesque that he stuck out like a landmark, he was well known to all the local cops, most of whom called him by his first name. He was Edmund Emil Kemper III—Big Ed to his friends—and he represented the ultimate and total failure of law and psychiatry. He was never "caught" in the actual sense; instead, after indulging in one final paroxysm of slaughter, he quietly turned himself in. His trial marked one of the rare occasions when the U.S. press found itself unable to report the full details. Some of them were unprintable.

Kemper first attracted official attention when, at age fifteen, he killed both his grandparents. Apparently he shotgunned and stabbed his grandmother because, like his mother, she dominated him, and his grandfather because, being an abject coward, he was afraid of the old man's reaction. He then dutifully rang his mother and the sheriff to tell them what he had done.

He spent the next five years in Atascadero State Mental Hospital, where he learned two important things. The first was to camouflage his smoldering hatred for his mother in particular and people in general, while similarly hiding his constant preoccupation with violence. (He used to mutilate his sister's dolls, slicing off their legs and heads, and later graduated to doing the same with neighborhood cats and dogs.) The second was to master the jargon employed by the medical staff and decipher the workings of the psychiatric tests performed on him. Being highly intelligent, he succeeded so well that the medical board declared him "fully recovered" in 1969. Against the strenuous protests of the prosecuting attorney in his case, Ed Kemper was released.

He never forgot those lessons. In September 1972 Kemper was able to persuade four learned psychologists to recommend the sealing of his criminal record—an imbecilic California legal ploy by which a murderer's past is effectively expunged. The four psychiatric specialists duly agreed that Kemper had become a perfectly normal, nonviolent, well-adjusted citizen whose record should be sealed. During his last two psychiatric interviews, the head of his latest victim was stowed in the trunk of his car, parked outside the office.

Eight months later District Attorney Chang voiced his bitterness over the so-called experts' performance. "Too many psychiatrists think they can determine a defendant's sanity, potential for violence, or degree of recovery by a simple one-hour 'tell me about it' interview," he said. "Many psychiatrists never bother to read the police files. Instead they take the defendant's rationalized version at face value. On occasion, they have been known to alter the defendant's version so that it does not conflict with their diagnosis." Mr. Chang's outburst was justified but a little belated. By then the "normal, well-adjusted" citizen with the duly expunged record had rapturously dismembered eight people. Nevertheless, the medicos concerned were still pontificating to their patients and collecting fat fees for their efforts.

Psychiatrists were not the only functionaries of the criminal justice system to be taken in by Ed Kemper. Big Ed made a habit of drinking at the Jury Room, a no-frills liquor dispensary that, being handy to the Santa Cruz courthouse, was frequented by off-duty patrolmen. Generally gathered around the bar, rattling the dice cup, the cops clearly liked Ed and took simple delight in the very size of him. Kemper stood six feet nine inches in his socks, weighed 280 pounds, and had a neck as large as the average thigh. His face seemed somehow mismatched. Despite his owlish spectacles and drooping mustache, it wore the expression of a petulant child about to have a temper tantrum. Ed was quiet and a good listener, particularly when the cops talked about guns. Occasionally he'd show off his enormous strength by seizing a man's elbows and, to the patrolmen's enthusiastic applause, hoisting him up on the bar.

Nothing indicated the wetter of furies, lusts, and complexes seething inside this lumbering buffalo. Kemper was driven by manic sex urges but saddled with a crippling sense of inferiority. He had a small penis, which on him looked minuscule, and was quite inept as a lover. The one woman who had accepted him refused a second date. Convinced that no *living* female would bear him,* Kemper's cravings gave fuel to his simmering rage against his mother, who in simultaneously protecting, browbeating, and disciplining him had made him feel "small as a mouse."

Nevertheless, his mother was to aid and abet his desires in at least one important way: She worked for the college administration, and was able to obtain a university parking sticker for his car—just what he needed to disarm any doubts that hitchhiking UCSC co-eds might harbor. Thus, when goaded beyond endurance by the sight of rows of warm young bodies with upraised thumbs along Ashby Avenue, Kemper had merely to smile and open his car door. In they climbed—smiling back and chattering as he greeted them over the roaring in his head. And then—sometimes—his fantasies came true. Not always, by any means. Kemper worked with remarkable caution, studying maps to find suitable locations, carrying cellophane bags so severed limbs wouldn't stain the upholstery, wearing special dark clothing that would show no bloodstains, delivering those girls who had been seen getting in his car safely to their destinations. Only with six of them were all the circumstances just right.

He killed quickly—sometimes shooting, more often strangling or knifing them. He raped only one girl while she was still gasping her dying breath. As a rule he waited until a bit later to undress a victim, gaze at her, caress her, take Polaroid snaps of her, and have intercourse with her. Sometimes he took the bodies home to bed with him, waiting until the next day to dismember and dispose of them. Certain portions, carefully wrapped in cellophane, he kept longer. He liked to masturbate in the mouths of severed heads before finally disposing of them. Other portions he ate, at first raw, later cooked—gaining immense pleasure from the thought of what he was eating as he progressed from tiny slices to fair-sized chunks.

---

* In this he resembled the London murderer John Christie, a man twice his age. Christie turned necrophiliac from similar reasons, and had intercourse with five women while throttling them. He was tried in January 1953 and hanged in July.

Such were the private joys of the "normal, well-adjusted" young man who spent his evenings drinking with the local constabulary. He learned useful things from them, just as he had from the psychiatrists, but the cops proved even more helpful. They gave him an official-looking training-school badge, which came in handy, and a pair of handcuffs. Kemper used those police cuffs to secure at least three of his victims who were putting up too much resistance.

We don't know what mounting inner pressures drove him to his culminating murders. Whatever twisted rationality had guided him so far evaporated at this stage. In the early morning of April 20, 1973, he crept into his mother's bedroom with a claw hammer, smashed the sleeping woman's skull, sliced off her head with his folding knife, carved out the larynx, and cut off both her hands. He threw these parts in the garbage disposal. The headless trunk he pushed into a walk-in closet.

But he wasn't finished yet—not quite. There was his mother's best friend, Mrs. Hallet. His mother had confided many nasty, embarrassing things about him to this woman. Now she would discover that they were true, and he would once again feel humiliated. He didn't want that. He rang Mrs. Hallet and invited her to a "surprise dinner" for his mother that evening. She arrived punctually at eight. After chatting for a few minutes, Kemper gripped the woman in a hammerlock that made her pass out, and then strangled her with a nylon cord. Having deposited her body alongside that of his mother in the closet, Kemper finally departed to have a farewell drink with his police friends at the Jury Room.

Three days later and nearly a thousand miles away, from Pueblo, Colorado, Big Ed phoned Santa Cruz police headquarters. He said that he had killed people in California and might kill still more unless someone came and got him. He then waited patiently until a patrol car arrived.

A most cooperative prisoner, Kemper confessed in such hair-raising detail that he had difficulty persuading investigators to believe him. At his trial the jury experienced similar incredulity, along with an unnerving sense of help-lessness. As public defender Jim Jackson put it: "There are no laws to cover Ed Kemper." * When the accused was asked what he considered a fit punishment, he replied, "Death by torture." Instead he received a simple life sentence.

When Voltaire wrote that those who refuse to learn from history are condemned to repeat it, he might have been referring specifically to Santa Cruz. The town resolutely refused to learn anything. After Kemper's trial, his deeds became history—therefore no longer true, certainly not part of "what's happening." Except that it was.

Thus, when in 1976 the dark mountains were turning up bodies again, the law was just as unprepared as it had been three years earlier. They found Karen Percifield stabbed in a wooded ravine, Mary Gorman and Vickie Bezore stripped and battered to death. But the county still lacked a trained criminologist, a crime lab, or enough manpower to patrol the hills. Despite an all-points alert, Mary's shiny new Mazda sat undiscovered on a main road for two days. Even when it was found, stained with her blood, it was simply towed to a local garage and left unattended. The garage owner's dog got its paw prints all over the sides.

The parents and friends of the murdered women were so appalled by the official torpor that they hired private investigators to search for clues.† But the basic malaise didn't lie in the police department; it only culminated there. Throughout history small towns have gotten by with minimal police protection by virtue of a highly developed sense of

---

* Jackson was also slated to defend Herb Mullin and was still handling an appeal on behalf of John Frazier. This made him the only attorney on record with three mass murderers as clients simultaneously.

† The bludgeon slayer of Gorman and Bezore turned out to be an ex-convict, Richard "Blue" Sommerhalder, who ran a head shop in Rio Del Mar. The tall, bushy-haired Sommerhalder had a criminal record two inches thick and was regarded as a street-wise cult hero by local youngsters, whom he supplied with dope. He drew two life sentences for the killings. His younger brother was already in Folsom Prison, serving a life stretch for triple murder. As a prison official remarked: "They were two great brothers. Sort of like Cain and Cain."

cohesion and a degree of mutual responsibility. Santa Cruz lacked cohesion and felt responsible for no one, clinging to verbiage and faith in magic—two decidedly inferior substitutes. Instead of communicating, it "psycho-babbled"— using trendy word balloons like *karma* to express fatalism and *energy* for violence. The counterculture gurus ceaselessly pour forth the idiot's tale, "full of sound and fury, signifying nothing," one of them proclaiming, "If you want openness of life, you have to put up with the risks. And the murders are part of it. It's all an outpouring of the same youthful energy that's trying to form itself into new shapes."

At last we know what it's all about! Not only are the Fraziers and Mullins and Kempers part of the "openness of life," but "new shapes" may take the form of decapitated corpses. In a similar vein, those inclined toward magic were content to believe that murderous impulses stemmed from geomagnetic fluctuations—from the alleged capacity of anti-magnetic effects of the topography to make certain individuals go berserk. To those folks, Santa Cruz was ground zero on the American murder map—nature's own incubator for homicides. This is roughly akin to believing that "pyramid power" will sharpen razor blades—which a great many of them believe as well. It had the added charm of letting everybody off the hook—like it's all cosmic, brother, so nobody is to blame. The only possible remedy would be to evacuate the place.

There appears to be little connection between the brutish necrophilia of Edmund Emil Kemper III and the pixilated malevolence of Arthur Frederick Goode III. Kemper raged because he couldn't become a man among men; Goode because he couldn't remain a child among children. Kemper's IQ was 136, while Goode passed as "borderline retarded." Kemper possessed the physique of an ox; Goode was nearly as frail as his victims. What links the two cases together is the compelling way they illuminate the failure of the legal and mental-health systems to cope with them—despite every conceivable warning. Failure due not to misguided "soft-ness" but to mind-boggling incompetence.

Arthur Goode, called Freddie by his family, grew up in Hyattsville, Maryland. A rather late youngest child, born when his mother was already into the change of life, Freddie received warm affection from his parents and three older sisters, but at every stage, he had trouble winning the accep-tance of his peer group. Constantly lagging in his develop-ment, he was always trying to get back into a lower age bracket. At twenty-two, he wore his hair styled in Little Lord Fauntleroy bangs, which gave him a passably cherubic look.

He began making sexual advances to small boys while in his early teens. Goode's tendencies ultimately became so notorious that local people took to warning new families in the area to keep their youngsters away from him. This was sound advice but difficult to follow. Arrested on three counts of indecent assault on minors, Freddie each time gained instant release on bonds posted by his parents. "He was always back in a few days, riding his bicycle around, looking for little boys," one neighbor remembered. "We didn't know what to do."

Neither did anyone else. Goode was obviously a homo-sexual pedophiliac, but so far as the state authorities were concerned, this might have been an altogether new and startling deviation instead of an ancient and familiar one. Pedophilia is an adult's sexual attraction to children—basic stuff for any psychiatrist. According to Dr. Harry Kozol, "Every child molester must be looked upon as potentially dangerous, a potential killer. Short-range psychiatric treat-ment is worthless. It is virtually certain that most child molesters will repeat their acts unless exposed to long-term, multi-year specialized treatment by sophisticated experts."

Few pedophiliacs are violent by nature. Indeed, they may be genuinely loving and tender. They will seduce or bribe rather than rape a child (although even then their shock effect on children can be traumatic). The real danger lies in their knowledge of the penalties involved—particularly if they are repeaters. This inevitably supplies them with a powerful motive for silencing their victims—and they do so with terrible frequency. The risk factor rises with every new assault. Under the circumstances, the treatment received by Goode was almost an invitation to homicide.

In March 1975 Freddie was arrested for five sexual assaults on a nine-year-old boy. The Goode family raised twenty-five thousand dollars to bail him out again. While on bail, Freddie attacked an eleven-year-old. This time the family attorney had to engage in plea-bargaining. In return for a guilty plea, Goode was handed five years' probation on the condition that he voluntarily undergo treatment at Spring Grove State Hospital.

The judge either didn't know or didn't care that "voluntary treatment" gave the hospital no right to hold Freddie against his will. Goode stayed for just fifteen weeks, then walked out of the institution and took a bus to his parents' new home in St. James City, Florida. Later the Goodes claimed that they had expected the hospital to pick up their son. But despite warnings from a probation officer and a judge's bench warrant, no one came to collect Freddie. Florida was, after all, a long way off.

On the afternoon of March 5, 1976, Goode met nine-year-old Jason VerDow from Fort Myers, who was waiting for his school bus. Telling the boy that he wanted help in "finding something" in a nearby wooded area, he persuaded Jason to come along. As Goode later testified, "I told him he was going to die and described how I would kill him. I asked him if he had any last words, and he said, 'I love you,' and then I strangled him."

When Jason's body was found, stripped naked except for his socks, the Cape Coral police questioned Goode twice. Unaware of the warrant for his arrest, they let him go. A week later—with the avowed intention of returning to the hospital—Freddie took a train to Spring Grove. His visit to the hospital lasted exactly five minutes. When he suspected that the receptionist was calling the police, he simply walked out a second time, without any attempt being made to stop him. The hospital authorities subsequently maintained that they had known nothing about an arrest warrant for their former patient.

Later that day Goode met Billy Arthe, aged ten, on his newspaper delivery route and somehow persuaded the boy to go to Washington, D.C., with him. He appears to have genuinely liked Billy, for he kept him around for ten days without doing him serious harm. But after the pair had wandered about the capital area for a few days, doing odd jobs for householders and staying in motels at night, Billy witnessed something he isn't likely to ever forget.

On March 20 the two encountered eleven-year-old Kenny Dawson and took him along on a bus to Tysons Corner, Virginia, to have lunch and explore some bicycle paths in the nearby woods. What happened then formed part of the testimony Billy later gave to a chilled courtroom:

> Fred told Kenny to take off his clothes. Kenny started to cry. Fred forced him to. He was with Kenny for a while. When he got up to get dressed he told Kenny to stay where he was, lying face down in the dirt. Fred took the belt off his pants, got Kenny's pants and put them over Kenny's head. He said he was going to play a little trick on Kenny.
>
> Fred put his belt around Kenny's neck so it would slide like a slip knot. He pushed down on his head and pulled on the belt. Kenny started squealing, then in a few minutes he was silent and Fred just kept on pulling on the belt. Then Fred got up and listened to Kenny's heart to see if it was beating or he was breathing. I guess it wasn't beating, so he took his money out of his wallet and put his clothes in Kenny's bag. Then we left.

After Billy Arthe's picture appeared on television as "Missing—believed kidnapped," the two were recognized by an alert Falls Church housewife. When she called her local police station, however, the duty officer said he knew nothing about the case and suggested she instead ring the Maryland state police. Although the state cops admitted to knowing about the case, they nevertheless insisted that it wasn't *their* case. They promised to call her back—uh, sometime. Undaunted, the lady phoned the Baltimore police, and this time—glory be—she scored. Detectives shortly cornered the pair in the woman's basement. As the handcuffs were snapped on, Goode said in his shrill, boyish voice, "You can't do nothing to me. I'm sick."

Almost immediately a major row erupted over the question of why and by whom Goode had been permitted to run around loose. Maryland Governor Marvin Mandel ordered a "thorough investigation" into the matter, and, with clockwork precision, every official finger pointed at someone else, while a cloud of accusations and countercharges neatly obscured any legible traces of blame—not to mention whatever chance of correcting the situation might have existed. Accordingly, no one bothered to explore the basic dilemma brought out by the case: the dichotomy between the court's knowledge that an accused person needs lengthy and specialized psychiatric treatment and its unwillingness or inability to compel him to undergo such a regimen. On the one hand, mental hospitals administering such treatment can't compel him to stay. On the other, maximum-security institutions, which are the only safe alternative to compulsory hospitalization, have no such treatment facilities. But that, happily, was beyond the jurisdiction of the governor's investigators.

Goode spent much of his pretrial detention time writing letters to the parents of boys he had attacked. His letter to the mother of Jason VerDow began, "I think now it's time that I confess to you about your poor son, Jason," then described the murder in such graphic detail that you could almost see him salivating over it. County officials had to get a court order restricting his mail for the sake of the grieving parents. This caused Goode to complain, "All my rights have been violated. They won't even let me write letters to people." Later, however, he added: "If I ever get my hands on another boy—a sexy little boy—he will never make it home."

Although he pleaded not guilty by reason of insanity, the Maryland court first gave him life imprisonment for the murder of Ken Dawson, then extradited him to Florida.

There the judge sentenced him to the electric chair for the killing of Jason VerDow.*

During the trials it emerged that Goode had been supplied with Depo-Provera as part of his earlier treatment. The drug, an "antagonist" to the male hormone, is quite effective in suppressing certain sex urges so long as it's taken regularly. Unfortunately, no one paid attention to whether Goode took it at all—which he didn't. As one of his sisters explained, "Freddie didn't like those drugs. He didn't like any drugs. . . . He liked everything to be nice and natural."

* Such mutually exclusive sentences are becoming quite common in America but exist nowhere else. The current record is held by Ralph Murphy, who kidnapped and murdered a young Indiana mother and her child. In July 1975 Murphy was sentenced to death for the slaying of the boy and to three consecutive terms of life imprisonment on the second murder and kidnap charges. There is little chance of any of these sentences being actually carried out.

14

The Tangled Scales of Justice

"Revolving door" justice convinces the criminal that
his chances of actually being caught, tried, convicted
and jailed are too slim to be taken seriously. In
short, our existing criminal justice system is
no deterrent at all to violent crime in our society.
—Senator Edward M. Kennedy

Although I couldn't pull the trigger myself, I don't
disagree with murder sometimes, especially political
assassinations, which have been a part of political
life since the beginning of recorded history. I'm not
entirely upset by the Kennedy assassinations. In many
ways two of the most dangerous men in the country
were eliminated.
—Lawyer William M. Kunstler

Let us for a moment imagine a Martian visiting our planet
for the purpose of studying the administration of criminal
justice in the United States in A.D. 1977. This Martian has
read that a Maryland circuit court found one Willie Lee
Jones, aged twenty-five, guilty of abducting and murdering
three men. Judge Jacob Levin sentenced Jones to three terms
of life imprisonment on three counts of first-degree murder,
one hundred and twenty years' imprisonment on four counts
of kidnapping, and sixty years' imprisonment on four counts
of using a handgun in connection with the murders. It
was, the newspaper noted with satisfaction, the stiffest sentence handed down in Prince George's County in recent
memory.

Our Martian adds up the figures on his pulse-operated
wrist calculator and looks up with a puzzled smile. "I do
not quite understand," he says. "The earthling's life span is
three score and ten years, yes? Three life sentences, therefore,
are two hundred and ten years. This plus one hundred

324

twenty and sixty years totals three hundred and ninety years' imprisonment. My calculator is maybe in need of repair?"

We assure him of its accuracy.

"Ah," says he, "the punishment, then, applies to reincarnation. The criminal must spend his next—let me see— four and a half lives in prison also?"

No, only this particular lifetime is concerned.

"Then, please, what is the purpose of all those centuries?"

The purpose, we explain, is to prevent the criminal from being paroled.

Our Martian nods. "Now I comprehend. This stern judge, he has made certain that the criminal remains confined for the rest of his days, yes?"

Well—er—not exactly. The stern judge, in fact, has made certain of nothing very much whatsoever. Because here's a statement from the Maryland Parole Commission. It says, "Under state law, anyone sentenced to life imprisonment is eligible for parole after serving fifteen years. As a rule, consecutive life sentences are treated as *one* sentence."

The Martian blinks his middle eye. "You are telling me that this Mr. Jones with his five and a half life sentences may actually be freed at the age of forty?"

Oh, probably well before then. They may deduct the time he had in jail while awaiting trial. Or let him out on furlough. Or to live in a halfway house. Something like that.

"But then—what is the point of the sentence?"

Why, to deter others, of course! Also to help rehabilitate Mr. Jones. So perhaps he'll think twice before killing any more people when he gets out.

Here we unfortunately lose our Martian, who wanders away, quietly giggling, while trying to pick the flowers off the wallpaper. But if, by chance, you think we were indulging in hyperbole, allow me to present a few further samples of contemporary practice in this area.

In October 1966 a slight, sandy-haired pianist named Charles Yukl lured aspiring entertainer Suzanne Reynolds to his Manhattan studio by offering her music lessons. Yukl strangled the girl with a necktie, had intercourse with her, mutilated her body, and dumped her clothes in the garbage. For this, Yukl spent exactly five years and four months in prison before being paroled.

During July 1974 the periodical *Show Business* carried an ad announcing that "Actresses, ages 17 to 25, non-Equity, college types" were being interviewed for a motion picture to be filmed in New York shortly. Hopefuls were asked to contact "Mr. Williamson" at a studio on Waverly Place in Greenwich Village. One who did so was twenty-five-year-old Karin Schlegel of New Jersey. Her naked, strangled, ripped, and violated body was found sprawled on the floor of an unoccupied studio at the Waverly Place address. The police didn't look any further when they discovered that "Mr. Williamson," the superintendent of the building, was Charles Yukl. He had replayed his previous murder in every detail. He received a life sentence but remains eligible for parole.

Richard Marquette was an Oregon plumber with a penchant for dismembering middle-aged women. In 1961 he was sentenced to life imprisonment for cutting up and scattering Joan Caudle of Portland. After twelve years behind bars, Marquette was granted parole in January 1973. A year later he killed another woman, but only cut off her head this time. Then, in April 1975, he completely carved up Betty Wilson —first severing her head, arms, legs, and breasts, then throwing the torso into a creek near Salem. When he pleaded guilty to this crime and drew a second life sentence, consecutive to his previous one, the Oregon Board of Parole announced that he would not be granted a hearing until the year 2005. It might be interesting to know how many more females Marquette has to dissect before being considered *beyond* parole.

In September 1974 an amiably weak-faced young man named Barry Austin Brown stood in San Mateo, California, Superior Court and pleaded guilty on three charges of first-degree murder. The first murder was that of Mrs. Lois McNamara, a wealthy Hillsborough matron. Brown had gone through high school with her son, had frequently visited her home, and had been treated "like a second son" by her. Murder No. 2 was that of Stephen Russell, a discharged sailor who was hitchhiking when Brown picked him up. No. 3 was that of Richard Pipes, who was shot dead when Brown held up the grocery store in Santa Cruz where he worked.

All three killings were committed for loot, with Mrs. McNamara netting Brown a car and around $1,500, but the sailor, only a backpack. Brown, however, saw himself in a rather benevolent light. "I don't believe murder is part of my character," he informed a probation officer. "I believe I can, if given the chance, offer a lot to the people around me. I want to discover why I committed those acts. I don't want to be put in prison to rot away. . . ." The court apparently felt that he had a point. Brown received three concurrent life sentences for his triple slayings, making him eligible for parole after seven years.

It requires no special insight to recognize that something is drastically askew with these court actions. There is a distinct flavor about them—theatrical entrepreneur's lingo in which "super-colossal record smasher" means that your show is just about breaking even. The punishments tossed around sound like heavy-handed parodies of legal procedure. Sentences that couple the death penalty with two, three, or more life terms, running concurrently or consecutively, plus a few extra decades thrown in for good measure, resemble nothing so much as the judge-and-jury satires that used to crack up Victorian music-hall audiences. They have little more bearing on reality.

A few years ago former Attorney General Edward H. Levi startled overseas listeners to the Voice of America by declaring: "Judges throughout the United States are afraid to enforce the criminal law." Levi couldn't have put it more wrongly if he'd tried. American judges aren't afraid, in the sense that somebody is intimidating them. But a great many of them are utterly at a loss on how to enforce laws that—for technical, sociological, or legislative reasons—have become unenforceable.

In 1968 Melvin Belli, one of the most flamboyant trial lawyers extant, produced a book called *The Law Revolution,* in which he enthused about the convulsions afflicting this country's judicial system. But, as you read through his volume you become more and more struck by the *absence* of revolutionary development, such as occurred in France, for instance, with the introduction of the Code Napoléon. What we find is the withering, erosion, reinterpretation, or circumvention of existing laws—usually by means of plea-bargaining. Of "revolution there isn't a trace." Instead, we see the undermining of all those characteristics without which no legal system can function effectively for any length of time: consistency, predictability, and constancy.

To these three we must add credibility—an essential quality that the courts themselves undermine whenever they hand down their *outré* sentences. Why, then, do they persist in the practice? Mainly because they are defending their traditional position against the steady encroachments of other agencies, whose powers cut across and often stymie the will of the courts. The most potent of these are the parole boards. To a large extent the use of such Kafkaesque penalties by the courts are devices aimed at keeping prisoners out of the reach of the parole people for as long as possible. But their efficacy is waning rapidly as the parole boards and their allies come up with new wrinkles of their own.

Thus two bodies whose activities were meant to be coordinated are locked in a power struggle that is threatening to choke the breath out of the criminal-justice system itself. It would be quite false to assume that courts favor harsher methods while parole boards espouse humanitarian principles. More often than not, parole decisions are governed purely by temporary expediency and are unaffected by moral considerations. The point is that they can and do short-circuit the intentions expressed by judges and jurors at the time of the trial verdict.*

---

* In November 1977 Chicago Circuit Judge James Bailey sentenced one Henry Brisbon to 1,000–3,000 years in prison—the longest term in Illinois history. Brisbon had murdered a young couple during a holdup, ordering

The power struggle is particularly intense in Washington, D.C., which in some respects has become a testing ground for judicial innovations. "Let me illustrate how the system works here," said U.S. District Attorney William Collins. "Under the D.C. code, first-degree murder carries a mandatory life sentence. The actual terms are twenty years to life. According to statute, a murderer is not entitled to parole until he has served a *minimum* of twenty years. But there are a couple of factors cutting across that. The D.C. Corrections Department has introduced programs such as work-release and furlough. I've tried a number of homicide cases where the defendant should now be serving those minimum twenty years. And what happens? He's out working every day in the city! Then there's furlough. We have a rather well-known defendant here—no, I won't mention his name— who is presently holding down a pretty important job in Washington. And officially he is under a twenty-years-to-life sentence for first-degree murder!"

The D.A. gave me a rather grim little smile. "Furthermore," he went on, "in the late 1960s we had the dawning of the so-called halfway-house concept. Now a person living in a halfway house is under—let me say—*very minimal* supervision. But he is still, technically, serving his sentence. And the law of the District of Columbia is still, technically, being followed. Because the law, you see, doesn't prescribe the *manner* of the sentence. Merely the length." *

Occasionally parole boards seem actually to be vying with courts in their determination to keep obviously lethal individuals at large until they produce at least one dead body. In 1975 a Washingtonian named Olen Lebby was convicted of assault with a dangerous weapon. When, out on parole on this conviction, he was hauled in and convicted of another assault with a dangerous weapon, the parole people

---

them to lie on the roadside and "kiss their last kiss" before shooting them both in the back. Bailey explained that he gave the extraordinarily long term to indicate to future parole boards that Brisbon should never be freed. (Some judges, you may note, no longer sentence—they "indicate.")

* For security conditions in halfway houses, see Chapter 9.

promptly sprang him again—this time to await sentencing on his second conviction. Still on parole, then, Mr. Lebby used his freedom to shoot and kill a D.C. policeman. Arrested once more, he was sentenced first to thirty to ninety months on the second dangerous-weapons count, then to nine to twenty-seven years for murder. Since the sentences are to run concurrently, Lebby will be eligible for parole once again after nine years.

The D.C. board has a record of granting parole two out of three times when a prisoner first becomes eligible for it. Its chairman, the Reverend H. Albion Ferrell, acknowledged that this proportion might appear somewhat high. But, he added with inimitable logic, only 10 percent of prisoners held in maximum security are paroled, because "If they are in maximum security, they're disciplinary problems. And if they can't adjust within an institution, how can we anticipate they'll adjust in the community?" Which, of course, begs the question of why those problem 10 percent should be released at all.

While the board acts like greased lightning in facilitating the earliest possible release of offenders, it turns tortoise when pondering revocation of parole for defendants who have committed violent crimes after being freed. At a 1976 hearing of the District's judiciary subcommittee, Ferrell explained that when the board decides to consider revoking the parole of a repeat offender, the decision is usually postponed until the court system has disposed of the charge for which the defendant was arrested—an adjudication that may take months or even years.

This seems to place the blame squarely on the courts. But Superior Court Judge Donald S. Smith told the hearing that he had waited "day after day, week after week" for the board to provide him with a recommendation as to whether it wished to pursue parole revocation for a particular defendant. Finally, Smith related, he had threatened to haul the Reverend Ferrell himself into court if a recommendation was not forthcoming immediately. Only then did the board finally comply.

The above will give you an inkling of the relationship between courts and parole boards. The character of their working methods can be best gauged from the fact that of all criminals arrested for murder in Washington, D.C., 28 percent were found to be free on parole, bail, or probation.

It might be gratifying to reveal that parole boards take bribes to spring prisoners, as intimated by J. Edgar Hoover. This, however, proves to be another F.B.I. myth. With rare exceptions, parole boards are far less corruptible than state governors—some of whom constantly favor selected underworld pals. By and large, the boards are staffed by honest mediocrities, appointed for no discernible merit and determined to hang on to their $32,000-a-year jobs. This determination often forces them into petty lying, such as feeding investigators crooked statistics that they hope won't be checked. They never lie on a grand scale in the manner of, say, lawyers or police departments. They just manicure the facts a little.

Their ignorance can be appalling. Several board members turned out not to know the difference between psychological and psychiatric reports or between neurotics and psychotics. Yet they base most of their parole decisions on what they fondly term a prisoner's "mental attitude."

How do they assess this attitude? "It's done in about ten to fifteen minutes," an ex-con—still on parole—told me. "That's what you wait for all year. You're in this room, with two members of the board facing you. They ask you questions and you answer fast because you keep thinking how you don't have much time to make a good impression. A good impression—that's being kinda middling smart, not *too* smart. And sounding like you feel guilty, but not *too* guilty. Not like you're all hung up about it. And you gotta sound *positive*, like you have a program ready: work or school or religion maybe. Religion is always good. You bring in Jesus, and that goes over great, mostly.

"The main thing, though, you gotta let on you'll put up with any amount of shit, really kiss ass. What I mean is you don't walk in there upright. You sort of crawl in and crawl out again. And talk real soft and gentle. I seen guys practice it in their cells—hundreds of times—how they'll walk and talk. Practice their mental attitudes. . . ."

The right "mental attitude," then, is mainly a matter of play-acting. The smoothies and hypocrites and Bible-spouters are the most likely to succeed. Although the boards are supposed to consider the prisoner's whole personality and background, in practice they concentrate almost solely on his behavior in custody—behavior that is apt to be totally misleading. His actual crime, which should be the chief criterion, weighs least of all. I had one board person tell me quite seriously that "The worse a prisoner's offense, the better, generally, he does on parole"—an assessment so devastatingly inaccurate that I wondered from what part of Oz she hailed.

But because the boards keep one ear cocked for public reaction, some prisoners are made to pay for the crimes of others. If popular outrage runs high over some particularly brutal bank robbery or rape, men convicted of that type of felony will have their parole deferred until things simmer down. Above all, the boards are sensitive to the fluctuating needs of the state governor's office—this being, after all, where their jobs are handled. It follows that whenever the governor requires a tough law-'n'-order image in order to counterbalance a political scandal or an especially heinous crime, the parole tap is turned down to a trickle. Then, when the cages begin to bulge at the seams and it becomes necessary to consider building expensive new prisons, there's a sudden and miraculous increase in the number of convicts developing the right mental attitudes, and the trickle turns into a flood. Expediency comes first, with genuine parole considerations lagging so far behind they're virtually lost from sight.

The wildest fluctuations occur in California, probably because it allows the greatest parole discretion. By state law a lifer becomes eligible for parole after serving seven years, those with lesser stretches after one-third of their *minimum* term. Which renders the meaning of "minimum" as ridiculous as that of "life" and further widens the credibility gap of the entire sentencing system.

California has no standard parole policy, only spasms dictated by politics, finances, and the public temper. In 1974, for example, the Adult Authority (the state parole board) released 4,717 prisoners, while the very next year the number shot up to 10,578—without there being any reason to suppose that more than twice as many convicts somehow qualified for freedom. All that had really happened was that, with the state's prison population swelling way beyond its housing capacity, the governor's office passed the word to "empty 'em out."

Reponding to protests, the Adult Authority distributed form letters declaring, "Only about two per cent of all felons released continue to commit highly violent crimes." While disseminating this comforting claim, the Adult Authority apparently never imagined that anyone might check it against figures compiled by the state's Bureau of Criminal Statistics. Those who did so found that this percentage comprised only felons rearrested while on parole, convicted of new violent crimes, and returned to prison. It did not include those who were caught but returned directly to prison without a new trial, those who plea-bargained down to a conviction for some nonviolent crime, or those sentenced to federal prison or locked up in another state. If you added these categories, the number ran anywhere from 20 percent to more than 50 percent!

James Reece was among those released in the 1975 parole deluge, despite a judge's recommendation that he never be paroled. Branded a "one-man crime wave" by the judge, Reece robbed a Hayward pharmacy in 1966, kidnapping an old man and a sheriff's deputy during his getaway. Captured, he twice attempted escape and succeeded the second time. Robbing an Oakland woman before his escape was even noticed, he was recaptured while trying to drive a stolen car across the Mexican border. He appeared in a San Diego court, which released him from custody through a clerical foul-up that still hasn't been explained, Reece vanished.

He reappeared a month later, when he tried to kidnap a top-less dancer named Yvonne D'Angers at gunpoint. After chasing her car down a winding road and running her into a ditch, he was foiled by a car crash in which he was badly injured.

He spent the next three years in a state hospital for the criminally insane, until the doctors declared him legally sane and fit to be tried. At his trial Reece tried to demolish the courtroom. It took five deputies to subdue him, even after he was handcuffed. Although the judge gave him five years to life, it was barely three and a half years before the Adult Authority decided that he had made a "social adjustment." They knew this because Reece had told them so himself. He was, he declared, eager for parole because it would allow him to work on the outside with juvenile offenders. "I want to deter them from a life of crime such as I have led."

Exactly fifty-two days after his release, Reece kidnapped young Debra Ann Rebiejo, a Hayward college student. He raped her, shot her five times, and dumped her corpse in a drainage ditch. Then he stole a car, robbed a woman clerk in a wig store, tried to rape her, and shot her when she screamed for help. He was critically wounded in a shootout with pursuing lawmen when finally captured. The D.A. of Alameda County, who had originally prosecuted Reece, learned only after the battle that the "crime wave" was back on the streets —the Adult Authority hadn't bothered to inform him of the release.

When the Adult Authority sprang Dr. Geza de Kaplany in 1975, they took the precaution of sneaking him out of the country six months ahead of the official date. Kaplany, the "acid doctor," had perpetrated perhaps the most horrendous single murder in American history—an atrocity that he airily euphemized as "my one-hour crackup." His case demonstrates the current meaninglessness of the life sentence, the worthlessness of promises made to jurors by state prison officials, and the astonishing lengths to which parole boards will go once they've taken it into their heads to turn someone loose.

Geza de Kaplany was a Hungarian of the type who hints that the "de" of his name denotes aristocratic lineage; which it didn't. A waxy-skinned, faintly effeminate individual, he impressed colleagues chiefly by an air of lip-curling arrogance. He worked as an anesthesiologist, lived in San Jose, and married one of the outstanding beauties of California's Hungarian community, largely on the strength of his professional status. Hajna was a striking twenty-five-year-old blonde and part-time fashion model when she wedded the thirty-six-year-old doctor in 1962. Kaplany was apparently unable to consummate the marriage. Within five weeks, this blot on his masculine ego had driven him into a state of cold frenzy. He imagined his wife was having affairs throughout the neighborhood, laughing at his impotence. He determined, in his own words, "to ruin her beauty."

The doctor assembled an elaborate torture kit in their San Jose honeymoon apartment, including a hi-fi to drown out screams. Before going home, he had a manicure—so as not to puncture the rubber gloves he would be wearing. Overpowering Hajna, he tied her to the bed. Then, with surgical knives, cut deep gashes in her face, body, and legs. With the music blasting away in the background, he took a bottle of nitric acid and began pouring the liquid into the cuts. Starting on her face, he poured acid into her eyes, nostrils, and mouth. Slowly and systematically, working downward, he proceeded to douse her neck, breasts, nipples, belly, and vagina. The whole process took more than an hour. At the end, the woman looked as if she had been scorched with a blowtorch.

Hajna had a tough constitution; she lived for three weeks in unspeakable agony. The hospital nurses found it hard to look at her. She no longer had anything resembling a human face. Her mother sat by her bedside, praying to God to let her daughter die. After twenty-one days, her prayers were granted.

In court, Dr. de Kaplany denied that he had intended to kill his wife—he had merely meant to mar her looks. In view of his medical knowledge, the claim was patently ridiculous. He got off with one life sentence, mainly because, during the penalty phase, a representative of the state prison system took the stand to assure the jurors that de Kaplany would be classed as a "special interest prisoner." The court did its feeble best to keep faith by ordering that photographs of Kaplany's acid-eaten victim be kept in his file. The pictures, however, soon vanished into the drawers of the Adult Authority, where they couldn't upset anyone.

The doctor was to serve only thirteen years of his sentence before gaining his release under somewhat mysterious circumstances. Six months ahead of his announced parole date, he was quietly put on an airplane to Taiwan. Although the Adult Authority later explained that speed was essential because a missionary hospital urgently needed his skills as a cardiac specialist, this hardly seems convincing. De Kaplany was an anesthesiologist, not a heart specialist, his skills had been rusting for thirteen years, and his medical license had been revoked when he entered prison.

In an attempt to shed some light on this point, I wrote to Ray Procunier, then head of the parole board, and asked for an interview. In reply I received a pleasant little note requesting me to call his office for an appointment. I did so daily for six consecutive days. On each occasion, Mr. Procunier was either unexpectedly absent or in conference; in any case, unavailable to me. I didn't have to call him a seventh time, for by then I had read the newspaper item reporting his resignation from the board "for personal reasons."

If misuse of parole is eroding the authority of the courts, plea-bargaining may be cutting their throats. No better process was ever devised to elicit contempt for a nation's judiciary system and to negate the very purposes for which it is supposed to function. A plea bargain is a legal ploy that allows a defendant to plead guilty to a reduced charge and thereby save the state the uncertain outcome and certain expense of a trial. In other words, it is a legal conspiracy between the prosecution and the defense aimed at rendering a trial unnecessary. While an efficient economy measure, it is perhaps the most disastrous fixture known to criminal justice.

Today, nationwide, 90 percent of all serious crimes are cleared by plea bargains—though "cleared" is hardly the right word for a procedure based essentially on falsehood.* The U.S. court structure is so overburdened that a reduction in plea-bargaining of even 10 to 15 percent would double the trial load and virtually bring the machine to a halt. Chicago Judge Marvin Aspen stated, "Sometimes you have to rely on things which are antagonistic to the system just so the system won't fall apart." But in the context of society's constitutional right to trial, the system already has fallen apart inasmuch as it fails to function some 90 percent of the time.

The perniciousness of plea-bargaining cuts both ways, shafting as many innocents as it allows guilty criminals to get off lightly. The ploy is exploited by the thousands of hack lawyers who spend their days hanging around courtrooms in order to fasten onto potential clients at the time of their arraignment. These clients—mostly poor, bewildered, and semiliterate—usually acquiese when their self-appointed mouthpiece suggests that their only chance of avoiding a stiff sentence lies in pleading guilty to a charge reduced down one rung from whatever they are facing—say, assault instead of armed robbery. The prosecutor will usually agree as well, particularly when his evidence is shaky. So the lawyer collects his fee, the prosecutor gets his conviction, and the accused receives a reduced sentence—although he might well have been acquitted or received an even milder sentence had the case gone to trial. The process is so irrational that it sometimes results in cellmates' serving radically different stretches for the same felony.

New York City is America's plea-bargain capital because it has the most logjammed courts, a ludicrously divided criminal-justice system, and a state legislature suffering from

---

* The most illustrious plea bargain in history was that of Vice-President Spiro Agnew. The Justice Department allowed him to plead nolo contendere (no contest) to a count of income-tax evasion. Agnew resigned as Vice-President and received a three-year suspended sentence and ten-thousand-dollar fine instead of imprisonment.

the periodic urge to commit hara-kiri. During one such fit the legislature narrowed the definition of first-degree murder so as to cover only the slaying of police and correctional officers. All other killings are relegated to the status of second-degree homicides—thus depriving the prosecution of one more chip in the bargaining game.

This doesn't mean, however, that cop-killers are automatically tried for first-degree murder—not when expediency suggests otherwise. Although Luis Velez had confessed to coldbloodedly gunning down officers Fred Reddy and Andrew Glover, in 1976, District Attorney Robert Morgenthau permitted him to plead guilty to two counts of second-degree murder. Why? A conviction for first-degree murder would have carried a mandatory death sentence, which, in the event that the Supreme Court chose to strike down the verdict, could have meant an expensive retrial. Rather than risk such a gruesome prospect, Mr. Morgenthau agreed to a bargain that demonstrated utter contempt not only for the lives of policemen but also for the law of the state. The dead officers' colleagues felt even more embittered when, as a sop thrown in their direction, the D.A. recommended that Velez never be granted parole. Everybody—including the D.A.—knows how parole boards treat such recommendations.

New York City currently averages about 1,700 homicides a year—nearly half of them in Manhattan alone. The fact that less than 60 percent of these cases are cleared annually may constitute a world record for lame justice. During the heyday of the gunfighters in Tombstone, Arizona, the clearance rate was 18 percent higher.

In 1973, an average year for Manhattan, grand juries returned 326 homicide indictments. Out of this total, 200 killers plea-bargained their way down to manslaughter or negligent-homicide raps, which differ quite drastically from murder. Since Manhattan had thus spared itself the expense of 200 trials, almost everybody was pleased—conservatives because it saved the taxpayers' money; liberals because it prevented the killers from languishing in jail for long; and the slayers because they collected two to five years for deeds that not so long ago might have meant the electric chair. The only unhappy ones were the cranks who believed that homicide laws should be enforced, and perhaps the families of the 200 victims.

Irving R. Kaufman, Chief Judge of the U.S. Circuit Court of Appeals, waxed very indignant about this state of affairs in the pages of the New York *Times*. "No criminal defendant or prosecutor should, in a properly functioning judicial system, be bludgeoned by cost or delay into bargaining for a plea," wrote the distinguished jurist—thereby revealing an almost touching innocence. A properly functioning judicial system? New York's system is barely functioning at all, much less functioning properly. The Manhattan D.A.'s Homicide Bureau can, with the resources it has at present, process a maximum of fifty murder trials a year—less than one sixth of the indictments handed down. Without plea-bargaining, this particular part of the system would grind to a complete halt.

The same applies to the entire American judiciary network, coast to coast, federal as much as local. Not only aren't there anywhere near enough judges and prosecutors, bailiffs and clerks, reporters and typists, courts, jails, or even enough washroom facilities, but what exists is generally of such inferior quality that it only adds to the problem.

The one commodity available in superabundance is lawyers, the only court personnel that has multiplied as fast as the crime rate. Attorneys are so thick on the ground that Virginia mass murderer James Leroy Breeden had three of them assigned to his defense after he fired his original one. At the beginning of this century there was approximately one lawyer to every 1,100 Americans. Today the ratio stands at one to 530. In contrast, England has one for every 1,600, Japan one for every 10,300.

Far from easing the overcrowded court dockets, this plethora of legal eagles is constantly adding to the burden. They will undertake the most harebrained of appeals or the most frivolous of judicial maneuvers simply in order to keep busy. And, while they may do their clients not a shred of good, these shysterish manipulations consume huge portions of the court's time. Some lawyers rely heavily on delaying tactics in court—tabling motions and raising objections for no purpose other than the prolongation of a trial.* In one California case, an attorney spent fifty-four weeks on pretrial motions and another eight weeks on jury selection. Thus, after fourteen and a half months of this strategy, the trial proper hadn't even begun. This kind of maneuvering means that American courts take four months to decide a case that elsewhere would be settled in as many days. The time wasted doesn't add an iota to the quality of justice dispensed; it merely skyrockets the costs.

New York's situation is further exacerbated by the partitioning of its criminal-justice machine. The city has five District Attorneys, each with his own Homicide Bureau, frequently at loggerheads with the others. Together they resemble a fishing net with holes big enough for most of the catch to swim through. Criminals operate across borough lines—committing, say, a murder in Manhattan, a car theft in Queens, and a robbery in the Bronx. This means that the city's 750 Assistant D.A.s, already thinly stretched, must duplicate their efforts by processing the same culprit. Information gets lost, evidence is withheld, and the opportunities for crossed wires are endless. The sole reason for this ramshackle structure is that it provides more jobs for political cronies than a unified apparatus.

"We had weekly meetings of the Homicide Bureau," a former Assistant D.A., now in private practice, told me. "When the statistics were up—and they were always going up—the bureau chief would order us to plea-bargain. Not a direct order, but he'd say we had to push harder for dispositions. 'Give 'em a little' was the phrase he used. So we gave a little. You wouldn't believe what was called 'little.' Like one guy, he'd tied his victim up, gagged him, then shot

* One counsel, notorious for foot-dragging, objected to a prosecution witness's stating his own name because, since he had first learned his name from his mother, it was "hearsay."

him five times. He was allowed to plead guilty to second-degree manslaughter. He got zero to five years in prison—minus time off for good behavior, naturally. And this was considered a good conviction—after all, we'd put him away, hadn't we?"

On the other hand, things can go hard on a defendant who refuses a bargain—chiefly because of the interminable delays and expense involved. In the fall of 1973 there was a series of rape-robberies within a few short blocks of one another on Manhattan's East Side. All followed the same pattern. A man knocked on a young woman's door, asking for pencil and paper in order to leave a message for another tenant. When the victim let him in, he held a knife at her throat, wrapped pantyhose around her neck, and threatened to strangle her if she didn't submit. Three of the victims—all exceptionally attractive—identified their attacker by photograph. His name was David Allweiss, and he had been arrested for a sex offense in Queens some years earlier.

A tall, natty twenty-one-year-old who called himself a writer, Allweiss, accompanied by an attorney, walked into the East Twenty-first Street station house on October 10 and turned himself in. He was arraigned and duly released on bail.

On the night of October 23 a friend found the body of Carol Hoffmann in her studio apartment on East Twenty-ninth Street. She had been a publishing assistant working for Harper & Row, a well-groomed, smartly dressed career woman with a divorce behind her. Now she lay face up on the white rug, pantyhose wound around her neck, the blade of a knife protruding from her abdomen. The medical examiner determined that Ms. Hoffmann had been manually strangled—not garroted—and that the killer afterward plunged the knife into her stomach ten times.

The amazing thing was that her boyfriend had actually talked to her murderer for about fifteen minutes just before she was killed. The friend had telephoned her at 9:00 P.M. and learned that a man was in her apartment—a man with a "problem." He had come in allegedly looking for another man who had raped his wife. The friend talked to him and tried to calm him down. When Carol came back on the line, he advised her to get rid of the fellow—fast—and then ring him back. "All right," she said quietly and hung up. When she failed to ring back, the friend went to her apartment and found her dead.

After the pantyhose clue—which smacked of fetishism—led the detectives to arrest Allweiss, Carol's friend identified his voice as positively that of the man on the telephone. The crime laboratory established that a strand of hair found in the dead girl's mouth had the same properties as the suspect's hair. But that was all the evidence linking Allweiss to the murder. It was a weak case, and grew no stronger when six young women identified Allweiss as the man who had raped them in their apartments. Proof of multiple rape was not proof of murder. Furthermore, Ms. Hoffmann had not been sexually assaulted.

Once begun, the bargaining dragged on for nearly two years, losing whatever resemblance it might have had to a legal procedure. The D.A. offered to drop four rapes if Allweiss would plead guilty to two—plus the murder. Allweiss refused, and the wrangling went on. In April 1974 he agreed to plead guilty to raping two women. Stipulated as covering all "pending cases," including the killing of Carol, this plea, it was agreed, would result in a sentence of eight to twenty-five years, which could get him out on parole after three years. Later Allweiss withdrew his plea, saying that he hadn't realized that he would, in effect, be admitting the murder. There was nothing for it but to try him in court, a prospect the prosecution dreaded.

The prosecutor, Assistant D.A. Paul Flaxman, asked for permission to employ the so-called Molineux Doctrine, a rarely used method of introducing evidence of the defendant's past crimes in order to prove a pattern that matches elements in the present case. The six women took the stand, described their rapes, and pointed out Allweiss as their attacker. There were certain matching elements—such as the lingerie fetish-ism—that also appeared in the murder. Nevertheless, the fact remained that the killing was not a rape-murder, and Flax-man utilized this point with remarkable skill.

"Each of these women complied with the defendant's order. Each is alive," he told the jury. "I suggest to you that you may reasonably draw the conclusion that Carol Hoff-mann is dead because she did not comply. Carol Hoffmann is dead precisely because she was *not* raped!"

The jurors found Allweiss guilty of second-degree murder. He received up to eighteen years' imprisonment for the rapes, twenty-five years to life for the murder. At Flaxman's re-quest, the sentences were consecutive, making Allweiss in-eligible for parole until he is sixty-seven. An example had been made—perhaps not of justice, but certainly of what happens to culprits who turn down a good bargain.

Among conservatives it is an article of faith that "soft judges" bear the main responsibility for our homicide crisis and that, accordingly, toughness from the bench would go a long way toward alleviating it. Like so many articles of faith, this doesn't stand up too well under scrutiny. There are, of course, a great many judges whose soft souls match their soft heads. But these judges are the products of a politicized selection system to which conservatives cling with iron te-nacity. Every attempt to change it runs into their furious op-position.

We have also seen how the power vested in parole boards can take the bite out of virtually any sentence; even Charles Manson will be eligible for parole in 1978. In 1977 Cali-fornia Superior Court Judge Harry V. Peetris did his damned-est to hand out a fitting penalty for Robert Leroy Biehler, with distinctly anemic results. Biehler, who aspired to become "the pimp of San Fernando Valley," murdered a woman and her fifteen-year-old son, an adult neighbor, and a roller-derby girl. In court the judge declared that only death would be an appropriate punishment for the quadruple killer, and since such a sentence was not possible under current law, life without possibility of parole. This, however, could be awarded only for crimes such as kidnap for ransom. "The next step downward in severity would be consecutive sentences for each murder," said Peetris. "Unfortunately, the Sentencing Law of 1976 does not permit this." He therefore gave the defendant life in prison, but added: "The reality of this sentence is that because of credit for time already spent in custody—450 days—Biehler will be eligible for parole in five years, ten months from today."

Where homicide is concerned, the ultra-complaisant judges are largely balanced out by their opposites. At one extreme, a Kansas City, Missouri, court gave holdup-slayer William Kline ten years in prison and then put him on five years' probation—with the result that he won't serve any time at all unless he violates his probation terms. At the other extreme, Cleveland double murderer Larry Kaiser was sentenced to be electrocuted twice in succession—and on the same day. Common Pleas Judge John T. Patton, who dreamed this impossible dream, explained that he bestowed his sentence because he felt that capital punishment was a deterrent to murder—ergo, it should be doubly deterrent when performed twice. Needless to say, Kaiser has so far not been executed even once. The sole difference between these judicial extremists is that the former stand a better chance of seeing their decisions upheld.*

The problem stems far less from indulgent judges than from incompetent ones. In New York, Chicago, and other large cities, political sachems determine who will be elevated to the bench, and their choices frequently waver between nonentities and outright disasters. Court reporters call a large proportion of these party appointees "old necessities" because, like necessity, they know no law. Legal ignorance, however, is often among their minor failings. As Pat Brown, former governor of California, once acknowledged, "There are some judges that are superannuated, senile, mentally ill or alcoholics, and they should be removed."

This is easier said than done. Federal judges are appointed

---

* In 1974 the U.S. Court of Appeals ruled improper a 320-year federal prison sentence imposed on Dallas Ray Delay for the murder of a bank president and his wife and daughter. The court reduced his term to 100

by the President and generally hold their jobs for life. They can be removed only by impeachment for misbehavior—which happens very rarely indeed. Gubernatorial appointees, who rank among the worst selections, can theoretically be ousted by the voters. In practice, however, incumbents have so many advantages going for them—such as patronage and political influence—that it becomes immensely difficult to vote them out. Since ordinary voters do not, as a rule, follow courtroom affairs very closely, a judge's behavior has to be spectacularly awful in order to jeopardize his seat at the polls. Lack of judicial knowledge alone is seldom sufficient.

San Francisco Superior Court Judge Bernard B. Glickfield once tried a rape case and—although the rapist had threatened to kill his victim—sentenced him only to weekends in jail. When the woman complained, Glickfield called her a "horse's ass" and made several derogatory remarks about her character. The Supreme Court censured him for "conduct prejudicial to the administration of justice," but was quite prepared to let it go at that. It took the efforts of newspaper columnist Guy Wright to elevate Glickfield's behavior into a regular campaign issue, and hence bring about his defeat in the 1974 city elections. This, to repeat, is quite exceptional. As a rule, judges can perpetrate almost any amount of courtroom inanities without having to fear either censure or ouster.

According to U.S. Attorney Ramon Child, Federal Judge Willis W. Ritter of Utah has been known to confiscate the court stenographer's notes after making particularly injudicious statements from the bench, thus escaping appellate-court censure. *Time* magazine reported that Ritter once hauled in thirty postal workers for contempt of court because the mail-sorting machine in his courthouse was noisy. He had a reporter confined for two hours without explanation; a bailiff said Ritter was angered by the journalist's picking his nose in court. Through 1975 Ritter's verdicts were reversed in 58 per-

---

years—which Delay will start serving after he completes twenty years in the Missouri State Penitentiary.

cent of his civil cases, 40 percent of his criminal cases, and 76
percent of his *habeas corpus* cases—possibly the worst record
in the U.S. He has also been ejected from the University
Club in Salt Lake City for encouraging a barroom fight. At
the time of this writing, the seventy-eight-year-old Ritter is
still on the bench.*

Judges can also, if they so choose, get by on the barest
minimum of work. Despite the severe shortage of judges, a
study conducted in Chicago found that the workday of the
average Cook County jurist consisted of no more than two
and three-quarter hours on the bench, plus one and three-
quarter hours in his chambers.

Undoubtedly the most corrosive feature is the constant
pressure of local politics on bench decisions. Steven Phillips,
former Assistant D.A. in New York's Bronx County, told
of a potentially explosive homicide case in which an Italian
boy had knifed a black high-school student simply to
prove his machismo. In the plea-bargaining wrangles that followed, Phillips proposed an open plea of first-degree manslaughter, with the question of an appropriate sentence being
left entirely in the hands of the judge—where it belongs. He
was not in the least surprised to hear his proposal turned
down on the spot. The judge adjourned the case for one
week, at which time, if the District Attorney's office was prepared to make a recommendation on sentence, he would
accept the plea and follow that recommendation. Otherwise,
the case would be set for trial.

It is this uncertainty, this pathetic lack of judicial self-
assurance, that creates much of the havoc in criminal jurisprudence. It tends to make judges go off the deep end in
opposite directions. Some act like Attila the Hun, curse,
bellow, and threaten to jail everybody within reach, imposing
penalties that any first-year law student knows will be overturned on review. Others, displaying marshmallow spines, let

---

* Judge Ritter died in March 1978, having resisted all efforts to get him
to retire. A suit filed by the Justice Department to have him removed from
cases involving the federal government was still pending at the time of his
death.

themselves be bullied by all participants—including obstreperous defendants—and watch benignly while their court becomes a shambles. In New York I saw a defendant spit repeatedly at witnesses without evoking any reprimand from His Honor. Only a minority seem to wield the calm, detached authority expected of British judges as a matter of course.

The result of such judicial incompetence is the debilitating frequency of mistrials and reversed decisions, which serve to add still further time and expense to cases that have already swallowed up too much of both. In Los Angeles, for example, an ordinary theft trial, involving only $100, ended up costing taxpayers $130,212. Most reversals are based on procedural errors or improper sentences that even moderately efficient judges could have avoided.

But even outstanding jurists may find it well-nigh impossible to administer some of the transcendental laws imposed on them by legislators. A prime specimen was the 1970 Bail Reform Act, which, while aiming at the abolition of some old evils, succeeded only in compounding them with new ones. Bail, an ancient Anglo-Saxon legal tradition that antedates the Magna Carta, has always worked unfairly against the poor. They had to stay in jail while the rich posted bond and went free until the time of their trial. The Reform Act, introduced in the District of Columbia as a "model law," sought to rectify this by requiring that an accused be set free without bail if he can demonstrate the kind of community ties that suggest he will show up for his trial. Among the pitfalls of the reform was the extent to which a term like "community ties" can be interpreted to mean just about anything. It can, for example, mean the woman the accused is currently living with. In one case I attended, the judge accepted the address of a prostitute the defendant had picked up in a bar three weeks previously as constituting his "established residence." A parole officer told me an even better one: "Quite often they give the name of a 'resident friend'— and he or she is a co-defendant in the crime for which they're going to be tried."

According to the U.S. Attorney's office, out of every two thousand cases that involve felony indictments, five hundred defendants fail to appear for trial. But even this is still a better record than that of Bonabond, an organization founded by ex-convicts that frequently gets "third-party custody" of defendants awaiting trial. Since 1966 over one third of Bonabond's clients either didn't show up in court or were re-arrested for other crimes before their appointment was due.

Most of the felonies mentioned above were offenses involving property. You might reasonably suppose that bail regulations are more stringent where murder and other violent crimes are concerned, particularly when the safety of prospective witnesses is at stake. Not so. Section 1321 of the Bail Reform Act states explicitly, "No financial condition may be imposed to assure the safety of any person or the community." This means that an armed bandit, whose fate hinges on the testimony of his victim, has as much right to bail as a shoplifter. Even if the victim or his family get threatening phone calls in the meantime, they have to *prove* that these calls came from the defendant before bail revocation can be considered.

Until 1972 judges had the option of detaining defendants charged with capital crimes as they saw fit. When the Supreme Court effectively abolished capital punishment in the District of Columbia that year, lawyers could henceforth argue that, since capital crimes no longer existed, their clients were entitled to the same bail benefits as others not charged with murder. Often they argued successfully, giving rise to grimly comic interludes in which judges called the accused "dangers to the community" in one breath and granted them bail in the next. High money bonds make little difference, except to give the judge a sterner image, since defendants usually have to put up only one tenth of the amount themselves.*

---

* According to the stipulations of the Reform Act, David Berkowitz, the mass murderer known as "Son of Sam," would have been legally entitled to immediate release on bail. He had a steady job, a permanent address, and no prior convictions.

Washington Police Chief Maurice Cullinane described "one of hundreds" of similar cases in his files to a House District subcommittee: In October 1975 a man was arrested for homicide, indicted for murder, then released on his personal recognizance. Arrested seven days later for carrying a dangerous weapon, he was again released on personal recognizance. Arrested on November 28 for unlawful entry, he was released yet another time on personal recognizance. Arrested once more on December 3 for grand larceny, he once more was released on personal recognizance. Finally, in February 1976, when the defendant was brought in again—this time for attempted petit larceny—the court's forbearance seemed to be wearing thin. The judge set bond at one thousand dollars, of which the defendant actually had to post *one hundred* dollars before being freed again.

Chief Cullinane gave his account in June 1976. He regretted that he couldn't mention the defendant's name. The man was still out on bail, awaiting his trials, and had to be presumed innocent until found otherwise.

15

Remedial Action

Every society gets precisely the criminals it deserves.
—Criminologist Jean Lacassagne

In April 1969, amid considerable fanfare, the Nixon administration announced the first allocation of funds by the Law
Enforcement Assistance Administration—thereafter known as
the LEAA. This organization, conceived by President Johnson but remolded in the Nixon-Mitchell image, was authorized to spend $300 million annually for the next few years
to help modernize individual police departments, courts, and
correctional systems.

The LEAA, which has since poured $5 billion into the war
against crime, bore the unique distinction of combining
nearly all the faults of American law enforcement in a single
body. From the start it resembled a doctor trying to treat a
German measles epidemic by dabbing at the individual spots
on his patients' skin. Its failure was virtually guaranteed
by the nature of one of its key provisions. This was the
so-called block-grant provision, which earmarked 85 percent
of its budget for the use—more or less as they pleased—of
state and local governments. What pleased them most were
more cops equipped with more hardware—more guns, helmets, gas grenades, and armored vehicles, which they needed
like the proverbial hole in the head. The result was a nationwide police army of more than half a million uniformed men
with enough munitions to conquer Mexico—but quite un-
suited for combating street muggers.

The LEAA expounded some excellent theories, only to
prove incapable of applying them. Its executives appeared to
be spiritual twins of James Flecker's Mandarin general in
The Golden Journey to Samarkand, "Who never left his

palace gates before,/But hath grown blind reading great
books on war." While repeatedly paying lip service to the
proposition that minorities are the main victims as well as
the major perpetrators of crime, the LEAA's policies showed
no glimmer of that recognition in practice. Of 184 LEAA
employees at administrative and management levels, exactly
nine were black. The LEAA allocated $250,000 a year to
seven white colleges within a crime-fighting consortium, while
nine black colleges received only $64,000 for the same
purpose.

Other allocations read like Art Buchwald at his most acidu-
lous: $27,000 for a study to determine why prison inmates
wish to escape. The study sought to reduce security costs
by predicting the least likely and most likely escapees; it
duly elucidated that an escapee is more likely to be someone who had been turned down for parole. A study that
aimed at improving courtroom design swallowed $280,000.
Its main conclusion was the suggestion that the judges'
benches be lowered one inch. The $176,000 granted to the
Chicago Alliance to End Repression was used by the Alliance
first to obtain information on the identity of police informers,
then to blow their covers. Community Design Analysis in
New York was awarded $650,072 for the study of why stable
neighborhoods have lower crime rates than those with a high
turnover of residents.

The LEAA was not directly responsible for many other
grotesqueries. It couldn't stop Indiana from using an aircraft,
purchased with an $84,000 grant, to fly its governor around
the country, nor California from spending $75,602 of anti-
crime money to assist kindergarten children with learning
problems. Nor could it prevent the blossoming of fifty-five
state and territorial agencies that had the sole function of
passing along the federal funds—after deducting their own
salaries.

The LEAA's dilemma was basically that of America's law
enforcement as a whole: It had no overall plan or system of
priorities, and was prohibited from formulating any because

that would have spoiled the political advantages of throwing money into the maws of as many civic bodies as possible.

"Throwing money at crime" is not necessarily futile. The billions puffed away by the LEAA might have had tremendous impact if the people in charge had known where to aim. They didn't know because they lacked the relevant information—for despite our positive mania for statistics, no industrialized nation knows less about its crime rate than the United States. Although we have at present fifty-seven different statistical systems deployed within a large variety of governmental branches in order to measure crime, their lack of coordination and the disparity of the various yardsticks they use render their figures useless as a basis for action.

One of the LEAA directors, Gerald M. Caplan, deplored this "deluge of meaningless statistics" and called for a centralized crime-statistics bureau within the Justice Department. Similar calls have been sounding for forty-seven years, but still no such office exists. It does not seem to have occurred to Dr. Caplan that he could have used some of the funds at his disposal to establish one. All his organization did was to occasionally bestow money on individual communities to computerize their particular crime data. What they discovered in this way was often appalling. It revealed that some police chiefs were understating felony figures by as much as 100 percent. But it provided only isolated glimpses of the whole problem. So far as the nationwide crime picture was concerned, these local spotlights contributed nothing except the uncomfortable feeling that things were considerably worse than we had supposed.

Back in 1931, the Wickersham Commission recommended the immediate creation of a central bureau for collecting crime statistics, such as nearly every industrial country on earth already possessed. But Washington's powers that be chose to have their crime fighters stumble around in the dark —thus insuring that every law-and-order crusade would turn into a game of blindman's buff.

Next in order of priority should have been the overhaul of

the court system, federal *and* state. For court facilities to meet the demands of them, they must be expanded all along the line—from judges and prosecutors, bailiffs and filing clerks, to holding cells and stenotype machines. This could have been accomplished with a fraction of the funds the LEAA poured into political gutters.

A beefed-up court system would automatically alleviate two of the worst headaches afflicting the judiciary: a defendant's right to a speedy trial and the related matter of bail. The right to a speedy trial is a constitutional principle the courts were forced to ignore frequently because of overloaded schedules, though sometimes through sheer maladroitness.* In 1974 Congress passed the Speedy Trial Act, requiring that an accused be tried within ninety days, but without allocating one cent to provide the additional personnel needed to comply with the Act. Hundreds of felons have had their sentences thrown out in consequence of this legislation.

In December 1971, a construction worker was stabbed to death in a street argument. Simply because there were not enough prosecuting D.A.s to cope with mounting case backlog, the accused's trial was postponed again and again. Nineteen months later, in July 1973, he pleaded guilty to manslaughter and was sentenced to a maximum ten years' imprisonment. In 1975, however, the State Court of Appeals overturned his conviction, dismissed the indictment, and ordered him released. The court ruled that he had been denied his constitutional right to a speedy trial.

Congress and the Appeals Court acted in the spirit of the Constitution. But this spirit becomes mere posturing in the absence of a judiciary capable of fulfilling its legal implications. As it was, the gesture simply voided one murder trial. It did nothing to speed the process of justice for others.

---

* The record for trial delays was set when two men were charged with shooting a Washington hospital patient in December 1972. Although their arrest came within twenty-four hours, their pretrial hearing was not held until October 1973, and the trial proper was duly slated for February 1977.

During that year, in Bronx County alone, no fewer than fifty-two men held on murder charges had been awaiting trial for more than twelve months. As Bronx District Attorney Mario Merola said at the time, "Since I took office, two years ago, I've lost twenty-five assistant D.A.s because of the city's freeze on hirings and pay rises. So what do you want me to do?"

One obvious remedy would be to shift the allocation of available criminal-justice funds. At present New York City spends about 80 percent of the available money on the Police Department, dividing the rest among the courts, the Department of Corrections, the district attorneys, and the probation and legal-aid services. This maintains a force of thirty-two thousand policemen—larger than most armies in history *—but provides nowhere near enough facilities to process the culprits this army hauls in.

Similar imbalances exist throughout the nation, creating bottlenecks that slow the mills of justice down to a tortoise crawl. The reason for this lopsidedness is once again political: Cops are visible, court facilities aren't. It is therefore essential that any federal funding be irrevocably earmarked for these vital purposes, rather than leaving their provision to the vote-courting expediencies of local governments.

Adequate court facilities would take much of the sting out of the controversy over bail laws. Civil libertarians of the gratis-bail-for-all persuasion can now make a case of the often unconscionably long confinements imposed on defendants awaiting trial. With waiting periods reduced to reasonable lengths, there would be less cause to release prisoners who— judged by their past actions—represent a danger to the community. Persons considered dangerous should not be able to buy their way out of jail. The court's option to impose money bond upon such persons should be removed from the law. The most maddeningly unnecessary murders are those com-

---

* London, with roughly the same population, has a police force of twenty-six thousand.

mitted by defendants free on bond.* Undoubtedly one of
the reasons for England's low homicide rate is the British
court practice of not letting violent individuals post bail.

To stick with the British example for a moment, English
sentences, while generally milder than ours, seem to have
vastly greater deterrent effect. This is due, above all, to the
greater surety that attends them—the feature most conspicu-
ously absent in U.S. justice. Sir Robert Mark, Chief of Scotland Yard, expressed this notion succinctly in a magazine
interview: "The best deterrent to deliberate, and therefore
preventable, crime is not so much severity of punishment as
the likelihood of being caught and, if caught, the near certainty of being convicted if guilty. And the more certain
justice is, the less severe it need be."

The British have several advantages in trial procedure,
some of very recent origin. In 1967, for instance, they
abolished the requirement of a unanimous jury verdict; it
now takes agreement by only ten of the twelve jurors, after
two hours' deliberation, for conviction. America could save
itself hundreds of mistrials by following suit, since the majority of our hung juries are the handiwork of one inflexible
jury member.

The lack of certainty extends over the entire criminal-
justice front. There is fatal scope for everybody concerned to
play games. Everyone has far more discretion than they can
handle: policemen on whether to arrest, district attorneys on
whether to prosecute, judges on whether to grant bail, parole
boards on whether and when to terminate sentences. The
whole field is a quagmire of contingencies. But a start could
be made in clearing it by building enough prisons to accom-

---

* In February, 1978, a twenty-three-year-old Chicago man appeared in
court charged with kidnapping, robbery and rape. He had been free under a
$25,000 bond. He left his car parked outside Maywood Court with *another*
victim—a doctor's wife he had abducted from a parking lot—locked in the
trunk. During a recess in the court proceedings he went out, opened the
trunk lid and talked to her. Later he murdered her. The woman would
still be alive today if the Chicago authorities hadn't seen fit to grant money
bail to an obviously violent and dangerous criminal.

modate those offenders we have duly convicted and wish to hold.

This sounds pretty rudimentary—until we remember that a large proportion of parolees gain freedom solely because we must, somehow, create room for the next batch. Under such circumstances the punitive process loses any connection with justice and becomes a mere matter of floor space. There are now roughly 250,000 men and women behind bars throughout the country—many of them in subhumanly over-crowded conditions that render supervision impossible and ignite one bloody mutiny after another. Few of the prisoners know how long they will be confined—it may be decades for an act of larceny, or months for willful murder. In various degrees, it depends on whether they are serving indetermi-nate stretches, on the outcome of random appeals, on the mood of the parole board, on the whim of the governor, or on the availability of cells in a particular year. It seems to depend on virtually anything or everything—except the sen-tence they have received. If surety is the chief deterrent factor, this system has virtually discarded it.

David Jacob Seiterle, for instance, received *three* death sentences and one life sentence, but was nevertheless paroled when it suited the board's convenience. In August 1960 Seiterle had been convicted of double murder—he and two companions having stabbed and strangled a California businessman and his wife after robbing them of two hundred dollars. Seiterle was sentenced to the gas chamber, but the state Supreme Court overturned the sentence because the judge had allegedly given faulty instructions to the jury. Two new penalty trials followed, with the same outcome: The sentences were overturned on technicalities—a fact that pro-vides a fairly good idea of the legal competence of California judges. Seiterle was awaiting his fourth trial in 1972 when California's capital-punishment law was declared uncon-stitutional, changing his sentence automatically to life im-prisonment.

"Life" in his case lasted until October 1975, when the parole board quietly released him from Folsom Prison. They gave him a new name as well—Michael Malone—a move that only helped to complicate matters when, exactly a year later, Seiterle/Malone was arrested for rape and attempted abduction. Having picked up a girl hitchhiking on Hollywood's Sunset Strip one night, he had held her at gunpoint, burned her arms with lit cigarettes, and forced her to have sex. When he tried the same stunt some nights later, however, his victim jumped out of the car and escaped when he pulled his gun. She had no trouble describing him, a wallowing blimp of a man, covered with vivid tattoos. Seiterle went back to prison on a sixteen-years-to-life term—a sentence that once again leaves his fate more or less in the laps of the parole gods.

California's parole board, rechristened the Community Release Board, is currently headed by Howard Way, a conservative Republican who favors capital punishment and takes pains to assure interviewers that he is not a "bleeding-heart liberal." At the same time, however, Mr. Way sees nothing terribly wrong with parole dictated by accommodation costs. "If the public doesn't want us to let anybody out, they'll have to tell us how much money it'll take to build prisons for 100,000 people or so," he informed a reporter. "It would be staggering."

It would be considerably less staggering if some of the squandered LEAA funds had been used for prison construction. At least there would then have been no economic reason to unleash the likes of Seiterle on the world.

The embodiment of our uncertainty is a sentencing system unique in the annals of penology. To the layman it sounds like a secret code devised by a gaga mathematician, but even the experts can only guess at how long a given term will actually work out to be. For example, a man who murdered his three children and attempted to kill his wife was handed three sentences of five years to life and one sentence of one to fourteen years, to run consecutively. Later these sentences were "aggregated" into a single ten-years-to-life term. This made him eligible for parole consideration after three years and four months. But it was his misfortune to have been sentenced by a persistently wrathful judge, who annually wrote the parole board asking that he not be released. It happened The parole board, although not obliged to accept the judge's advice, chose to do so. Consequently, the prisoner served time for as long as the judge kept writing letters—fifteen years. Only when the judge died was he freed. Thus, the prisoner's penalty hinged on the life span of the man who had sentenced him—by Western ethics a monstrosity paralleled only by the ancient practice of Turkish sultans who condemned their prisoners to be incarcerated "for as long as I draw breath."

The irony is that the indeterminate sentence was devised as a measure of judicial enlightenment. Introduced some sixty years ago, it stipulated terms ranging from the minimum to the maximum number of years prescribed by law for a given felony. According to the state, offenders came up for parole after serving varying fractions of their minimum time. This could be further adjusted downward to reflect time off for good behavior and periods spent in pretrial confinement. No one, therefore, was sentenced to *any* specific term. For an assault conviction carrying six months to life an offender could serve sixty days or literally his lifetime.

The humane motivation of the scheme was to offer criminals recurring chances for rehabilitation. It held out the possibility of freedom should they succeed in convincing a parole board of their "release readiness." In order to do this, they had to "act rehabilitated"—a process criminologist Hans Mattick described as "turning prisons into drama schools." It also turned them into psychological torture chambers, assembly lines for paranoiacs.

Every ex-convict I questioned voiced hatred for indeterminate sentencing. "Almost anything was easier to take than the uncertainty," said a former inmate of Reidsville, Georgia. "This never knowing *when.* No use striking days off a calendar because you don't know how many days you got. You see other guys go free, and they're serving the same stretch you got. But they go out and come back and get sprung maybe two, three times while you're still inside. They're no more ready than you are, but they get around the parole board again and again—while a sad-assed bastard like me can't do it even once. Drives you nuts. I'm telling you: I'd rather do six years flat time than five years dangling, like I had to."

It is the capriciousness of the system—its constantly changing and unpredictable character—that undermines prisoners' recuperative powers far more profoundly than brutality and degradation. They are forced to play a game in which the rules are altered and the terms shifted by hostile forces completely beyond their control. And the fact that this game can go on indefinitely seems to breed a degree of despair or frustration that when combined with infantile helplessness, far exceeds even the harshest certainty. And this is done for almost purely idealistic reasons.

Rehabilitation, the foundation stone of indeterminate sentencing, was an Anglo-Saxon ideal that arose about the time we began to incarcerate people as part of the criminal-justice process.* It never influenced the French or other Latin nations. The Code Napoléon, a body of civil law very advanced for its period, saw imprisonment as simply retribution for flouting the rules of society. The offender had to endure it, but was not expected to undergo changes in his or her psyche as a result. Even though the punishments have been lightened, this concept still forms the practical basis of the French penal system. In America, in contrast, the principle of criminal rehabilitation has become interwoven with a vision of human perfectibility to be achieved by means of social engineering—the same quasi-religious impulse that has inspired half a thousand flourishing self-improvement cults. The idea took root, fired the imagination of reformers, and slowly

---

* Prison sentences are a relatively new historical innovation, only about as old as the United States. Until then lawbreakers were dealt with more swiftly by means of the whip, the stocks, the branding iron, or the gallows—chiefly the last. It was Pennsylvania Quaker Dr. Benjamin Rush who, in 1790, devised the world's first "Penitentiary House," where criminals were held in solitary confinement "to reflect upon their sins and become penitent."

hardened into a judicial doctrine demanding that every penalty be framed from a rehabilitative viewpoint.

As Norman A. Carlson, Director of the Federal Bureau of Prisons, wrote:

> Correctional administrators would be glad to rehabilitate all offenders—if they only knew how. Society's illusion that they can is a result of the language that has surrounded corrections in recent years. . . . Gradually a medical model was created that implied offenders were sick, that we could diagnose their ailments as we do with people who are physically or mentally ill, and then prescribe a "treatment" program which would bring about a cure.

But if crime is a sickness—an inflammation of the social fiber, so to speak—it follows that even the most heinous acts are merely aggravations of similar conditions, to be eliminated by still bigger doses of the same medicine. Thus, the rehabilitative concept, which was first applied only to minor offenders, climbed up the entire penal ladder until—in a relentless progression toward *reductio ad absurdum*—it covers pickpockets and mass murderers alike. This is the rationale underlying statements like that delivered by parole-board chairman Howard Way: "I don't want to sound liberal, but beyond a certain time for a specific crime, incarceration doesn't do any good."

What possible "good" can the imprisonment of, say, an Edmund Kemper or a Charles Manson achieve, other than that of keeping them out of circulation? Yet the law insists that they and their ilk remain within the framework of a program of rehabilitation—that is, within the grasp of some future parole board, whatever title it may adopt.

Psychoanalyst and social critic Ernest van den Haag has given short shrift to the theory that criminals are necessarily sick, pointing out that "Those who feel that all offenders suffer from some disorder to be corrected by treatment confuse their moral disapproval with a clinical diagnosis." Which, of course, is merely the modern expression of the old inability of religious moralists to distinguish between crime and sin.

The real absurdity of the current system lies in the compulsory nature of the treatment, which negates whatever good may possibly have come out of it. Rehabilitation programs consist of assorted mixtures of vocational and academic training, plus mental therapy. Prisoners who refuse to participate virtually wreck their parole chances and suffer worse living conditions as well. The psychotherapy offered is little more than a ritual—sometimes consisting of only one half-hour session a week of group counseling, in which progress is measured by the vehemence with which cons beat their breasts and shout "mea culpa." This may prove entertaining but achieves little else. Although some of the participants are undoubtedly psychotic and in need of therapy, every psychologist knows that such treatment is utterly futile unless sought voluntarily by the patient and backed by a genuine desire to be cured—not merely to gather points toward release.

Behind these futile charades, however, lurks a Frankensteinian monster that the more perceptive prisoners can sense quite clearly. For once the principle of compulsory therapy for the "sickness of crime" has been established, it follows that the *type* of treatment applied can be changed at will. It might eventually include forms of "behavior modification" whose very wording is enough to send icy trickles down one's spine. Several noted criminologists are even now recommending that remote physiological-monitoring devices be implanted in the parolee's brain:

> The use . . . of telemetric systems as a method . . . of stimulating his brain electrically from a distance, seems . . . entirely feasible and possible as a method of control. . . . It will be possible to maintain twenty-four-hour-a-day surveillance over the subject and to intervene electronically or physically to influence and control selected behavior. . . .

Here we enter the realm of vintage science fiction, in which Flash Gordon's interplanetary nemesis, Ming the Merciless, turns opponents into robots by fitting them with will-destroying helmets—except, of course, that *our* helmets would bear therapeutic stencils.

Meanwhile, our supposedly curative formulas have been so thoroughly discredited that the word "failure" is an understatement. Connecticut's Commissioner of Corrections, John R. Manson, who heads one of the most advanced and innovative prison systems in America, told the New York *Times*: "With few exceptions the rehabilitative approach to imprisonment, the whole framework of indeterminate sentencing, education and job training in prison and, finally, of parole have provided a structure in which prisoners outwit the people who imprison them and gain an easier time in prison and earlier release than society expects." Similarly, Columbia sociologist Robert Martinson concluded, after studying several hundred programs over a period of years, "The prison which makes every effort at rehabilitation succeeds no better than the prison which leaves its inmates to rot."

Proof of these findings leaps at you from the figures. Recidivism (repeat crime by released offenders) runs at around 70 percent for all former inmates. Of those put on probation instead of behind bars, an estimated 55 percent either have their probation revoked for new crimes or flee the control of their probation officers. "Control," in any case, is a grandiose term for the kind of supervision most of them receive. Probation officers (another species in desperately short supply) now carry a caseload of 50 to 150 offenders each—a load that makes it difficult for them to do more than shuffle through the files of their charges, assuming these files have not been lost or mislaid. Some of the probation programs about which the courts intone consist of nothing more than a telephone conversation once a week. I overheard one such conversation between a lady probationist and her charge, a twice-convicted holdup man. The lady asked, "Well, how're things going with you, Steve?" She listened to Steve's reply, beamed into the receiver, said, "Well, that's okay then," and hung up. End of session. Later that day a Chicago police detective gave me another view: "We just keep arresting the same people over and over, sometimes before we even know they're out. It's like an annual class reunion—same faces, longer histories."

Indeterminate sentencing is currently being modified through legislation, which doesn't mean it's being replaced by finite and equitable prison terms. After all, that would put parole boards out of business. Instead, the new system merely narrows the range of penalties that can be imposed by judges, abolishing such extreme metaphysics as five-years-to-life stretches. And the innovation stops short exactly where an overhaul is most needed—at the gravest crimes, including first-degree murder.

It is in the handling of convicted killers that the punitive and rehabilitative viewpoints collide head on; in the confrontation, they cancel each other out. Thus, we hand down bizarre sentences spanning several lifetimes and simultaneously temper them with contingencies that may reduce them to a couple of years. They can neither rehabilitate nor deter; they resemble legal eccentricities rather than acts of justice.

Our treatment of murderers reflects a terrible uncertainty as to the value of human lives—the killers' as well as the victims'. We cannot decide how many years of the slayer's life the victim is worth, and prefer to leave the answer to a convoluted game of chance rather than settle it in court. This is moral cowardice at its ultimate and most destructive, and stems from the nation's increasing doubts about its entire value system. The liberal columnist and sometime philosopher Max Lerner pointed out how the failure of liberals to formulate a practical anticrime program could be traced to their conviction that the roots of crime are embedded in an unjust society:

> If their view is true, two things must follow. One is that most crimes, being social in origin, become acts of political conflict. The second is that our compassion must go out not to the victim but to the criminal, whom we must shield with all our legal and constitutional energies. How any society that accepts these ideas can hope to survive is beyond me. How this idiocy came to be enshrined as accepted doctrine is one for future historians to puzzle out as they sit by the ruins. . . .

On the right of the spectrum, conservatives are just as irrational in their assessment of the value of life. Most of them would be willing to liquidate any number of socially underprivileged felons. *Their* compassion instead goes out to alcoholized motorists who slaughter people in batches, to hunters whose spastic trigger-happiness claims scores of human game each season, to slumlords who let entire families fry in their firetraps after bribing city inspectors to ignore the peril. Whenever one of *those* killers faces jail (as they do in Scandinavia, Switzerland, and other uncivilized regions), conservative stalwarts rise en masse to thunder "Nay!"

In truth, despite incessant prattle about the "sanctity of life," both sides readily accept wholesale sacrifices for the sake of political principles. This moral dementia has produced an astonishing degree of callousness toward the victims involved. One judge, famous for his kindness toward offenders, referred to a holdup slaying as an "obscure murder," implying that the prey was of minor consequence. The good judge undoubtedly would have been horrified to hear a surgeon label a patient "an obscure tumor case"—particularly if he happened to be that patient.

Middle-class guilt obsessions have so clouded the basic issue of crime and punishment that it requires a process of judicial neutralization to get the system on an even keel. Justice must be blindfolded, exactly as she is portrayed symbolically. Sentences must fit the *deed*—not the slayer's sobriety, color, background, lingual handicap, or childhood deprivation.

The law will have to decide what value to set on human life and then abide by the decision. This means a new range of penalties for the various categories of homicide. The terms imposed must be "flat time," precluding parole, work-release, furlough, or any other form of remission. Convicted murderers could still enter rehabilitation programs, but on a truly voluntary basis and with the knowledge that participation would in no way affect their release date. If a sentence decrees *x* number of years, that figure must remain unaltered whether a prisoner joins every available program or none.

Then—and only then—we could hope that prison terms would act as deterrents to murder. And only then could this be accomplished by relatively humane sentences.

According to the experience of other nations, the actual lengths of sentences seem to be of secondary importance. What counts is their unequivocal certainty—the assurance that murder means imprisonment for a definite period and that no judge in the country can hand out probation instead. Plea-bargaining would have to be eliminated in homicide cases, and with it the possibility of trading down from a murder to a manslaughter indictment.

The new range of sentences should be divided into two broad categories, each serving a distinct purpose: corrective and incapacitating. The former would constitute a punitive jolt, a forceful expression of society's disapproval. Incapacitation, in contrast, would aim at isolating certain individuals from society during their violence-prone youth, perhaps through middle age, and possibly for life. Assignment to one or the other bracket should depend on the nature of the killing as well as the offender's past record—not on nebulous psychiatric reports or the assessments of social workers.

Past records *must* influence sentencing, and for this they have to be available. It is quite typical of New York's hankering for self-immolation that it denies judges legal access to the juvenile criminal records of an accused—as if armed robberies committed in his teens had no bearing on a holdup killing in his twenties.

For the "mildest" forms of homicide—lovers' quarrels, barroom brawls, domestic fights ending in death—sentences could run a modest six or seven years, providing the offender has no previous record of violence. And this should be considered the rock-bottom price for extinguishing a human life, except accidentally or in demonstrable self-defense. The maximum of three years' imprisonment suggested by American Civil Liberties Union director Aryeh Neier is a tic rather than a jolt. It might help our sense of proportion to recall that less than two decades ago we were executing people for such crimes of passion.

The upward range of penalties needn't differ greatly from those in force now—except that they would actually have to be served. A fifteen-year stretch for a robbery-murder could be both incapacitating and deterring, *if* the certainty existed that the killer would do every day of it.

At the risk of redundancy, I will add that this scale should apply for single murders only. It might appear obvious that anyone who deliberately kills two, three, or more people ought to be permanently isolated, either in prison or in an asylum, and does in every nation except America. Only in America could a double slayer like Seiterle emerge on parole at the age of thirty-four. Only in America would an attempt be made—and almost succeed—to spring a seven-victim killer like Freeman from a mental hospital. Only in America would authorities stage the clownish solemnities of holding annual parole hearings for Richard Speck, who murdered eight nurses and received 1,200 years' imprisonment.

The most depressing aspect of these legalistic grasshopper jumps is that they don't arise from an excess of human kindness. They are manifestations of a jungle growth of haphazard, often irrational and conflicting legislation distilled into ordinances by lawyers for the exclusive benefit of lawyers. Their prime purpose is to keep the ball rolling indefinitely, to eliminate any sense of finality from court decisions, to give employment to more and still more lawyers through endless rounds of writs and appeals that terminate only with the death of the offender, and sometimes not even then.

If the fact that the liberation of driven creatures like Freeman might result in further massacres does not have any impact on the legal establishment, then it is up to us, his prospective victims, to revise the law so as to keep him and his kind at a safe distance. If we are incapable of accomplishing this—incapable of effectively isolating a handful of homicidal maniacs—then perhaps the moment has come to ring down the curtain, turn out the lights, and get the hell off the stage.

Despite the legal profession's aversion to finality, we will have to establish a point of no return, an ultimate cutoff line. A terminal penalty must exist in one form or another, not only for the protection of jail personnel but also as a moral imperative: society's conclusive gesture of revulsion. It could be reserved for very few—for child-murderers like Goode, for torture killers like de Kaplany, for convicts who kill a guard while already serving a life sentence. So long as this ultimate punishment is available, it doesn't matter greatly whether it consists of solitary confinement for life or execution.

Capital punishment per se is fairly irrelevant to an effective penal code. Its opponents are losing the battle against its return not because the public is roaring for blood but because the anti-death forces are fighting under false slogans. They keep harping on life imprisonment as an alternative, knowing full well that we have no such alternative at present. By now most people are aware that a life sentence can mean seven years if the parole gods so deign, or less if the organizers of work-release programs feel in the mood. The clamor for executions comes from a majority that feels hoodwinked by the authorities as well as threatened by the killers. Both feelings are only too valid. If the foes of the death penalty supported legislation to eliminate parole, pardons, and other types of release for lifers, they might well win the struggle.

Instead, they offer pious cant laced with unconscious mockery. Former U.S. Attorney General Ramsey Clark argued that capital punishment spawns even more violence "because it demeans life." He also suggested that the maximum prison term for any crime should be five years. For Herbert Mullin, this would work out at twenty weeks' confinement per victim—about as long as you'd get for stealing a car. But, according to Mr. Clark's logic, *that* would not demean life. After the execution of Gary Gilmore, Washington columnist Carl T. Rowan—another opponent of capital punishment asked, quite pertinently: "But who among us honestly feels one whit more secure because Gilmore is dead, rather than locked up?" He did not follow through by asking "Locked up for how long?"

The death penalty as such has little to recommend it

beyond the simple economy of not having to feed, house, and guard the criminal. Its deterrent power is unproven. Undoubtedly, some people would be deterred by it, just as some would be deterred by the threat of a flogging. The moot point is, how many?

At least one is on record: Allen Leroy Anderson, who ran amok through seven states but carefully avoided Texas because he believed—erroneously—that Texas was the only state with the death penalty. Capital-punishment advocates like to quote him as an argument in favor, but he is not a very convincing one. Anderson, a known homosexual, had spent eleven of his thirty-four years in prison for burglary, auto theft, and forgery—all nonviolent felonies. In January 1976 he was paroled to a halfway house in Seattle, where he had a drama-charged romance with another inmate. After six months, his lover rejected him, and this seems to have propelled Anderson into his weirdly patterned trail of violence.

On June 1 he stole the car and credit cards of the halfway-house director and drove off. Over the next five months he drove thousands of miles, through twenty or more states, piling up corpses as he went. Police across the nation believe he was responsible for at least eight murders, though he admitted to only two. Seven of the victims were shot, execution-style, in the back of the head, "because dead people aren't very good witnesses." Inexplicably, he let other witnesses live. In Richland, Iowa, a returning family surprised Anderson as he was burgling their home. He drew a gun and forced the father, mother, and child to sit on the bathroom floor. While the husband pleaded for their lives, Anderson stood over them, cocking the hammer of his weapon, letting it down slowly, cocking it again—over and over. Finally he left without having harmed anyone.

On October 28, Anderson was driving a van and trailer stolen from a murdered man in Chowchilla, California, when Los Angeles police pounced on him. The joyride was over; now the legal minuet began. According to his attorney, public defender Lester Gendron, the first question Anderson asked was whether California had the death penalty. Since it didn't at that time, Anderson agreed to plead guilty to the bludgeon killing in Chowchilla. "The death penalty," said Gendron, "was the only thing he worried about."

But there was another murder charge against him in Northfield, Minnesota. Anderson promptly waived extradition and pleaded guilty there as well. He was a native of Minnesota, had served time there, and preferred the prisons of his home state to the California variety. The authorities were glad to trade. In California Anderson would have been eligible for parole after seven years; in Minnesota he will have to wait seventeen. Gendron told reporters that his client was contemplating writing a book about his experiences. With both homosexuality and mass murder as basic ingredients, it would have best-seller potential.

Anderson's fear of execution, however, offers no indication of the effectiveness of the death sentence as a deterrent. People in eighteenth-century England were also afraid of the gallows, but that did not stop them from doing what was liable to get them hanged. In 1785 England boasted more than two hundred capital offenses, including handkerchief stealing, rabbit poaching, and willful destruction of machinery. As historian J. Christopher Herold observed: "It is difficult to see how a pauper could avoid hanging, except for the virtual absence of a police system." Weekly executions were held at London's Marble Arch, attended by large, boisterous crowds. While the townspeople watched, thieves picked their pockets—the very crime for which others were being noosed.

Mass hanging did not diminish thefts any more than boiling in oil had prevented coining two centuries earlier. What curbed the country's staggering crime rate was the introduction of a "preventive police"—the first of its kind in the Western world. Founded by Robert Peel in 1829, the "Peelers" eventually developed into today's Scotland Yard. Their crime-reducing methods still represent the only feasible means of achieving results: fewer but rigorously enforced laws, high certainty of apprehension, and a police force whose primary task is protection.

America doggedly pursues the opposite course. Laws proliferate, like laboratory rats, at a dazzling rate but get minimal enforcement. Simultaneously, the police take pains to assure citizens that they are *not* concerned with their protection, discovering new reasons for their unconcern every day. I heard one Chicago cop tell the victim of a street assault after his assailant was captured: "We're not arresting this guy—*you* are. We're only transporting him for you."

The same self-defeating haphazardness has governed capital punishment, nullifying whatever deterrent effect it might have had. Between 1930 and 1967 a total of 3,859 persons were executed in the United States. They represented a small handful of those convicted of capital offenses—and by no means the worst handful. They died for crimes ranging from homicide, rape, and kidnapping to aggravated assault and espionage. Thousands of others, found guilty of the same crimes, spent but a few years in prison before being paroled.

Although plenty of wealthy people perpetrated capital offenses, those executed were nearly all either poor or black—often both. In practice, America was the only democratic society in the world in which having money was virtually certain to save your neck. Even England occasionally hanged peers of the realm—their sole privilege in that respect being the right to trial by their peers (the House of Lords).

But above all, those put to death were unlucky—the losers in a protracted roulette game with human lives as chips. The rules of the game were such that even mediocre lawyers could postpone doomsday at least a few times. The action was in the form of appeals—first in the state courts, then through the federal courts, eventually to the U.S. Supreme Court. Defeat in that ultimate court still wasn't final, providing attorneys could discover or invent new grounds for more appeals. Then the game began all over again, up the same ladder of courts, continuing for five, eight, ten, a dozen years, exhausting one round of appeals after another. At some point the appeals ran out, the wheel stopped, a loser was declared. That loser, the one with the unlucky number, was then taken out and ceremoniously exterminated.

Thus, Caryl Chessman, who killed nobody, had to die, while underworld torpedos with hit lists as long as your arm retired to villas in Florida.* The sheer blatant frivolity of this Las Vegas–style death game had begun to turn the public's stomach long before the Supreme Court decided to declare it "cruel and unusual punishment."

The system of nominating executees was certainly unusual, but the cruelty depended on the state. Of the forty-two states practicing capital punishment, twenty-four killed by electrocution, nine by lethal gas, eight by hanging, and one (Utah) offered a choice between the rope and the firing squad. As methods of execution go, nothing in modern times, not even the Spanish garrote, could approach the gas chamber for diabolical cruelty. Every other device makes it impossible for the victim to postpone death—even for a brief moment. In the lethal chamber, he can do so as long as he holds his breath, knowing that once he exhales he must inhale again. His life lasts as long as his lung power, which can be an eternity. He has to aid in his own destruction, which is a crime against human decency—the brainchild of sadistic adolescents playing with chemistry sets.

Here is how reporter Dan Frishman saw Caryl Chessman go: "He dies hard, gasping, drooling, rolling his head—surviving the engulfing gas for several minutes, apparently, despite assurance of Warden Fred R. Dickson that 'they're unconscious about thirty seconds after the pellets are dropped.'"

There were no executions for nearly a decade after 1967. Capital punishment lay dormant partly because of public distaste, partly because of a Supreme Court ruling that *sounded* like a constitutional ban—you couldn't be sure.

---

* Chessman committed several rape-robberies in a Los Angeles lovers' lane in late 1947. He was sentenced under California's "Little Lindbergh" law, which stipulated death for kidnapping with bodily harm, despite the fact that he hadn't actually kidnapped anyone. Chessman lodged thirty-nine appeals, had his execution date deferred eight times, and wrote three books while on death row. He became the center of an international controversy that caused demonstrations the world over. He was gassed in San Quentin on May 2, 1960, eleven years and two months after his arrest.

But the rate of violent crime went on soaring, and in 1976 the moratorium ended. The Supreme Court uttered another pronouncement as magnificently obtuse as the first: "We hold that the death penalty is not a form of punishment that may never be imposed. . . ." Immediately, thirty-five states began revamping their criminal codes, trying to accommodate the Delphic vagueness of the nation's highest court. All the decision settled, in fact, was that the roulette wheel could spin again.

For the 578 men and ten women in the country's "condemned" cells, it simply meant a return to square one— back to watching the little ball bounce. America's justice system, like the defunct Bourbon kings of Europe, had learned nothing and forgotten nothing.

When a Utah firing squad felled double murderer Gary Gilmore, the six rifles cut off a flurry of legal maneuvering that very nearly had canceled the volley. It was the old cliff-hanger; right up to the last moment, nobody knew whether or when Gilmore would die. What the performance lost in surety it gained in ballyhoo. Gilmore kept demanding death and cursing the "bleeding hearts" who insisted on trying to save him. His attorney enthusiastically supported his death wish and announced that he was going to write a book about the case. Meanwhile, he sold an interview with Gilmore to a London newspaper for $250 spot cash. "If people say this is unethical, let them define ethics," he declared. "If they say this is immoral, let them define morals. I don't care what the profession says."

Any deterrent impact of this *danse macabre* got lost in the P. T. Barnum atmosphere that surrounded Gilmore's final squalor. The fact that he was executed had no relevance to our crime problems. But the tawdry circus air of the proce-dure—and the fumbling uncertainty of those who staged— it had.

There was never any possibility of a death sentence for George Adorno. George was a teenager whose crime career began at the age of four and ended—temporarily, anyway—at eighteen. Yet Adorno is not merely relevant to our homicide scourge; he almost symbolizes it. In February 1977, Adorno shot and killed taxi driver Steven Robinson during a robbery in New York's Harlem, which netted him twenty dollars. Adorno was a dark-skinned Puerto Rican who couldn't pass a first-grade reading test. Robinson was a black law student who drove a cab to pay for his education and kept a copy of Antoine de Saint-Exupery's classic *Wind, Sand and Stars* in his glove compartment. The illiterate with the gun snuffed out the scholar with the book on an impulse. Someone in his gang had said, "Let's go grab a couple of bucks from a cabbie."

The deed carried less significance than what preceded it. For, throughout George Adorno's life, the New York City authorities seemed determined to teach him that *nothing* he did—not even murder—mattered very much. At four, he set fire to his sister. At fifteen he was charged with triple murder. He confessed to one of the killings before a district attorney and in the presence of his sister, who had been called in because his mother spoke not a word of English. But a juvenile court judge threw out the confession, because his mother had not been present when he made it. Instead, the learned judge gave him three years in prison on downgraded robbery charges. In accordance with New York's juvenile laws the three murder charges, along with Adorno's sixteen arrests for theft, were ordered sealed.

Adorno served exactly half of his sentence. Nineteen days after his release he shot Steven Robinson.

He stood before Justice Burton Roberts for sentencing wearing a green T-shirt and red sneakers, his eyes fastened on the ceiling with an expression of gentle boredom while the judge made a speech. "Nothing ever happened to Adorno," the judge said. "He plays the courts like a concert player plays the piano. Is there ever a time when a red light goes on and you say 'We have to control this person'? So, at age sixteen, he finally gets a three-year sentence and he is out in eighteen months."

Justice Roberts sentenced Adorno to fifteen years to life, the maximum permitted by the accused's guilty plea, then added: "But at the end of fifteen years, the parole board does not have to release him. The court states that the parole board should seriously reflect whether he should be allowed out at the end of fifteen years."

One of the detectives present in court voiced skepticism bred by experience. "The citizens of New York know in their hearts that George will be paroled in eight and a half years," he commented. "And I promise you his days of killing are not over."

Adorno had grown up in the city without going to school. He had stolen, robbed, assaulted and slain without punishment. He was able to do this because nobody in New York cared enough either to educate or to restrain him. The trouble and expense involved outweighed whatever concern might have been generated by George *or* his victims.

But in this process of weighing human lives against effort and expenditure lies our choice between a bearable rate of violence and one that will eventually destroy the fabric of our existence. The scales won't descend in our favor until we decide that we are indeed our brothers' keeper.

Selected Bibliography

This book is based on personal interviews and extensive correspondence, as well as hundreds of newspapers, periodicals, brochures, reports, pamphlets, circulars, and press releases. Listed below are only the basic reference sources.

Adler, Freda. *Sisters in Crime.* New York: McGraw-Hill, 1975.

Allen, Frederick Lewis. *Only Yesterday.* New York: Harper & Bros., 1931.

Alvarez, N. *The James Boys in Missouri.* Clyde, Ohio: Ames Publishing Co., 1907.

Asbury, Herbert. *The Gangs of New York.* New York: Alfred A. Knopf, 1927.

————. *The Barbary Coast.* New York: Alfred A. Knopf, 1933.

Bach, George R., and H. Goldberg. *Creative Aggression.* New York: Doubleday & Co., 1974.

Bedau, Hugo O., ed. *The Death Penalty in America.* New York: Doubleday & Co., Anchor Books, 1964.

Belli, Melvin. *The Law Revolution.* Los Angeles: Sherbourne Press, 1968.

Bolitho, William. *Murder for Profit.* New York: Harper & Bros., 1926.

Bonney, Edward. *Banditti of the Prairies.* Chicago: Homewood Publishing Co., 1890.

Borodin, Michael. *Die Memoiren des General Borodin.* Berlin: Internationale Bibliothek, 1930.

Brearley, H. C. *Homicide in the United States.* Montclair, N.J.: Patterson Smith, 1969.

Brussel, James A. *Casebook of a Crime Psychiatrist.* New York: Bernard Geis Associates, 1968.

Bryant, Will. *Great American Guns and Frontier Fighters.* New York: Grosset & Dunlap, 1961.

Bugliosi, Vincent, and Curt Gentry. *Helter Skelter.* New York: W. W. Norton & Co., 1974.

Bush, Francis X. *Enemies of the State.* New York: Bobbs-Merrill, 1954.

Capote, Truman. *In Cold Blood.* New York: Random House, 1965.

Chaplin, J. P. *Rumor, Fear and the Madness of Crowds.* New York: Ballantine Books, 1959.

Clark, Ramsey. *Crime in America.* New York: Simon and Schuster, 1970.

Cockburn, Claude. *In Time of Trouble.* London: Rupert Hart-Davis, 1956.

Daley, Robert. *Target Blue.* New York: Dell Publishing Co., 1971.

Dickson, Grierson. *Murder by Numbers.* London: Robert Hall, 1958.

Eshelman, Byron. *Death Row Chaplain.* Englewood Cliffs, N.J.: Prentice-Hall, 1962.

Frank, Gerold. *The Boston Strangler.* New York: New American Library, 1967.

Fromm, Erich. *The Anatomy of Human Destructiveness.* New York: Holt, Rinehart and Winston, 1973.

Gelb, Barbara. *On the Track of Murder.* New York: William Morrow & Co., 1975.

Godwin, John. *Killers in Paradise.* London: Herbert Jenkins, 1962.
————. *Alcatraz.* New York: Doubleday & Co., 1963.
————. *Unsolved, The World of the Unknown.* New York: Doubleday & Co., 1976.

Graham, H. D., and T. R. Gurr. *Violence in America.* New York: Bantam Books, 1969.

Gurwell, J. K. *Mass Murder in Houston.* Houston: Cordovan Press, 1974.

Hardin, John Wesley. *The Life of John Wesley Hardin.* Norman, Okla.: University of Oklahoma Press, 1961.

Hoover, J. Edgar. *Persons in Hiding.* Boston: Little, Brown & Co., 1938.

Jackson, Sir Richard. *Occupied with Crime.* New York: Doubleday & Co., 1967.

Jesse, F. Tennyson. *Murder and Its Motives.* London: Pan Books, 1958.

Kling, Samuel G. *Sexual Behavior and the Law.* New York: Bernard Geis Associates, 1965.

Kobler, John. *Capone.* New York: G. P. Putnam's Sons, 1971.

Lake, Stuart N. *Wyatt Earp.* Boston: Houghton Mifflin Co., 1931.

Loomis, Stanley. *Paris in the Terror.* New York: J. B. Lippincott Co., 1964.

Louderback, Lew. *The Bad Ones.* New York: Fawcett Publications, 1968.

Lunde, Donald T. *Murder and Madness.* Stanford: The Portable Stanford, 1975.

Maas, Peter. *The Valachi Papers.* New York: G. P. Putnam's Sons, 1968.

Menninger, Karl. *The Crime of Punishment.* New York: Viking Press, 1966.

Nash, Jay R. *Bloodletters and Badmen.* New York: Warner Paperback Library, 1975.

Neier, Aryeh. *Crime and Punishment: A Radical Solution.* New York: Stein & Day Publishers, 1975.

Nelson, Bruce. *Land of the Dacotahs.* Lincoln, Neb.: University of Nebraska Press, 1967.

Neustatter, Lindesay W. *The Mind of the Murderer*. London: Christopher Johnson, 1957.

Olsen, Jack. *The Man with the Candy*. New York: Simon & Schuster, 1974.

Packer, Herbert L. *The Limits of Criminal Sanction*. Stanford, Calif.: Stanford University Press, 1968.

Sherrill, Robert. *The Saturday Night Special*. New York: Charterhouse, 1973.

Sorel, Georges. *Réflexions sur la violence*. Paris: Pages Libres, 1908.

Toland, John. *The Dillinger Days*. New York: Random House, 1963.

Tuchman, Barbara. *The Proud Tower*. New York: Macmillan Co., 1966.

van den Haag, Ernest. *Punishing Criminals*. New York: Basic Books, 1975.

West, Don. *Sacrifice Unto Me*. New York: Pyramid Books, 1974.

Whitehead, Don. *The FBI Story*. New York: Random House, 1956.

Wilson, Colin. *Order of Assassins*. London: Rupert Hart-Davis, 1972.

Wilson, James Q. *Thinking About Crime*. New York: Basic Books, 1973.

Wolfgang, Marvin. *Patterns of Criminal Homicide*. Philadelphia: University of Pennsylvania Press, 1958.

————, ed. *Studies in Homicide*. New York: Harper & Row, 1967.

Notes

Abbreviations

FBIU	FBI *Uniform Crime Report*
IWA	Interview with author
LAT	*Los Angeles Times*
NK	*Newsweek*
NYD	*New York Daily News*
NYP	*New York Post*
NYT	*New York Times*
SFC	*San Francisco Chronicle*
SFE	*San Francisco Examiner*
TI	*Time*
UNW	*U.S. News & World Report*
WP	*Washington Post*
WS	*Washington Star*

Prologue on a Crisis

Page

1: I got a . . . WS, November 4, 1977.

4: "Considering how much . . ." TI, June 30, 1975.

5: From 1972 to 1974 . . . FBIU, 1974.

6: With only 31 percent . . . D. T. Lunde, *Murder and Madness* (Stanford, 1975).

6: "I'd be surprised . . ." IWA.

8: Ellsworth Smith, . . . *Readers Digest*, December 1976.

11: "Maybe it's something . . ." IWA.

13: As a cheaper . . .WS, January 14, 1976.

1   Murder as a Family Affair

17: Epigraph: Ramsey Clark, *Crime in America* (New York, 1970).

17: "I'd rather arrest . . ." IWA.

18: However, they still . . . FBIU, 1974.

19: The case of . . . *Newsday*, February 1975.

20: Dr. Bach's subjects . . . George R. Bach, *Creative Aggression* (New York, 1974).

22: "The first time . . ." IWA.

22: I was married . . . IWA.

24: "useful only . . ." IWA.

25: Diane Hallman, . . . American Law Institute Report 1976.

30: The one known victim . . . *True Detective*, January 1976.

33: "You told the cops . . ." *Life*, May 1972.

36: The classic example . . . Truman Capote, *In Cold Blood* (New York, 1965).

39: Eben went through . . . SFC, SFE, February 1975.

2 The Bloody Background

Page
48: In New York this . . . Herbert Asbury, *The Gangs of New York* (New York, 1927).
50: For example, New Orleans Police Chief . . . *Police Gazette*, December 1890.
54: The same blithe . . . Frederick Lewis Allen, *Only Yesterday* (New York, 1931).
56: "spreading a coat . . ." IWA.
57: Foremost among them . . . J. Kobler, *Capone* (New York, 1971).
57: "All my rackets, . . ." Claud Cockburn, *In Time of Trouble* (London, 1951).
60: Despite similar backgrounds . . . John Toland, *The Dillinger Days* (New York, 1963).
63: Footnote: J. Edgar Hoover, *Persons in Hiding* (Boston, 1938).
63: When Alvin Karpis . . . J. Godwin, *Alcatraz* (New York, 1963).

3 Crimes Passionel

65: Footnote: Frederick Lewis Allen, *Only Yesterday* (New York, 1931).
67: "I can't be responsible . . ." *Front Page Detective*, February 1975.
69: "Dear Kenny, . . ." WP, September 3, 1976.
70: "If you looked . . ." IWA.
72: Shelley Sperling . . . NYT, February 20, 1975.
74: Footnote: *Cosmopolitan*, March 1976.
77: "She was always stronger . . ." *True Detective*, February 1976.
81: Footnote: S. Loomis, *Paris Under the Terror* (New York, 1964).
82: The fact was that she had . . . *Police Gazette*, November 1910.

4 They Come Younger Every Year

84: Epigraph: IWA.
86: "We are not allowed . . ." IWA.
88: The four boys, . . . WP, WS, February 1976.
90: Michele was riding . . . NYT, November 30, 1975.
91: Take the case of . . . IWA.
93: Criminologist Gerald Haslip . . . IWA.
96: "Society seems to be flying apart . . ." NK, October 8, 1975.
97: This at a time . . . Subcommittee to Investigate Juvenile Delinquency report, 1974.
97: "In effect, . . ." IWA.
99: In February 1976, . . . SFE, February 22, 1976.
101: "The number of American students . . ." Senate Subcommittee to Investigate Juvenile Delinquency report, 1974.
108: In December 1975, . . . Document on file with author.
109: "Clearing her, . . ." IWA.
110: "Don't buy any of that nonsense . . ." IWA.
111: In October 1975, . . . *East Los Angeles Tribune*, October 16, 1975.

5 Sisterhood of Cain

113: Epigraph: WS, February 27, 1976.
114: "outraged by correlations . . ." WP, February 28, 1976.
114: "Adler is the one person . . ." WS, February 27, 1976.
115: "A frail woman . . ." Freda Adler, *Sisters in Crime* (New York, 1975).

Page
115: between 1960 and 1974 . . . FBIU.
116: During the spring of 1975 . . . *Inside Detective*, August 1975.
118: Frances, a hatched-faced woman . . . *Inside Detective*, October 1976.
118: "If all women were . . ." IWA.
123: "I started to freak out . . ." SFC, November 21, 1975.
124: Even the awesome . . . *Official Detective*, October 1976.
128: In San Francisco, . . . SFC, March 25, 1975.
128: In Baltimore, . . . WP, May 21, 1976.
129: Linda Agurs . . . WS, June 25, 1976.
130: "Those broads . . ." IWA.
130: "Aw, I dunno . . ." IWA.
131: In California, . . . California State Department of Corrections report, 1976.
131: In 1970, Texas motorcycle-gang . . . *Inside Detective*, May 1970.
131: It took the FBI . . . *Inside Detective*, January 1972.
132: Garcia, a very pretty, . . . J. Wood, *The Rape of Inez Garcia* (New York, 1976).
133: "A rapist is not trying . . ." *Ms.*, July 1975.
136: "One thing I found . . ." *Der Spiegel*, May 1974.

6 The Syndicate Wars
137: Entering quickly, . . . B. Turkus, *Murder, Inc.* (New York, 1951).
138: The composition of . . . Peter Maas, *The Valachi Papers* (New York, 1968).
139: The brainchild of . . . J. R. Nash, *Bloodletters and Badmen* (New York, 1973).
140: Their commander was changed . . . B. Turkus, *Murder, Inc.* (New York, 1951).
143: Bugsy died in a hail . . . *Playboy's History of Organized Crime*, 1976.
145: Chicago, long known as . . . TI, June 30, 1975.
146: A short, bulb-nosed Brooklyn man . . . WP, October 18, 1976.
146: Colombo organized a . . . *Playboy's History of Organized Crime*, 1976.
148: "Joe had little formal . . ." IWA.
149: The place of the paralyzed . . . NYT, July 12, 1975.
150: Now in his seventies . . . *Oui*, April 1976.
156: "If only, . . ." IWA.
158: The three liquor-soaked goons, . . . WS, September 4, 1976.

7 The Gay and the Dead
159: Footnote: SFC, December 22, 1977.
161: "Listen, ya better . . ." J. Olsen, *The Man with the Candy* (New York, 1974).
162: In the sticky afternoon . . . TI, February 4, 1974.
164: "Wanna come to a party . . ." J. K. Gurwell, *Mass Murder in Houston* (Houston, 1974).
166: "Hell, he hardly . . ." IWA.
166: In 1973 . . . FBIU.
168: Footnote: W. Bolitho, *Murder for Profit* (London, 1926).
169: It doesn't mean that inverts . . . IWA.
169: It revealed that . . . LAT, November 19, 1976.
171: The accused was a tall . . . *True Detective*, November 1976.
172: Knight inhabited . . . NK, December 22, 1975.
174: The girl was one . . . WP, December 24, 1975.

Page
175: The go-go girl remembered . . . *Village Voice,* January 26, 1976.
176: The killings fell into . . . SFC, January 19, 1976.
176: "It's highly likely . . ." SFC, January 20, 1976.
177: "Knowing that these guys . . ." IWA.
178: "It could be regarded . . ." IWA.
180: "Stand off or . . ." *Front Page Detective,* September 1974.

8   Ghettocide

182: Epigraph: IWA.
185: In round figures, . . . TI, June 30, 1975.
185: Footnote: U.N. survey, 1976.
185: Not many Detroit whites . . . *Detroit News,* December 18, 1973.
187: "You have a release . . ." WS, December 23, 1975.
188: The kind of crimes . . . LAT, February 1, 1975.
190: According to Police . . . LAT, February 1, 1975.
191: Six times in two years . . . WS, February 8, 1976.
193: "It's just like . . ." IWA.
193: "The problem is ours, . . ." NYT, March 7, 1976.
196: Harlem is the distribution . . . NYT, December 8, 1975.
197: In June 1975, . . . *Village Voice,* November 3, 1975.
197: "perhaps the closest . . ." *New Times,* July 1975.
199: Slowly but steadily, . . . T. Walker, *Fort Apache* (New York, 1976).
201: Illegal immigrants, . . . UNW, April 5, 1976.
202: "They come over . . ." IWA.
205: My small sister . . . IWA.

9   No Rhyme and Little Reason

206: Kenneth Bryant, . . . WS, December 22, 1976.
209: "Did it come as a surprise . . ." WS, December 23, 1976.
210: The three teenagers, . . . WS, November 14, 1976.
211: "We want your wallet, . . ." IWA.
212: On the evening of . . . *Front Page Detective,* June 1976.
213: When Richard Turner . . . *Front Page Detective,* December 1976.
218: In September 1976, . . . WP, September 23, 1976.
218: One week later, . . . WP, June 11, 1976.
218: Even so, . . . WS, October 26, 1976.
219: We can only assume . . . WP, June 11, 1976.
220: But this is nothing . . . *Official Detective,* March 1976.
222: Ruzicka was the loser type . . . IWA.
225: "I can't give it to you . . ." IWA.
226: We don't know what . . . WS, February 18, 1976.

10   The Politics of Homicide

228: "Down in the lower depths . . ." Barbara Tuchman, *The Proud Tower* (New York, 1966).
229: In the eighteen years . . . G. Sorel, *Reflexions sur la violence* (Paris, 1908).
230: People like the Tullers, . . . NK, July 21, 1975.
232: "a feeling of total impotence . . ." Letter to author.
235: Footnote: SFC, October 2, 1975.
235: So far the Weather people . . . FBI Bulletin.
239: "They were killed because . . ." *Spring 3100.*

Page
240: "Here are the license plates . . ." Robert Daley, *Target Blue* (New York, 1971).
243: "Stealing," wrote the . . . LAT.
243: We found that banditry . . . G. Borodin, *Die Memoiren des General Borodin* (Berlin, 1930).
244: Having finally reemerged . . . SFC, January 3, 1977.
246: An entire generation . . . TI, January 22, 1975.
246: This was done through . . . NYP, December 1, 1975.
246: "Many of the activities . . ." SFE, May 9, 1976.

11 While of Unsound Mind
249: On Palm Sunday morning, . . . WP, March 25, 1977.
252: Consider the career . . . WS, February 4, 1976.
253: "No way . . ." IWA.
256: John Gilbert Freeman, . . . *Detective World*, February 1976.
258: Frazier was convinced . . . D. T. Lunde, *Murder and Madness* (Stanford, 1975).
260: Herbert William Mullin, . . . D. West, *Sacrifice Unto Me* (New York, 1974).
262: During the seventeen-month period . . . NYT, May 25, 1977.
263: "That place was wall-to-wall . . ." IWA.
265: "That doesn't mean . . ." IWA.
266: "Those jurors aren't stupid . . ." WS, February 4, 1976.
272: Michael Butcher, . . . SFC, March 9, 1976.
273: "We may know that a patient . . ." IWA.
274: The trouble with mentally . . . J. Brussel, *Casebook of a Crime Psychiatrist* (New York, 1968).
277: "That's because it isn't one, . . ." IWA.

12 Have Gun, Will Use
280: Only a portion of these deaths . . . *Good Housekeeping*, March 1974.
281: "that part of the United States . . ." Robert Sherrill, *The Saturday Night Special* (New York, 1973).
282: In 1974 in New York City, . . . National Coalition to Ban Handguns report.
284: At twenty he had been . . . L. Thoresen, *It Gave Everybody Something to Do* (New York, 1976).
287: Slaughter will continue . . . *Psychology Today*, November 1975.
287: When Marvin Helfgott, . . . LAT, August 2, 1976.
288: "We believe that Americans . . ." *Point Blank*.
288: "There are just as many . . ." WS, February 11, 1976.
289: During a summer weekend . . . IWA.
290: A husky brunette . . . IWA.
291: "one of our most outstanding . . ." NYD, December 18, 1975.
292: In September 1976 . . . SFC, September 28, 1976.
294: On top of this, . . . Police Foundation report.

13 Chamber of Horrors
298: The three whites . . . *New Times*, January 1977.
301: He never ceased to . . . William F. Buckley column, 1976.
305: Their rampage began . . . *Startling Detective*, March 1976.
308: "You bastards shot me, . . ." W. Allen, *Starkweather* (New York, 1976).

Page
308: The scene was the . . . NYT, October 20, 1975.
311: "I'll never forget . . ." IWA.
312: "They made life . . ." IWA.
314: "Too many psychiatrists . . ." SFC, May 10, 1973.
315: He killed quickly . . . Trial testimony by Dr. Joel Fort.
317: The parents and friends . . . IWA.
317: Footnote: SFC, July 7, 1977.
318: "If you want openness . . ." IWA.
319: "He was always back . . ." IWA.
320: "I told him he was going . . ." WP, April 3, 1977.
323: Footnote: WS, March 25, 1976.

14   The Tangled Scales of Justice
324: Epigraph 2: WP, January 29, 1976.
324: Judge Jacob Levin . . . WP, May 9, 1977.
325: In October 1966 . . . *Inside Detective*, December 1974.
326: Richard Marquette . . . *True Detective*, December 1975.
328: Footnote: SFC, November 2, 1977.
329: "Let me illustrate . . ." IWA.
330: In 1975 a Washingtonian . . . *Washington Monthly*, January 1976.
330: "If they are in maximum . . ." UNW, May 10, 1976.
331: Several board members . . . IWA.
331: "It's done in about ten . . ." IWA.
332: "The worse a prisoner's offense, . . ." IWA.
333: In 1974, for example, the Adult Authority . . . SFC, March 5, 1976.
334: among those released . . . SFE, September 18, 1975.
335: When the Adult Authority . . . SFC, February 19, 1976.
335: Starting on her face, . . . Guy Wright column.
338: New York City currently . . . *New York*, 1976.
340: At the beginning . . . UNW, March 25, 1974.
340: Footnote: Vincent Bugliosi and Curt Gentry, *Helter Skelter* (New York, 1974).
341: "We had weekly meetings . . ." IWA.
341: In the fall of . . . *Official Detective*, July 1976.
343: "Each of these women . . ." NYT, November 26, 1975.
344: "The next step downward . . ." LAT, March 30, 1977.
344: At the other extreme, . . . WS, January 8, 1976.
345: When the woman complained, . . . *San Francisco Bay Guardian*, September 17, 1976.
348: Since 1966 over one third of Bonabond's . . . *Washington Monthly*, January 1976.
349: Washington Police Chief . . . WP, June 22, 1976.

15   Remedial Action
350: The LEAA . . . WP, August 24, 1975.
351: While repeatedly paying . . . Carl T. Rowan column, WS, May 14, 1976.
351: Other allocations read . . . Jack Anderson column, November 29, 1975.
354: At present New York . . . *New York*, 1976.
355: "The best deterrent . . ." IWA.
356: David Jacob Seiterle, . . . LAT, October 22, 1976.
357: Later these sentences were . . . *Human Behavior*, January 1972.
358: In order to do this, . . . UNW, August 25, 1975.

Page
358: "Almost anything was easier . . ." IWA.
359: As Norman A. Carlson, . . . UNW, August 25, 1975.
360: "Those who feel . . ." E. Van Den Haag, *Punishing Criminals* (New York, 1975).
361: The use . . . of telemetric systems . . . L. S. Coleman, *Perspectives on the Medical Research of Violence* (Berkeley, 1974).
367: Former U.S. Attorney General . . . SFC, April 12, 1977.
367: At least one is on record . . . WS, January 20, 1977.
368: "The death penalty, . . ." WS, January 22, 1977.
369: "It is difficult . . ." J. C. Herold, *The Age of Napoleon* (New York, 1964).
371: The system of nominating . . . H. A. Bedau, *The Death Penalty in America* (New York, 1964).
371: "He dies hard, . . ." SFE, May 2, 1960.

Index